THE BROADVIEW
Introduction to
Literature

Poetry

THE BROADVIEW
Introduction to
Literature

Poetry

General Editors
Lisa Chalykoff
Neta Gordon
Paul Lumsden

broadview press

Library and Archives Canada Cataloguing in Publication

The Broadview introduction to literature, poetry / general editors, Lisa Chalykoff, Neta Gordon, Paul Lumsden.

Includes index.
ISBN 978-1-55481-179-3 (pbk.)

1. English poetry. 2. American poetry. 3. Canadian poetry (English). 4. Poetry—Translations into English. I. Chalykoff, Lisa, editor of compilation II. Gordon, Neta, 1971-, editor of compilation III. Lumsden, Paul, 1961-, editor of compilation IV. Title: Introduction to literature, poetry.

PN6101.B78 2013   808.81   C2013-903883-3

Broadview Press is an independent, international publishing house, incorporated in 1985. We welcome comments and suggestions regarding any aspect of our publications—please feel free to contact us at the addresses below or at broadview@broadviewpress.com.

North America
PO Box 1243, Peterborough, Ontario, Canada K9J 7H5
2215 Kenmore Ave., Buffalo, New York, USA 14207
Tel: (705) 743-8990; Fax: (705) 743-8353
email: customerservice@broadviewpress.com

UK, Europe, Central Asia, Middle East, Africa, India, and Southeast Asia
Eurospan Group,
3 Henrietta St., London WC2E 8LU, United Kingdom
Tel: 44 (0) 1767 604972; Fax: 44 (0) 1767 601640
email: eurospan@turpin-distribution.com

Australia and New Zealand
NewSouth Books c/o TL Distribution,
15-23 Helles Ave., Moorebank, NSW, Australia 2170
Tel: (02) 8778 9999; Fax: (02) 8778 9944
email: orders@tldistribution.com.au

www.broadviewpress.com

Broadview Press acknowledges the financial support of the Government of Canada through the Canada Book Fund for our publishing activities.

This book is printed on paper containing 50% postconsumer fibre.

PRINTED IN CANADA

Contributors to *The Broadview Introduction to Literature*

MANAGING EDITORS	Don LePan
	Marjorie Mather
DEVELOPMENTAL AND TEXTUAL EDITOR	Laura Buzzard
EDITORIAL COORDINATORS	Tara Bodie
	Bryanne Miller
CONTRIBUTING EDITORS AND TRANSLATORS	Lisa Chalykoff
	Neta Gordon
	Ian Johnston
	David Swain
CONTRIBUTING WRITERS	Laura Buzzard
	Paul Johnston Byrne
	Tara Bodie

EDITORIAL ASSISTANTS

Tara Bodie	Amanda Mullen
Alicia Christianson	Virginia Philipson
Joel DeShaye	Anja Pujic
Victoria Duncan	Andrew Reszitnyk
Rose Eckert-Jantzie	David Ross
Emily Farrell	Nora Ruddock
Travis Grant	Kate Sinclair
Karim Lalani	Jack Skeffington
Phil Laven	Kaitlyn Till
Kellen Loewen	Morgan Tunzelmann

PRODUCTION COORDINATOR	Tara Lowes
PRODUCTION ASSISTANT	Allison LaSorda
COPY EDITOR	Colleen Franklin
PROOFREADERS	Joe Davies
	Judith Earnshaw
DESIGN AND TYPESETTING	Eileen Eckert
PERMISSIONS COORDINATOR	Merilee Atos
COVER DESIGN	Michel Vrana

Contents

PREFACE   xix

ACKNOWLEDGEMENTS   xxi

THE STUDY OF LITERATURE: INTRODUCTION   xxiii

POETRY

POETRY: INTRODUCTION   1

THE EXETER BOOK (C. 970–1000 CE)   25

"The Wife's Lament"   26

Exeter Book Riddles: Riddle 23   27

Riddle 33   28

Riddle 81   28

GEOFFREY CHAUCER (C. 1343–1400)   29

"To Rosemounde"   29

SIR THOMAS WYATT (C. 1503–1542)   32

["The long love that in my thought doth harbour"]   32

["They flee from me that sometime did me seek"]   33

["Whoso list to hunt, I know where is an hind"]   34

EDMUND SPENSER (1552?–1599)   35

from *Amoretti*

1 ["Happy ye leaves when as those lilly hands"]   35

75 ["One day I wrote her name upon the strand"]   36

SIR WALTER RALEGH (C. 1554–1618)   37

"The Nymph's Reply to the Shepherd"   38

CHRISTOPHER MARLOWE (1564–1593)   39

"The Passionate Shepherd to His Love"   39

WILLIAM SHAKESPEARE (1564–1616)   41

Sonnets: 18 ["Shall I compare thee to a summer's day?"]   41

29 ["When in disgrace with fortune and men's eyes"]   42

73 ["That time of year thou mayst in me behold"]   42

116 ["Let me not to the marriage of true minds"]   43

130 ["My mistress' eyes are nothing like the sun"]   43

THOMAS CAMPION (1567–1620)   44

["There is a garden in her face"]   44

JOHN DONNE (1572–1631)   46

"The Flea"   46

from *Holy Sonnets*

10 ["Death be not proud, though some have called thee"]   47

14 ["Batter my heart, three personed God; for you"]   48

"A Valediction: Forbidding Mourning"   48

LADY MARY WROTH (1587–1653?)   50
  from *Pamphilia to Amphilanthus*
      Song ["Love, a child, is ever crying"]   50
      77 ["In this strange labyrinth how shall I turn?"]   51
ROBERT HERRICK (1591–1674)   52
  "Delight in Disorder"   52
  "To the Virgins, to Make Much of Time"   53
  "Upon Julia's Clothes"   53
GEORGE HERBERT (1593–1633)   54
  "The Altar"   55
  "Easter Wings"   56
JOHN MILTON (1608–1674)   57
  "On Shakespeare"   57
  ["When I consider how my light is spent"]   58
  "Lycidas" (sites.broadviewpress.com/BIL)
ANNE BRADSTREET (1612–1672)   59
  "The Author to Her Book"   59
ANDREW MARVELL (1621–1678)   61
  "The Garden"   61
  "To His Coy Mistress"   64
ANNE FINCH, COUNTESS OF WINCHILSEA (1661–1720)   66
  "There's No Tomorrow"   66
ALEXANDER POPE (1688–1744)   68
  from *An Essay on Criticism*   68
  The Rape of the Lock   69
THOMAS GRAY (1716–1771)   96
  "Elegy Written in a Country Churchyard"   96
ANNA LAETITIA BARBAULD (1743–1825)   102
  "The Caterpillar"   102
PHILLIS WHEATLEY (1753–1784)   104
  "On Being Brought from Africa to America"   104
WILLIAM BLAKE (1757–1827)   105
  from *Songs of Innocence*
      "The Lamb"   105
      "The Chimney Sweeper"   107
  from *Songs of Experience*
      "The Chimney Sweeper"   108
      "The Sick Rose"   108
      "The Tyger"   108
      "London"   110
WILLIAM WORDSWORTH (1770–1850)   111
  "Lines Written a Few Miles above Tintern Abbey"   112
  ["The world is too much with us"]   116

SAMUEL TAYLOR COLERIDGE (1772–1834) 117
    "Frost at Midnight" 117
    "Kubla Khan" 119
    "The Rime of the Ancient Mariner" (sites.broadviewpress.com/BIL)
PERCY BYSSHE SHELLEY (1792–1822) 122
    "Ozymandias" 122
    "Ode to the West Wind" 123
JOHN KEATS (1795–1821) 127
    "When I Have Fears that I May Cease to Be" 127
    "La Belle Dame sans Merci: A Ballad" 128
    "Ode to a Nightingale" 130
    "Ode on a Grecian Urn" 132
    "To Autumn" 134
ELIZABETH BARRETT BROWNING (1806–1861) 136
    from *Sonnets from the Portuguese*
        Sonnet 22 ["When our two souls stand up erect and strong"] 136
        Sonnet 24 ["Let the world's sharpness like a clasping knife"] 137
        Sonnet 43 ["How do I love thee? Let me count the ways"] 137
EDGAR ALLAN POE (1809–1849) 138
    "The Raven" 138
ALFRED, LORD TENNYSON (1809–1892) 142
    "The Lady of Shalott" 142
    "The Lotos-Eaters" 148
    "Ulysses" 154
    "The Charge of the Light Brigade" 156
ROBERT BROWNING (1812–1889) 159
    "Porphyria's Lover" 159
    "My Last Duchess" 161
EMILY BRONTË (1818–1848) 163
    ["No coward soul is mine"] 163
    ["Often rebuked, yet always back returning"] 164
    ["I'll come when thou art saddest"] 165
WALT WHITMAN (1819–1892) 166
    from *Song of Myself*: 1 ["I celebrate myself, and sing myself"] 166
    "I Hear America Singing" 167
    "When I Heard the Learn'd Astronomer" 167
MATTHEW ARNOLD (1822–1888) 168
    "Dover Beach" 168
EMILY DICKINSON (1830–1886) 170
    249 ["Wild Nights—Wild Nights!"] 170
    288 ["I'm Nobody! Who are you?"] 171
    341 ["After great pain, a formal feeling comes"] 171
    465 ["I heard a Fly buzz—when I died"] 172
    712 ["Because I could not stop for Death"] 172

754 ["My Life had stood—a Loaded Gun"]   173
1129 ["Tell all the Truth but tell it slant"]   174
CHRISTINA ROSSETTI (1830–1894)   175
   "Goblin Market"   175
   "Cobwebs"   192
   "In an Artist's Studio"   192
THOMAS HARDY (1840–1928)   193
   "The Darkling Thrush"   193
   "The Convergence of the Twain"   195
   "During Wind and Rain"   196
GERARD MANLEY HOPKINS (1844–1889)   198
   "God's Grandeur"   198
   "The Windhover"   199
A.E. HOUSMAN (1859–1936)   200
   "Terence, This Is Stupid Stuff"   200
W.B. YEATS (1865–1939)   203
   "Easter 1916"   203
   "The Second Coming"   206
   "Leda and the Swan"   207
   "Sailing to Byzantium"   207
PAUL LAURENCE DUNBAR (1872–1906)   209
   "We Wear the Mask"   209
ROBERT FROST (1874–1963)   210
   "The Road Not Taken"   210
   "Stopping by Woods on a Snowy Evening"   211
   "Design"   212
WALLACE STEVENS (1879–1955)   213
   "Thirteen Ways of Looking at a Blackbird"   213
   "Anecdote of the Jar"   216
WILLIAM CARLOS WILLIAMS (1883–1963)   217
   "The Red Wheelbarrow"   217
   "Spring and All"   218
   "This Is Just to Say"   218
   "Landscape with the Fall of Icarus"   219
EZRA POUND (1885–1972)   220
   "The River-Merchant's Wife: A Letter"   220
   "In a Station of the Metro"   221
MARIANNE MOORE (1887–1972)   222
   "Poetry"   222
   "Poetry" (Revised version)   223
T.S. ELIOT (1888–1965)   224
   "The Love Song of J. Alfred Prufrock"   225
   "Journey of the Magi"   229

EDNA ST. VINCENT MILLAY (1892–1950)   231
["I, being born a woman and distressed"]   231
["What lips my lips have kissed, and where, and why"]   232
WILFRED OWEN (1893–1918)   233
"Anthem for Doomed Youth"   233
"Dulce et Decorum Est"   234
E.E. CUMMINGS (1894–1962)   235
["in Just-"]   235
["(ponder,darling,these busted statues"]   236
["somewhere i have never travelled,gladly beyond"]   237
["anyone lived in a pretty how town"]   238
["l(a"]   239
LANGSTON HUGHES (1902–1967)   240
"The Negro Speaks of Rivers"   240
"Harlem (2)"   241
STEVIE SMITH (1902–1971)   242
"Not Waving but Drowning"   242
EARLE BIRNEY (1904–1995)   243
"Vancouver Lights"   243
"The Bear on the Delhi Road"   245
JOHN BETJEMAN (1906–1984)   246
"In Westminster Abbey"   246
W.H. AUDEN (1907–1973)   248
"Funeral Blues"   249
"Musée des Beaux Arts"   249
"September 1, 1939"   250
"The Unknown Citizen"   253
GEORGE OPPEN (1908–1984)   255
"Psalm"   255
"The Forms of Love"   256
"Latitude, Longitude"   257
THEODORE ROETHKE (1908–1963)   258
"My Papa's Waltz"   258
"Root Cellar"   259
"I Knew a Woman"   259
DOROTHY LIVESAY (1909–1996)   261
"Green Rain"   261
"The Three Emilys"   262
ELIZABETH BISHOP (1911–1979)   264
"First Death in Nova Scotia"   264
"One Art"   266
DOUGLAS LEPAN (1914–1998)   267
"A Country without a Mythology"   267
"Aubade"   269
"The Haystack"   269

RANDALL JARRELL (1914–1965)   270
    "The Death of the Ball Turret Gunner"   270
DYLAN THOMAS (1914–1953)   271
    "The Force That Through the Green Fuse Drives the Flower"   271
    "Fern Hill"   272
    "Do Not Go Gentle into That Good Night"   274
P.K. PAGE (1916–2010)   275
    "The Stenographers"   275
    "Stories of Snow"   277
AL PURDY (1918–2000)   279
    "Trees at the Arctic Circle"   279
    "Lament for the Dorsets"   281
GWEN HARWOOD (1920–1995)   284
    "In the Park"   284
HOWARD NEMEROV (1920–1991)   285
    "The Vacuum"   285
    "A Way of Life"   286
PHILIP LARKIN (1922–1985)   288
    "Church Going"   288
    "Talking in Bed"   290
    "This Be the Verse"   291
    "The Old Fools"   291
ALLEN GINSBERG (1926–1997)   293
    "A Supermarket in California"   293
JOHN ASHBERY (B. 1927)   295
    "Civilization and Its Discontents"   295
    "The Improvement"   297
THOM GUNN (1929–2004)   298
    "Tamer and Hawk"   298
    "To His Cynical Mistress"   299
    "The Hug"   300
ADRIENNE RICH (1929–2012)   301
    "Aunt Jennifer's Tigers"   301
    "Living in Sin"   302
    "Diving into the Wreck"   302
TED HUGHES (1930–1998)   306
    "The Thought-Fox"   306
    "Pike"   307
    "Hawk Roosting"   309
    "Heptonstall Old Church"   309
DEREK WALCOTT (B. 1930)   311
    "A Far Cry from Africa"   311
    "Ruins of a Great House"   313
    from Midsummer
        52 ["I heard them marching the leaf-wet roads of my head"]   315
    "Central America"   316

SYLVIA PLATH (1932–1963)   317
   "Daddy"   318
   "Lady Lazarus"   320
ADRIAN HENRI (1932–2000)   324
   "Mrs. Albion You've Got a Lovely Daughter"   324
LUCILLE CLIFTON (1936–2010)   326
   "Miss Rosie"   326
   "The Lost Baby Poem"   327
ROGER MCGOUGH (B. 1937)   328
   "Comeclose and Sleepnow"   328
LES MURRAY (B. 1938)   330
   "Pigs"   330
   "The Shield-Scales of Heraldry"   331
   "The Early Dark"   333
MARGARET ATWOOD (B. 1939)   334
   "Death of a Young Son by Drowning"   334
   ["you fit into me"]   335
   "Variation on the Word *Sleep*"   336
   "The Door"   337
SEAMUS HEANEY (B. 1939)   339
   "Digging"   339
   "Mid-Term Break"   341
   "The Grauballe Man"   342
   "Cutaways"   344
BILLY COLLINS (B. 1941)   346
   "Pinup"   346
GWENDOLYN MACEWEN (1941–1987)   348
   "Dark Pines Under Water"   348
   "The Discovery"   349
DON MCKAY (B. 1942)   350
   "Some Functions of a Leaf"   350
   "Meditation on a Geode"   351
   "Meditation on Shovels"   352
   "Song for the Song of the Wood Thrush"   352
ROY MIKI (B. 1942)   353
   "attractive"   353
   "on the sublime"   355
   "make it new"   356
SHARON OLDS (B. 1942)   358
   "The One Girl at the Boys Party"   358
   "Sex without Love"   359
MICHAEL ONDAATJE (B. 1943)   360
   "Letters & Other Worlds"   360
   "The Cinnamon Peeler"   363
   "To a Sad Daughter"   364

EAVAN BOLAND (B. 1944)   367
    "Night Feed"   367
    "Against Love Poetry"   369
BPNICHOL (1944–1988)   370
    "Blues"   370
    ["dear Captain Poetry"]   371
CRAIG RAINE (B. 1944)   372
    "A Martian Sends a Postcard Home"   372
TOM WAYMAN (B. 1945)   374
    "Did I Miss Anything?"   374
ROBERT BRINGHURST (B. 1946)   376
    "Leda and the Swan"   376
MARILYN NELSON (B. 1946)   379
    "Minor Miracle"   379
BRIAN PATTEN (B. 1946)   381
    "Somewhere Between Heaven and Woolworths, A Song"   381
DIANE ACKERMAN (B. 1948)   383
    "Sweep Me through Your Many-Chambered Heart"   383
LORNA CROZIER (B. 1948)   384
    from *The Sex Lives of Vegetables*
        "Carrots"   384
        "Onions"   385
    "The Dark Ages of the Sea"   385
    "When I Come Again to My Father's House"   387
TIMOTHY STEELE (B. 1948)   389
    "Sapphics Against Anger"   389
AGHA SHAHID ALI (1949–2001)   391
    "Postcard from Kashmir"   391
    "The Wolf's Postscript to 'Little Red Riding Hood'"   392
ANNE CARSON (B. 1950)   394
    from *Short Talks*
        "On Rain"   394
        "On Sylvia Plath"   395
        "On Walking Backwards"   395
DANA GIOIA (B. 1950)   396
    "Thanks for Remembering Us"   396
    "Planting a Sequoia"   397
ROO BORSON (B. 1952)   398
    "Water Memory"   398
RITA DOVE (B. 1952)   400
    "Persephone, Falling"   400
DIONNE BRAND (B. 1953)   402
    from *thirsty*
        30 ["Spring darkness is forgiving. It doesn't descend"]   402
        32 ["Every smell is now a possibility, a young man"]   403

KIM ADDONIZIO (B. 1954)   404
"First Poem for You"   404
SARAH ARVIO (B. 1954)   405
"Wood"   405
CAROL ANN DUFFY (B. 1955)   407
"Drunk"   407
"The Good Teachers"   408
"Crush"   409
"Rapture"   409
"Treasure"   410
MARILYN DUMONT (B. 1955)   411
"Not Just a Platform for My Dance"   411
"The White Judges"   412
ROBIN ROBERTSON (B. 1955)   414
"The Park Drunk"   414
"What the Horses See at Night"   415
LI-YOUNG LEE (B. 1957)   417
"Persimmons"   417
BENJAMIN ZEPHANIAH (B. 1958)   420
"Dis Poetry"   420
GEORGE ELLIOTT CLARKE (B. 1960)   422
from *Whylah Falls*
"Blank Sonnet"   422
"Look Homeward, Exile"   423
"Casualties"   424
JACKIE KAY (B. 1961)   426
"In My Country"   426
"Her"   427
"High Land"   427
"Late Love"   428
LAVINIA GREENLAW (B. 1962)   429
"Electricity"   429
"Zombies"   430
SIMON ARMITAGE (B. 1963)   431
"Poem"   431
"Very Simply Topping Up the Brake Fluid"   432
"It Could Be You"   433
IAN IQBAL RASHID (B. 1965)   434
"Could Have Danced All Night"   434
CHRISTIAN BÖK (B. 1966)   436
"Chapter I"   436
"Vowels" (sites.broadviewpress.com/BIL)
ALICE OSWALD (B. 1966)   440
"Wedding"   440

"Woods etc."   441
"Dunt"   441
KAREN SOLIE (B. 1966)   444
    "Sturgeon"   444
    "Nice"   445
    "Self-Portrait in a Series of Professional Evaluations"   446
ARUNDHATHI SUBRAMANIAM (B. 1967)   447
    "To the Welsh Critic Who Doesn't Find Me Identifiably Indian"   447
RITA WONG (B. 1968)   450
    "opium"   451
    "nervous organism"   452
RACHEL ZOLF (B. 1968)   453
    from *Human Resources*
        ["The job is to write in 'plain language.' No adjectives,
            adornment or surfeit"]   454
        ["New performance weightings a bit of a moving target
            the future liability of make this sing"]   454
        ["Given enough input elements, a writing machine can spew
            about anything"]   455
        ["I don't want to trip over this in the future from where
            I'm sitting can you suggest massages"]   455
STEPHANIE BOLSTER (B. 1969)   456
    from *White Stone*
        "Portrait of Alice, Annotated"   456
        "Portrait of Alice with Christopher Robin"   457
R.W. GRAY (B. 1969)   460
    "How this begins"   460
SHARON HARRIS (B. 1972)   462
    "99. Where Do Poems Come From?"   462
    "70. Why Do Poems Make Me Cry?"   463

POETRY IN TRANSLATION

POETRY IN TRANSLATION: INTRODUCTION   465
SAPPHO (C. 630-612 BCE–C. 570 BCE)   467
    2 ["here to me from Krete to this holy temple"]   468/469
    55 ["Dead you will lie and never memory of you"]   471
FRANCESCO PETRARCH (1304–1374)   472
    294 ["In my heart she used to stand lovely and live"]   473
ARTHUR RIMBAUD (1854–1891)   474
    "À la Musique" / "Scene Set to Music"   475
    "Voyelles" / "Vowels"   478
FEDERICO GARCÍA LORCA (1898–1936)   479
    "Romance de la luna, luna"   480
    ["The moon came to the forge"]   481
    "Ballad of the Moon, Moon, Moon"   482

Pablo Neruda (1904–1973)   483
   "Exilio" / "Exile"   484/485
   "Un Perro Ha Muerto" / "A Dog Has Died"   488/489
Paul Celan (1920–1970)   492
   "Totenhemd" / "Shroud"   493
   "Todesfuge" / "Death Fugue"   494/495
Nicole Brossard (b. 1943)   498
   "Geste" / "Gesture"   499
   ["tous ces mois passés"] / ["all these months spent"]   500
Yehuda Amichai (1924–2000)   501
   " תַּיָּרִים " / "Tourists"   502/503
Reesom Haile (1946–2003)   504
   "ስደት" / "Knowledge"   505
   "አመሪካ ኢ.ሉ.ኩ.ም" / "Dear Africans"   506/507

Glossary   509
Permission Acknowledgements   529
Index of First Lines   539
Index of Authors and Titles   545

Preface

On hearing that Broadview was planning a new anthology designed to provide an overview of literature at the first-year level, more than a few people have expressed surprise. What could a new anthology have to offer that really is different—that gives something new and valuable to academics and students alike? We hope that you will find your own answers to that question once you have looked through this volume. Certainly our intent has been to offer something that is in many ways different. We have brought fresh eyes to the process of choosing a table of contents; from Alice Oswald's "Wedding" to R.W. Gray's "How this begins," from Sharon Harris's "Where Do Poems Come From?" to the Old English riddles of the Exeter Book, you'll find selections here that have not been widely anthologized elsewhere. You'll also find more visual material than in competing anthologies.

Although the emphasis of the anthology is very much on literature in English (in recognition of the reality that most "introduction to literature" courses in Canada are taught in English departments), we have also included rather more literature in translation than is to be found in most competing anthologies. Particularly noteworthy is the special section on Poetry in Translation that discusses some of the many issues involved and provides a concise but wide-ranging sample of poems in translation, with the original offered for comparison.

Not everything about *The Broadview Introduction to Literature* is entirely new, of course. Many of the selections will, we hope, be familiar to instructors; as to which of the "old chestnuts" continue to work well in a teaching context we have in large part been guided by the advice provided to us by academics at a variety of institutions across Canada. But even where familiar authors and selections are concerned, we think you'll find quite a bit here that is different. We have worked hard to pitch both the author introductions and the explanatory notes at a consistent level throughout—and, in both introductions and notes, to give students more by way of background.

Finally, you'll find fresh material posted on the companion website associated with the anthology. The site <http://sites.broadviewpress.com/BIL/> features additional material on many literary sub-genres and movements; material on reading poetry (including exercises that will help those unfamiliar with the patterns of accentual-syllabic metre in English); material on writing essays about literature—and on referencing and citation; a much fuller glossary of literary terms than it is possible to include in these pages; self-test quizzes on the information provided in the introductions to the various genres; and several additional selections that we were unable to find space for in the bound book. We have included Rossetti's "Goblin Market" in its entirety here; those looking to incorporate more long poems into a course will find several options on the website (including Milton's "Lycidas" and Coleridge's "The Rime of the Ancient Mariner"). All are introduced and annotated according to the same principles and presented in the same format as the selections in the bound-book anthology. Those wishing to go beyond these choices may assign any one of the more than 300 volumes in the acclaimed Broadview Editions series, and we can arrange to have that volume bundled together with the bound book anthology in a shrink-wrapped package, at little or no additional charge to the student.

Any of the genre volumes of the anthology may also be bundled together in special-price shrink-wrapped packages; whatever genres your course covers, and whatever works you would like to cover within those genres, we will do our best to put together a package that will suit your needs. (Instructors should note that, in addition to the main companion website of materials that may be of interest both to students and to instructors, we have posted instructor-related materials on a separate website.)

I do hope you will like what you see—and I hope as well that you will be in touch with any questions or suggestions; we will always be on the lookout for good ideas as to what we should add to the anthology's companion web-site—and/or for what we should look to include in the next edition of *The Broadview Introduction to Literature.*

[D.L.]

Acknowledgements

The general editors, managing editors, and all of us at Broadview owe a debt of gratitude to the academics who have offered assistance and feedback at various stages of the project:

Rhonda Anderson
Trevor Arkell
Veronica Austen
John Ball
David Bentley
Shashi Bhat
Nicholas Bradley
Jocelyn Coates
Richard Cole
Alison Conway
Heidi J. Tiedemann Darroch
Celeste Daphne Derksen
Lorraine DiCicco
Kerry Doyle
Monique Dumontet
Michelle Faubert
Rebecca Gagan
Jay Gamble
Dana Hansen
Alexander Hart
Linda Harwood
Chandra Hodgson
Kathryn Holland
Ashton Howley
Renee Hulan
Kathleen James-Cavan
Karl Jirgens
Diana Frances Lobb

Kathyrn MacLennan
Shelley Mahoney
Joanna Mansbridge
Mark McDayter
Lindsey McMaster
Susan McNeill-Bindon
Craig Melhoff
Bob Mills
Stephanie Morley
Andrew Murray
Russell Perkin
Allan Pero
Mike Perschon
John Pope
Phyllis Rozendal
Cory Rushton
Laura Schechter
Stephen Schryer
Peter Slade
Marjorie Stone
Daniel Tysdal
Linda Van Netten Blimke
Molly Wallace
David Watt
Nanci White
David Wilson
Dorothy Woodman
Gena Zuroski-Jenkins

The Study of Literature

The Nobel prize-winning physicist Paul Dirac reportedly said, "The aim of science is to make difficult things understandable in a simple way; the aim of poetry is to state simple things in an incomprehensible way." More recently, noted Language poet Charles Bernstein—whose work typically challenges the limits of simple comprehension—published the poem "Thank you for saying thank you," in which he explicitly takes up the issue of how poetry "states" things:

> This is a totally
> accessible poem.
> There is nothing
> in this poem
> that is in any
> way difficult.
> All the words
> are simple &
> to the point.

Though Bernstein's work is undoubtedly meant to register as ironic, both his poem and Dirac's comment draw attention to the idea that literature uses language in a peculiar way, and that one of the most fundamental questions readers of literature must ask themselves is: "How is this said?" Or—with apologies to Dirac—the question might be: "How do the language choices in this text make a seemingly simple thing—for example, a statement about love, or family, or justice, or grief—not incomprehensible, but rather more than just something simple?"

Another way of approaching the question of how literature works is to consider the way this anthology of literature is organized around the idea of genre, with texts chosen and categorized according to the way they fit into the classifications of poetry, short fiction, drama, and literary non-fiction. One way of organizing an introductory anthology of literature is the historical, in which selections are sorted from oldest to most recent, usually grouped together according to what have become acknowledged as distinctive historical periods of literary output. Another is the topical or thematic, in which historically and generically diverse selections are grouped together according to subject matter, so that students may compare differing attitudes toward, for example, gender relations, personal loss, particular historical events, or the process of growing up. The decision by an editor of an anthology—or the instructor of a course—to select one organizing principle over another is not arbitrary, but reflects a choice in terms of teaching students how to approach the reading of literature. In very simple terms, one might regard the three options thus: the historical configuration emphasizes discovering the "what" and "when" of literature—what is the body of written work that has come to be considered "literature" (especially in terms of tracing the outlines of a national literature), and when were examples from this distinguished corpus written? The thematic configuration emphasizes sorting through the "why" of literature—why do writers turn to literature to work through complex ideas, and what can we make of our complex responses to differing, often competing, stances on various topics? The generic configuration, finally, emphasizes the "how" of literature—how is the text put together? What are its working parts? How does an attention to the formal attributes of a literary piece help the reader understand the way it achieves its intellectual and emotional—its more than just simple—effects?

What do literary critics mean when they refer to genre? The word was introduced into the English language sometime in the late eighteenth century, borrowed from the French word *genre*, which meant "kind" or "style" of art, as when the British agricultural reformer Arthur Young refers in his travel narratives to the "genre" of Dutch painting, which he finds wanting in comparison to the work of the Italian masters. We can look back further to the Latin root *genus*, or even the Greek γένος (*génos*), a term which also refers to the idea of a distinct family or clan; thus, the notion of "kind" might helpfully be thought of as a way of thinking about resemblances, relationships, and keys to recognition among the literary genres. Another helpful analogy is the way biologists have taken up the term *genus* as part of the taxonomy of organisms. The term *genus felis*, for example, refers to a particular order of small cats, including such species as the domestic cat (*felis catus*) and the wildcat (*felis silvestris*); both species share common generic attributes, such as a similar size and a preferred diet of small rodents. For biologists and literary critics alike, the concept of genus or genre, respectively, is used to group things together according to a system of shared, identifiable features, with both terms allowing for the idea that larger groupings can be further broken down into even more specific ones (thus we can refer to the various breeds of domestic cats, or the distinctions among the Petrarchan, Shakespearian, and Spenserian sonnets).

Biologists tend to use the word "characteristics" to designate the features of a genus; literary critics, on the other hand, make use of the word "convention," a somewhat more complicated term. Like *characteristics*, the term *conventions* refers to distinguishing elements of a genre, which is why the study of literature requires a thorough understanding of the specialized descriptive vocabulary used to discuss such elements as a text's metre, its narrative point of view, its use of figurative language, etc. The introductions to each section of this anthology will draw attention to this specialized vocabulary, and students will also want to refer to the extensive glossary of literary terms located at the end of the anthology. The idea of convention, though, has additional conceptual importance relating to the way texts are built to be read. While a domestic cat is simply born with retractable claws and a taste for mice, a literary text is constructed, written in a particular way, often with the aim of eliciting a particular response from a reader. The word convention, in this sense, harks back to the legal concept of agreement, so that when writers make use of conventions associated with a genre, they set up a kind of contract with the reader whereby the reader has a sense of what to expect from the text. For example: when the first five minutes of a film include a long shot of the Pentagon, along with a few quickly edited shots of grim-looking military personnel moving quickly through underground hallways, and perhaps a shot of someone in a dark suit yelling into a cellphone, "Operation Silvestris has been aborted!" the audience understands that they are in for some sort of political thriller. They need not know anything about the details of Operation Silvestris to make this interpretive leap, as the presence of a few conventions of the political thriller (the shot of the Pentagon, the phrase "Operation [blank] has been aborted!") are enough to provide the general outline of a contract entered into between film and audience. Likewise, recognizing that a poem has 14 lines and makes use of a rhyming couplet at the end will provide knowledgeable readers of literature with an inkling as to what they should expect, as these readers will be familiar with the structural conventions of the Shakespearean sonnet.

Whereas a legal contract is a fairly straightforward affair—it outlines the terms of agreement for both sides and more or less explicitly refers to the penalties for undermining those terms—the contract between text and reader is multifaceted. One of the most fascinating things about the way writers make use of literary convention is that the terms of agreement are constantly subject to further consideration, thoughtful challenge, or outright derision. Thus, when the speaker of Shakespeare's sonnet 130 refers to his lady's "dun" breasts and "reek[ing]" breath, the point is not to insult his mistress, or even to admire her in a new, more realistic way; rather, the point is to ridicule the way other poets slavishly adhere to the convention that sonnets glorify a woman's beauty, comparing her eyes to the sun and her breath to the smell of roses. This reading is available for the reader who knows that by the time Shakespeare decided to try his hand at the genre, translations and imitations of the Petrarchan sonnet had been circulating at the Elizabethan court for many decades. Like organisms, or even laws, conventions of literature evolve over time as writers seek to rethink the rules of the form they wish to explore. In the prologue to her recent collection *XEclogue*, Lisa Robertson declares, "I needed a genre to gloss my ancestress' complicity with a socially expedient code"; she explains how, in turning to the conventions of the eclogue—a collection of pastoral poems, often satiric—she has found a suitable formal framework for her exploration of the way social insiders and outsiders are marked by class and gender.

Is it somehow problematic to inquire too tenaciously into the working parts of a literary text? Does one risk undermining the emotional force of a poem, the sharp wit of a play, or the exciting plot of an adventure tale if one pays too much attention to seemingly mundane issues of plot structure or metre? To paraphrase a common grievance of the distressed student: by examining the way literature works, are we, somehow, just wrecking it? These questions might, paradoxically, recall Dirac's complaint that literature makes simple things incomprehensible: while we know that literature can manage to communicate difficult notions, making what is mysterious more comprehensible, it is often difficult to articulate or make a viable argument about how it does so. By paying attention to the way a text is built and to the way an author constructs his or her end of the contract, the reader can begin to understand and respond explicitly to the question of how literature produces its particular effects.

Consider the following two textual excerpts:

> Come live with me and be my love,
> And we shall all the pleasures prove.
> (Christopher Marlowe, 1590)

> Boom, boom, boom, let's go back to my room,
> And we can do it all night, and I can make you feel right.
> (Paul Lekakis, 1987)

Based on a quick reading: which excerpt is more appropriate for inclusion in a Valentine's Day card? A poll of employees at Hallmark, not to mention the millions of folks invested in the idea that Valentine's Day is a celebration of romance, would likely make an overwhelming case for the Marlowe excerpt. But why? Answering that question might involve a methodological inquiry into how each excerpt produces a particular response, one which might be broken down into five stages:

Level One: Evaluation—Do I like this text? What is my gut reaction to it?
No doubt, most students of literature have heard an instructor proclaim, with
more or less vitriol, "It doesn't matter if you like the poem/story/play! This
is a literature class, not a book club!" And, while it is true that the evaluative
response does not constitute an adequate final critical response to a text, it's
important to acknowledge one's first reaction. After all, the point of literature
is to produce an effect, sometimes an extreme response. When a text seems
confusing, or hilarious, or provocative, or thrilling, it prompts questions: How
are such effects produced using mere words in particular combinations? Why
would an author want to generate feelings of confusion, hilarity, provocation,
etc.? How am I—the reader—being positioned on the other end of such effects?

Level Two: Interpretation—What is the text about? This is a trickier level
of reading than it might seem. Students sometimes think, mistakenly, that
all literature—and especially poetry—is "open to interpretation," and that
all interpretations are therefore correct. This line of thinking leads to snap,
top-down interpretations, in which the general "mood" of the text is felt
at a gut level (see above), and the ensuing reading of the poem is wrangled
into shape to match that feeling. It is sometimes helpful to think about interpretation as a kind of translation, as in the way those who work at the
United Nations translating talking points from Arabic to Russian are called
"interpreters." Though no translation is flawless, the goal of simultaneous
translation is to get as close as possible to the meaning of the original. Thus,
an interpretation should be thought of as a carefully paraphrased summary
or, for particularly dense works, a line by line explication of the literary text,
both of which may require several rereadings and some meticulous use of
a dictionary. As with reading for evaluation, reading for interpretation can
help generate useful critical questions, such as: How does the way this text
is written affect my attitude toward the subject matter? What is the point of
all the fancy language, which makes this text more or less difficult to interpret? Now that I've figured out what this text is about—at least in terms of
its subject matter—can I begin to determine what sorts of themes are being
tackled?

A note about the distinction between subject matter and **theme**: while
these terms are sometimes used interchangeably, the notion of theme differs
from subject matter in that it implies an idea about or attitude toward the
subject matter. A good rule of thumb to remember is that theme can never be
summed up in just one word (so, there is no such thing as the theme of "Love"
or "Family" or "Women"). Whereas the subject matter of Shakespeare's sonnet
"Shall I compare thee to a summer's day" is admiration or the nature of beauty,

one theme of the poem, arguably, is that the beloved's good qualities are best made apparent in poetry, and that art is superior to nature. Another theme of the poem, arguably, is that the admiration of youth is best accomplished by someone older. Thus, identifying a text's subject matter via interpretation aims to pinpoint a general topic, while the process of contemplating a text's theme is open to elaboration and argumentation.

Level Three: Description—What does the text look like, at least at first glance? Can you give a quick account of its basic formal features? At this level of reading, one starts to think about how a text is built, especially in terms of basic generic features. For example, are we dealing with poetry? Short fiction? Drama? If poetry, can we identify a sub-genre the text fits into—for instance, the sonnet, the ode, or the elegy—and can we begin to assess whether the author is following or challenging conventions associated with that genre? Of course, answering these questions requires prior knowledge of what, for example, a conventional ode is supposed to look like, which is why the student of literature must have a thorough understanding of the specific terminology associated with the discipline. At this level of reading, one might also begin to think about and do some preliminary research on when and where the text was written, so that the issues of literary history and cultural context are broached; likewise, one might begin to think about who is writing the poem, as the matter of the author's societal position might prove a fruitful avenue for further investigation. Thus, a consequent objective at this level of reading is to map the terrain of inquiry, establishing some general facts about the text as building blocks that underpin critical analysis.

Level Four: Analysis—How are particular formal features working, especially as they interact with content? The word analysis comes from the Greek terms ἀνά- (ana-), meaning "throughout," and λύειν (lysis), meaning "to loose." Thus, the procedure for analysis involves taking a text and shaking it apart in order to see more clearly all its particular bits and pieces. This level of reading is akin to putting a text under a microscope. First, one has to identify individual formal features of the text. Then one needs to consider how all the parts fit together. It is at this level that one's knowledge of generic conventions and particular literary techniques—the way figurative language works, the ways in which rhythm and rhyme affect our response to language, the way plotting and point of view can be handled, and so on—is crucial. It may be the case that not everything one notices will find its way into an essay. But the goal at this level of reading should be to notice as much as possible (and it is usually when working at this level that an instructor will be accused of "reading too much into a text," as if that image of a moth beating its wings against a window means nothing more than that the moth is trapped, and that it just happens to have been included in a work). Careful analysis shows that nothing in a text "just happens" to be there. A text is constructed out of special uses of language that beg to be "read into." Reading at this level takes time and a certain amount of expertise so as to tease out how the work is built and begin to understand the connections between form and content.

Level Five: Critical Analysis—How do the formal elements of a literary work connect with what the work has to say to the reader? It is at this level of reading that one begins to make an argument, to develop a thesis. In order to construct a viable thesis, one needs to answer a question, perhaps one of the questions that arose at an earlier level of reading. For example, why does this poem, which seems on the surface to be about love, make use of so many images that have to do with science? What is up with this narrator, who seems to be addressing another character without in any way identifying who he is speaking to? What is significant about the fact that the climax of this play hangs on the matter of whether a guy is willing to sell a portrait? It is at this level of reading, rather than at the level of interpretation, that the literary critic is able to flex his or her creative muscles, as a text poses any number of viable questions and suggests any number of viable arguments. Note, however, that the key word here is "viable." In order to make an argument—in order to convincingly answer a question posed—one must have the textual evidence to make the case, evidence that has been gleaned through careful, meticulous, and thoughtful reading.

Returning now to the two texts, let's see if we can come up with one viable argument as to why Marlowe's text seems more likely to show up in a Valentine's Day card, going through each level of reading to build the foundation—the case—for making that argument.

Level One: Evaluation. At first glance, the Marlowe text just seems more romantic than the Lekakis text: it uses flowery words and has a nice flow to it, while the phrase "do it all night" is kind of blunt and unromantic. On a gut level, one might feel that a Valentine's Day card should avoid such blunt language (although this gut reaction might suggest a first useful research question: why should romance be associated with flowery language rather than blunt expressions?).

Moving on to **Level Two: Interpretation.** Well, the Lekakis text is certainly the more straightforward one when it comes to interpretation, though one has to know that the phrase "do it" refers to having sex as opposed to some other activity (and it is interesting to note that even in the more straightforward text, the author has used a common euphemism). The phrase "Boom boom boom" seems to be untranslatable, which begs the question of why the author used it. Is the phrase still meaningful, even if it's just a series of sounds?

As for the Marlowe text, a careful paraphrase would go something like this: "Move in with me and be my lover, and we can enjoy all kinds of pleasures together." Hmmm—wait a minute: what does the author mean by "pleasures"? Eating good food? Playing card games? Though the word is arguably vague, the references in the first line to moving in together and love make it pretty clear that "pleasures" is another euphemism for having sex (though perhaps a more elegant one than "doing it").

If both texts can be interpreted similarly—both are the words of a would-be lover trying to convince the object of his/her affection to have sex—why does it matter which phrase ends up in a Valentine's Day card? What are the significant differences between each text that cause them to generate distinct gut responses?

Level Three: Description. The Marlowe text, at least this piece of it, is a **couplet**, written in iambic **tetrameter** (or eight syllables in each line that follow the rhythmic pattern of unstressed/stressed). The language is flowery, or, to use a slightly more technical phrase, the **diction** is elevated, which means that this is not the way people normally talk in everyday life. In fact, there seems to have been a lot of attention paid to making the words sound pleasing to the ear, through patterns of rhythm and rhyme, and also through patterns of alliteration in the consonants (of the soft "l" sound in the first line, and then of powerful plosives at the end of the second).

The Lekakis text also makes use of rhyme, but in a different way: each line includes an **internal rhyme**, so that "boom" rhymes with "room" and "night" rhymes with "right." The rhythmic pattern is harder to make sense of, as there are a different number of syllables in each line and a lot of short, sharp words that undermine a sing-song effect. The sound effects of the text are comparatively harsher than in the Marlowe text, with many "b" and "k" and "t" sounds.

The Marlowe text was written in the 1590s, while the Lekakis text is a popular dance song from the 1980s; it might be interesting to follow up on the distinct cultural contexts out of which each work emerges. It might also be interesting to examine how each text thematizes the subject of having sex: whereas the Marlowe text seems to promote the attitude that the "pleasures" of sex should be tried out (to "prove" in sixteenth-century English meant to test or to try out) within the context of "living with" someone, or that love and sex go hand-in-hand, the Lekakis text seems to suggest that even sex on one "night" in someone's "room" can make one feel "right." Or, good sex has nothing at all to do with love.

Because these texts are so short and are fairly simple, much of the work of **Level Four: Analysis** has already been touched on. A closer inspection of the use of rhyme and **alliteration** in the Marlowe text demonstrates the way the poem insists on the idea that love can be "proved" by sex, while the internal rhyming of the words "me," "be," and "we" further indicates a strong emphasis on how the joining of two people represents a significant change. The use of elevated diction is consistent, suggesting that discussions of love and sex are worthy of serious consideration.

As for the Lekakis text, a major point to analyze is the phrase "boom boom boom." Is this **onomatopoeia**? If so, what "sense" is the sound trying to express? The sound of sex? If so, what kind of sex are we talking about here? Or is it the sound of something else, perhaps dancing (as is suggested by the cultural context of which the text emerges)? Maybe the phrase is simply meant to express excitement? What do we make of the plain speech the text employs? Does the use of such diction debase notions of sex, or is it simply more candid about the way sex and love might be separated?

As you can see, the level of **Critical Analysis**, or argument, is quickly and organically developing. If the research question one decides on is, What is interesting about the distinct way each text thematizes the relationship between love and sex?, a viable argument, based on evidence gleaned from close reading, might be: "Whereas Marlowe's text suggests that the pleasures of sex are best discovered within the context of a stable, long-term relationship, the text by Lekakis asserts that sex can be enjoyed in and of itself, undermining the importance of the long-term relationship." One might take this argument further. Why is what you have noted significant or particularly interesting? A possible answer to that question—and an even more sophisticated thesis—might be: "Thus, while the Lekakis text is, on the surface, less romantic, its attitude toward sex is much less confining than the attitude presented in Marlowe's text." Or, one might pursue an entirely different argument: "Whereas Marlowe's text indicates that sex is to be enjoyed mutually by two people, the Lekakis text implies that sex is something one 'does' to another person. Further, it implies that sex is a fairly meaningless and potentially aggressive activity."

The above description of the steps taken toward critical analysis shows how students of literature are meant to approach the works they read. What the description does not convey is why one would bother to make the effort at all, or why the process of critical literary analysis is thought to be a meaningful activity. In order to answer that question, it is helpful to consider how the discipline of literary studies came to be considered a worthwhile course of study for university and college students.

The history of literary studies is both very old and, in terms of the study of English literature, very fresh. In the fifth century, Martianus Capella wrote the allegory *De nuptiis Philologiae et Mercurii* ("The Marriage of Philology and Mercury"), in which he described the seven pillars of learning: grammar, dialectic, rhetoric, geometry, arithmetic, astronomy, and musical harmony. Collectively, such subjects came to be referred to as the liberal arts; as such, they were taken up by many of the high medieval universities as constituting the core curriculum. During the Early Modern period, the study of the so-called *trivium* (grammar, dialectic, rhetoric) was transformed to include the critical analysis of classical texts, i.e., the study of literature. As universities throughout Europe, and later in North America, proliferated and flourished between the sixteenth and nineteenth centuries, the focus remained on classical texts. As Gerald Graff explains, "In theory, the study of Greek and Latin was supposed to inspire the student with the nobility of his cultural heritage." (Somewhat paradoxically, classical texts were studied primarily in terms of their language use as opposed to their literary quality, perhaps because no one read or spoke Greek or Latin outside the classroom.) Until the late nineteenth century, the university system did not consider literary works written in English (or French or German or Italian) to be worthy of rigorous study, but only of *appreciation*. As Terry Eagleton notes in *Literary Theory: An Introduction*, the reading of works of English Literature was thought best left to working-class men, who might attend book clubs or public lectures, and to women; it was "a convenient sort of non-subject to palm off on the ladies, who were in any case excluded from science and the professions." It was only in the early twentieth century— hundreds of years after the founding of the great European universities—that literature came to be taken seriously as a university or college subject.

Over the past century and more, the discipline of literary studies has undergone a number of shifts. In the very early twentieth century, literature was studied largely for the way in which it embodied cultural tradition; one would learn something about being American or British by reading so-called great works of literature. (As British subjects, Canadians were also taught what it was to be a part of the British tradition.) By mid-century the focus had shifted to the aesthetic properties of the work itself. This fresh approach was known as Formalism and/or the New Criticism. Its proponents advocated paying close attention to literary form—in some cases, for an almost scientific approach to close reading. They tended to de-emphasize authorial biography and literary history. The influence of this approach continues to be felt in university and college classrooms (giving rise to such things as, for example, courses organized around the concept of literary genre). But it is important to keep in mind here that the emphasis on form—on generic conventions, on literary terminology, on the aesthetic as opposed to the cultural, philosophical, or moral qualities of literature—is not the only way to approach the study of literature, but was, rather, institutionalized as the best, most scholarly way. The work of close reading and producing literary criticism is not in any way "natural," but is how the study of literature has been "disciplined"; thus the student in a literature classroom should not feel discouraged if the initial steps of learning what it is he or she is supposed to be doing are challenging or seem strange.

The most recent important shift to have occurred in the "disciplining" of literary studies was the rise in the 1960s and 1970s of what became known as "literary theory." There is not room enough here to adequately elucidate the range of theories that have been introduced into literary studies, but a crude comparison between how emerging methods were set in opposition to New Criticism (which is itself a type of literary theory) may be useful. John Crowe Ransom's *The World's Body*—a sort of manifesto for New Criticism—argues that the work of the literary critic must strenuously avoid, among other things, "Any other special studies which deal with some abstract or prose content taken out of the work ... [such as] Chaucer's command of medieval sciences ... [or] Shakespeare's understanding of the law." In other words, the New Critic should focus solely on the text itself. In contrast, those today who make use of such theoretical frameworks as New Historicism, Gender Studies, or Postcolonial Studies will strenuously *embrace* all manner of "special studies" in order to consider how the text interacts with context. As Graff puts it, "Theory is what is generated when some aspect of literature, its nature, its history, its place in society, its conditions for production and reception, its meaning in general ... ceases to be a given and becomes a question to be argued." What this means for the student of literature trying to work out what to do with a text is that the question "Why is what I have noticed in the text significant?" can be approached from an almost limitless set of knowledge contexts. How might a particular poem illuminate historical notions of class divisions? How might a particular play tell us something about how technological advances have changed the way humans think about identity? And, though it might seem that the focus on form that so defines the New Critical approach becomes irrelevant once Literary Theory arrives on the disciplinary scene, the fact is that most field practitioners (i.e., writers of literary criticism) still depend heavily on the tools of close reading; formal analysis becomes the foundation on which a more theoretical analysis is built.

Thus, we might consider a sixth level of reading: advanced critical analysis. At this level the stakes are raised as arguments about why a text's formal construction is meaningful are set within a larger conceptual framework. The work of advanced critical analysis requires that the literary critic think about and research whatever conceptual framework is being pursued. For example, after noticing that the Marlowe text and the Lekakis text are written about 400 years apart, one might further research cultural attitudes toward sex in the two time periods to come up with another, even more sophisticated, layer of argumentation, one which would not only provide insight into two literary texts, but show how the comparative analysis of such texts tells us something about how viewpoints on sex have shifted. Or, after noticing that both texts are written by male authors, one might further research and consider what they reveal about masculine approaches to sex and seduction. Or, after discovering that Marlowe's poem follows the conventions of **pastoral** poetry, or that "Boom boom boom (let's go back to my room)" became popular within the LGBT community, one might contemplate and develop an argument about the implications of the way sex is idealized and/or becomes part of a complex cultural fantasy. Or, after discovering that Marlowe presented homoerotic material frequently in his other writing (in his poem "Hero and Leander," for example, he writes of one of the male protagonists that "in his looks were all that men desire"), one might inquire into the ways in which the author's or narrator's sexual orientation may or may not be relevant to a discussion of a love poem. To put it bluntly (and anachronistically), does it matter if Marlowe was gay?

Because the reading of literature entails a painstaking, thoughtful interaction with some of the most multifaceted, evocative, and provocative uses of language humans have produced, thinking about such work critically may tell us something about what it means to be human.

[N.G.]

Poetry

Why poetry? Why, when we hear so much of the value of making one's meaning plain to others, of striving for clarity, of avoiding ambiguity, should we pay attention to writing that much of the time seems to willfully ignore all of that? Is poetry important? Is poetry meaningless? What *is* it, anyway! And why should we study it?

If the human animal were so constructed as to always think without feeling, and feel without thinking, the human world would have no place for poetry. In the twenty-first century, what poetry may do best is to explore through words the places where reason and the emotions and senses meet. When we "think" of death, of loss, or of love, our powers of reasoning are unlikely to be untouched by our emotions—or by our senses. And much the same is often true when we think of morning, or of light, or of the sea. Poetry at its best can give full expression to the ways in which our thoughts and feelings come together with our sense impressions—and can itself give rise to powerful sense impressions. Not infrequently, indeed, poetry has been defined by the physical reactions it is capable of producing. "If I read a book and it makes my whole body so cold no fire can ever warm me," wrote the American poet Emily Dickinson, "I know that is poetry." "If I feel physically as if the top of my head were taken off, I know *that* is poetry," she added.

It seems safe to conclude that few lose their heads to poetry in the way Dickinson describes—but a great many others find there is a natural association between poetry and intensity of feeling. Carol Ann Duffy tells us that poems, above all, "are a series of intense moments." Of her own poetry she writes, "I'm not dealing with facts. I'm dealing with emotions." The Australian poet Les Murray suggests that "a true poem is dreamed and danced as well as thought."

Murray knows perfectly well that a poem cannot be danced—not in any literal sense. Like Dickinson, in attempting to describe poetry he has resorted to the language of poetry: language that suggests and likens and associates as it moves toward meaning. Even more than in prose fiction or in drama, language is central to the ways in which poems work. In a poem the connotations of a word or phrase—the things that it is capable of suggesting—are often at least as important as the word's denotative meaning. Poetry works above all through association. Associations of thought and emotion and sense impressions; associations of sound and of sense; associations between physical images; and associations between what we see on a printed page and what goes on in our minds. Let's turn to that last one first.

The Look of Poetry

The layers of an onion have frequently been a metaphorical reference point when people talk about trying to get to the centre of something. Let's begin this section by looking at a few lines from a poem about the real thing— "Onions," by Lorna Crozier:

> If Eve had bitten it
> Instead of the apple
> How different
> Paradise

Compare that with how the same words would look on the page written as prose:

> If Eve had bitten it instead of the apple how different paradise.

Why do these words work better set out in the way that Crozier has chosen? Does setting them out this way on the page make them more easily intelligible? In prose, arguably, one would have to add not only punctuation but also extra words to convey the same meaning:

> If Eve had bitten it instead of the apple, how different paradise would have been.

As is often the case, poetry is here a means of expression more concise than prose. It also gives the words different emphases; giving "Paradise" a line on its own draws attention to the notion of paradise itself.

Laying out words in the way that Crozier has done may also encourage the reader to feel suggestions of a variety of meanings; ambiguity, which we generally take to be a fault if it occurs in essay writing, can add interest and richness to poetry. A poem's presence as words and lines upon a page can open up a rich world of suggestion for the reader—and open up too the possibility of surprise. Let's turn to another example. The following lines are taken from a poem by Al Purdy about the experience of pioneers trying to farm in early Ontario, "The Country North of Belleville":

> a lean land
>   not like the fat south
> with inches of black soil on
>   earth's round belly —

And where the farms are
       it's as if a man stuck
both thumbs in the stony earth and pulled
       it apart
         to make room
   enough between the trees
    for a wife
        and maybe some cows and
        room for some
  of the more easily kept illusions

Which are the lines here that end in ways that open up different possible meanings? Where are we surprised? Does that surprise happen differently because the words and lines are laid out in verse? Perhaps the most notable thing about the layout of these lines is the way in which the lines "it apart" and "to make room" are set with plenty of space to each side, suggesting through the look of the words on the page their literal meaning. Do the lines "for a wife" and "of the more easily kept illusions" also surprise? Surely they strike the reader in a slightly different way than they would if they were set out as prose.

Laying the words of a poem out on the page in irregular lines in this way (as **free verse**) has become commonplace—so much so that many now think of it as the primary form in which poetry is written. But until the late nineteenth century in France, and until well into the twentieth century in the English-speaking world, such poetry was unheard of. Before the **imagist** verse of Ezra Pound and of H.D. and, even more influentially, the early poetry of T.S. Eliot, the layout of a poem on the page was typically governed by formal metrical patterns (and also, often, by rhyme)—governed, in short, by structures of sound.

Poetry and Sound

There are many ways in which poetry can be organized according to sound. In a language such as Shona (a Bantu language), tonal patterns may provide the structure; much of Shona poetry is characterized by a drifting downwards in pitch from the beginning to the end of each line. In ancient Greece and Rome the organizing principle was the lengths of the sounds, with each line organized into patterns of alternating long and short sounds. The length of a sound is also referred to as its **quantity**, and poetry based on a system of alternating lengths of sound as **quantitative verse**. The Greeks developed a set of terms to describe sound combinations with this system—terms we still use today (albeit with a twist, as discussed below). A pattern in which short sounds were followed by long sounds was called iambic, and a single grouping of a short sound followed by a long sound was called an **iamb**. Other possible patterns of long and short sounds were similarly categorized. A long sound followed by a short sound was called a **trochee**; a long sound followed by two short sounds was called a **dactyl**; two short sounds followed by a long sound was called an **anapest**; a group of two long sounds together was called a **spondee**, and so on. Each group of sounds was termed a **foot**, and lines of poetry would be formed with a set number of poetic feet. If each line in a poem comprised five iambs in a row, then the **metre**, or pattern of poetic rhythm, was called **iambic pentameter**—the most common metre in ancient Greek and Roman poetry.

The Anglo-Saxon (or Old English) language was organized according to very different structures of sound. What mattered was not which syllables were long and which were short, but which were **stressed** (or **accented**) and which were not. A line of poetry in Old English is typically divided into two halves, in each of which there are two stressed syllables. Here, for example, are two lines from the most famous poem in Old English, *Beowulf*:

Swa sceal geong guma	gode gewyrcean
Fromum feohgiftum	on faeder bearme

So shall [a] young man	good make-happen
[with] pious gifts	from [his] father's coffers

In the first of these lines the syllables "geong" and "gu-" are stressed, as are the syllables "gode" and "wyrc"; in the next line the syllables "From-" and "gift" are stressed, as are the syllables "fae-" and "bear-." It is a structure of sound that does not take into account the *total* number of sounds or syllables in each line; what matters is the number of *stressed* syllables in each line.

Even without any knowledge of Old English, it's easy to notice that another organizing principle is operating in the sounds of these lines: **alliteration**. In Old English poetry there is typically alliteration between one or both of the stressed syllables in the first half-line and the first stressed syllable of the second half-line. (There is often also a good deal of alliteration beyond that—as there is here.)

A third way of structuring a poem according to sounds may also be found in Old English poetry, but it appears in only a single poem that has survived. It is a poem known as "The Rhyming Poem," and **rhyme** is indeed its organizing principle, with lines organized into rhyming pairs, or **couplets**. Aside from that one example, rhyme is nowhere present in the Anglo-Saxon literature that has come down to us; rhyme evidently never took hold in Anglo-Saxon poetry. It became a staple of later English poetry due to the influence of French poetry on English—specifically, songs of love and chivalry of the twelfth- and thirteenth-century French poets known as troubadours. Rhyme is a strong presence in the poetry of Geoffrey Chaucer (most of whose work comprises lines of 10 syllables with no clear pattern of stressed and unstressed syllables but with a rhyme at the end of every line). But there is no uniformity in the sound structures of medieval English poetry; some of the most important medieval poems (notably *Sir Gawain and the Green Knight*) use alliterative structures of sounds very similar to those found in Old English poetry.

Metre and Rhythm

The English Renaissance of the sixteenth century breathed new life into the ideas and the literary works of ancient Greece and Rome. It also picked up on the literary work and intellectual currents of the Italian Renaissance that had begun more than a century earlier. By the late sixteenth century the metrical patterns of ancient Greek and Latin poetry had become dominant in English poetry as well. But where the ancient Greeks and Romans had structured poetic metre on the basis of *long* and *short* syllables, English substituted a system based on *stressed* and *unstressed* syllables. In ancient Greece a line of iambic pentameter was a line in which a short syllable was followed by a long syllable five times in a row; in Renaissance England it became a line in which an unstressed syllable is followed by a stressed syllable five times in a row. Because it is based on counting the syllables in each line (and in each group of sounds, or poetic foot, within that line), this system of metre is syllabic; because it is also based on stress, or accent, it is accentual. The system, then, is known as **accentual-syllabic verse**.

Given that spoken English tends toward substantial variation in levels of stress (far more so than Greek or Latin or French or Italian), it is perhaps not very surprising that English would emphasize alternation between stressed and unstressed syllables rather than between longer and shorter syllables. But the degree to which the new accentual-syllabic approach to structuring the sounds of poetry came to dominate—and the speed with which it came to dominate—is remarkable. At the beginning of the sixteenth century accentual-syllabic poetry was still a rarity in England; by the end of the century virtually all poetry written in English used some form of accentual-syllabic metre.

Where accentual-syllabic metre is strictly adhered to, the alternation of stressed and unstressed syllables follows an absolutely regular pattern. Such is the case, for example, in these lines from Sir Walter Ralegh's "The Nymph's Reply to the Shepherd":

> If all the world and love were young,
> And truth in ev'ry shepherd's tongue,
> These pretty pleasures might me move
> To live with thee and be thy love.

These lines are written in iambic tetrameter—an accentual-syllabic metre in which each line is composed of four iambic feet; that is to say, each group of syllables (or foot) is made up of an unstressed syllable followed by a stressed syllable, with four such groups in every line. Here are the lines again with the feet and the stressed syllables marked:

   /   /   /   /

If all / the world / and love / were young,

       /   /   /   /

And truth / in ev'- / ry shep- / herd's tongue,

     /   /   /   /

These pret- / ty pleas- / ures might / me move

   /   /   /   /

To live / with thee / and be / thy love.

Iambic tetrameter is one common accentual-syllabic metre; more common still is iambic pentameter—in which each line has five feet rather than four. A metre in which the lines have three feet is call **trimeter**; a metre in which the lines have six feet is called **hexameter**.

Together with an accentual-syllabic metre, Ralegh employs rhyme as a second structure of sound in the poem; the lines are in couplets, with the last words in each couplet rhyming (*young* and *tongue*) or almost rhyming (*move* and *love*[1]).

It is worth noticing here that in the interests of maintaining the regular pattern of metre and of rhyme, the ordering of the words has been made (to modern ears at least) less regular; Ralegh writes "might me move" instead of using the more common syntactical arrangement "might move me." Such alterations of word order are called **syntactical inversions**.

Rhyme is very commonly used in poems that follow an accentual-syllabic metrical structure, but there is no necessary connection between the two. Indeed, some of the best-known poetry in English is written in **blank verse**— lines in iambic pentameter that do not rhyme. Such verse is found frequently in William Shakespeare's plays and is used throughout John Milton's epic poem *Paradise Lost*. Here are the final four lines of that poem:

The world was all before them, where to choose
Their place of rest, and Providence their guide.
They, hand in hand, with wand'ring steps and slow
Through Eden took their solitary way.

---

1   It is entirely possible that "move" and "love" may have rhymed fully in England in Ralegh's time.

The syllables at the ends of these lines (*choose, guide, slow, way*) do not rhyme—but the lines do follow a regular pattern of unstressed and stressed syllables. Here are the lines again, this time with the feet and the stressed syllables[1] marked:

> /　　　　/　　　/　　　　　　/　　　　/
> The world / was all / be-fore / them, where / to choose
> 　/　　　　/　　　　　/　　　　/　　　　　/
> Their place / of rest, / and Pro- /vi- dence / their guide.
> 　　/　　　　/　　　　　/　　　　　/　　　　　/
> They, hand / in hand, / with wand'- / ring steps / and slow
> 　　/　　　　　/　　　　/　　　　/　　　/
> Through E- /den took / their sol- / i-tar- / y way.

The lines have a very different feel to them than do the lines from the Ralegh poem—and that's more than a matter of their being unrhymed, or than their having five feet in each line rather than four. Three of the four lines from the Ralegh poem are **end stopped**—that is, they end with punctuation such as a comma or period that brings a marked pause in the verse. And none of the Ralegh lines is written with a significant pause in the middle of the line. In contrast, there are significant pauses in the middle of three of the four lines from *Paradise Lost*—and only two of the four are end stopped. Both these features have names. The practice of carrying sense and grammatical construction past the end of a line in poetry is called **enjambment**; a pause in the middle of a line of poetry is called a **caesura**. By using enjambment and caesura, poets can vary the rhythm of a poem while the underlying metre—the arrangement of stressed and unstressed syllables—remains the same.

Enjambment and caesura are two of several aspects of rhythm that do not depend on metre. Another is the *degree* to which the sounds of syllables may be stressed or unstressed. A widely unappreciated aspect of rhythm is that not all accented syllables are stressed to the same degree. Compare for example the lines from the Ralegh poem quoted above with the first two lines of Philip Larkin's "This Be the Verse":

> If all the world and love were young,
> And truth in ev'ry shepherd's tongue,
>
> They fuck you up, your mum and dad.
> They may not mean to, but they do.

---

1   To some degree the accenting of syllables is subjective, of course. One might, for example, read these lines with a stress placed on *They* at the beginning of the third line.

Here are the Larkin lines again, with the stressed syllables and the poetic feet marked:

        /   /   /   /
They fuck / you up, / your mum / and dad.
        /   /   /   /
They may / not mean / to, but / they do.

The pattern of stressed and unstressed syllables in these lines is exactly the same as with the Ralegh lines (or, to put it another way, the lines **scan** identically). Yet the rhythm is very different. The reader naturally places a stronger stress on the second syllable of the first line here ("they *fuck* you up") than on the second syllable of the first line from Ralegh ("if *all* the world ...").

What about the levels of stress on other syllables? Overall, the first two lines of the Larkin poem read far less smoothly than do the first lines of Ralegh's; that has something to do with the caesuras in both the Larkin lines. But just as important are the levels of emphasis that we naturally put on the syllables, which vary far more widely in the Larkin lines. In the lines from Ralegh the stressed syllables are stressed to roughly the same degree, and the unstressed syllables are unstressed to roughly the same degree. That consistency imparts a good deal of smoothness to the sound of the lines—a smoothness entirely appropriate to the sense of the lines. In the Larkin the wider variation in levels of stress, together with the caesuras, creates an aural sense of disorder that is entirely appropriate to the sense of those lines.

If variation in levels of stress is one underappreciated element of poetic rhythm, another is variation in quantity—in the length of time it takes to say different syllables. Of course everyone speaks at a different rate; no two people are likely to take exactly the same time to say the same group of syllables or the same poetic line, any more than any two people are likely to place exactly the same level of stress on a particular group of syllables. But no one is likely to put as much emphasis on the stressed syllables of "level sands" as on the stressed syllables of "break, blow, burn." By the same token, no one is likely to take as long to say the three syllables "bit of it" as to say the three syllables "lengths of sound," or take as long to say the two syllables "so-so" as to say the two syllables "skunks cringe." Everyone has long accepted that an entire system based on quantity—such as that of the ancient Greeks and Romans—would not work in English. But that should not be taken as evidence that the local effects of quantity in a poem are unimportant. To get a sense of how greatly such things can affect the rhythm of a line of poetry, let's compare another pair of lines: the final line of Thomas Hardy's "During Wind and Rain" and the final line of Larkin's "This Be the Verse." Each has eight syllables:

Down their carved names the rain drop ploughs.

And don't have any kids yourself.

Larkin's eight quick, no-nonsense syllables bring the poem skidding to a close. The eight syllables that end the Hardy poem, in contrast, move as slowly as a plough—the sound entirely suggestive of the sense of the line.

The idea that a poem works most effectively when its sounds suggest its sense is an old one; the eighteenth-century poet Alexander Pope gave memorable expression to it in *An Essay on Criticism*, asserting that in poetry, "the sound must seem an echo to the sense." Poets have in many cases continued to strive for these aural effects. The effect they are striving for might perhaps be termed broad onomatopoeia. In an individual word or phrase, **onomatopoeia** occurs when the sounds of the words in themselves seem to imitate the sound they are naming—as do, for example, the words *burst* or *scrape*. A broader sort of imitation is involved in phrases such as Tennyson's "as moving seems asleep," Milton's "with wandering steps and slow," or Hardy's "the rain drop ploughs." And perhaps something that might be called onomatopoeia may operate more broadly still. Arguably, some form of onomatopoeia—of the sounds of a poem imitating its sense—can operate throughout entire poems, such as Robert Herrick's "Delight in Disorder" and Theodore Roethke's "My Papa's Waltz."

Rhyme

The examples of patterns of rhyme we have touched on thus far have been rhyming couplets. That is only one way of rhyming; many possible **rhyme schemes** may be used as part of the organizing principle of a poem: rhyming every other line; carrying on patterns of rhyme from one stanza to another; returning at the end of a poem to rhymes used at the beginning.

Ever since the dramatic break with the past that modernism ushered in early in the twentieth century, poets in the English-speaking world have generally chosen not to rhyme. In North America, rhyme is thought of as appropriate to certain forms of music—from folk music to hip-hop. But the thought of rhyming in *poetry* often conjures up images of verse that is childish or sentimental or hopelessly old fashioned, or all of the above. Those who disparage rhyme as an adult activity think of a conventional rhyme scheme operating in conjunction with a highly regular metre—and of rhymed verse where it seems the poet has been entirely willing to meddle with normal grammar and syntax for no better purpose than to achieve rhymes at the end of each line. A few lines from Letitia Landon's "The Improvisatrice" may be enough to convey the idea:

And fondly round his neck she clung;
Her long black tresses round him flung,
Love-chains, which would not let him part;
And he could feel her beating heart,
The pulses of her small white hand,
The tears she could no more command.

It was no doubt with this sort of poetry in the back of her mind that the modern Irish poet Eavan Boland wrote "Against Love Poetry"—as a prose poem, without lines, without stanzas, without metre, without rhyme. But rhyme has no necessary connection to particular sentiments or poetic traditions, and it may be used quite independently of any accentual-syllabic metrical system. It may be used loosely in free verse—as T.S. Eliot does in these lines from *The Waste Land*:

The river sweats
Oil and tar
The barges drift
With the turning tide
Red sails
Wide
To leeward, swing on the heavy spar.

It may also be used to provide a structure of sound through an entire poem that lacks any strict pattern of metre—as is the case in Larkin's "The Old Fools." It may be used within the framework of a traditional form such as a sonnet, but in ways that are entirely varied and fresh. Such is the case, for example, in Alice Oswald's "Wedding," in which **slant rhymes** and other imperfect rhymes help to create a sense of exuberant abandon:

And this, my love, when millions come and go
Beyond the need of us, is like a trick;
And when the trick begins, it's like a toe
Tip-toeing on a rope, which is like luck;
And when this luck begins, it's like a wedding,
Which is like love, which is like everything.

As every child senses intuitively, rhyme gives the human ear an opportunity to recognize and confirm a regular pattern—something the mind delights in. Because it has served this purpose for so long, it's sometimes used by modern and contemporary poets to suggest the very idea of regularity and order—or to suggest a sense of delight. An excellent example of this is Dorothy Livesay's "The Three Emilys," which begins with a regular rhyme scheme of three rhyming couplets (aabbcc). Then, as the speaker's thought processes become more complex and confused, the rhyme scheme falls away, and the poem's form becomes increasingly disordered, its sounds suggesting the speaker's mental state.

A more contemporary, and equally inventive, use of rhyme to convey meaning is found in Kim Addonizio's "First Poem for You," which uses the rhyme scheme of the Shakespearian sonnet to perfection, but makes such extensive use of enjambment that the human ear has to strain to actually detect the rhyme. Here's how the poem begins:

> I like to touch your tattoos in complete
> darkness, when I can't see them. I'm sure of
> where they are, know by heart the neat
> lines of lightning pulsing just above
> your nipple,

We may sometimes think of rhyme as being an inherently intrusive aural element in a poem—something that will inevitably draw attention to itself rather than to the meaning of the lines. But if the rhyming syllables are only lightly stressed, as is the case here, rhyme can operate quite unobtrusively. And that is all the more true if, again as here, the poet employs enjambment and caesura, so that the reader never stops and lingers at the rhymes.

"First Poem for You" continues in the same vein for 12 of its 14 lines. Not until the final two lines are there any end-stopped lines. And that creates an ongoing gentle tension. The quiet regularity with which the rhyme scheme operates pulls in one direction, the thoughts running past the ends of the lines in another. Is there a similar tension in the speaker's mind? She is attracted to the tattoo, but at the same time terrified by its permanence. Are her feelings toward the tattoo suggestive of her feelings toward her lover and the possibility of a commitment that might be permanent?

In the Shakespearian sonnet form the final two lines are a rhymed couplet—and here too Addonizio holds to the form. But now the poem abandons enjambment; both these final lines are end-stopped, thus giving strong emphasis to each line's final word.

> … whatever persists
> or turns to pain between us, they will still
> be there. Such permanence is terrifying.
> So I touch them in the dark; but touch them, trying.

In a poem that seems in large part to be about trying to deal with the terror of permanence in a relationship, it is wonderfully appropriate to have the two words "trying" and "terrifying" rhymed in a couplet at the poem's end. There are many tensions and harmonies in "First Poem for You"—and throughout the poem, sound echoes sense. To observe such unity is to be reminded that rhyme isn't just a sound effect; it can be a lovely "aha!" shared by mind and ear together.

• • •

It is sometimes imagined that sound is only an important element of poetry when some sound-related organizing principle is involved—metre, or rhyme, or some wholly different aural principle (such as that involved in Christian Bök's *Eunoia*, in which each section uses one vowel only). But even poets who tend not to organize their poems according to aural principles are often highly attuned to sound. Margaret Atwood is a good example. She remains a poet better known for the striking ways in which her poems lay words out on a page than she is for the sounds of her poems. Yet here is how she responded in 1984 to an interviewer's question about "words on the page":

> First of all, a poem is not words on a page. A poem is words in the air; or I should say words in the ear, because a poem is heard. And the words on the page are a notation like a musical score. We would not say that Beethoven was a bunch of black marks on a page; you would say that Beethoven is what we hear when we transcribe those black marks. And it's the same with a poem; when you are reading a poem the words are in your ear.

Is she right? Interestingly, when Atwood reads her own poems, her voice is quite flat. That is to say, it does not vary much in pitch; there are no "high notes" or "low notes" as there are in most pieces of music. The effect is to focus one's ears more strongly on the aural elements that *do* vary in any poem in English—levels of stress and lengths of sound chief among them.

Imagery, Metaphor and Simile, Symbol

If poetry is very largely about the power of suggestion, the **images** that a poem conjures up are often central to that power. When readers think of imagery, they often think first of imagist poets such as Ezra Pound, H.D., and William Carlos Williams—poets who use the spacing of the words on the page (and the sounds those words convey) in ways that draw attention to the physical images the words name. This is what Williams does in poems such as "The Red Wheelbarrow" and "This Is Just to Say," poems that offer the reader fragments of experience.

I have eaten
the plums

that were in
the icebox

and which
you were probably
saving
for breakfast

Forgive me
they were delicious
so sweet
and so cold

It is often imagined that what gives an image specificity must be purely a matter of physical description. But an image may also be made specific by human circumstance; what gives the plums specificity here is not only the physical attributes of sweetness and coldness but also their "history"—the small part they play in the relationship between the speaker and the one he is addressing.

It is useful in discussing poetic imagery to distinguish between the two axes concrete/abstract and specific/general. Whereas the opposite of concrete is abstract, the opposite of specific is general. The terms "concrete" and "specific" are often used almost interchangeably in discussing imagery, and certainly there is an overlap between the two. Yet they are in fact distinct from each other. The word "fruit" expresses something concrete but general; the word "nourishment" expresses a far more abstract concept. To speak of "plums" is to be both more specific and more concrete than to speak of "fruit." To speak of "ripe plums" is again both more concrete and more specific. "The plums that were in the icebox," though, is not a more concrete image than "the plums"; it adds a degree of specificity to the image without adding to the concreteness of it.

It is sometimes implied when attention is drawn to the specificity of images in such poems as these, that it is inherently better poetically if particular plums are referenced. Is there in fact anything inherently poetic about specificity? Certainly specificity helps to make William Carlos Williams's images memorable. But it is also true that many of the best loved and most admired poems are remembered at least as much for images that convey a very general sense of the physical—even a sense of vagueness. Would not the door in Atwood's "The Door," to choose one recent example, lose much of its suggestive power if it were made more specific, located more clearly in a specific place or time?

Even in poems inspired by very specific things or places, the images in the resulting poetry may often appeal to us through images that are far from specific—that are quite general or even vague. "Tintern Abbey" is a good example. Inspired by a specific place familiar to him, William Wordsworth appeals to us through images that have a high degree of generality, as he speaks of how he has been affected by his experiences:

> ... changed, no doubt, from what I was when first
> I came among these hills; when like a roe
> I bounded o'er the mountains, by the sides
> Of the deep rivers, and the lonely streams,
> Wherever nature led.

Much as specificity in images can be of value, it may also be the case that imagery with a certain vagueness or generality to it can be particularly effective in allowing the imagination of the reader to enter the poem.

Imagery in poetry is sometimes imagined to consist almost entirely of metaphor or simile—of using figures of speech to liken one thing to another. We will get to those in a moment. But the pure description found in poems such as the ones referenced above by Williams and Wordsworth may help to remind us that metaphor is not everything when it comes to imagery. Another example of how powerful imagery can be without metaphor or simile is Douglas LePan's "The Haystack." In that poem there are likenesses drawn between the still-alive soldier writing the poem, with his sunburn, and the soldier immolated by the haystack—but they are simple comparisons, not figures of speech.

If metaphor and simile are not everything when it comes to imagery, they are nevertheless central to a very great deal of what poetry does. In essence, **metaphor** is a way of likening one thing to another thing through language. In its simplest form, the **simile**, the likeness is made explicit through the use of words such as *like* or *as if*. "Like a roe I bounded o'er the mountains" is a simile in which Wordsworth is likening himself to an animal. That example—like the line so often used as the paradigm of a simile, Robert Burns's "My love is like a red, red rose"—offers a likeness that is easy for almost any reader to comprehend. Many similes, though, draw connections that are far more tenuous. Such is the case, for example, with the simile in the last line of Dylan Thomas's "Fern Hill" ("I sang in my chains like the sea"), or this simile from John Ashbery's "The Improvement": "the leopard is transparent, like iced tea." Such is the case also with the famous simile at the opening of "The Love Song of J. Alfred Prufrock":

> Let us go then, you and I,
> When the evening is spread out against the sky
> Like a patient etherized upon a table

The suggestive power of a simile can often be arresting in ways that are surprising or puzzling or disturbing; the same is true of other forms of metaphorical language. Sometimes such metaphors may be compressed into a powerful phrase, as is the case when Karen Solie writes of a sturgeon landed on the water's edge being unable to contain

> the old current he had for a mind, its pull
> and his body a muscle called river, called spawn.

Using highly concentrated metaphorical language, Solie likens the fish's body to the river that is its natural home, the fish's mind to the current of the river—and then ends by drawing a further likeness.

In a longer poem patterns of imagery and metaphor may appear and reappear, taking on different shadings each time. In *Maud*, for example—Alfred, Lord Tennyson's long 1856 poem about love and war—the first part ends with the protagonist imagining flowers blooming over the grave of the woman he loves: "blossom in purple and red." Much later in the poem, the final section of Tennyson's original version ends with the protagonist, having lost all hope of love, leaving for the Crimean War, where he imagines that from the

> ... deathful-grinning mouths of the fortress flames
> The blood-red blossom of war with a heart of fire.

The suggestiveness of such contrasting images as these takes us about as far as could be imagined from the simplicity of "like a red, red rose."

The rose appears and reappears in different contexts in *Maud*, but at no point does the poet dwell on it in extended or elaborate fashion. Some poems, however, do precisely that: elaborate on a single metaphor in a sustained way over several stanzas. Such is the case with the comparison between two souls and the twin feet of a compass in the final stanzas of John Donne's "A Valediction: Forbidding Mourning." An elaborate and sustained metaphor such as Donne's twin feet is often referred to as a **conceit** or a Petrarchan conceit; many of the poems of Petrarch include this sort of extended metaphor. Indeed, a metaphor may be extended throughout an entire poem—as it is, for example, when Lady Mary Wroth compares love to a child in "Love, a Child, is Ever Crying."

When a comparison (metaphorical or otherwise) is made or implied between something non-human and human qualities, it is often referred to as **personification**. Thus Sir Philip Sidney personifies the moon in this opening to one of his sonnets:

> With how sad steps, O Moon, thou climb'st the skies!
> How silently, and with how wan a face!

And thus Allen Ginsberg personifies his country in his poem "America":

America, when will you be angelic?
When will you take off your clothes?

A figure of speech that is sometimes grouped with metaphor and simile is **metonymy**. Like metaphors and similes, metonyms do bring together different things. But whereas with metaphor and simile the connection is a matter of comparison, with metonymy it is a matter of association. The following sentences may clarify the distinction:

Numerous scientists have criticized Ottawa's plan to close the environmental research centre.

What dish are you cooking tonight?

In the first of these examples the word "Ottawa" is standing for "the federal government of Canada"; as the capital, Ottawa is the home of the federal government and is thus naturally associated with it, but it is not being compared to the federal government. Nor, in the second example, is the dish being compared to the food; it is associated with the food rather than likened to it. When T.S. Eliot writes in "The Love Song of J. Alfred Prufrock" of "sawdust restaurants" he is employing metonymy; the restaurants are not being likened to sawdust but rather associated with one particular characteristic: the sawdust on the floor.

A related literary device is **synecdoche**—the practice of referring to a part of something in a way that stands for the whole. If someone asks "Have you got wheels?" the rhetorical device of synecdoche is being used—as it is in a number of vulgar expressions in which a person's sexual organs are named as a way of referring to an entire person ("The prick followed me all the way home"). Synecdoche may be thought of as one form of metonymy: wheels are part of a car and that is one way of being associated with a car. But (unlike with metaphor and simile) they are not being *likened* to a car. Eliot's "The Love Song of J. Alfred Prufrock" may again provide a poetic example; he employs synecdoche when he writes "after the teacups" rather than saying "after we had finished with the tea and the teacups and the sandwiches...." It is useful to be aware of devices such as metonymy and synecdoche—but it is also useful to be aware that they occur far less frequently in poetry than do metaphor, simile, and personification.

One other concept that is important to the understanding of poetic imagery—and of poetry generally—is **symbol**. This is a term used more loosely than most of the terms discussed above—it is one that may overlap with many of them (a metaphor may act as a symbol, but so may a metonym). In Christian tradition a cross evokes the crucifix but may also symbolize Christianity or Christ's body. The beaver and the maple leaf are symbols of Canada, as the bald eagle is a symbol of the United States. But not all symbols are entrenched in tradition as are these—and not all are cast in stone. A bird is often in poetry a symbol of freedom, but in Ted Hughes's poem "Heptonstall Old Church," a bird is a symbol for Christian religion. The rose is traditionally a symbol of love, but it may also carry other associations. As Atwood's "The Door" illustrates, a door may be a symbol of possibilities opening up—but it may also symbolize their final closing.

Meaning

In every age there have been poets and poems whose meanings are more difficult to discern than others. There have also been significant shifts over time in the ways in which poets strive to express meaning—or, in some cases, to problematize the very idea that a poem should have a meaning. One such shift began in France in the second half of the nineteenth century. The young poet Arthur Rimbaud was one who rejected the conventions both of Western poetry and of Western society altogether. Here is how he put it in his 1871 collection *Une Saison en Enfer* (*A Season in Hell*):

> Un soir, j'ai assis la Beauté sur mes genoux—et je l'ai trouvée amère— et je l'ai injuriée. (One night I set Beauty down on my lap—and I found her bitter—and I gave her a rough time.)

When Edgar Allan Poe, writing in 1849, described the poetry of words as "the rhythmical creation of beauty," he was giving memorable expression to an idea that for centuries had been generally assumed to be central to the art of poetry. Rimbaud turned all that on its head: the rejection of any idea that the poet should be creating something beautiful is a consistent theme in his work, with images of vomit and of mucus jostling together with images of children and of the sea. What is the reader to make of such poetry? How are we to construct meaning out of it?

The modernist revolution in English poetry that poets such as Ezra Pound and T.S. Eliot ushered in early in the twentieth century has deep roots in the work of nineteenth-century French poets such as Rimbaud, Jules Laforgue, and Stéphane Mallarmé. Both Pound and Eliot rejected the conventionally beautiful, and both rejected conventional order in poetry. No longer was it felt that incidents or images should connect clearly and coherently with meaning, or that the images and meanings of one line should follow from that of the previous one in ways that could be clearly understood. "What branches grow Out of this stony rubbish?" Eliot asked in *The Waste Land*—

and answered, "You cannot say, or guess, for you know only A heap of broken images."

Modernism forged its own traditions, which have remained strong through the twentieth century and on into the twenty-first. The disconnectedness of the images in John Ashbery's poems is striking, but so too is the *sense* that there is meaning here, even if it may be impossible to express in words other than those used by the poet himself. What meaning is there in the sort of suggestive "heap of images" that we find in a poem such as Ashbery's "Civilization and Its Discontents"?

> ... What is agreeable
> Is to hold your hand. The gravel
> Underfoot. The time is for coming close. Useless
> Verbs shooting the other words far away.
> I had already swallowed the poison
> And could only gaze into the distance at my life
> Like a saint's with each day distinct.
> No heaviness in the upland pastures. Nothing
> In the forest. Only life under the huge trees
> Like a coat that has grown too big, moving far away,
> Cutting swamps for men like lapdogs, holding its own,
> Performing once again, for you and for me.

That some sense of meaning can emerge out of apparently disconnected images may be psychologically less strange than it might seem, given what is now being discovered about the human brain. "What is the sound of the gravel underfoot?" seems a question that asks for unsurprising associations to be made. But research conducted by scientists such as Anne-Sylvie Crisinel and Charles Spence of the University of Oxford suggests that associations that cross sense barriers may operate far more widely than has been suspected. It's not only that loud sounds suggest brightness, or that high-pitched sounds suggest smallness. Experiments have shown, for example, that the smell of blackberries evokes the sound of a piano in many people's minds, and that bitter tastes suggest lower pitched sounds to most people. Such research is still in its infancy, but it may be far from ludicrous to ask, in responding to lines such as Ashbery's, such questions as these: Do the sounds he gives us lead us to smell the upland pastures? Does it feel right to have the distance low-pitched, a saint high-pitched? What colour is heaviness? Though this introduction has for convenience treated sound and sense and visual image as largely separate phenomena, it has recognized that they are inter-related. How deeply and broadly the connections extend—and how far they may take the suggestiveness of images in the direction of poetic meaning—is something we are still finding out.

In the medieval period and through the Renaissance the accepted view was that poetry should have both a clear meaning and a clear moral purpose. One way of conveying a moral message was simply to tell a story, and have the good characters end up rewarded and the bad characters punished—though to put it so crudely is to grossly oversimplify the poetic theory of the time. Even when poetry was not telling a story, it was felt that moral improvement was a natural accompaniment to the art of poetry. Poetry should imitate the world—but in doing so should always make plain the world as it *should* be. As Sir Philip Sidney put it in the late sixteenth century, poetry is "an art of imitation, a speaking picture with this end, to teach and delight."

The consensus that instruction and delight were twin purposes of poetry (and indeed of all literature) remained powerful through to the late eighteenth century, when the French Revolution and the birth of Romanticism brought a shift; the idea that poetry should provide moral instruction began to lose favour, while the idea that poetry should give expression to the truths of nature, and to unbridled human feeling (including feelings of romantic love, certainly, but including as well strong political feeling) came to the fore. It was during this era that Wordsworth defined poetry as "the spontaneous overflow of powerful feelings: it takes its origin from emotion recollected in tranquility." It was in this era too that Percy Shelley argued that poetry had to it "something divine," but that it also could and should be used to further political causes. He wrote with equal passion of the spiritual force of nature and of the oppressive force of the wealthy landlords and heartless manufacturers of the era. Here, for example, is how he addresses the labouring classes in "Song to the Men of England," a poem widely taken up by the British labour movement:

Men of England, wherefore plough
For the lords who lay ye low?
Wherefore weave with toil and care
The rich robes your tyrants wear?

The notion that conveying a political message can be as appropriate to poetry as conveying thoughts of nature or of love did not begin with Shelley, nor did it end with him; it remained a powerful sub-current in nineteenth-century aesthetics. The modernism of the early twentieth century, however, was antithetical not only to the notion that poetry should try to teach, but also to the idea that it should have any clear meaning. Perhaps the most extreme expression of this view (on the face of it, at least) appears in "Ars Poetica," a poem by the American modernist Archibald MacLeish, which concludes as follows:

A poem should be equal to:
Not true.

> For all the history of grief
> An empty doorway and a maple leaf.
>
> For love
> the leaning grasses and two lights above the sea—
>
> A poem should not mean
> But be.

Does MacLeish really mean that a poem should be without meaning? Or is he simply trying to argue that what comes naturally to poetry is suggestion and association—that poetry does not naturally convey meaning in any fixed or conventional sense?

Eliot, the most important figure of modernism, did not go so far as to suggest that a poem should be without meaning. But he did feel that it was natural to the spirit of the age for poetry to be difficult. Here is how he put it in his 1926 essay "The Metaphysical Poets":

> … it appears likely that poets in our civilization, must be *difficult*.…
> The poet must become more and more comprehensive, more allusive,
> more indirect, in order to force, to dislocate if necessary, language
> into his meaning.

The idea that meanings in poetry should be allusive and indirect—perhaps even by their very nature inexpressible in words other than those chosen by the poet—remained strong through the twentieth century and into the twenty-first. It is the governing idea in Les Murray's "The Meaning of Existence":

> Everything except language
> knows the meaning of existence.
> Trees, planets, rivers, time
> know nothing else. They express it
> moment by moment as the universe.
>
> Even this fool of a body
> lives it in part, and would
> have full dignity within it
> but for the ignorant freedom
> of my talking mind.

Does language truly get in the way of meaning, as Murray suggests? It is one irony of the poem that, even as it suggests that the meaning of existence is inexpressible through language, it conveys that thought in a wonderfully clear and coherent fashion, through language.

A great many poems from the past hundred years are less paradoxical than this, but also less clear in the ways that they convey meaning. To appreciate them we have to be open to the ways in which meanings can be suggested even when they are not stated clearly. And we must be able to recognize a central truth about poetry: the fact that meaning is not always plain does not mean it is absent.

None of the above should be taken to imply that all twentieth- and twenty-first-century poets eschew plain speaking. Some strive quite consistently for clarity of meaning in writing about a wide range of topics, while remaining attuned to the ways in which their poems can suggest meanings above and beyond those stated. Others write with a clear ethical or political stance, and have wanted for those reasons to make their meanings plain. Perhaps not surprisingly, strong political poetry in the twentieth and twenty-first centuries has come disproportionately from poets belonging to groups who have been in one way or another disadvantaged, or have been lacking in power—women, the colonized, visible minorities, Native North Americans, gays and lesbians. No reader is likely to be unclear about what W.H. Auden is driving at in "Unknown Citizen," or Langston Hughes in "Let America Be America Again":

> From those who live like leeches on the people's lives,
> We must take back our land again,
> America!

It is important not to presume, however, that once one has acknowledged the most transparent meaning of a poem which makes a clear point, nothing is left to be said. Even in a poem that aims to convey a clear political message there may be layered or multiple meanings.

Point of View

One of the most important ways in which the genres of literature differ one from another is in the way that they present human characters. Whereas the presentation of different human characters is central to prose fiction and to drama, it is often much less important to poetry. If one wishes to give direct expression to one's feelings or thoughts about nature, or death, or love, poetry is the natural medium to write in. But it is not always that simple.

As readers, how do we know who is behind a poem? If it is an "I" or a "we"—if it is written in the first person, in other words, how do we know who that "I" or "we" is? Sometimes we may need to bring historical or biographical information to bear. If we read the late nineteenth-century African American poet Paul Laurence Dunbar's "We Wear the Mask" without knowing the identity of "we," we will be missing a detail that greatly affects our reading of the poem. And sometimes the poem will say "I" or "we" but we cannot and should not be confident that the poet means what she says.

To say that poetry is often the most personal of the genres is not to say that we should read all poems as being direct expressions of the poet's thoughts or feelings. When we read a work of prose fiction in which a narrator tells a story, we should never assume that narrator to be the author; very frequently the author narrates a story through a *persona*, in order to provide a particular perspective on the events being narrated. The character of that persona may be very different indeed from that of the author. Much the same can be true in poetry. In some cases the poet may adopt a persona radically different from herself—as Margaret Atwood does, for example, in "Death of a Young Son by Drowning" and the other poems in her book *The Journals of Susanna Moodie*, in which she writes from the point of view of a woman who emigrated to Canada in the nineteenth century.

In *The Journals of Susanna Moodie* it is usually quite obvious who the "I" in the poems is. In other cases it may be much less clear whether the "I" in a poem is a persona. To what extent is the "I" in a love poem by John Donne the poet speaking directly? Or a sonnet by Shakespeare? Or, for that matter, any one of the thousands of love poems written in the first person, with an "I" addressing a "you"? In the case of a poem such as "Tintern Abbey," where there is external evidence that Wordsworth saw the proper function of poetry as being the direct expression of personal feeling, we may be reasonably confident that the "I" of the poem is indeed the poet himself, though even with such a seemingly direct poem, one must refer to the "speaker" in the poem, not the author. Further, poetry that reads as "personal" may be expressing a point of view quite independent from that of the poet. Such may be the case even with poetry that is highly intimate, even confessional (as the poetry of Sylvia Plath is often described as being).

With some poems written in the first person (or the first and second person), we may gradually come to realize as we read the poem not only that the "I" behind the poem is someone other than the poet, but also that this "I" is someone we should not trust. In a dramatic monologue such as Robert Browning's "My Last Duchess," we need to pay attention to character in much the same way as we do when trying to respond to a work of prose fiction in which we recognize that the narrator is unreliable. In a poem such as that one, the point of view is maintained consistently throughout the poem. Such is the case as well with dramatic monologues such as Tennyson's "Ulysses." A poem such as "The Love Song of J. Alfred Prufrock," however, begins very much like a dramatic monologue, but then seems to shift from time to time in its point of view. Is the "we" of "We have lingered in the chambers of the sea" near the poem's end written from the same point of view as that of the "I" with which the poem begins—or the "I" of "Do I dare to eat a peach?" a few lines earlier? Or is the viewpoint unstable in a poem such as this one?

The dramatic monologue is not the only form poets use to adopt an entirely different persona. Ted Hughes's "Hawk Roosting" and Les Murray's "Pig" are examples of poems in which traditional forms are used to give expression to the imagined point of view of a non-human animal.

One often unappreciated aspect of point of view in poetry is the degree to which a wide range of poems may be written very largely in the second person. This is true of a great deal of love poetry, certainly, and also of many dramatic monologues. It is true as well of a poem such as Tom Wayman's "Did I Miss Anything?"—a poem consisting entirely of a professor's answers to the question posed by a student in the title of the poem. And it is true of Carol Ann Duffy's "The Good Teachers," a very different sort of poem about education, in which "you" is used not in the way we usually use the second person, but in the way we use "one" when speaking in the third person.

Another interesting aspect of point of view is how subtle shifts in grammatical person may help to signal shifts in tone. Such is the case with the Larkin poems "Church Going" and "The Old Fools." In "Church Going," a poem written in the first person through its first six stanzas shifts in the final stanza to the third person: "someone will forever be surprising / A hunger in himself to be more serious." And in "The Old Fools" the sudden appearance in the final line of the first person plural—"We shall find out"—at the end of a poem that until then has been written entirely in the third person brings us up short. It is worth asking how these shifts tie in with the sense of the lines, and contribute to the feelings we are left with at the end of each poem.

Form

This introduction has already touched on a number of aspects of the formal properties a poem may exhibit. It may follow a particular metrical form, for example, and it may have a set rhyme scheme. The **stanza** is another aspect to the form a poem may take. Stanzas are groups of lines into which a poem may be divided; each stanza follows a pattern in its metre and/or in its rhyme scheme. Conventional stanza forms include **tercets** (stanzas of three lines, often linked by an interlocking rhyme scheme) and **quatrains** (stanzas of four lines, also usually rhymed).

There are also various forms in which complete poems may be written. The most common of these by far in English poetry is the **sonnet**—a poem of 14 lines, usually written in iambic pentameter, and generally following a strict rhyme scheme. Details concerning several of the main types of sonnet (including the **Petrarchan**, the **Spenserian**, the **Shakespearian**, and the **Miltonic**), as well as many more technical aspects of poetry than are dealt with in this introduction, will be found in the glossary of this anthology.

The sonnet is itself only one of several different complete poem forms. The **villanelle**, for example, is a poem generally consisting of 19 lines, with 5 tercets rhyming aba followed by a quatrain rhyming abaa. Dylan Thomas's "Do Not Go Gentle Into That Good Night" is one example of a villanelle included in these pages; Elizabeth Bishop's "One Art" is another.

Many other poetic forms—including the **ballad**, the **ghazal**, the **rondelle**, and the **sestina**—are also described in the glossary. So too are various categories of poem—the **elegy**, for example—that are defined less by such characteristics as metre or rhyme scheme than by subject matter and tone. The reader will also find in the glossary far more detail than is provided in this introduction on such things as the various forms of accentual-syllabic metre, the various forms of rhyme, and the various figures of speech commonly used in poetry.

Almost all of the above applies to **lyric** poetry, the sort of poetry that has been dominant in Western culture since the Renaissance. A lyric is a relatively short poem expressive of an individual's thoughts or feelings, and often appreciated for its aural qualities. Sonnets, elegies, dramatic monologues—all these are different sorts of lyric, as are poems as diverse as Andrew Marvell's "To His Coy Mistress," Emily Dickinson's "[Tell all the Truth, but tell it slant]," E.E. Cummings's "anyone lived in a pretty how town," Margaret Atwood's "[you fit into me]," George Elliott Clarke's "blank sonnet," and Alice Oswald's "Woods etc." But in other cultures and in other eras poetry has taken very different shapes. Nowadays Carol Ann Duffy speaks for a great many poets (and a great many readers of poetry too) in her belief that "poetry's power is not in narrative." To the ancient Greeks, however, the **epic** poem—a long poem telling a story, or a series of stories—was considered the most important form of poetry. The ancient Greeks also wrote plays in verse, and most plays in English-speaking cultures were also written largely or entirely in verse until the eighteenth century. In other times and other cultures even science and philosophy have been thought fit matter for poetry. *De Rerum Natura*, a long Latin poem about the nature of physical things and of life and death by the first century BCE writer Lucretius, is written entirely in verse—some 7,400 lines in total, all in dactylic hexameter. What poet today could even imagine writing such a work? Yet Stephen Greenblatt, a prominent critic and scholar of our time, has written a series of recent books and articles on Lucretius that have helped to bring *On The Nature of Things* (as the poem's title translates into English) to the admiring attention of fresh generations of readers, two millennia after it was written. When a poet writes with intensity and feeling of life and of death and of nature, there seem to be few limits to how widely read or how long lasting the resulting work may turn out to be.

—D.L.

The Exeter Book

c. 970–1000 CE

"Saga hwæt ic hatte (Say what I am called)": thus do many of the riddles compiled in the Exeter Book challenge the reader to identify their true subjects. Named for the cathedral in which it has resided for nearly a millennium, the Exeter Book is one of just four extant manuscripts consisting entirely of Anglo-Saxon writing. On its calfskin pages are preserved some 200 anonymous poems—roughly half of them riddles—written predominantly in the West Saxon vernacular and traditional four-stress line of Old English alliterative metre.

In some respects, the group of "elegies," serious meditative poems that constitute a portion of the Exeter Book, are as ambiguous as the riddles they accompany. Most, such as *The Wanderer* and *The Wife's Lament*, are monologues spoken by an unidentified character whose situation is unclear but who seems to be cut off from human society and the comforts of home and friendship. The meaning of individual lines is sometimes difficult to unravel because, in Old English poetic language, sentence boundaries and relationships between clauses are often uncertain. And yet despite these interpretive challenges, the Exeter Book elegies are among the most moving and powerful poems in Old English; their vision of life as both infinitely precious and inevitably transitory still resonates with many readers.

That the riddles were transcribed alongside these elegies and other serious works suggests that, though probably intended primarily as entertainments, the riddles were also esteemed for their poetry. Undoubtedly they are much more than cunning descriptions of objects in terms intended to suggest something else: their elaborate extended metaphors prompt the reader to consider even the most mundane articles in a different light, challenging fixed habits of mind and perception and revealing unlooked-for connections between things apparently unlike.

Many riddles rely on *prosopopoeia*, a device whereby a creature or object cryptically addresses itself to the reader in the first person. Others draw on double meanings to lure the reader astray and playfully expose misguided assumptions. Still others juxtapose contrasting states of being to present a single subject as fundamentally double in nature.

The Wife's Lament[1]

I make this song of myself, deeply sorrowing,
my own life's journey. I am able to tell
all the hardships I've suffered since I grew up,
but new or old, never worse than now—
5 ever I suffer the torment of my exile. .
     First my lord left his people
over the tumbling waves; I worried at dawn
where on earth my leader of men might be.
When I set out myself in my sorrow,
10 a friendless exile, to find his retainers,
that man's kinsmen began to think
in secret that they would separate us,
so we would live far apart in the world,
most miserably, and longing seized me.
15   My lord commanded me to live here;[2]
I had few loved ones or loyal friends
in this country, which causes me grief.
Then I found that my most fitting man
was unfortunate, filled with grief,
20 concealing his mind, plotting murder
with a smiling face. So often we swore
that only death could ever divide us,
nothing else—all that is changed now;
it is now as if it had never been,
25 our friendship. Far and near, I must
endure the hatred of my dearest one.
     They forced me to live in a forest grove,
under an oak tree in an earthen cave.[3]
This earth-hall is old, and I ache with longing;
30 the dales are dark, the hills too high,
harsh hedges overhung with briars,
a home without joy. Here my lord's leaving
often fiercely seized me. There are friends on earth,
lovers living who lie in their bed,

---

1   *The Wife's Lament* Translation by R.M. Liuzza, copyright Broadview Press.
2   *live here* Or, "take up a dwelling in a grove" or "live in a (pagan) shrine." The precise
    meaning of the line, like the general meaning of the poem, is a matter of dispute and
    conjecture.
3   *earthen cave* Or "an earthen grave" or barrow.

while I walk alone in the first light of dawn   35
under the oak-tree and through this earth-cave,
where I must sit the summer-long day;
there I can weep for all my exiles,
my many troubles; and so I can never
escape from the cares of my sorrowful mind,   40
nor all the longings that seize me in this life.
    May the young man always be sad-minded
with hard heart-thoughts, yet let him have
a smiling face along with his heartache,
a crowd of constant sorrows. Let to himself   45
all his worldly joys belong! let him be outlawed
in a far distant land, so my friend sits
under stone cliffs chilled by storms,
weary-minded, surrounded by water
in a sad dreary hall! My beloved will suffer   50
the cares of a sorrowful mind; he will remember
too often a happier home. Woe to the one
who must wait with longing for a loved one.[1]

                         —10th century

Exeter Book Riddles[2]

Riddle 23

I am a wondrous thing, a joy to women,
Of use to close companions; no one
Do I harm, except the one who slays me.
High up I stand above the bed;
Underneath I am shaggy. Sometimes   5
Will come to me the lovely daughter
Of a peasant—will grab me, eager girl, rushing to grip
My red skin, holding me fast,
Taking my head. Soon she feels
What happens when you meet me,   10
She with curly hair. Wet will be her eye.

---

1   *May the young man ... loved one* These difficult lines have been read as a particular reflection, imagining the mental state of her distant beloved, or as a general reflection on
the double-faced nature of the world; here, following the reading of some critics, they
are taken as a kind of curse.

2   *Exeter Book Riddles* Translations by R.M. Liuzza, copyright Broadview Press.

Riddle 33

Creature came through waves, sailed strangely
As if a ship's stem, shouting at land,
Sounding loudly. Its laughter horrible,
Chilling to all. Sharp were her sides.
5 She was spiteful, sluggish in battle,
Biting in her bad works, smashing any ship's shield wall.
Hard in her taking, binding with spells
Spoke with cunning of her own creation:
"My mother is of the dearest race of women,
10 And my mother is my daughter too,
Grown big, pregnant. It is known to men of old
And to all people that she stands
In beauty in all lands of the world."

Riddle 81

Not silent is my house; I am quiet.
We are two together, moving
As our Maker meant. I am faster than he is,
Sometimes stronger; he runs harder, lasts longer.
5 Sometimes I rest; he must run on.
He is my house all my life long
If we are parted death is my destiny.

—10th century

Solutions to the Exeter Book Riddles are provided with the Permissions Acknowledgements on page 537.

Geoffrey Chaucer

c. 1343–1400

Geoffrey Chaucer is generally considered the father of English poetry, a title bestowed by John Dryden, who held his forebear "in the same degree of veneration as the Grecians held Homer, or the Romans Virgil." Together with William Langland and the anonymous author of *Sir Gawain and the Green Knight*, Chaucer was among the first poets to craft sophisticated literary expressions in a Middle English vernacular. But whereas Langland and the *Gawain* poet wrote in an unrhymed alliterative style characteristic of Old English verse, Chaucer's poetry reflects the fashions and influences of the Continent and is written in a dialect more closely related to modern English.

Chaucer was born at a time that saw the beginnings of a breakdown in strict divisions between the aristocracy, the Church, and the commoners. Born into the newly expanding mercantile class, he was able to transcend the restrictions of the old social order to procure a variety of high positions— including Controller of Customs and Justice of the Peace—and to marry a lady-in-waiting to the queen. It is speculated that he began his literary career as a translator when, in 1359, he took part in the war in France, where he was captured and held until the king paid his ransom in 1360. Most of his best work, however, was composed after a 1372 diplomatic trip to Italy, where he probably acquired his knowledge of the Italian literary masters, who strongly influenced his later work.

Though Chaucer wrote some short poems (such as "To Rosemounde"), he is best known for his longer works, most notably *The Parliament of Fowls* (1380), an early dream vision; *Troilus and Criseyde* (c. 1385), a masterly romance of great psychological complexity; and *The Canterbury Tales*, generally considered his masterpiece. Frequently hilarious, sometimes bawdy, and often revealing, *The Canterbury Tales* presents itself as a series of stories told by a group of pilgrims on their way from London to Canterbury. Chaucer worked on *The Canterbury Tales* during the last decades of his life, producing 24 tales totalling over 17,000 lines, but leaving the work unfinished when he died.

To Rosemounde

A Balade

Madame, ye ben of al beaute shryne°   *shrine*
As fer as cercled° is the mapamounde,°[1]   *rounded / map of the world*

---

1   *ye ben of al ... mapamounde* You are the shrine of all beauty throughout the world.

For as the cristal glorious ye shyne,
And lyke ruby ben your chekes rounde.
5 Therwith ye ben so mery and so jocounde°   *pleasant, joyful*
That at a revel° whan that I see you daunce,   *festival*
It is an oynement° unto my wounde,   *ointment*
Thogh ye to me ne do no daliaunce.[1]

For thogh I wepe of teres ful a tyne,°   *barrel*
10 Yet may that wo myn herte nat confounde;°   *destroy*
Your semy° voys that ye so smal out twyne°   *small, high / twist out*
Maketh my thoght in joy and blis habounde.°   *abound, be full of*
So curtaysly I go with love bounde
That to myself I sey in my penaunce,
15 "Suffyseth me to love you, Rosemounde,
Thogh ye to me ne do no daliaunce."[2]

Nas never pyk walwed° in galauntyne[3]   *immersed*
As I in love am walwed and ywounde,°   *wound*
For which ful ofte I of myself devyne°   *discover, understand*
20 That I am trewe Tristam[4] the secounde.
My love may not refreyde° nor affounde,°   *grow cold / founder, grow numb*
I brenne° ay in an amorous plesaunce.°   *burn / desire*
Do what you lyst,° I wyl your thral be founde,[5]   *wish*
Thogh ye to me ne do no daliaunce.

tregentil————————//————————chaucer[6]

—c. 1477

---

1   *Thogh … daliaunce* Even though you give me no encouragement.
2   *daliaunce* Sociable interaction, or more explicitly amorous or sexual exchange.
3   *Nas … galauntyne* No pike was ever steeped in galantine sauce.
4   *Tristam* Tristan, lover of Isolde, often presented as the ideal lover in medieval romance.
5   *I … founde* I will remain your servant.
6   *tregentil … chaucer* Although the words appear joined (or separated) by a line or flourish
    in the manuscript, the status of *tregentil* is uncertain. It may be an epithet (French: very
    gentle) or a proper name.

The first page of Chaucer's Tale of Melibee, *from the Ellesmere manuscript of* The Canterbury Tales, *1400–05. The figure on horseback is generally taken to be a representation of Chaucer. The actual size of pages in the Ellesmere manuscript is approximately 15¾ × 11⅛".*

Sir Thomas Wyatt

c. 1503–1542

Thomas Wyatt lived his entire adult life amidst the political intrigue and turmoil that accompanied the reign of King Henry VIII, and was twice imprisoned in the Tower of London. Even his poems on subjects far from the machinations of the king and his courtiers—subjects such as love and idyllic country life—can carry a subtext about the court's political dramas. Wyatt wrote in many poetic forms, but is best known for the artistry of his satires and songs and, along with Henry Howard, Earl of Surrey (1517–47), for introducing the Italian sonnet to England.

Wyatt was born into a family of wealth and status. He was a man of many accomplishments, adept at music and poetry as well as politics, and he soon became a valued member of King Henry VIII's court. He began a diplomatic career in 1526 with missions to France, Rome, and Venice, where he may have acquired his knowledge of Italian sonnets. He was knighted in 1536 but soon afterward had his first falling out with the king and was imprisoned in the Tower of London—possibly because of a past relationship with the queen, Anne Boleyn, who would be executed that year. Wyatt temporarily regained the king's favour, but in 1541 he was imprisoned again, this time on trumped-up charges of treason. He was spared and returned to favour a second time, but died the next year, succumbing to fever in 1542.

Few of Wyatt's poems were printed in his lifetime, but many appeared in Richard Tottel's 1557 volume *Songes and Sonettes* (later to become known as *Tottel's Miscellany*). Some years later, the Elizabethan critic George Puttenham summarized Sir Thomas Wyatt's importance to the English literary tradition in terms that remain broadly accepted today: "[Wyatt and Surrey] travailed into Italie, and there tasted the sweet and stately measures and stile of the Italian Poesie.... They greatly pollished our rude & homely maner of vulgar Poesie, from that it had been before, and for that cause may justly be said the first reformers of our English meetre and stile."

[The long love that in my thought doth harbour][1]

The long love that in my thought doth harbour
And in mine heart doth keep his residence
Into my face presseth with bold pretence
And therein campeth, spreading his banner.
5 She that me learneth° to love and suffer   *teaches*

---

1   *[The long love ... doth harbour]* This poem is an adaptation of Sonnet 140 from the
Italian poet Petrarch's *Rime sparse* (*Scattered Rhymes*).

And will° that my trust and lust's negligence   *wishes*
Be reined by reason, shame,° and reverence,   *modesty*
With his hardiness° taketh displeasure.   *daring*
Wherewithal unto the heart's forest he fleeth,
Leaving his enterprise with pain and cry,   10
And there him hideth and not appeareth.
What may I do when my master feareth,
But in the field with him to live and die?
For good is the life ending faithfully.

—1557

[They flee from me that sometime did me seek]

They flee from me that sometime did me seek
With naked foot stalking° in my chamber.   *treading softly*
I have seen them gentle, tame, and meek
That now are wild and do not remember
That sometime they put themself in danger   5
To take bread at my hand; and now they range,
Busily seeking with a continual change.

Thanked be fortune it hath been otherwise
Twenty times better; but once in special,
In thin array after° a pleasant guise,°   *in accordance with* / *style*   10
When her loose gown from her shoulders did fall
And she me caught in her arms long and small,
Therewithal sweetly did me kiss
And softly said, "Dear heart, how like you this?"

It was no dream; I lay broad waking.°   *wide awake*   15
But all is turned, through my gentleness,
Into a strange fashion of forsaking.
And I have leave to go of her goodness,[1]
And she also to use newfangleness.°   *inconstancy*
But since that I so kindly[2] am served,   20
I would fain° know what she hath deserved.   *gladly*
—1557

---

1   *I have ... goodness* I have her permission to go from her.
2   *kindly* Naturally, according to natural laws (i.e., that women are fickle). The word also
     ironically suggests the modern "with kindness." In the original printing after Wyatt's
     death, the text was amended to "unkindly," removing the irony.

[Whoso list to hunt, I know where is an hind][1]

Whoso list° to hunt, I know where is an hind,°   *likes / female deer*
But as for me, alas, I may no more:
The vain travail hath wearied me so sore.
I am of them that farthest cometh behind;
5 Yet may I by no means my wearied mind
Draw from the deer: but as she fleeth afore,
Fainting I follow. I leave off therefore,
Since in a net I seek to hold the wind.
Who list her hunt, I put him out of doubt,
10 As well as I may spend his time in vain:
And, graven with diamonds, in letters plain
There is written her fair neck round about:
"*Noli me tangere*, for Caesar's I am,[2]
And wild for to hold, though I seem tame."

—1557

---

1   *[Whoso list ... an hind]* This poem is an adaptation of Sonnet 190 from Petrarch's *Rime sparse* (*Scattered Rhymes*).

2   *Noli me tangere* Latin: Touch me not; words spoken by Christ after his resurrection; *for Caesar's I am* It was thought that Caesar's deer wore collars with this inscription to ensure they would not be hunted. Wyatt's readers who identified the deer with Anne Boleyn (whom Wyatt knew and perhaps loved) would have read the lines as suggesting that the "hind" belongs to Henry VIII.

Edmund Spenser

1552?–1599

Best known for his epic poem *The Faerie Queene* (1590–96), Edmund Spenser was an extraordinarily accomplished poet in other forms as well. Born to parents of modest means, he nevertheless earned two degrees from Cambridge and embarked on a career as a servant of the Crown. It was a successful career—though nowhere near as successful as Spenser's poetic work turned out to be. He was a secretary to the Earl of Leicester, then to the Lord Deputy of Ireland, and served briefly as Sheriff of Cork.

In 1579 Spenser used the pseudonym "Immerito" on his first significant publication, *The Shepheardes Calender*, a set of illustrated pastoral poems for each month of the year. He spent the following decade working on the first three books of *The Faerie Queene* (1590), an allegorical examination of the virtues set in a magical romance world. This work was politically as well as poetically motivated: the poem was a bid for more direct royal patronage from Queen Elizabeth. Its central if often absent figure is Prince Arthur, the future British king, who is seeking the always absent heroine, the "Faerie Queene" Gloriana—an allegorical "mirror" of Queen Elizabeth in her public role as ruler. Spenser had hoped to write twelve books, but completed only six, the second set of three books being published in a 1596 edition. Spenser won a pension from the queen, but Elizabeth's patronage seems to have gone no further, perhaps because his satirical "Mother Hubberds Tale," included in his *Complaints* (1591), angered the authorities.

In between the two installments of *The Faerie Queene*, Spenser wrote several other volumes, including *Colin Clouts Come Home Againe* (1595), a sometimes satirical anti-court pastoral; and *Astrophel* (1596), an elegy for fellow poet Philip Sidney. During this time he also completed his *Amoretti* (1595), a series of sonnets commemorating his courtship of Elizabeth Boyle, issued with *Epithalamion*, a marriage hymn celebrating their union. Spenser died early in 1599 and is buried in Westminster Abbey, next to Chaucer.

from *Amoretti*[1]

1

Happy ye leaves° when as those lilly hands,	*pages*
which hold my life in their dead doing° might,	*death-dealing*
shall handle you and hold in loves soft bands,°	*bonds*
lyke captives trembling at the victors sight.	

---

1   *Amoretti* Italian: Little Loves.

5   And happy lines, on which with starry light,
        those lamping° eyes will deigne sometimes to look   *blazing*
        and reade the sorrowes of my dying spright,°   *spirit*
        written with teares in harts close bleeding book.
    And happy rymes bath'd in the sacred brooke,
10   of *Helicon*[1] whence she derivèd is,
        when ye behold that Angels blessèd looke,
        my soules long lackèd foode, my heavens blis.
    Leaves, lines, and rymes, seeke her to please alone,
        whom if ye please, I care for other none.

75

    One day I wrote her name upon the strand,°   *shore*
        but came the waves and washèd it away:
        agayne I wrote it with a second hand,
        but came the tyde, and made my paynes his pray.°   *prey*
5   Vayne man, sayd she, that doest in vaine assay,°   *attempt*
        a mortall thing so to immortalize.
        for I my selve shall lyke to this decay,
        and eek° my name bee wypèd out lykewize.   *also*
    Not so, (quod° I) let baser things devize   *said*
10   to dy in dust, but you shall live by fame:
        my verse your vertues rare shall eternize,
        and in the hevens wryte your glorious name.
    Where whenas° death shall all the world subdew,   *whenever*
        our love shall live, and later life renew.

                                                                        —1595

---

1   *Helicon* One of the mountains sacred to the Nine Muses, the goddesses of the arts and
    sciences. The sacred spring that flows from Helicon is the Hippocrene.

Sir Walter Ralegh
c. 1554–1618

Known as an explorer, courtier, writer, and adventurer—and as a knight and captain of the Queen's Guard who was later accused of treason—Sir Walter Ralegh was a controversial figure. A great portion of his writing has been lost over the centuries, but the remaining works reveal a dynamic voice imaginatively relaying his experiences and boldly critiquing the social and political climate in which he lived.

Born in Hayes Barton, Devonshire, Ralegh was a student at Oxford and a soldier in France and Ireland before becoming a favourite of Elizabeth I in the early 1580s. A secret marriage to one of Elizabeth's ladies-in-waiting caused him to fall out of favour, and in 1592 he was imprisoned for several months in the Tower of London—the occasion of his long poem *The Ocean to Cynthia*, lamenting Elizabeth's displeasure. Before and after his imprisonment Ralegh made attempts to establish colonies in what is now Virginia and the Carolinas, and he undertook several expeditions to the New World, including a 1595 voyage to Guiana in search of the legendary golden city of El Dorado. In 1596 he wrote *The Discovery of Guiana*, a vivid and partly fantastical account of his travels that influenced the popular European conception of South America as an exotic locale.

After his tumultuous relationship with Elizabeth I, Ralegh found a less sympathetic ruler in James I, who had him condemned under dubious charges of treason and imprisoned in the Tower from 1603 to 1616. Upon his release Ralegh embarked on another failed search for El Dorado. During this expedition, his crew attacked a Spanish settlement in contradiction of James's diplomatic policy, and when Ralegh returned home he was executed for his defiance.

Ralegh's poetry is characterized by an intensely personal treatment of such conventional themes as love, loss, beauty, and time. The majority of his poems are short lyrics—many of them occasional, written in response to particular events. Although he wrote throughout his eventful life, he was most prolific during the period of his imprisonment, producing poetry, political treatises, and an unfinished *History of the World* intended to chronicle life on Earth from the time of creation to Ralegh's own era.

And I will make thee beds of roses
10 And a thousand fragrant posies,
A cap of flowers, and a kirtle°   *tunic or skirt*
Embroidered all with leaves of myrtle;

A gown made of the finest wool
Which from our pretty lambs we pull;
15 Fair linèd slippers for the cold,
With buckles of the purest gold;

A belt of straw and ivy buds,
With coral clasps and amber studs:
And if these pleasures may thee move,
20 Come live with me, and be my love.

The shepherd swains° shall dance and sing   *rustic lovers*
For thy delight each May morning:
If these delights thy mind may move,
Then live with me and be my love.

—1599

William Shakespeare
1564–1616

As his fellow poet-playwright Ben Jonson declared, William Shakespeare "was not of an age, but for all time." Without doubt, the "Bard of Avon" has proved worthy of this monumental phrase: nearly four centuries after his death, Shakespeare's histories, comedies, tragedies, and romances continue to be staged the world over.

Today, Shakespeare's name is connected less with a flesh-and-blood human being—the son of a glover, born in the small town of Stratford-on-Avon, who left for London to pursue a career in the theatre after fathering three children—than with an extraordinary body of work. Shakespeare's oeuvre includes as many as 38 plays, many of them masterpieces; two narrative poems, *Venus and Adonis* (1593) and *The Rape of Lucrece* (1594), both much admired in Shakespeare's lifetime; and 154 sonnets, which were not necessarily conceived as a sequence but were published as one in 1609, perhaps without Shakespeare's consent.

In the sonnets the chief object of the poet's desire is not a chaste fair-haired lady but an idealized young man who prefers the praises of a rival poet and who occupies the centre of a psychologically complex love triangle in which the poet-speaker and a promiscuous "dark lady" are entangled. Because of their intensely intimate expression of love, lust, jealousy, and shame, the sonnets have been the subject of endless biographical speculation, yet it is by no means certain whether the poet-speaker is Shakespeare himself or a persona constructed for dramatic effect.

The enduring power of the sonnets resides not merely in what they mean but in how they produce meaning, that is, in the emotional and intellectual tensions and continuities between their several interworking parts.

Sonnets

18

Shall I compare thee to a summer's day?
Thou art more lovely and more temperate:
Rough winds do shake the darling buds of May,
And summer's lease hath all too short a date:
Sometime too hot the eye of heaven shines,   5
And often is his gold complexion dimmed;
And every fair° from fair sometime declines,   *beauty*
By chance, or nature's changing course, untrimmed:
But thy eternal summer shall not fade,

10 Nor lose possession of that fair thou ow'st,°   *own*
   Nor shall death brag thou wander'st in his shade
   When in eternal lines to time thou grow'st:
      So long as men can breathe or eyes can see,
      So long lives this, and this gives life to thee.

29

   When in disgrace with fortune and men's eyes
   I all alone beweep my outcast state,
   And trouble deaf heav'n with my bootless° cries,   *unavailing*
   And look upon myself, and curse my fate,
5 Wishing me like to one more rich in hope,
   Featured like him,[1] like him with friends possessed,
   Desiring this man's art° and that man's scope,   *skill*
   With what I most enjoy contented least;
   Yet in these thoughts myself almost despising,
10 Haply° I think on thee, and then my state,   *by chance*
   Like to the lark at break of day arising,
   From sullen° earth sings hymns at heaven's gate;   *dark, gloomy*
      For thy sweet love remembered such wealth brings
      That then I scorn to change my state with kings.

73

   That time of year thou mayst in me behold,
   When yellow leaves, or none, or few do hang
   Upon those boughs which shake against the cold,
   Bare ruined choirs[2] where late the sweet birds sang;
5 In me thou seest the twilight of such day
   As after sunset fadeth in the west,
   Which by and by black night doth take away,
   Death's second self[3] that seals up all in rest;
   In me thou seest the glowing of such fire
10 That on the ashes of his youth doth lie,
   As the deathbed, whereon it must expire,
   Consumed with that which it was nourished by;
      This thou perceiv'st, which makes thy love more strong,
      To love that well, which thou must leave° ere long.   *lose*

---

1   *Featured like him* With physical attractions like his.
2   *choirs* Parts of churches designated for singers.
3   *Death's second self* Sleep.

116

Let me not to the marriage of true minds
Admit impediments;[1] love is not love
Which alters when it alteration finds,
Or bends with the remover[2] to remove.
O no, it is an ever-fixèd mark,   5
That looks on tempests and is never shaken;
It is the star to every wand'ring bark,°   *boat*
Whose worth's unknown, although his height be taken.[3]
Love's not Time's fool, though rosy lips and cheeks
Within his bending sickle's compass° come;   *sweep*   10
Love alters not with his brief hours and weeks,
But bears it out even to the edge of doom.
        If this be error and upon me proved,
        I never writ, nor no man ever loved.

130

My mistress' eyes are nothing like the sun;
Coral is far more red than her lips' red;
If snow be white, why then her breasts are dun;°   *greyish-brown*
If hairs be wires, black wires grow on her head;
I have seen roses damasked,° red and white,   *parti-coloured*   5
But no such roses see I in her cheeks;
And in some perfumes is there more delight
Than in the breath that from my mistress reeks.
I love to hear her speak, yet well I know
That music hath a far more pleasing sound;   10
I grant I never saw a goddess go;°   *walk*
My mistress when she walks treads on the ground.
        And yet, by heaven, I think my love as rare
        As any she[4] belied with false compare.

—1609

---

1   *impediments* Cf. the marriage service in the Book of Common Prayer (c. 1552): "If any
     of you know cause, or just impediment, why these two persons should not be joined
     together in holy Matrimony, ye are to declare it."
2   *remover* One who changes, i.e., ceases to love.
3   *Whose ... taken* Referring to the "star" of the previous line, most likely the North Star,
     whose altitude can be reckoned for navigation purposes using a sextant, but whose es-
     sence remains unknown.
4   *any she* Any woman.

Thomas Campion
1567–1620

Thomas Campion was both a poet and a composer who, as he wrote in the introduction to one of his volumes of lyric poems, "chiefly aymed to couple [his] Words and Notes louingly together."

Campion was born in London and attended the University of Cambridge and Gray's Inn, one of England's four Inns of Court for the study of law. While he never did take up a legal profession, he had an active social life at the Inns of Court and formed many friendships with musicians and poets. His first collection, *Poemata* (1595), was a volume of Latin verse, but it was *A Booke of Ayres* (1601), his first book in English, that cemented his reputation as a lyric poet. Written in collaboration with the lutist Philip Rosseter, *A Booke of Ayres* was the first of several volumes of lyrics with lute accompaniment that Campion would produce. He followed it with the manifesto *Observations in the Art of English Poesie* (1602), in which he championed the use of classical metres and deplored the "vulgar and unarteficiall custome of riming"—although he frequently disregarded this philosophy and used traditional English rhyme and metre in much of his own work.

In 1605, Campion completed a medical degree at Caen University in France. He practised medicine for the rest of his life, but he continued to write songs and poetry, as well as the libretti for several elaborate masques that were performed at important court weddings. His last book, *Third and Fourth Booke of Ayres*, was published in 1617, three years before his death.

[There is a garden in her face]

There is a garden in her face,
Where roses and white lilies grow;
A heav'nly paradise is that place,
Wherein all pleasant fruits do flow.
There cherries grow, which none may buy
5   Till cherry ripe[1] themselves do cry.

Those cherries fairly do enclose
Of orient pearl[2] a double row,
Which when her lovely laughter shows,
10 They look like rosebuds filled with snow.

---

1   *cherry ripe* The cry of a London street seller.
2   *orient pearl* High-quality pearl.

Yet them nor peer nor prince can buy,
Till cherry ripe themselves do cry.

Her eyes like angels watch them still;
Her brows like bended bows do stand,
　　Threat'ning with piercing frowns to kill   15
All that attempt with eye or hand
　　Those sacred cherries to come nigh,
　　Till cherry ripe themselves do cry.

—1617

John Donne
1572–1631

John Donne was an innovator who set out to startle readers with his disdain for convention, writing poems that challenged expectations about what was appropriate in poetic subject matter, form, tone, language, and imagery.

As with the speaker of his "Holy Sonnet 19," in Donne "contraries meet in one." Some critics and readers try to resolve these "contraries" by separating Donne's career in two: in early life, a witty man-about-London whose love poems combine erotic energy with high-minded argument; in later life, a learned minister famous for his religious verse and his sermons. But Donne frequently blurs the differences between the sacred and the secular, sometimes presenting erotic love as a form of religious experience, and sometimes portraying religious devotion as an erotic experience. His poetic voice, moreover, ranges across a multitude of roles and postures, from misogynist cynicism to tender idealism and devout religious passion.

Donne was the son of a prosperous ironmonger, and his family was Catholic at a time when the government viewed all Catholics with suspicion. Donne studied at both Oxford and Cambridge but took no degree—perhaps because graduation required accepting the Church of England's 39 "articles of religion." In 1592 he began legal studies in London, and over the next few years wrote many of the love lyrics for which he later became famous; like most of his poems, these were circulated in manuscript but not published during his lifetime.

Donne eventually converted to Anglicanism, and in 1615 he became a clergyman. In 1621, he was appointed Dean of St. Paul's Cathedral in London, where he attracted large audiences for his intellectually challenging and emotionally stirring sermons. His *Poems* first appeared in 1633, two years after his death.

The Flea

Mark but this flea, and mark in this,
How little that which thou deny'st me is;
It sucked me first, and now sucks thee,
And in this flea, our two bloods mingled be;[1]
5   Thou know'st that this cannot be said
A sin, nor shame, nor loss of maidenhead,
    Yet this enjoys before it woo,

---

1   *mingled be* The speaker's subsequent argument hinges on the traditional belief that blood mixed during sexual intercourse.

And pampered swells with one blood made of two
And this, alas, is more than we would do.

Oh stay, three lives in one flea spare,   10
Where we almost, yea more than married are.
This flea is you and I, and this
Our marriage bed, and marriage temple is;
Though parents grudge, and you, we're met,
And cloistered in these living walls of jet.   15
    Though use° make you apt to kill me,   *habit*
    Let not to that, self murder added be,
    And sacrilege, three sins in killing three.

Cruel and sudden, hast thou since
Purpled thy nail, in blood of innocence?   20
Wherein could this flea guilty be,
Except in that drop which it sucked from thee?
Yet thou triumph'st, and sayest that thou
Find'st not thy self, nor me the weaker now;
    'Tis true, then learn how false, fears be;   25
    Just so much honour, when thou yield'st to me,
    Will waste, as this flea's death took life from thee.

                                                        —1633

from *Holy Sonnets*

10

Death be not proud, though some have called thee
Mighty and dreadful, for thou art not so,
For, those, whom thou think'st thou dost overthrow
Die not, poor death, nor yet canst thou kill me.
From rest and sleep, which but thy pictures be,   5
Much pleasure, then from thee, much more must flow,
And soonest our best men with thee do go,
Rest of their bones, and soul's delivery.
Thou art slave to Fate, Chance, kings, and desperate men,
And dost with poison, war, and sickness dwell,   10
And poppy, or charms, can make us sleep as well,
And better than thy stroke; why swell'st thou then?
One short sleep past, we wake eternally,
And death shall be no more; death, thou shalt die.

14

Batter my heart, three personed God; for you
As yet but knock, breathe, shine, and seek to mend;
That I may rise and stand, o'erthrow me, and bend
Your force, to break, blow, burn and make me new.
5 I, like an usurped town, to another due,
Labour to admit You, but oh, to no end,
Reason Your viceroy in me, me should defend,
But is captived, and proves weak or untrue.
Yet dearly I love You, and would be loved fain,
10 But am betrothed unto Your enemy:
Divorce me, untie, or break that knot again,
Take me to you, imprison me, for I
Except you enthrall me, never shall be free,
Nor ever chaste, except you ravish me.

—1633

A Valediction: Forbidding Mourning

As virtuous men pass mildly away,
    And whisper to their souls to go,
Whilst some of their sad friends do say,
    The breath goes now, and some say, no:

5 So let us melt, and make no noise,
    No tear-floods, nor sigh-tempests move,
  'Twere profanation of our joys
    To tell the laity our love.

Moving of th'earth° brings harms and fears,   *earthquake*
10   Men reckon what it did and meant,
But trepidation of the spheres,[1]
    Though greater far, is innocent.

---

1   *the spheres* According to Ptolemaic theory, a concentric series of spheres revolved around
    the earth; the heavenly bodies were set into these spheres. Enveloping all the rest was an
    outer sphere known as the "*Primum Mobile*" ("First Mover"), thought to give motion to
    the other spheres, and to introduce variations into the times of the equinoxes.

Dull sublunary[1] lovers' love
    (Whose soul is sense) cannot admit
Absence, because it doth remove   15
    Those things which elemented it.

But we by a love, so much refined,
    That our selves know not what it is,
Inter-assured of the mind,
    Care less, eyes, lips, and hands to miss.   20

Our two souls therefore, which are one,
    Though I must go, endure not yet
A breach, but an expansion,
    Like gold to airy thinness beat.

If they be two, they are two so   25
    As stiff twin compasses[2] are two,
Thy soul, the fixed foot, makes no show
    To move, but doth, if th'other do.

And though it in the centre sit,
    Yet when the other far doth roam,   30
It leans, and hearkens after it,
    And grows erect, as that comes home.

Such wilt thou be to me, who must
    Like th'other foot, obliquely run;
Thy firmness draws my circle just,   35
    And makes me end, where I begun.

—1633

---

1   *sublunary* Beneath the moon, hence earthly (as opposed to heavenly) and therefore corruptible and subject to change.

2   *twin compasses* Single drawing compass (with twin "feet").

Lady Mary Wroth
1587–1653?

Lady Mary Wroth wrote the first work of prose romance and the first ama-
tory sonnet sequence published by a woman in English. Her work was admired by a number of poets of her day—Ben Jonson proclaimed that her
verse had made him "a better lover, and much better poet"—and although
her reputation faded during the ensuing centuries, today she is recognized
as a significant Jacobean writer and pioneer.

Born Mary Sidney, Wroth was a member of an illustrious political and
literary family. She was educated by tutors and was already an accomplished
scholar and musician by the time of her arranged marriage in 1604. The
marriage was unhappy; when her husband died in 1614, Wroth was left with
crushing debts, but was also free to pursue more openly a long-time illicit
affair with her cousin, William Herbert. This affair, and financial constraints,
may have limited Wroth's access to court and spurred her to write more seriously.

Wroth published a court romance, *The Countess of Montgomery's Urania*, in 1621. A groundbreaking work, *Urania* exploits a genre traditionally
written by men—pastoral romance—in untraditional ways to examine the
social situation of women in actual court society. Appended to *Urania* was
a sequence of 83 sonnets and 20 songs entitled *Pamphilia to Amphilanthus*.
These poems highlight love's tensions and contradictions with great poetic
skill; the climax of *Pamphilia to Amphilanthus* is a technical *tour de force*,
a "corona" or "crown" of 14 sonnets in which the last line of each poem
becomes the first line of the next.

from *Pamphilia to Amphilanthus*

Song [Love, a child, is ever crying]

Love, a child, is ever crying,
    Please him, and he straight is flying;
    Give him, he the more is craving,
    Never satisfied with having.

5 His desires have no measure,
    Endless folly is his treasure;
    What he promiseth he breaketh;
    Trust not one word that he speaketh.

He vows nothing but false matter,
    And to cozen° you he'll flatter;   *deceive* 10
    Let him gain the hand, he'll leave you,
    And still glory to deceive you.

He will triumph in your wailing,
    And yet cause be of your failing:
    These his virtues are, and slighter   15
    Are his gifts, his favours lighter.

Feathers are as firm in staying,
    Wolves no fiercer in their preying.
    As a child then leave him crying,
    Nor seek him, so giv'n to flying.   20

77[1]

In this strange labyrinth how shall I turn?
    Ways° are on all sides while the way I miss: *paths*
    If to the right hand, there in love I burn;
    Let me go forward, therein danger is;
If to the left, suspicion hinders bliss;   5
    Let me turn back, shame cries I ought return,
    Nor faint, though crosses° with my fortunes kiss;   *troubles*
    Stand still is harder, although sure to mourn.[2]
Thus let me take the right, or left-hand way,
    Go forward, or stand still, or back retire: 10
    I must these doubts endure without allay°   *relief*
    Or help, but travail[3] find for my best hire.
Yet that which most my troubled sense doth move,
Is to leave all, and take the thread of Love.[4]

                                      —1621

---

1   *77* The first sonnet in the 14-poem sequence *A Crown of Sonnets Dedicated to Love*, part
    of the larger sequence of *Pamphilia to Amphilanthus*.
2   *sure to mourn* Sure to make me mourn.
3   *travail* Take pains to; possibly meant as a pun on "travel," which was the word used in an
    early edition of the poem.
4   *thread of Love* Referring to the myth of Ariadne, who gave her beloved Theseus a spool of
    thread to unwind behind him as he travelled through the labyrinth of the Minotaur; by
    following the thread he could find his way back out.

Robert Herrick
1591–1674

Of the "sons of Ben" who basked in the genius of poet and playwright Ben Jonson in 1620s London, Robert Herrick is the poet most familiar to modern readers—more so, to many readers, than Jonson himself. "Gather ye rosebuds while ye may," the opening line of Herrick's "To the Virgins, to Make Much of Time," is the most famous version of a classical refrain, while poems such as "Delight in Disorder" are fixtures in anthologies. That Herrick's fame rests on a few crystalline lyrics obscures the fact that he possessed a fairly varied repertoire. His major collection, *Hesperides* (1648), containing over 1,400 poems, includes epigrams, epistles, odes, eclogues, and other lyric forms. The introduction to *Hesperides* genially invites the reader to enjoy the book in a spirit of "cleanly wantonness," to share the poet's delight in such things as good food, drink, and company; female beauty; and love of the countryside. Whether playful or earnest, many of Herrick's poems are exhortations in the *carpe diem* tradition: since all things are subject to "Time's trans-shifting," we must seize every fleeting chance for happiness, but we must do so with due regard for the classical virtue of moderation.

Although *Hesperides* was published during the English Civil Wars (1642–51), Herrick, a staunch Royalist, often seems insensible of the political upheaval that is embraced by his more rebellious contemporaries, such as Milton. Partly because its light bucolic tone did not match the seriousness of the time, *Hesperides* achieved little notice during Herrick's life; in the nineteenth century, however, the Romantic attraction to pastoral and rural themes made Herrick popular with anthologists. More recent critics, appreciating his cunning and delicate artistry, have accorded him a high status among seventeenth-century poets.

Delight in Disorder

A sweet disorder in the dress
Kindles in clothes a wantonness:
A lawn[1] about the shoulders thrown
Into a fine distractiòn;
5   An erring lace, which here and there
Enthralls the crimson stomacher:[2]
A cuff neglectful, and thereby
Ribbons to flow confusedly:

---

1   *lawn* Shawl or scarf of finely woven cotton or linen.
2   *stomacher* Decorative garment worn over the breast and stomach and secured by lacing.

A winning wave, deserving note,
In the tempestuous petticoat;   10
A careless shoestring, in whose tie
I see a wild civility:
Do more bewitch me than when art
Is too precise in every part.

—1648

To the Virgins, to Make Much of Time

Gather ye rosebuds while ye may,
    Old time is still a-flying;[1]
And this same flower that smiles today,
    Tomorrow will be dying.

The glorious lamp of heaven, the sun,   5
    The higher he's a-getting;
The sooner will his race be run,[2]
    And nearer he's to setting.

That age is best, which is the first,
    When youth and blood are warmer;   10
But being spent, the worse, and worst
    Times still succeed the former.

Then be not coy, but use your time,
    And while ye may, go marry;
For having lost but once your prime,   15
    You may for ever tarry.

—1648

Upon Julia's Clothes

Whenas° in silks my Julia goes,   *Whenever*
Then, then, methinks, how sweetly flows
That liquefaction of her clothes.

Next, when I cast mine eyes and see
That brave° vibration each way free,   *beautiful*   5
Oh, how that glittering taketh me!

—1648

---

1   *Old ... a-flying* Paraphrase of the Latin *tempus fugit* ("time flies").
2   *his race be run* The sun's movement was pictured in Greek mythology as the chariot of
     Phoebus Apollo racing across the sky.

George Herbert
1593–1633

George Herbert was born in Wales to a well-connected family and was educated at Trinity College in Cambridge, becoming a university orator, a member of Parliament, and later an Anglican priest. Deeply religious, he bemoaned the number of "love poems that are daily writ and consecrated to Venus" and the much smaller number of poems that "look toward God and Heaven." His own work opposed this trend: Herbert is known for devotion poetry that employs varied metre, unusual figurative language, and visual effects in the expression of faith.

Herbert experimented with poetic form: the words of his poem "Easter Wings," for example, are assembled on the page to depict two pairs of wings, while the text of "The Altar" takes the shape of an altar. Such typographical pattern poems influenced nineteenth- and twentieth-century poets such as Lewis Carroll, E.E. Cummings, and bpNichol, among others, and his work is considered a precursor to the "concrete poetry" movement of the 1950s. *The Temple* (1633), Herbert's major collection of poetry, was published in the year of his death.

Herbert had immense influence on the devotional poets of the 1600s, but by the nineteenth century his reputation had waned. In the twentieth century he rejoined the poetic mainstream when T.S. Eliot praised his fusion of emotion and intellect. Herbert was, Eliot wrote, "an anatomist of feeling and a trained theologian too; his mind is working continually both on the mysteries of faith and the motives of the heart."

The Altar

A broken A L T A R, Lord, thy servant rears,
Made of a heart, and cemented with tears:[1]
    Whose parts are as thy hand did frame;
    No workman's tool hath touched the same.[2]
          A H E A R T alone   5
          Is such a stone,
          As nothing but
          Thy pow'r doth cut.
          Wherefore° each part   *accordingly*
          Of my hard heart   10
          Meets in this frame,
          To praise thy name.
    That, if I chance to hold my peace,
    These stones to praise thee may not cease.[3]
O let thy blessed S A C R I F I C E be mine,   15
And sanctify this A L T A R to be thine.

                —1633

---

1   *A broken ... tears* See Psalms 51.17: "The sacrifices of God are a broken spirit: a broken
and a contrite heart, O God, thou wilt not despise."

2   *No ... same* See Exodus 20.25: "And if thou wilt make me an altar of stone, thou shalt
not build it of hewn stone: for if thou lift up thy tool upon it, thou hast polluted it."

3   *That ... cease* In Luke 19.40, Jesus says of his disciples, "if these should hold their peace,
the stones would immediately cry out."

Easter Wings

Lord, who createdst man in wealth and store,
Though foolishly he lost the same,
Decaying more and more,
Till he became
Most poor: 5
With thee
O let me rise
As larks, harmoniously,
And sing this day thy victories:
Then shall the fall further the flight in me.   10

My tender age in sorrow did begin:
And still with sicknesses and shame
Thou didst so punish sin,
That I became
Most thin.   15
With thee
Let me combine,
And feel this day thy victory:
For, if I imp¹ my wing on thine,
Affliction shall advance the flight in me.   20

—1633

---

1   *imp* Graft feathers from one falcon onto the wing of another, a technique used in falconry to mend damaged wings and improve flight.

John Milton
1608–1674

Missionary poet, Puritan sage, and radical champion of religious, domestic, and civil liberties, John Milton is among the most influential figures in English literature, a writer who, as the critic Matthew Arnold wrote, was "of the highest rank in the great style." In *Paradise Lost* (1667), his culminating achievement, Milton at once works within and transforms the epic tradition of Homer, Virgil, and Dante, casting off "the troublesome and modern bondage of rhyming" for majestic blank verse (unrhymed lines of iambic pentameter).

Milton was a Puritan, a Protestant who wanted to "purify" and simplify English religion, and, like other Puritans during the English Civil Wars (1642–51), he supported rebellion against the king—a support he expressed in an array of tracts and polemics. However, his religious opinions diverged from Puritanism to become increasingly heretical in his later years. Denounced for his pamphlets advocating divorce, which were prompted by his troubled marriage, Milton wrote the *Areopagitica* (1644), one of history's most rousing defences of a free press. He later reconciled with his wife only to lose her in childbirth, the first in a series of personal crises that saw the death of his son, his second wife, and their infant daughter, as well as the complete loss of his sight. Despite these blows, Milton continued late into his life to produce poetry of vast ambition.

On Shakespeare

What needs my Shakespeare for his honoured bones
The labour of an age in pilèd stones,
Or that his hallowed relics should be hid
Under a star-ypointing pyramid?
Dear son of memory,[1] great heir of Fame,   5
What need'st thou such weak witness of thy name?
Thou in our wonder and astonishment
Hast built thyself a livelong monument.
For whilst to th'shame of slow-endeavouring art,
Thy easy numbers flow, and that each heart   10
Hath from the leaves of thy unvalued° Book   *invaluable*
Those Delphic[2] lines with deep impression took,

---

1   *memory* Mnemosyne, mother of the muses.
2   *Delphic* Apollo, god of poetry, had his temple at Delphi.

Then thou our fancy of itself bereaving,
Dost make us marble with too much conceiving;
15 And so sepùlchered in such pomp dost lie,
That kings for such a tomb would wish to die.

—1632

[When I consider how my light is spent][1]

When I consider how my light is spent,
   Ere half my days, in this dark world and wide,
   And that one talent[2] which is death to hide,
   Lodged with me useless, though my soul more bent
5 To serve therewith my maker, and present
   My true account, lest he returning chide,
   Doth God exact day-labour, light denied,
   I fondly° ask; but patience to prevent   *foolishly*
That murmur, soon replies, God doth not need
10   Either man's work or his own gifts; who best
   Bear his mild yoke, they serve him best, his state
Is kingly. Thousands at his bidding speed
   And post° o'er land and ocean without rest: *ride*
   They also serve who only stand and wait.

—1673 (written c. 1652–55)

---

1   *[When ... spent]* Milton became blind in 1651.
2   *talent* Reference to the biblical parable of the talents; see Matthew 25.14–30. In this parable, a master gives varying amounts of money to three servants: five talents, two talents, and one talent, respectively. The servants that received larger sums invest the money, double it, and are celebrated, while the servant with one talent buries it for safekeeping and is punished for his failure to collect interest.

Anne Bradstreet
1612–1672

A member of an affluent and well-connected English family, Anne Bradstreet was well read and well learned in languages and literatures. At 18, she left England with her husband and parents aboard the *Arbella*, a ship headed for Massachusetts. Twenty years later, Bradstreet would become the first published female writer in the new colonies with her poetry collection *The Tenth Muse Lately Sprung Up in America* (1650).

Bradstreet's early writing bears the impress of her education, but her later poetry was also deeply influenced by her new life in America. Initially, she wrote, her "heart rose up" in protest at the "new world and new manners" that she found there. However, she continued to write under the difficult conditions of colonial life, while also raising eight children in the country so different from her birthplace. Her poetry conveyed familial devotion toward her husband and children as well as documenting the hardships endured by early settlers. Much of Bradstreet's poetry expressed strong Puritan faith, and the ornate diction and forms of her earlier work gave way to mature work distinguished by a lyrical voice, biblical themes, and biblical language.

The Tenth Muse was admired upon its publication, and Bradstreet has long been counted among the early literary lights of American poetry.

The Author to Her Book[1]

Thou ill-formed offspring of my feeble brain,
Who after birth didst by my side remain,
Till snatched from thence by friends, less wise than true
Who thee abroad, exposed to public view,
Made thee in rags, halting to th' press to trudge,   5
Where errors were not lessened (all may judge).
At thy return my blushing was not small,
My rambling brat (in print) should mother call,
I cast thee by as one unfit for light,
Thy visage° was so irksome in my sight;   *face*   10
Yet being mine own, at length affection would
Thy blemishes amend, if so I could:

---

1   *The Author to Her Book* These lines are thought to be a preface intended for a new edition of Bradstreet's collection *The Tenth Muse*, which was first published without her permission.

I washed thy face, but more defects I saw,
And rubbing off a spot still made a flaw.
15 I stretched thy joints to make thee even feet,
Yet still thou run'st more hobbling than is meet;°   *appropriate*
In better dress to trim thee was my mind,
But nought save homespun cloth i' th' house I find.
In this array 'mongst vulgars may'st thou roam.
20 In critic's hands beware thou dost not come,
And take thy way where yet thou art not known;
If for thy father asked, say thou hadst none;
And for thy mother, she alas is poor,
Which caused her thus to send thee out of door.

—1678

Andrew Marvell
1621–1678

Andrew Marvell's poems are complex, full of paradox and irony, and frequently employ naïve or ambivalent personae who present debates or balance competing claims. His poem "An Horation Ode upon Cromwell's Return from Ireland" (1650), for example, oscillates between admiration for King Charles I and praise for (and veiled criticism of) Oliver Cromwell, who choreographed the abolition of the monarchy through the English Civil Wars (1642–51), executing Charles I in the process. Marvell was known primarily as a politician and satirist during his lifetime, and his reputation as one of the best lyric poets of his era was not fully established until the twentieth century.

The son of a clergyman, Marvell grew up in Hull in northeast England. At age 12 he was admitted to the University of Cambridge, where he studied for seven years and where he published his first poems, written in Latin and Greek. Instead of completing his degree, Marvell left England in 1642 for four years of travel in continental Europe, perhaps to wait out the period of the English Civil Wars. In 1650, he began working as a tutor to the 12-year-old daughter of Thomas, Lord Fairfax, the recently retired Commander-in-Chief of Cromwell's army. It was likely during his two years on the Fairfax estate that Marvell composed many of his most famous works, including the sensuous and witty "To His Coy Mistress."

Marvell served in Cromwell's government as Latin Secretary and was elected in 1659 as Member of Parliament for Hull, a seat he would maintain until his death. He was highly critical of Charles II (who was restored to the monarchy in 1660 after the collapse of Cromwell's Commonwealth), but Marvell's harshest criticisms were published anonymously. When he died in 1678, there was still an outstanding government reward offered for the name of the man who had written "An Account of the Growth of Popery and Arbitrary Government in England" a year earlier.

The Garden

1

How vainly men themselves amaze
To win the palm, the oak, or bays,[1]
And their uncessant labours see
Crowned from some single herb or tree,

---

1   *the palm, the oak, or bays* Wreaths or garlands; the traditional rewards signifying military (palm leaves), civic or political (oak leaves), or poetic (bay laurel leaves) achievement.

5 Whose short and narrow vergèd shade
Does prudently their toils upbraid,
While all flow'rs and all trees do close
To weave the garlands of repose.

2

Fair Quiet, have I found thee here,
10 And Innocence, thy sister dear!
Mistaken long, I sought you then
In busy companies of men.
Your sacred plants, if here below,
Only among the plants will grow.
15 Society is all but rude,°   *ignorant*
To this delicious solitude.

3

No white nor red[1] was ever seen
So am'rous as this lovely green.
Fond lovers, cruel as their flame,
20 Cut in these trees their mistress' name.
Little, alas, they know, or heed,
How far these beauties hers exceed!
Fair trees! wheres'e'er your barks I wound,
No name shall but your own be found.

4

25 When we have run our passions' heat,
Love hither makes his best retreat.
The gods, that mortal beauty chase,
Still in a tree did end their race.
Apollo hunted Daphne so,
30 Only that she might laurel grow.
And Pan did after Syrinx speed,
Not as a nymph, but for a reed.[2]

---

1   *white nor red* Colours traditionally associated with female beauty.
2   *Apollo ... reed* Reference to two classical myths associated with erotic pursuit and transformation. While being chased by Apollo, the god of poetry, Daphne was transformed into the laurel tree that became Apollo's sacred emblem. Syrinx, chased by Pan, god of flocks and shepherds, was transformed into a reed, the basis of the pan-pipe, emblem of pastoral poetry.

5

What wondrous life is this I lead!
Ripe apples drop about my head;
The luscious clusters of the vine   35
Upon my mouth do crush their wine;
The nectarine, and curious peach,
Into my hands themselves do reach;
Stumbling on melons, as I pass,
Ensnared with flow'rs, I fall on grass.   40

6

Meanwhile the mind, from pleasures less,
Withdraws into its happiness:
The mind, that ocean where each kind
Does straight its own resemblance find;[1]
Yet it creates, transcending these,   45
Far other worlds, and other seas,
Annihilating all that's made
To a green thought in a green shade.

7

Here at the fountain's sliding foot,
Or at some fruit-tree's mossy root,   50
Casting the body's vest aside,
My soul into the boughs does glide:
There like a bird it sits, and sings,
Then whets,° and combs its silver wings;   *preens*
And, till prepared for longer flight,   55
Waves in its plumes the various light.

8

Such was that happy garden-state,
While man there walked without a mate:
After a place so pure, and sweet,
What other help could yet be meet?[2]   60

---

1   *that ocean ... own resemblance find* Alluding to the Renaissance belief that the ocean
     contains a counterpart for every plant and animal on land.
2   *help ... meet* See Genesis 2.18: "And the Lord God said, It is not good that the man
     should be alone; I will make him an help meet for him."

But 'twas beyond a mortal's share
To wander solitary there:
Two Paradises 'twere in one
To live in Paradise alone.

9

65 How well the skilful gardener drew
Of flowers and herbs this dial[1] new,
Where from above the milder sun
Does through a fragrant zodiac run;
And, as it works, the industrious bee
70 Computes its time as well as we.
How could such sweet and wholesome hours
Be reckoned but with herbs and flowers!

—1681 (probably written in the early 1650s)

To His Coy Mistress

Had we but world enough, and time,
This coyness Lady were no crime.
We would sit down, and think which way
To walk, and pass our long love's day.
5 Thou by the Indian Ganges' side
Should'st rubies find: I by the tide
Of Humber[2] would complain. I would
Love you ten years before the Flood:
And you should, if you please, refuse
10 Till the conversion of the Jews.[3]
My vegetable love should grow[4]
Vaster than empires, and more slow.
An hundred years should go to praise
Thine eyes, and on thy forehead gaze.
15 Two hundred to adore each breast:
But thirty thousand to the rest.

---

1   *dial* Floral sundial.
2   *Humber* River in northern England; it flows alongside Hull, Marvell's home town.
3   *conversion of the Jews* Event supposed to usher in the final millennium leading to the end of time.
4   *vegetable love should grow* His love (or its physical manifestation) would grow slowly and steadily: Aristotle (384-322 BCE) defined the vegetative part of the soul as that characterized only by growth.

An age at least to every part,
And the last age should show your heart.
For Lady you deserve this state;
Nor would I love at lower rate.   20
But at my back I always hear,
Time's wingèd chariot hurrying near:
And yonder all before us lie
Deserts of vast eternity.
Thy beauty shall no more be found;   25
Nor, in thy marble vault, shall sound
My echoing song; then worms shall try
That long preserved virginity:
And your quaint honour turn to dust;
And into ashes all my lust.   30
The grave's a fine and private place,
But none I think do there embrace.
Now therefore, while the youthful glew
Sits on thy skin like morning dew,[1]
And while thy willing soul transpires   35
At every pore with instant fires,
Now let us sport us while we may;
And now, like am'rous birds of prey,
Rather at once our time devour,
Than languish in his slow-chapt[2] pow'r.   40
Let us roll all our strength, and all
Our sweetness, up into one ball:
And tear our pleasures with rough strife,
Thorough° the iron gates[3] of life.   *through*
Thus, though we cannot make our sun   45
Stand still,[4] yet we will make him run.

—1681

---

1   *youthful glew … morning dew* This wording is as it appears in Marvell's original manu-
    script, but there are many early variants on the final words in each line of this couplet.
    Most of these changes occurred in printer's attempts to correct "glew" (which may mean
    "sweat," or be a variant spelling of "glow").
2   *slow-chapt* Slowly devouring; "chaps" are jaws.
3   *gates* "Grates" in the 1681 printed edition with manuscript corrections, but many editors
    see "gates of life" as a typically Marvellian inversion of the biblical "gates of death" (see
    Psalm 9.13).
4   *sun / Stand still* Refers both to the love poetry convention in which lovers ask for time to
    stop when they are together, and to Joshua 10.12–14, in which Joshua made the sun and
    moon stand still while his army slaughtered the Amorites.

Anne Finch, Countess of Winchilsea
1661–1720

One of very few women to publish poetry in the early part of the eighteenth century, Anne Finch was a versatile poet who wrote in all of the traditional neoclassical forms and addressed a broad range of subjects including gender politics, art, nature, and religion. Her best-known poem during her lifetime was "The Spleen," which concerns what today we would categorize as depression—an affliction from which Finch herself suffered.

Finch began writing poetry in the 1680s, and she first circulated her work in manuscript form in the 1690s, but it was not until 1713 that she openly published a book, *Miscellany Poems on Several Occasions*. She had become a countess the year before, but publishing poetry was nonetheless a bold move for a woman, as Finch acknowledges in "The Introduction": "a woman that attempts the pen, / Such an intruder on the rights of men, / Such a presumptuous creature is esteemed, / The fault can by no virtue be redeemed." *Miscellany Poems*, however, was well-received and praised by her friends in London's literary circles, among them Jonathan Swift and Alexander Pope, who included seven of her poems in a 1717 anthology.

After her death, Finch's work fell into obscurity until the nineteenth century, when William Wordsworth commended her poem "Nocturnal Reverie" for its nature imagery. In the early twentieth century, her unpublished "Wellesley manuscript" came to light, adding more than 50 poems to her known oeuvre.

There's No Tomorrow

A fable imitated from Sir Roger L'Estrange[1]

Two long had loved, and now the nymph[2] desired,
The cloak of wedlock, as the case required;
Urged that, the day he wrought her to this sorrow,
He vowed, that he would marry her tomorrow.
5 Again he swears, to shun the present storm,
That he, tomorrow, will that vow perform.

---

1   *Sir Roger L'Estrange* English translator and political writer; Finch's poem retells a fable included in his translation *Fables of Aesop and Other Eminent Mythologists, with Morals and Reflections* (1692).

2   *nymph* Beautiful young woman.

The morrows in their due successions came;
Impatient still on each, the pregnant dame
Urged him to keep his word, and still he swore the same.
When tired at length, and meaning no redress,   10
But yet the lie not caring to confess,
He for his oath this salvo° chose to borrow,   *excuse*
That he was free, since there was no tomorrow;
For when it comes in place to be employed,
'Tis then today; tomorrow's ne'er enjoyed.   15
The tale's a jest, the moral is a truth;
Tomorrow and tomorrow, cheat our youth:
In riper age, tomorrow still we cry,
Not thinking, that the present day we die;
Unpractised all the good we had designed;   20
There's no tomorrow to a willing mind.

—1713

Alexander Pope
1688–1744

▬▬▬▬ "The proper study of mankind is man," declared Alexander Pope, who based his enormously successful literary career on social commentary and the documentation of contemporary experience. Almost all of his work is composed in closed heroic couplets (a popular verse form consisting of self-contained pairs of rhymed ten-syllable lines), but Pope adapted this form to an astonishing range of poetic modes—among them pastoral, lyric, and mock-epic—and to approaches ranging from the viciously satiric to the earnestly philosophical.

Disabled as a boy by tuberculosis of the spine, Pope was scarcely four and a half feet tall when fully grown. But this was merely one among many disadvantages he overcame in his career: as a Roman Catholic, Pope was forbidden to vote, hold public office, own land, or live within ten miles of London. As he once bitterly observed, "The life of a wit is a warfare upon the earth," and his religion, Tory political leanings, and disability made him the frequent subject of savage critical attack. Pope got the better of his critics in his *The Dunciad* (1728–43), an ironic epic of praise to hack writers; it ranges far beyond personal insult to expose pettiness, mediocrity, and dullness as forces capable of destroying culture.

The number of Pope's enemies only increased with the release of *The Dunciad*, but Pope is much better remembered for his circle of friends—especially the fellow members of the Scriblerus Club, which he formed in 1714 with Jonathan Swift, Lord Bolingbroke, and other influential intellectuals of the day. The club was named for a character of their own invention, Martinus Scriblerus, a learned fool to whom they attributed all that was tedious, narrow-minded, and pedantic in contemporary scholarship.

In addition to his satire, Pope was famous for his ambitious verse essays, such as *An Essay on Criticism* (1711), a sweeping overview of literary history and literary criticism; and *Essay on Man* (1733–34), which analyzes aspects of human nature and discusses humanity's place in the universe.

from *An Essay on Criticism*

True ease in writing comes from art, not chance,
As those move easiest who have learned to dance.
'Tis not enough no harshness gives offence,
The sound must seem an echo to the sense:
5 Soft is the strain when Zephyr° gently blows,   *the west wind*
And the smooth stream in smoother numbers flows;

But when loud surges lash the sounding shore,
The hoarse, rough verse should like the torrent roar.
When Ajax[1] strives some rock's vast weight to throw,
The line too labours, and the words move slow;   10
Not so when swift Camilla[2] scours the plain,
Flies o'er th'unbending corn, and skims along the main.°   *sea*
Hear how Timotheus'[3] varied lays surprise,
And bid alternate passions fall and rise!

—1711

The Rape of the Lock

An Heroi-Comical Poem in Five Cantos

To Mrs. Arabella Fermor[4]

Madam,

It will be in vain to deny that I have some regard for this piece, since I dedicate it to you. Yet you may bear me witness, it was intended only to divert a few young ladies, who have good sense and good humour enough, to laugh not only at their sex's little unguarded follies, but at their own. But, as it was communicated with the air of a secret, it soon found its way into the world. An imperfect copy having been offered to a bookseller,[5] you had the good nature for my sake to consent to the publication of one more correct; this I was forced to before I had executed half my design, for the machinery was entirely wanting to complete it.

The machinery, Madam, is a term invented by the critics to signify that part which the deities, angels, or demons are made to act in a poem; for the ancient poets are in one respect like many modern ladies: let an action be never so trivial in itself, they always make it appear of the utmost importance.

---

1   *Ajax* Greek mythological figure who is proverbially strong; in Homer's *Iliad* he throws a
      large rock at his opponent Hector during a duel.
2   *Camilla* In classical mythology, a warrior virgin; she appears in Book 7 of Virgil's *Aeneid*,
      where the poet describes her as so swift that she "Flew o'er the fields, nor hurt the bearded
      grain: / She swept the seas."
3   *Timotheus* Accomplished Greek poet and musician (4th century BCE).
4   *Mrs. Arabella Fermor* Arabella Fermor, the daughter of a prominent Catholic family,
      was celebrated for her beauty. Lord Robert Petre snipped off a lock of her hair, occa-
      sioning Pope's poem. Mrs. was a title of respect for married or unmarried women.
5   *bookseller* Publisher.

These machines I determined to raise on a very new and odd foundation, the Rosicrucian[1] doctrine of spirits.

I know how disagreeable it is to make use of hard words before a lady, but 'tis so much the concern of a poet to have his works understood, and particularly by your sex, that you must give me leave to explain two or three difficult terms.

The Rosicrucians are a people I must bring you acquainted with. The best account I know of them is in a French book called *Le Comte de Gabalis*,[2] which both in its title and size is so like a novel that many of the fair sex have read it for one by mistake. According to these gentlemen, the four elements are inhabited by spirits, which they call Sylphs, Gnomes, Nymphs, and Salamanders.[3] The Gnomes, or demons of earth, delight in mischief, but the Sylphs, whose habitation is in the air, are the best-conditioned creatures imaginable. For they say any mortals may enjoy the most intimate familiarities with these gentle spirits, upon a condition very easy to all true adepts, an inviolate preservation of chastity.

As to the following Cantos, all the passages of them are as fabulous[4] as the vision at the beginning, or the transformation at the end (except the loss of your hair, which I always mention with reverence). The human persons are as fictitious as the airy ones, and the character of Belinda, as it is now managed, resembles you in nothing but in beauty.

If this poem had as many graces as there are in your person, or in your mind, yet I could never hope it should pass through the world half so uncensured as you have done. But let its fortune be what it will, mine is happy enough, to have given me this occasion of assuring you that I am, with the truest esteem,

Madam,
Your most obedient humble servant.

A. POPE

---

1   *Rosicrucian* Religious sect, originating in Germany, which existed in the seventeenth and eighteenth centuries. Its members were devoted to the study of arcane philosophy and mystical doctrines.
2   *Le Comte de Gabalis* Written by Abbé de Monfaucon de Villars and published in 1670, this was a lighthearted exploration of Rosicrucian philosophy. It was printed in duodecimo (about five by eight inches), a common size for novels and other inexpensive books.
3   *Salamanders* Salamanders were believed to be able to withstand, and live in, fire.
4   *fabulous* Mythical, fictional.

CANTO 1

What dire offence from am'rous causes springs,
What mighty contests rise from trivial things,
I sing—This verse to Caryll,[1] Muse! is due;
This, ev'n Belinda may vouchsafe to view:
Slight is the subject, but not so the praise,   5
If she inspire, and he approve my lays.°   *verses*
    Say what strange motive, Goddess! could compel
A well-bred lord t' assault a gentle belle?
Oh say what stranger cause, yet unexplored,°   *undiscovered*
Could make a gentle belle reject a lord?   10
In tasks so bold can little men engage,
And in soft bosoms dwells such mighty rage?
    Sol° through white curtains shot a tim'rous ray,   *sun*
And oped those eyes that must eclipse the day;
Now lapdogs give themselves the rousing shake,   15
And sleepless lovers, just at twelve, awake:
Thrice rung the bell, the slipper knocked the ground,[2]
And the pressed watch[3] returned a silver sound.
Belinda still her downy pillow pressed,
Her guardian Sylph prolonged the balmy rest.   20
'Twas he had summoned to her silent bed
The morning dream[4] that hovered o'er her head.
A youth more glitt'ring than a birthnight beau[5]
(That ev'n in slumber caused her cheek to glow)
Seemed to her ear his winning lips to lay,   25
And thus in whispers said, or seemed to say:
    "Fairest of mortals, thou distinguished care
Of thousand bright inhabitants of air!
If e'er one vision touched thy infant thought,
Of all the nurse and all the priest have taught,   30
Of airy elves by moonlight shadows seen,

---

1   *Caryll* Pope's friend John Caryll (c. 1666–1736), who requested the poem.
2   *slipper … ground* She bangs her slipper on the floor to summon the maid.
3   *pressed watch* "Repeater" watches would chime the time, to the nearest quarter hour, when the stem was pressed.
4   *morning dream* Morning dreams were believed to be particularly portentous.
5   *birthnight beau* On the birthday of the sovereign, members of the court dressed in their most lavish attire.

The silver token, and the circled green,[1]
Or virgins visited by angel pow'rs,
With golden crowns and wreaths of heav'nly flow'rs,
35   Hear and believe! thy own importance know,
Nor bound thy narrow views to things below.
Some secret truths, from learned pride concealed,
To maids alone and children are revealed.
What though no credit doubting wits may give?
40   The fair and innocent shall still believe.
Know then, unnumbered spirits round thee fly,
The light militia of the lower sky;
These, though unseen, are ever on the wing,
Hang o'er the box, and hover round the Ring.[2]
45   Think what an equipage thou hast in air,
And view with scorn two pages and a chair.°   *sedan chair*
As now your own, our beings were of old,
And once enclosed in woman's beauteous mould;
Thence, by a soft transition, we repair
50   From earthly vehicles to these of air.
Think not, when woman's transient breath is fled,
That all her vanities at once are dead:
Succeeding vanities she still regards,
And though she plays no more, o'erlooks the cards.
55   Her joy in gilded chariots, when alive,
And love of ombre,[3] after death survive.
For when the fair in all their pride expire,
To their first elements[4] their souls retire:
The sprites° of fiery termagants[5] in flame   *spirits*
60   Mount up, and take a Salamander's name.
Soft yielding minds to water glide away,
And sip, with Nymphs, their elemental tea.

---

1   *silver token* Fairies were said to skim the cream from the top of jugs of milk left overnight, leaving a silver coin in exchange; *circled green* Rings in the grass were said to be produced by dancing fairies.

2   *box* Private compartment in a theatre; *the Ring* Circular drive that divides Hyde Park from Kensington Gardens. The most fashionable members of society would drive around the Ring, displaying themselves and their equipages (coaches with attendants).

3   *ombre* Popular card game.

4   *first elements* All things on earth had been thought to be made from the four elements (earth, air, fire, and water), with one of these elements predominant in the temperament of each person.

5   *termagants* Quarrelsome, turbulent, or hot-tempered women.

The graver prude sinks downward to a Gnome,
In search of mischief still on earth to roam.
The light coquettes in Sylphs aloft repair,   65
And sport and flutter in the fields of air.
    "Know further yet, whoever fair and chaste
Rejects mankind, is by some Sylph embraced:
For spirits, freed from mortal laws, with ease
Assume what sexes and what shapes they please.[1]   70
What guards the purity of melting maids
In courtly balls, and midnight masquerades,
Safe from the treach'rous friend, the daring spark,°   *suitor*
The glance by day, the whisper in the dark,
When kind occasion prompts their warm desires,   75
When music softens, and when dancing fires?
'Tis but their Sylph, the wise celestials know,
Though *honour* is the word with men below.
    "Some nymphs° there are, too conscious of their face,   *maidens*
For life predestined to the Gnomes' embrace.   80
These swell their prospects and exalt their pride
When offers are disdained, and love denied.
Then gay ideas° crowd the vacant brain,   *images*
While peers° and dukes, and all their sweeping train,   *nobles*
And garters, stars, and coronets[2] appear,   85
And in soft sounds, 'your Grace' salutes their ear.
'Tis these that early taint the female soul,
Instruct the eyes of young coquettes to roll,
Teach infant cheeks a bidden blush to know,
And little hearts to flutter at a beau.   90
    "Oft, when the world imagine women stray,
The Sylphs through mystic mazes guide their way,
Through all the giddy circle they pursue,
And old impertinence expel by new.
What tender maid but must a victim fall   95
To one man's treat,° but for another's ball?   *feast*
When Florio speaks, what virgin could withstand,
If gentle Damon did not squeeze her hand?
With varying vanities, from ev'ry part,

---

1   *spirits ... please* See Milton's *Paradise Lost* 1.423–24: "For spirits when they please /
    Can either sex assume, or both." This is one of many allusions to Milton's epic poem.
2   *garters, stars, and coronets* Emblems of noble ranks.

100   They shift the moving toyshop[1] of their heart;
       Where wigs with wigs, with sword-knots[2] sword-knots strive,
       Beaux banish beaux, and coaches coaches drive.
       This erring mortals levity may call,
       Oh blind to truth! the sylphs contrive it all.
105   "Of these am I, who thy protection claim,
       A watchful sprite, and Ariel is my name.
       Late, as I ranged the crystal wilds of air,
       In the clear mirror of thy ruling star
       I saw, alas! some dread event impend,
110   Ere to the main° this morning sun descend;   *sea*
       But Heav'n reveals not what, or how, or where:
       Warned by thy Sylph, oh pious maid beware!
       This to disclose is all thy guardian can:
       Beware of all, but most beware of man!"
115   He said; when Shock,[3] who thought she slept too long,
       Leaped up, and waked his mistress with his tongue.
       'Twas then, Belinda, if report say true,
       Thy eyes first opened on a billet-doux;°   *love letter*
       Wounds, charms, and ardours were no sooner read,
120   But all the vision vanished from thy head.
            And now, unveiled, the toilet° stands displayed,   *dressing table*
       Each silver vase in mystic order laid.
       First, robed in white, the nymph intent adores,
       With head uncovered, the cosmetic pow'rs.
125   A heav'nly image in the glass appears,
       To that she bends, to that her eyes she rears.°   *lifts*
       Th' inferior priestess,[4] at her altar's side,
       Trembling begins the sacred rites of pride.
       Unnumbered treasures ope at once, and here
130   The various off'rings of the world appear;
       From each she nicely culls with curious toil,
       And decks the goddess with the glitt'ring spoil.
       This casket India's glowing gems unlocks,
       And all Arabia breathes from yonder box.

---

1   *toyshop* Store that sold not only toys but various trinkets, accessories, and ornaments.
2   *sword-knots* Fashionable men of society wore ribbons knotted around the hilts of their
     swords. They also wore wigs.
3   *Shock* Belinda's lapdog, named after a popular breed of long-haired, Icelandic toy poo-
     dle called the "shough," or "shock."
4   *Th' inferior priestess* Betty, Belinda's maid.

The tortoise here and elephant unite,   135
Transformed to combs, the speckled and the white.
Here files of pins extend their shining rows,
Puffs, powders, patches,[1] Bibles, billet-doux.
Now awful° beauty puts on all its arms;   *awe-inspiring*
The fair each moment rises in her charms,   140
Repairs her smiles, awakens ev'ry grace,
And calls forth all the wonders of her face;
Sees by degrees a purer blush arise,
And keener lightnings quicken in her eyes.[2]
The busy Sylphs surround their darling care,   145
These set the head, and those divide the hair,
Some fold the sleeve, whilst others plait the gown;
And Betty's praised for labours not her own.

CANTO 2

Not with more glories, in th' ethereal plain,
The sun first rises o'er the purpled main,   150
Than issuing forth, the rival of his beams
Launched on the bosom of the silver Thames.[3]
Fair nymphs and well-dressed youths around her shone,
But every eye was fixed on her alone.
On her white breast a sparkling cross she wore,   155
Which Jews might kiss, and infidels adore.
Her lively looks a sprightly mind disclose,
Quick as her eyes, and as unfixed as those:
Favours to none, to all she smiles extends;
Oft she rejects, but never once offends.   160
Bright as the sun, her eyes the gazers strike,
And, like the sun, they shine on all alike.
Yet graceful ease, and sweetness void of pride,
Might hide her faults, if belles had faults to hide:
If to her share some female errors fall,   165
Look on her face, and you'll forget 'em all.
        This nymph, to the destruction of mankind,

---

1   *patches* Artificial beauty marks made of silk or plaster cut into various shapes and
     placed on the face, either for decoration or to hide imperfections.
2   *keener ... eyes* As a result of drops of belladonna, or deadly nightshade, which enlarges
     the pupils.
3   *Launched ... Thames* Belinda voyages upstream to Hampton Court for the day. By tak-
     ing a boat she avoids the crowds and filth in the streets.

Nourished two locks, which graceful hung behind
In equal curls, and well conspired to deck
170 With shining ringlets the smooth iv'ry neck.
Love in these labyrinths his slaves detains,
And mighty hearts are held in slender chains;
With hairy springes° we the birds betray;   *snares*
Slight lines of hair surprise the finny prey;
175 Fair tresses man's imperial race ensnare,
And beauty draws us with a single hair.
        Th' adventurous Baron the bright locks admired;
He saw, he wished, and to the prize aspired.
Resolved to win, he meditates the way,
180 By force to ravish, or by fraud betray;
For when success a lover's toil attends,
Few ask if fraud or force attained his ends.
        For this, ere Phoebus¹ rose, he had implored
Propitious Heav'n, and every pow'r adored,°   *worshipped*
185 But chiefly Love—to Love an altar built,
Of twelve vast French romances, neatly gilt.
There lay three garters, half a pair of gloves,
And all the trophies of his former loves.
With tender billet-doux he lights the pyre,
190 And breathes three am'rous sighs to raise the fire.
Then prostrate falls, and begs with ardent eyes
Soon to obtain, and long possess the prize:
The pow'rs gave ear, and granted half his prayer;
The rest the winds dispersed in empty air.
195   But now secure the painted vessel glides,
The sunbeams trembling on the floating tides,
While melting music steals upon the sky,
And softened sounds along the waters die.
Smooth flow the waves, the zephyrs gently play,
200 Belinda smiled, and all the world was gay.
All but the Sylph—with careful thoughts oppressed,
Th' impending woe sat heavy on his breast.
He summons strait his denizens of air;
The lucid squadrons round the sails repair:
205 Soft o'er the shrouds² aerial whispers breathe

---

1   *Phoebus* One of the names of Apollo, god of the sun.
2   *shrouds* Ropes that brace the mast of the ship.

That seemed but zephyrs° to the train beneath.   *mild breezes*
Some to the sun their insect-wings unfold,
Waft on the breeze, or sink in clouds of gold.
Transparent forms, too fine for mortal sight,
Their fluid bodies half dissolved in light,   210
Loose to the wind their airy garments flew,
Thin glitt'ring textures of the filmy dew,
Dipped in the richest tincture of the skies,
Where light disports in ever-mingling dyes,
While every beam new transient colours flings,   215
Colours that change whene'er they wave their wings.
Amid the circle, on the gilded mast,
Superior by the head, was Ariel placed;
His purple pinions° op'ning to the sun,   *wings*
He raised his azure wand, and thus begun: 220
    "Ye Sylphs and Sylphids, to your chief give ear!
Fays, Fairies, Genii, Elves, and Demons, hear!
Ye know the spheres and various tasks assigned,
By laws eternal, to th' aerial kind.
Some in the fields of purest ether[1] play,   225
And bask and whiten in the blaze of day.
Some guide the course of wand'ring orbs on high,
Or roll the planets through the boundless sky.
Some, less refined, beneath the moon's pale light
Pursue the stars that shoot athwart the night,   230
Or suck the mists in grosser[2] air below,
Or dip their pinions in the painted bow,
Or brew fierce tempests on the wintry main,
Or o'er the glebe° distill the kindly rain.   *fields*
Others on earth o'er human race preside,   235
Watch all their ways, and all their actions guide:
Of these the chief the care of nations own,
And guard with arms divine the British Throne.
    "Our humbler province is to tend the fair,
Not a less pleasing, though less glorious care: 240
To save the powder from too rude a gale,
Nor let th' imprisoned essences° exhale;   *perfumes*
To draw fresh colours from the vernal flow'rs;

---

1   *fields of purest ether* Clear regions above the moon.
2   *grosser* Material, as opposed to ethereal.

To steal from rainbows ere they drop in show'rs
245　A brighter wash;° to curl their waving hairs,　　　　　　　*liquid cosmetic*
　　　Assist their blushes, and inspire their airs;
　　　Nay, oft in dreams invention we bestow,
　　　To change a flounce, or add a furbelo.°　　　　　　　　　*pleated trim*
　　　　　"This day, black omens threat the brightest fair
250　That e'er deserved a watchful spirit's care;
　　　Some dire disaster, or by force or slight,
　　　But what, or where, the Fates have wrapped in night.
　　　Whether the nymph shall break Diana's law,[1]
　　　Or some frail China jar receive a flaw,
255　Or stain her honour, or her new brocade,
　　　Forget her prayers, or miss a masquerade,
　　　Or lose her heart, or necklace, at a ball;
　　　Or whether Heav'n has doomed that Shock must fall.
　　　Haste then, ye spirits! To your charge repair:
260　The flutt'ring fan be Zephyretta's care;
　　　The drops° to thee, Brillante, we consign;　　　　　　　*diamond earrings*
　　　And, Momentilla, let the watch be thine;
　　　Do thou, Crispissa,[2] tend her fav'rite lock;
　　　Ariel himself shall be the guard of Shock.
265　　　"To fifty chosen Sylphs, of special note,
　　　We trust th' important charge, the petticoat:
　　　Oft have we known that sev'nfold fence[3] to fail,
　　　Though stiff with hoops, and armed with ribs of whale.
　　　Form a strong line about the silver bound,
270　And guard the wide circumference around.
　　　　　"Whatever spirit, careless of his charge,
　　　His post neglects, or leaves the fair at large,
　　　Shall feel sharp vengeance soon o'ertake his sins,
　　　Be stopped in vials, or transfixed with pins,
275　Or plunged in lakes of bitter washes lie,
　　　Or wedged whole ages in a bodkin's[4] eye;
　　　Gums and pomatums° shall his flight restrain,　　　　　　*hair ointments*
　　　While clogged he beats his silken wings in vain,

1　*break Diana's law*　Lose her virginity (Diana was the Roman goddess of chastity).
2　*Crispissa*　From the Latin verb *crispere*, meaning "to curl."
3　*sev'nfold fence*　Allusion to Achilles's "sevenfold shield" in the *Iliad*.
4　*bodkin*　Blunt needle with both a large and a small eye, used to draw ribbon through a hem.

Or alum styptics[1] with contracting pow'r
Shrink his thin essence like a riveled° flow'r.   *shriveled* 280
Or, as Ixion[2] fixed, the wretch shall feel
The giddy motion of the whirling mill,
In fumes of burning chocolate shall glow,
And tremble at the sea that froths below!"
    He spoke; the spirits from the sails descend;   285
Some, orb in orb, around the nymph extend;
Some thread the mazy° ringlets of her hair;   *maze-like*
Some hang upon the pendants of her ear.
With beating hearts the dire event they wait,
Anxious, and trembling for the birth of fate.   290

Canto 3

Close by those meads° forever crowned with flow'rs,   *meadows*
Where Thames with pride surveys his rising tow'rs,
There stands a structure of majestic frame,[3]
Which from the neighb'ring Hampton takes its name.
Here Britain's statesmen oft the fall foredoom   295
Of foreign tyrants, and of nymphs at home;
Here thou, great Anna! whom three realms obey,
Dost sometimes counsel take—and sometimes tea.
    Hither the heroes and the nymphs resort,
To taste awhile the pleasures of a court;   300
In various talk th' instructive hours they passed,
Who gave the ball, or paid the visit last;
One speaks the glory of the British Queen,
And one describes a charming Indian screen;
A third interprets motions, looks, and eyes;   305
At every word a reputation dies.
Snuff, or the fan, supply each pause of chat,
With singing, laughing, ogling, and all that.
    Meanwhile, declining from the noon of day,
The sun obliquely shoots his burning ray;   310
The hungry judges soon the sentence sign,

---

1   *alum styptics* Astringent substances applied to cuts to contract tissue and stop bleeding.
2   *Ixion* Zeus punished Ixion, who had attempted to seduce Hera, by tying him to a continuously revolving wheel in Hades. Here the wheel would be that of a machine that beats hot chocolate to a froth.
3   *structure … majestic frame* Hampton Court, the largest of Queen Anne's residences, located about 12 miles up the Thames from London.

And wretches hang that jurymen may dine;
The merchant from th' Exchange[1] returns in peace,
And the long labours of the toilette cease.
315 Belinda now, whom thirst of fame invites,
Burns to encounter two adventurous knights
At ombre,[2] singly to decide their doom,
And swells her breast with conquests yet to come.
Straight the three bands prepare in arms to join,
320 Each band the number of the sacred nine.[3]
Soon as she spreads her hand, th' aerial guard
Descend, and sit on each important card:
First Ariel perched upon a Matadore,[4]
Then each according to the rank they bore;
325 For Sylphs, yet mindful of their ancient race,
Are, as when women, wondrous fond of place.°   *social status*
Behold, four Kings in majesty revered,
With hoary whiskers and a forky beard;
And four fair Queens whose hands sustain a flow'r,
330 Th' expressive emblem of their softer pow'r;
Four Knaves in garbs succinct,[5] a trusty band,
Caps on their heads, and halberds[6] in their hand;
And parti-coloured troops, a shining train,
Draw forth to combat on the velvet plain.
335 The skilful nymph reviews her force with care;
"Let Spades be trumps!" she said, and trumps they were.
Now move to war her sable Matadores,
In show like leaders of the swarthy Moors.

---

1   *th' Exchange* The Royal Exchange, located in the commercial centre of London, was
     the principal market where merchants traded and where bankers and brokers met to do
     business.
2   *ombre* In the game of ombre that Belinda plays against the two men, Pope conveys an
     accurate sense of the game, the rules of which are similar to those of bridge. Each of the
     three players receives 9 cards from the 40 that are used (8s, 9s, and 10s are discarded).
     Belinda, as the challenger, or "ombre" (from the Spanish *hombre*, "man"), names the
     trumps. To win, she must make more tricks than either of the other two. For a complete
     description of the game, see Geoffrey Tillotson's Twickenham edition of Pope's poems,
     volume 2.
3   *sacred nine* Muses.
4   *Matadore* Matadores are the three highest cards of the game. When spades are trump,
     as they are here, the highest card is the ace of spades ("Spadillio"), followed by the two
     of spades ("Manillio"), and then the ace of clubs ("Basto").
5   *succinct* Brief, short. The knaves are wearing short tunics.
6   *halberds* Weapons that combine the spear and battle axe.

Spadillio first, unconquerable lord!
Led off two captive trumps, and swept the board.   340
As many more Manillio forced to yield,
And marched a victor from the verdant field.
Him Basto followed, but, his fate more hard,
Gained but one trump and one plebeian card.
With his broad sabre next, a chief in years,   345
The hoary Majesty of Spades appears,
Puts forth one manly leg, to sight revealed,
The rest his many-coloured robe concealed.
The rebel Knave, who dares his prince engage,
Proves the just victim of his royal rage.   350
Ev'n mighty Pam,[1] that kings and queens o'erthrew,
And mowed down armies in the fights of Loo,
Sad chance of war! now, destitute of aid,
Falls undistinguished by the victor Spade!
    Thus far both armies to Belinda yield;   355
Now to the Baron fate inclines the field.
His warlike Amazon[2] her host invades,
Th' imperial consort of the crown of Spades.
The Club's black tyrant first her victim died,
Spite of his haughty mien° and barb'rous pride.   *look*   360
What boots the regal circle on his head,
His giant limbs in state unwieldy spread?
That long behind he trails his pompous robe,
And of all monarchs only grasps the globe?
    The Baron now his Diamonds pours apace;   365
Th' embroidered King, who shows but half his face,
And his refulgent Queen, with pow'rs combined,
Of broken troops an easy conquest find.
Clubs, Diamonds, Hearts, in wild disorder seen,
With throngs promiscuous strew the level green.   370
Thus when dispersed a routed army runs,
Of Asia's troops, and Afric's sable sons,
With like confusion diff'rent nations fly,
Of various habit, and of various dye,
The pierced battalions disunited fall   375
In heaps on heaps; one fate o'erwhelms them all.

---

1   *Pam* Jack (knave) of clubs, the highest card in Loo, another popular card game.
2   *Amazon* Female warrior; here, the Queen of Spades.

The Knave of Diamonds tries his wily arts,
And wins (oh, shameful chance!) the Queen of Hearts.
At this, the blood the virgin's cheek forsook,
380   A livid paleness spreads o'er all her look;
She sees, and trembles at th' approaching ill,
Just in the jaws of ruin, and Codille.[1]
And now (as oft in some distempered state)
On one nice trick depends the gen'ral fate.
385   An Ace of Hearts steps forth: the King unseen
Lurked in her hand, and mourned his captive Queen.
He springs to vengeance with an eager pace,
And falls like thunder on the prostrate Ace.
The nymph, exulting, fills with shouts the sky;
390   The walls, the woods, and long canals reply.
        O thoughtless mortals! ever blind to fate,
Too soon dejected, and too soon elate!
Sudden these honours shall be snatched away,
And cursed forever this victorious day.
395   For lo! the board with cups and spoons is crowned,
The berries crackle, and the mill turns round.[2]
On shining altars of Japan[3] they raise
The silver lamp; the fiery spirits blaze.
From silver spouts the grateful liquors glide,
400   While China's earth[4] receives the smoking tide.
At once they gratify their scent and taste,
And frequent cups prolong the rich repast.
Straight hover round the fair her airy band;
Some, as she sipped, the fuming liquor fanned,
405   Some o'er her lap their careful plumes displayed,
Trembling, and conscious of the rich brocade.
Coffee (which makes the politician wise,
And see through all things with his half-shut eyes)
Sent up in vapours to the Baron's brain
410   New stratagems, the radiant lock to gain.
Ah, cease, rash youth! desist ere 'tis too late,

---

1   *Codille* Defeat of the ombre.
2   *berries … round* Coffee beans ("berries") roasted and then ground.
3   *altars of Japan* I.e., lacquered, or "japanned" tables, highly decorated and varnished.
     The style originated in Japan.
4   *China's earth* China cups.

Fear the just gods, and think of Scylla's[1] fate!
Changed to a bird, and sent to flit in air,
She dearly pays for Nisus' injured hair!
    But when to mischief mortals bend their will,   415
How soon they find fit instruments of ill!
Just then, Clarissa drew with tempting grace
A two-edged weapon° from her shining case;   *pair of scissors*
So ladies in romance assist their knight,
Present the spear, and arm him for the fight.   420
He takes the gift with rev'rence, and extends
The little engine° on his fingers' ends;   *instrument*
This just behind Belinda's neck he spread,
As o'er the fragrant steams she bends her head.
Swift to the lock a thousand sprites repair,   425
A thousand wings, by turns, blow back the hair,
And thrice they twitched the diamond in her ear;
Thrice she looked back, and thrice the foe drew near.
Just in that instant, anxious Ariel sought
The close recesses of the virgin's thought;   430
As on the nosegay in her breast reclined,
He watched th' ideas rising in her mind.
Sudden he viewed, in spite of all her art,
An earthly lover lurking at her heart.
Amazed, confused, he found his pow'r expired,   435
Resigned to fate, and with a sigh retired.
    The Peer now spreads the glitt'ring forfex° wide,   *scissors*
T' enclose the lock; now joins it, to divide.
Ev'n then, before the fatal engine closed,
A wretched Sylph too fondly interposed;   440
Fate urged the sheers, and cut the Sylph in twain
(But airy substance soon unites again).
The meeting points the sacred hair dissever
From the fair head, forever and forever!
    Then flashed the living lightning from her eyes,   445
And screams of horror rend th' affrighted skies.
Not louder shrieks to pitying heav'n are cast,
When husbands or when lapdogs breathe their last,

---

1   *Scylla* According to Ovid's *Metamorphoses*, Scylla was turned into a seabird by her father, King Nisus, after she cut off his purple lock of hair (on which the kingdom's safety
depended) to please her lover, Minos, who was besieging the city.

Or when rich china vessels, fall'n from high,
450 In glitt'ring dust and painted fragments lie!
    "Let wreaths of triumph now my temples twine,"
The victor cried, "the glorious prize is mine!
While fish in streams, or birds delight in air,
Or in a coach and six the British fair,
455 As long as *Atalantis*[1] shall be read,
Or the small pillow grace a lady's bed,
While visits shall be paid on solemn days,
When num'rous wax-lights in bright order blaze,
While nymphs take treats, or assignations give,
460 So long my honour, name, and praise shall live!
    "What time would spare, from steel receives its date,
And monuments, like men, submit to fate!
Steel could the labour of the Gods destroy,
And strike to dust th' imperial towers of Troy;
465 Steel could the works of mortal pride confound,
And hew triumphal arches to the ground.
What wonder then, fair nymph! thy hairs should feel
The conqu'ring force of unresisted steel?"

CANTO 4

But anxious cares the pensive nymph oppressed,
470 And secret passions laboured in her breast.
Not youthful kings in battle seized alive,
Not scornful virgins who their charms survive,
Not ardent lovers robbed of all their bliss,
Not ancient ladies when refused a kiss,
475 Not tyrants fierce that unrepenting die,
Not Cynthia when her manteau's pinned awry,
Ev'r felt such rage, resentment, and despair,
As thou, sad virgin! for thy ravished hair.
    For, that sad moment when the sylphs withdrew,
480 And Ariel weeping from Belinda flew,
Umbriel, a dusky, melancholy sprite
As ever sullied the fair face of light,
Down to the central earth, his proper scene,

---

1   *Atalantis* Delarivier Manley's *New Atalantis* was an enormously creative rendering of the latest political scandals and social intrigues, which she recreated as fiction.

Repaired to search the gloomy Cave of Spleen.[1]
    Swift on his sooty pinions flits the Gnome,   485
And in a vapour reached the dismal dome.
No cheerful breeze this sullen region knows,
The dreaded east[2] is all the wind that blows.
Here, in a grotto, sheltered close from air,
And screened in shades from day's detested glare,   490
She sighs forever on her pensive bed,
Pain at her side, and megrim° at her head.   *migraine*
    Two handmaids wait the throne: alike in place,
But diff'ring far in figure and in face.
Here stood Ill-Nature like an ancient maid,   495
Her wrinkled form in black and white arrayed;
With store of prayers for mornings, nights, and noons
Her hand is filled; her bosom with lampoons.
    There Affectation, with a sickly mien,
Shows in her cheek the roses of eighteen,   500
Practised to lisp, and hang the head aside,
Faints into airs, and languishes with pride;
On the rich quilt sinks with becoming woe,
Wrapped in a gown, for sickness and for show.
The fair ones feel such maladies as these,   505
When each new nightdress gives a new disease.
    A constant vapour o'er the palace flies,
Strange phantoms rising as the mists arise;
Dreadful as hermit's dreams in haunted shades,
Or bright as visions of expiring maids.   510
Now glaring fiends and snakes on rolling spires,°   *coils*
Pale spectres, gaping tombs, and purple fires;
Now lakes of liquid gold, Elysian° scenes,   *of paradise*
And crystal domes, and angels in machines.°   *vehicles*
    Unnumbered throngs on every side are seen   515
Of bodies changed to various forms by spleen.
Here living teapots stand, one arm held out,
One bent; the handle this, and that the spout.

---

1   *Cave of Spleen* The spleen was thought to be the seat of melancholy or morose feelings, and "spleen" became a term used to cover any number of complaints including headaches, depression, irritability, hallucinations, or hypochondria.

2   *dreaded east* An east wind was thought to bring on attacks of spleen (also called "the vapours").

A pipkin° there like Homer's tripod[1] walks;   *small earthen pot*
520 Here sighs a jar, and there a goose pie[2] talks;
Men prove with child, as pow'rful fancy works,
And maids turned bottles call aloud for corks.
     Safe passed the Gnome through this fantastic band,
A branch of healing spleenwort[3] in his hand.
525 Then thus addressed the pow'r: "Hail, wayward Queen!
Who rule the sex to fifty from fifteen,
Parent of vapours and of female wit,
Who give th' hysteric or poetic fit,
On various tempers act by various ways,
530 Make some take physic,° others scribble plays;   *medicine*
Who cause the proud their visits to delay,
And send the godly in a pet,[4] to pray.
A nymph there is that all thy pow'r disdains,
And thousands more in equal mirth maintains.
535 But oh! if e'er thy Gnome could spoil a grace,
Or raise a pimple on a beauteous face,
Like citron-waters[5] matrons' cheeks inflame,
Or change complexions at a losing game;
If e'er with airy horns[6] I planted heads,
540 Or rumpled petticoats, or tumbled beds,
Or caused suspicion when no soul was rude,
Or discomposed the headdress of a prude,
Or e'er to costive lapdog gave disease,
Which not the tears of brightest eyes could ease—
545 Hear me, and touch Belinda with chagrin;
That single act gives half the world the spleen."
     The Goddess with a discontented air
Seems to reject him, though she grants his prayer.
A wondrous bag with both her hands she binds,

---

1   *Homer's tripod* In Homer's *Iliad* (Book 18), the god Vulcan makes three-legged stools
    that move by themselves.
2   [Pope's note] Alludes to a real fact, a Lady of distinction imagined herself in this condi-
    tion.
3   *spleenwort* Herb said to cure ailments of the spleen. Here it is reminiscent of the golden
    bough that Aeneas carries for protection on his journey to the underworld (*Aeneid*,
    Book 6).
4   *pet* Fit of ill-humour.
5   *citron-waters* Lemon-flavoured brandy-based liquor.
6   *horns* Sign of a cuckold. The horns here are "airy" because the wife's infidelity is only
    imagined by her jealous husband.

Like that where once Ulysses held the winds;[1]   550
There she collects the force of female lungs:
Sighs, sobs, and passions, and the war of tongues.
A vial next she fills with fainting fears,
Soft sorrows, melting griefs, and flowing tears.
The Gnome rejoicing bears her gifts away,   555
Spreads his black wings, and slowly mounts to day.
   Sunk in Thalestris'[2] arms the nymph he found,
Her eyes dejected and her hair unbound.
Full o'er their heads the swelling bag he rent,
And all the Furies issued at the vent.   560
Belinda burns with more than mortal ire,
And fierce Thalestris fans the rising fire.
"O wretched maid!" she spread her hands, and cried
(While Hampton's echoes, "Wretched maid!" replied),
"Was it for this you took such constant care   565
The bodkin, comb, and essence to prepare?
For this your locks in paper durance[3] bound,
For this with tort'ring irons wreathed around?
For this with fillets strained your tender head,
And bravely bore the double loads of lead?   570
Gods! shall the ravisher display your hair,
While the fops envy, and the ladies stare!
Honour forbid! at whose unrivaled shrine
Ease, pleasure, virtue, all, our sex resign.
Methinks already I your tears survey,   575
Already hear the horrid things they say,
Already see you a degraded toast,[4]
And all your honour in a whisper lost!
How shall I, then, your helpless fame defend?
'Twill then be infamy to seem your friend!   580
And shall this prize, th' inestimable prize,
Exposed through crystal to the gazing eyes,

---

1   *Ulysses ... winds* In Homer's *Odyssey*, Aeolus, keeper of the winds, gives Ulysses a bag
    filled with all the winds that, if they blew, would hinder his journey home.
2   *Thalestris* Queen of the Amazons; here, suggesting a fierce, pugnacious woman.
3   *paper durance* Curling papers, which were fastened to the hair with strips of hot lead.
    The head was then encircled by a fillet, or thin crown.
4   *toast* Woman whose health is drunk. Since toasting a woman implied familiarity with
    her, it was detrimental to a lady's reputation if it was done too frequently, or by too
    many men.

And heightened by the diamond's circling rays,
On that rapacious hand forever blaze?[1]
585   Sooner shall grass in Hyde Park Circus[2] grow,
And wits take lodgings in the sound of Bow;[3]
Sooner let earth, air, sea, to chaos fall,
Men, monkeys, lapdogs, parrots, perish all!"
      She said; then raging to Sir Plume repairs,
590   And bids her beau demand the precious hairs
(Sir Plume, of amber snuffbox justly vain,
And the nice conduct of a clouded° cane).   *marbled*
With earnest eyes and round unthinking face,
He first the snuffbox opened, then the case,
595   And thus broke out—"My Lord, why, what the devil?
Z—ds!° damn the lock! 'fore Gad, you must be civil!   *zounds*
Plague on't! 'tis past a jest—nay prithee, pox!
Give her the hair"—he spoke, and rapped his box.
      "It grieves me much," replied the Peer again,
600   "Who speaks so well should ever speak in vain.
But by this lock, this sacred lock I swear
(Which never more shall join its parted hair;
Which never more its honours shall renew,
Clipped from the lovely head where late it grew)
605   That while my nostrils draw the vital air,
This hand, which won it, shall forever wear."
He spoke, and, speaking, in proud triumph spread
The long-contended honours of her head.
      But Umbriel, hateful Gnome! forbears not so;
610   He breaks the vial whence the sorrows flow.
Then see! the nymph in beauteous grief appears,
Her eyes half languishing, half drowned in tears;
On her heaved bosom hung her drooping head,
Which with a sigh she raised, and thus she said:
615   "Forever cursed be this detested day,
Which snatched my best, my fav'rite curl away!
Happy! ah ten times happy had I been,
If Hampton Court these eyes had never seen!

---

1   *Exposed ... blaze* I.e., the Baron will set the hair in a ring.
2   *Hyde Park Circus* Another name for the Ring road in Hyde Park.
3   *in the sound of Bow* Within the sound of the church bells of St. Mary-le-Bow in Cheap-
    side, an unfashionable part of town.

Yet am not I the first mistaken maid
By love of courts to num'rous ills betrayed.   620
Oh, had I rather unadmired remained
In some lone isle, or distant northern land;
Where the gilt chariot never marks the way,
Where none learn ombre, none e'er taste bohea!¹
There kept my charms concealed from mortal eye,   625
Like roses that in deserts bloom and die.
What moved my mind with youthful lords to roam?
Oh, had I stayed and said my prayers at home!
'Twas this the morning omens seemed to tell;
Thrice from my trembling hand the patch box fell;   630
The tott'ring china shook without a wind,
Nay, Poll² sat mute, and Shock was most unkind!
A Sylph too warned me of the threats of fate,
In mystic visions, now believed too late!
See the poor remnants of these slighted hairs!   635
My hands shall rend what ev'n thy rapine spares.
These, in two sable ringlets taught to break,
Once gave new beauties to the snowy neck.
The sister lock now sits uncouth, alone,
And in its fellow's fate foresees its own;   640
Uncurled it hangs, the fatal shears demands,
And tempts once more thy sacrilegious hands.
Oh, hadst thou, cruel! been content to seize
Hairs less in sight, or any hairs but these!"

CANTO 5

She said; the pitying audience melt in tears,   645
But Fate and Jove³ had stopped the Baron's ears.
In vain Thalestris with reproach assails,
For who can move when fair Belinda fails?
Not half so fixed the Trojan could remain,
While Anna begged and Dido raged in vain.⁴   650

---

1   *bohea* Expensive Chinese black tea.
2   *Poll* Belinda's parrot.
3   *Jove* King of the Roman gods.
4   *the Trojan ... vain* Commanded by the gods, Aeneas left his distraught lover, Dido, to
     found the city of Rome. Dido's sister Anna begged him to return, but he refused.

Canto 5, illustration from the 1714 edition of The Rape of the Lock.

Then grave Clarissa[1] graceful waved her fan;
Silence ensued, and thus the nymph began:
  "Say, why are beauties praised and honoured most,
The wise man's passion, and the vain man's toast?
Why decked with all that land and sea afford,   655
Why angels called, and angel-like adored?
Why round our coaches crowd the white-gloved beaux,
Why bows the side box from its inmost rows?
How vain are all these glories, all our pains,
Unless good sense preserve what beauty gains;   660
That men may say, when we the front box grace,
'Behold the first in virtue, as in face!'
Oh! if to dance all night, and dress all day,
Charmed the smallpox, or chased old age away,
Who would not scorn what housewife's cares produce,   665
Or who would learn one earthly thing of use?
To patch, nay ogle, might become a saint,
Nor could it sure be such a sin to paint.
But since, alas! frail beauty must decay,
Curled or uncurled, since locks will turn to grey;   670
Since painted, or not painted, all shall fade,
And she who scorns a man must die a maid;
What then remains but well our pow'r to use,
And keep good humour still, whate'er we lose?
And trust me, dear! good humour can prevail,   675
When airs and flights and screams and scolding fail.
Beauties in vain their pretty eyes may roll;
Charms strike the sight, but merit wins the soul."
  So spoke the dame, but no applause ensued;[2]
Belinda frowned, Thalestris called her prude.   680
"To arms, to arms!" the fierce virago[3] cries,
And swift as lightning to the combat flies.
All side in parties, and begin th' attack;
Fans clap, silks rustle, and tough whalebones crack;

---

1 [Pope's note] A new character introduced in the subsequent editions to open more
   clearly the moral of the poem, in a parody of the speech of Sarpedon to Glaucus in
   Homer. [See Homer's *Iliad* 12, in which Sarpedon reflects on glory and urges Glaucus
   to join the attack on Troy.]
2 [Pope's note] It is a verse frequently repeated in Homer after any speech, "So spoke
   ——, and all the heroes applauded."
3 *virago* Female warrior.

685 Heroes' and heroines' shouts confus'dly rise,
    And base and treble voices strike the skies.
    No common weapons in their hands are found;
    Like Gods they fight, nor dread a mortal wound.
        So when bold Homer makes the Gods engage,
690 And heav'nly breasts with human passions rage;
    'Gainst Pallas, Mars; Latona, Hermes[1] arms;
    And all Olympus rings with loud alarms.
    Jove's thunder roars, heav'n trembles all around;
    Blue Neptune[2] storms, the bellowing deeps resound;
695 Earth shakes her nodding tow'rs, the ground gives way,
    And the pale ghosts start at the flash of day!
        Triumphant Umbriel on a sconce's[3] height
    Clapped his glad wings, and sat to view the fight.
    Propped on their bodkin spears, the sprites survey
700 The growing combat, or assist the fray.
        While through the press enraged Thalestris flies,
    And scatters deaths around from both her eyes,
    A beau and witling° perished in the throng—   *inferior wit*
    One died in metaphor, and one in song.
705 "O cruel nymph! a living death I bear,"
    Cried Dapperwit, and sunk beside his chair.
    A mournful glance Sir Fopling upwards cast,
    "Those eyes are made so killing"—was his last.
    Thus on Maeander's flow'ry margin lies
710 Th' expiring swan, and as he sings he dies.[4]
        When bold Sir Plume had drawn Clarissa down,
    Chloe stepped in, and killed him with a frown;
    She smiled to see the doughty° hero slain,   *valiant*
    But at her smile the beau revived again.
715 Now Jove suspends his golden scales[5] in air,
    Weighs the men's wits against the lady's hair;
    The doubtful beam long nods from side to side;
    At length the wits mount up, the hairs subside.

---

1   *Pallas* Athena, goddess of wisdom; *Mars* God of war; *Latona* Goddess of light;
    Hermes Among other attributions, god of deceit.
2   *Neptune* Roman god of the sea.
3   *sconce* Wall bracket for holding a candle; also a small fort or earthwork.
4   *Maeander ... dies* River in Phrygia (present-day Turkey). Swans were said to sing before
    their deaths.
5   *golden scales* Used by the god to weigh the fates of mortals, particularly in battle.

See, fierce Belinda on the Baron flies
With more than usual lightning in her eyes;   720
Nor feared the chief th' unequal fight to try,
Who sought no more than on his foe to die.[1]
But this bold lord, with manly strength endued,
She with one finger and a thumb subdued:
Just where the breath of life his nostrils drew,   725
A charge of snuff the wily virgin threw;
The Gnomes direct, to every atom just,
The pungent grains of titillating dust.
Sudden, with starting tears each eye o'erflows,
And the high dome re-echoes to his nose.   730
    "Now meet thy fate," incensed Belinda cried,
And drew a deadly bodkin from her side.
(The same, his ancient personage to deck,
Her great-great-grandsire wore about his neck
In three seal rings;[2] which after, melted down,   735
Formed a vast buckle for his widow's gown.
Her infant grandame's whistle next it grew,
The bells she jingled, and the whistle blew;
Then in a bodkin graced her mother's hairs,
Which long she wore, and now Belinda wears.)   740
    "Boast not my fall," he cried, "insulting foe!
Thou by some other shalt be laid as low.
Nor think to die dejects my lofty mind;
All that I dread is leaving you behind!
Rather than so, ah let me still survive,   745
And burn in Cupid's flames—but burn alive."
    "Restore the lock!" she cries, and all around,
"Restore the lock!" the vaulted roofs rebound.
Not fierce Othello in so loud a strain
Roared for the handkerchief that caused his pain.[3]   750
But see how oft ambitious aims are crossed,
And chiefs contend 'till all the prize is lost!
The lock, obtained with guilt and kept with pain,
In every place is sought, but sought in vain;
With such a prize no mortal must be blessed,   755

---

1   *to die* Metaphorically, to experience an orgasm.
2   *seal rings* Rings used to imprint the wax that seals an envelope.
3   *fierce Othello … pain* See Shakespeare's *Othello* 3.4.

So Heav'n decrees! with Heav'n who can contest?
    Some thought it mounted to the lunar sphere,
Since all things lost on earth are treasured there.
There heroes' wits are kept in pond'rous vases,
760 And beaux' in snuffboxes and tweezer cases.
There broken vows and deathbed alms are found,
And lovers' hearts with ends of ribbon bound;
The courtier's promises, and sick man's prayers,
The smiles of harlots, and the tears of heirs,
765 Cages for gnats, and chains to yoke a flea,
Dried butterflies, and tomes of casuistry.[1]
    But trust the Muse—she saw it upward rise,
Though marked by none but quick poetic eyes
(So Rome's great founder[2] to the heav'ns withdrew,
770 To Proculus alone confessed in view);
A sudden star, it shot through liquid° air,   *transparent*
And drew behind a radiant trail of hair.
Not Berenice's[3] locks first rose so bright,
The heav'ns bespangling with dishevelled light.
775 The Sylphs behold it kindling as it flies,
And, pleased, pursue its progress through the skies.
    This the beau monde shall from the Mall[4] survey,
And hail with music its propitious ray.
This the blessed lover shall for Venus take,
780 And send up vows from Rosamonda's Lake.[5]
This Partridge[6] soon shall view in cloudless skies
When next he looks through Galileo's eyes;[7]

---

1   *casuistry* The application of general rules of ethics or morality to specific matters of conscience (often through minutely detailed, yet ultimately false or evasive reasoning).

2   *Rome's great founder* Romulus, who was apparently transported from earth in a storm cloud, never to be seen again except by Proculus, who claimed Romulus came to him in a vision from heaven.

3   *Berenice* Berenice dedicated a lock of her hair to Aphrodite to ensure her husband's safe return from war. She placed the lock in Aphrodite's temple, but it disappeared the next day, and was reputed to have ascended to the heavens, where it became a new constellation.

4   *the Mall* Walk in St. James's Park.

5   *Rosamonda's Lake* Pond in St. James's Park that is associated with unhappy lovers. (According to legend, Rosamond was Henry II's mistress and was murdered by his queen.)

6   [Pope's note] John Partridge was a ridiculous star-gazer who, in his almanacs every year, never failed to predict the downfall of the Pope, and the King of France, then at war with the English.

7   *Galileo's eyes* Telescope.

And hence th' egregious wizard shall foredoom
The fate of Louis, and the fall of Rome.
    Then cease, bright nymph! to mourn thy ravished hair,   785
Which adds new glory to the shining sphere!
Not all the tresses that fair head can boast
Shall draw such envy as the lock you lost.
For, after all the murders of your eye,
When, after millions slain, yourself shall die;   790
When those fair suns shall set, as set they must,
And all those tresses shall be laid in dust;
This lock the Muse shall consecrate to fame,
And 'midst the stars inscribe Belinda's name!
            —1717 (original, two-canto version published 1712)

Thomas Gray
1716–1771

A scholar and a recluse who produced only a handful of poems, Thomas Gray nevertheless occupies a pivotal position in the history of English literature. His reputation is secured by his "Elegy Written in a Country Churchyard" (1751), which brought him immediate (and unwelcomed) fame. The poem represents an important moment in the gradual transition from the Neoclassical to the Romantic period: its style embodies neoclassical restraint while its themes echo the sentiments of sensibility, the mid-century movement toward the expression of "universal feelings."

Gray had published only a few poems—all anonymously—before the "Elegy." The poem, which draws on traditions that included landscape poetry, the funeral elegy, and graveyard poetry, received immediate and widespread praise from both critics and readers. It went through twelve editions by 1763, appeared in several periodicals, was imitated, parodied, and translated into numerous languages, and became arguably the most quoted poem in English.

After the success of the "Elegy" six of Gray's poems were published in an illustrated collection (1753), and he turned to writing more elaborate poetry. In 1757, he was offered the Poet Laureateship, which he declined, and he published two odes, "The Progress of Poesy" and "The Bard"—complex, allusive poems that puzzled many readers (and were parodied in two odes to "Oblivion" and "Obscurity"). In later years he travelled, studied more and wrote less, and, in 1768, accepted a professorship of modern history at Cambridge, but never delivered a lecture. In temperament, he described himself as melancholic and others described him as socially withdrawn, but his letters reveal a lively wit and superior intellect.

Elegy Written in a Country Churchyard

The curfew tolls the knell of parting day,
The lowing herd wind slowly o'er the lea,[1]
The plowman homeward plods his weary way,
And leaves the world to darkness and to me.

5 Now fades the glimm'ring landscape on the sight,
And all the air a solemn stillness holds,
Save where the beetle wheels his droning flight,
And drowsy tinklings lull the distant folds;

---

1   *lea* Meadow or area of grassland.

Save that from yonder ivy-mantled tow'r
The moping owl does to the moon complain   10
Of such as, wand'ring near her secret bow'r,
Molest her ancient solitary reign.

Beneath those rugged elms, that yew-tree's shade,
Where heaves the turf in many a mould'ring heap,
Each in his narrow cell for ever laid,   15
The rude° forefathers of the hamlet sleep.   *unlearned*

The breezy call of incense-breathing morn,
The swallow twitt'ring from the straw-built shed,
The cock's shrill clarion or the echoing horn,
No more shall rouse them from their lowly bed.   20

For them no more the blazing hearth shall burn,
Or busy housewife ply her evening care:
No children run to lisp their sire's return,
Or climb his knees the envied kiss to share.

Oft did the harvest to their sickle yield,   25
Their furrow oft the stubborn glebe° has broke;   *soil*
How jocund° did they drive their team afield!   *merrily*
How bowed the woods beneath their sturdy stroke!

Let not Ambition mock their useful toil,
Their homely joys, and destiny obscure;   30
Nor Grandeur hear, with a disdainful smile,
The short and simple annals of the poor.

The boast of heraldry, the pomp of pow'r,
And all that beauty, all that wealth e'er gave,
Awaits alike th' inevitable hour.   35
The paths of glory lead but to the grave.

Nor you, ye Proud, impute to these the fault,
If Mem'ry o'er their tomb no trophies raise,
Where through the long-drawn aisle and fretted[1] vault
The pealing anthem swells the note of praise.   40

---

1   *fretted* Carved with decorative patterns.

Can storied urn or animated bust
Back to its mansion call the fleeting breath?
Can Honour's voice provoke the silent dust,
Or Flatt'ry soothe the dull cold ear of Death?

45 Perhaps in this neglected spot is laid
Some heart once pregnant with celestial fire;
Hands that the rod of empire might have swayed,
Or waked to ecstasy the living lyre.

But Knowledge to their eyes her ample page
50 Rich with the spoils of time did ne'er unroll;
Chill Penury repressed their noble rage,[1]
And froze the genial current of the soul.

Full many a gem of purest ray serene
The dark unfathomed caves of ocean bear:
55 Full many a flow'r is born to blush unseen
And waste its sweetness on the desert air.

Some village-Hampden[2] that with dauntless breast
The little tyrant of his fields withstood;
Some mute inglorious Milton[3] here may rest,
60 Some Cromwell[4] guiltless of his country's blood.

Th' applause of list'ning senates to command,
The threats of pain and ruin to despise,
To scatter plenty o'er a smiling land,
And read their hist'ry in a nation's eyes,

65 Their lot forbade: nor circumscribed alone
Their growing virtues, but their crimes confined;
Forbade to wade through slaughter to a throne,
And shut the gates of mercy on mankind,

---

1 *rage* Ardour, enthusiasm.
2 *Hampden* John Hampden (1594–1643), member of Parliament who defied Charles I and died early in the ensuing civil war.
3 *Milton* John Milton (1608–74), English poet and dramatist.
4 *Cromwell* Oliver Cromwell, military and political leader during the English Civil Wars (1642–51) and Lord Protector of England (1653–58).

The struggling pangs of conscious truth to hide,
To quench the blushes of ingenuous shame,   70
Or heap the shrine of Luxury and Pride
With incense kindled at the Muse's flame.[1]

Far from the madding crowd's ignoble strife,
Their sober wishes never learned to stray;
Along the cool sequestered vale of life   75
They kept the noiseless tenor of their way.

Yet ev'n these bones from insult to protect
Some frail memorial still erected nigh,
With uncouth rhymes and shapeless sculpture decked,
Implores the passing tribute of a sigh.   80

Their name, their years, spelt by th' unlettered muse,
The place of fame and elegy supply:
And many a holy text around she strews,
That teach the rustic moralist to die.

For who to dumb Forgetfulness a prey,   85
This pleasing anxious being e'er resigned,

---

1   *With ... flame* After this line, the earliest extant draft of the poem contains four stanzas
     that appear to be an earlier ending to the poem:

> The thoughtless World to Majesty may bow
> Exalt the brave, and idolize Success
> But more to Innocence their Safety owe
> Than Power and Genius e'er conspired to bless

> And thou, who mindful of the unhonoured Dead
> Dost in these Notes their artless Tale relate
> By Night and lonely Contemplation led
> To linger in the gloomy Walks of Fate

> Hark how the sacred Calm, that broods around
> Bids ev'ry fierce tumultuous Passion cease
> In still small Accents whisp'ring from the Ground
> A grateful Earnest of eternal Peace

> No more with Reason and thyself at strife;
> Give anxious Cares and endless Wishes room
> But thro' the cool sequestred Vale of Life
> Pursue the silent Tenor of thy Doom.

Left the warm precincts of the cheerful day,
Nor cast one longing ling'ring look behind?

On some fond breast the parting soul relies,
90 Some pious drops the closing eye requires;
Ev'n from the tomb the voice of nature cries,
Ev'n in our ashes live their wonted fires.

For thee who, mindful of th' unhonoured dead,
Dost in these lines their artless tale relate;
95 If chance, by lonely Contemplation led,
Some kindred spirit shall inquire thy fate,

Haply some hoary-headed swain[1] may say,
"Oft have we seen him at the peep of dawn
Brushing with hasty steps the dews away
100 To meet the sun upon the upland lawn.

"There at the foot of yonder nodding beech
That wreathes its old fantastic roots so high,
His listless length at noontide would he stretch,
And pore upon the brook that babbles by.

105 "Hard by yon wood, now smiling as in scorn,
Mutt'ring his wayward fancies he would rove,
Now drooping, woeful wan, like one forlorn,
Or crazed with care, or crossed in hopeless love.

"One morn I missed him on the customed hill,
110 Along the heath and near his fav'rite tree;
Another came; nor yet beside the rill,
Nor up the lawn, nor at the wood was he;

"The next with dirges due in sad array
Slow through the church-way path we saw him borne.
115 Approach and read (for thou can'st read) the lay,
Graved on the stone beneath yon aged thorn."

---

1   *hoary-headed swain* I.e., white-haired farmer.

THE EPITAPH

Here rests his head upon the lap of earth
A youth to fortune and to fame unknown.
Fair Science° frowned not on his humble birth,   learning
And Melancholy marked him for her own.

Large was his bounty and his soul sincere,   5
Heav'n did a recompense as largely send:
He gave to Mis'ry all he had, a tear,
He gained from Heav'n ('twas all he wished) a friend.

No farther seek his merits to disclose,
Or draw his frailties from their dread abode,   10
(There they alike in trembling hope repose)
The bosom of his Father and his God.

—1751

Anna Laetitia Barbauld
1743–1825

Anna Laetitia Barbauld's diverse accomplishments established her as a leading figure in London's intellectual life: she was as an educational reformer, critic, editor, radical political writer, and well-regarded poet of early Romanticism and children's literature. Her career as a published poet began in 1773 with her wide-ranging debut collection *Poems*, which was so popular that it would be re-issued and revised several times over the next 20 years. The varied subject matter of her work reflects a wide range of interests, from politics to animal rights to religious devotion.

Barbauld's father superintended one of the Protestant alternatives to England's exclusive Anglican schools; from him she learned languages such as Greek and Latin and received an education in literary classics. She followed in her father's footsteps when she and her husband co-founded their own boarding school for boys. Her work there inspired her *Lessons for Children* (1778–79) and *Hymns in Prose for Children* (1781), primers with literacy and faith as their respective goals. The large type in these small texts was an innovation that popularized children's books, and *Lessons* and *Hymns* were influential in both England and the newly formed United States.

Barbauld was also a political writer whose essays, pamphlets, and persuasive verse addressed topics such as freedom of religion, the abolition of slavery, and Britain's engagement in the Napoleonic Wars.

The Caterpillar

No, helpless thing, I cannot harm thee now;
Depart in peace, thy little life is safe,
For I have scanned thy form with curious eye,
Noted the silver line that streaks thy back,
5   The azure and the orange that divide
Thy velvet sides; thee, houseless wanderer,
My garment has enfolded, and my arm
Felt the light pressure of thy hairy feet;
Thou hast curled round my finger; from its tip,
10 Precipitous descent! with stretched out neck,
Bending thy head in airy vacancy,
This way and that, inquiring, thou hast seemed
To ask protection; now, I cannot kill thee.
Yet I have sworn perdition° to thy race,   *damnation, destruction*

And recent from the slaughter am I come 15
Of tribes and embryo nations: I have sought
With sharpened eye and persecuting zeal,
Where, folded in their silken webs they lay
Thriving and happy; swept them from the tree
And crushed whole families beneath my foot; 20
Or, sudden, poured on their devoted heads
The vials of destruction.[1]—This I've done,
Nor felt the touch of pity: but when thou—
A single wretch, escaped the general doom,
Making me feel and clearly recognize 25
Thine individual existence, life,
And fellowship of sense with all that breathes—
Present'st thyself before me, I relent,
And cannot hurt thy weakness.—So the storm
Of horrid war, o'erwhelming cities, fields, 30
And peaceful villages, rolls dreadful on:
The victor shouts triumphant; he enjoys
The roar of cannon and the clang of arms,
And urges, by no soft relentings stopped,
The work of death and carnage. Yet should one, 35
A single sufferer from the field escaped,
Panting and pale, and bleeding at his feet,
Lift his imploring eyes—the hero weeps;
He is grown human, and capricious Pity,
Which would not stir for thousands, melts for one 40
With sympathy spontaneous: 'Tis not Virtue,
Yet 'tis the weakness of a virtuous mind.

—1825

---

1   *vials of destruction* I.e., pesticides.

Phillis Wheatley
1753–1784

The first black person of African heritage to have a book published, Phillis Wheatley gained an international readership for her poetry, yet died impoverished and largely forgotten. During her lifetime, she published some 50 poems in American newspapers, an exceptional number for the time, and had a collection of poetry, *Poems on Various Subjects, Religious and Moral* (1773), published in London.

Born in Africa, Wheatley was transported to the British colonies in America on the slave ship *Phillis* in 1761. She was purchased as a slave-servant by a businessman and his wife, John and Susannah Wheatley, who gave her an education in English, Latin, classics, and the Bible. Her first published poem appeared in a Rhode Island newspaper when she was only 14 years old.

The 38 *Poems on Various Subjects* include several on nature and morality, a number of poems written to mark specific occasions (called occasional poems), and a racially self-conscious poem on religious transformation, "On Being Brought from Africa to America." Many of the poems are elegies for the dead, which display a reluctance to mourn and instead celebrate the passage of the departed to a happier and better life.

Wheatley gained her freedom in 1778, and in the same year she married a free black man. They lived in extreme poverty, which contributed to the death of all three of her children in infancy—and to Wheatley's own premature death at age 31.

On Being Brought from Africa to America

'Twas mercy brought me from my Pagan land,
Taught my benighted soul to understand
That there's a God, that there's a Saviour too:
Once I redemption neither sought nor knew.
5 Some view our sable race with scornful eye—
"Their colour is a diabolic dye."
Remember, Christians, Negroes, black as Cain,[1]
May be refined, and join th' angelic train.

—1773

---

1   *Cain* In Genesis 4.1–15, the son of Adam and Eve, who murdered his brother Abel and was cursed and marked by God as punishment. A popular interpretation of this story was that the mark of Cain turned his skin dark.

William Blake
1757–1827

"I labour upwards into futurity," wrote William Blake on the back of one of the "tablets" of his visionary art. Blake's genius was largely unrecognized during his own lifetime, but the mysterious and powerful poetry that he crafted—perhaps most memorably in *Songs of Innocence and Experience* (1789, 1794)—would eventually be recognized as having revolutionary significance.

As a child living above his parents' hosiery shop in London, Blake once received a thrashing for declaring he had seen the face of God. Apprenticed at 14 to a highly respected engraver, he spent seven years learning the trade that would earn him his keep. As an adult, Blake claimed to communicate daily with the spirit of his brother Robert, who had died of tuberculosis; the unique style of "illuminated printing" that Blake later devised came to him in a visitation from Robert. Etching words backwards into copper plates so that they would reverse to normal upon printing, Blake in 1788 created his first illuminated texts. Over the next 20 years he would produce an extraordinary series of works in which he used both words and images to express his artistic vision.

The Bible was a tremendous imaginative reserve upon which Blake drew all of his life, and one vision to which he often returns is that of an earthly Eden triumphing over forces of repression. He also had associations with decidedly non-mystical movements calling for political reforms, although he never fully participated in any organization, religious or political.

Blake found his soul mate in Catherine Boucher, a market gardener's daughter whom he taught to read and trained in the printing business. Catherine was evidently a submissive, devoted wife, and some have denigrated Blake's approach to marriage, citing his pronouncement that "the female … lives from the light of the male." But at the same time, Blake abjured sexual domination and celebrated "the moment of desire!" as a portal to the divine.

Against the grain of the times—he lived during the Industrial Revolution—Blake continued producing labour-intensive, elaborately illustrated books, none of which was commercially successful. Only 20 copies of *Songs of Experience* had been sold at the time of his death.

from *Songs of Innocence*

The Lamb

Little lamb, who made thee?
　Dost thou know who made thee,
Gave thee life & bid thee feed
By the stream & o'er the mead—

William Blake, "The Lamb," Songs of Innocence, *1789. Blake produced his illuminated books, including* Songs of Innocence *and* Songs of Experience, *by etching both text and illustrations onto copper plates, which he then used for printing. Often, he coloured the printed images by hand.*

5 Gave thee clothing of delight,
   Softest clothing, woolly bright,
   Gave thee such a tender voice,
   Making all the vales rejoice?
        Little lamb, who made thee,
10   Dost thou know who made thee?

   Little lamb, I'll tell thee,
   Little lamb, I'll tell thee!

He is called by thy name,
For he calls himself a Lamb;
He is meek & he is mild,[1]   15
He became a little child:
I a child, & thou a lamb,
We are called by his name.
  Little lamb, God bless thee,
  Little lamb, God bless thee!   20

The Chimney Sweeper[2]

When my mother died I was very young,
And my father sold me while yet my tongue
Could scarcely cry 'weep! 'weep! 'weep! 'weep![3]
So your chimneys I sweep, & in soot I sleep.[4]

There's little Tom Dacre, who cried when his head,   5
That curl'd like a lamb's back, was shav'd; so I said,
"Hush Tom! never mind it, for when your head's bare,
You know that the soot cannot spoil your white hair."

And so he was quiet, & that very night,
As Tom was a-sleeping he had such a sight!   10
That thousands of sweepers, Dick, Joe, Ned, & Jack,
Were all of them lock'd up in coffins of black;

And by came an Angel who had a bright key,
And he open'd the coffins & set them all free;
Then down a green plain leaping, laughing they run,   15
And wash in a river and shine in the Sun.

Then naked & white, all their bags left behind,
They rise upon clouds and sport in the wind.
And the Angel told Tom, if he'd be a good boy,
He'd have God for his father & never want joy.   20

---

1 *He is ... is mild* See Charles Wesley's hymn "Gentle Jesus, Meek and Mild" (1742).

2 *The Chimney Sweeper* Children were often forced to climb up chimneys to clean them—a filthy, dangerous, and unhealthy job. A law ameliorating their working conditions was passed in 1788, but it was rarely enforced.

3 *'weep ... 'weep* The child is attempting to say "sweep," the chimney-sweeper's street cry. The act of 1788 should have prevented the apprenticing of children younger than eight.

4 *in soot I sleep* The sweeps used their bags of soot as blankets.

And so Tom awoke; and we rose in the dark,
And got with our bags & our brushes to work.
Tho' the morning was cold, Tom was happy & warm;
So if all do their duty, they need not fear harm.

—1789

from *Songs of Experience*

The Chimney Sweeper

A little black thing among the snow
Crying 'weep! 'weep! in notes of woe!
"Where are thy father & mother, say?"
"They are both gone up to the church to pray.

5   "Because I was happy upon the heath
And smil'd among the winter's snow,
They clothed me in the clothes of death
And taught me to sing the notes of woe.

"And because I am happy & dance & sing,
10 They think they have done me no injury,
And are gone to praise God & his Priest & King,
Who make up a heaven of our misery."

The Sick Rose

O Rose, thou art sick:
The invisible worm,
That flies in the night,
In the howling storm,

5   Has found out thy bed
Of crimson joy;
And his dark secret love
Does thy life destroy.

The Tyger

Tyger! Tyger! burning bright
In the forests of the night,
What immortal hand or eye
Could frame thy fearful symmetry?

In what distant deeps or skies   5
Burnt the fire of thine eyes?
On what wings dare he aspire?[1]
What the hand dare seize the fire?[2]

And what shoulder, & what art,
Could twist the sinews of thy heart?   10
And when thy heart began to beat,
What dread hand? & what dread feet?

William Blake, "The Tyger," Songs of Experience,
1794.

---

1   *wings ... aspire* In Greek mythology, Icarus flew using wings made of wax and feathers;
     these melted when he attempted to fly too close to the sun.
2   *hand ... fire* In Greek mythology, Prometheus stole fire from heaven to give to humans.

What the hammer? What the chain?
In what furnace was thy brain?
15 What the anvil? what dread grasp
Dare its deadly terrors clasp?

When the stars threw down their spears
And water'd heaven with their tears,
Did he smile his work to see?
20 Did he who made the Lamb make thee?

Tyger! Tyger! burning bright
In the forests of the night,
What immortal hand or eye
Dare frame thy fearful symmetry?

London

I wander thro' each charter'd[1] street
Near where the charter'd Thames does flow,
And mark in every face I meet
Marks of weakness, marks of woe.

5 In every cry of every Man,
In every Infant's cry of fear,
In every voice, in every ban,
The mind-forg'd manacles I hear.

How the Chimney-sweeper's cry
10 Every black'ning Church appalls,
And the hapless Soldier's sigh
Runs in blood down Palace walls.

But most thro' midnight streets I hear
How the youthful Harlot's curse[2]
15 Blasts the new-born Infant's tear,[3]
And blights with plagues the marriage hearse.

—1794

---

1   *charter'd* Licensed. Charters grant freedoms, often for a select minority (such as mer-
    chants).
2   *Harlot's curse* Referring to both the oaths she utters and the venereal diseases she spreads.
3   *Blasts ... tear* Reference to the blindness caused in infants if they contract certain vene-
    real diseases (such as gonorrhea) from their mother.

William Wordsworth

1770–1850

William Wordsworth is often credited with initiating the shifts in poetic form and content that characterized the Romantic era in British poetry. The most frequent subjects of his poems are nature, the sublime, and the lives of ordinary country people—of interest because, according to Wordsworth, in "low and rustic life ... the essential passions of the heart find a better soil in which they can attain their maturity, are less under restraint, and speak a plainer and more emphatic language." Wordsworth himself viewed poetry as a divine gift and, in addition to celebrating "rustic living" and nature, many of his poems celebrate the imaginative capacity of the author.

Wordsworth was born in the English Lake District. His parents were both dead by the time he was 13, and he was sent by relatives to be educated at a boarding school, later completing his degree at Cambridge. He spent parts of his young adulthood walking throughout Europe, an experience which deepened his interest in politics as well as in nature; his time spent in Revolutionary France had an especially profound impact on his poetry. After these travels were concluded, Wordsworth would spend much of the rest of his life sharing a home with his "beloved sister" Dorothy, whom he described as one of "the two beings to whom my intellect is most indebted" (the other was his friend and fellow poet Samuel Taylor Coleridge).

Lyrical Ballads (1798), which Wordsworth co-authored with Coleridge, is often considered the most important single volume of poetry of the period. Wordsworth's self-stated ambition to write about "incidents and situations from common life" in "language really used by men" was a shift from the impersonal, formulaic poetry of the eighteenth century. This deviation stirred up a great deal of criticism, but by the last decades of his life, Wordsworth's skill and mastery as a poet were widely acknowledged. He was awarded the title of Poet Laureate at the age of 73. In the year after his death, his long poem *The Prelude* was published; originally written in 1798–99, and expanded then revised over the next 40 years, it is often regarded as Wordsworth's crowning achievement.

Lines Written a Few Miles above Tintern Abbey

On Revisiting the Banks of the Wye during a Tour, July 13, 1798 [1]

Five years have passed; five summers, with the length
Of five long winters! and again I hear
These waters, rolling from their mountain-springs
With a sweet inland murmur.[2] Once again
5 Do I behold these steep and lofty cliffs,
Which on a wild secluded scene impress
Thoughts of more deep seclusion; and connect
The landscape with the quiet of the sky.
The day is come when I again repose
10 Here, under this dark sycamore, and view
These plots of cottage-ground, these orchard-tufts,
Which, at this season, with their unripe fruits,
Among the woods and copses lose themselves,
Nor, with their green and simple hue, disturb
15 The wild green landscape. Once again I see
These hedge-rows, hardly hedge-rows, little lines
Of sportive wood run wild; these pastoral farms
Green to the very door; and wreaths of smoke
Sent up, in silence, from among the trees,
20 With some uncertain notice, as might seem,
Of vagrant dwellers in the houseless woods,
Or of some hermit's cave, where by his fire
The hermit sits alone.

             Though absent long,
25 These forms of beauty have not been to me,
As is a landscape to a blind man's eye:
But oft, in lonely rooms, and 'mid the din
Of towns and cities, I have owed to them,
In hours of weariness, sensations sweet,
30 Felt in the blood, and felt along the heart,

---

1   [Wordsworth's note] No poem of mine was composed under circumstances more
pleasant for me to remember than this. I began it upon leaving Tintern, after crossing
the Wye, and concluded it just as I was entering Bristol in the evening, after a ramble
of 4 or 5 days, with my sister. Not a line of it was altered, and not any part of it was
written down till I reached Bristol.

2   [Wordsworth's note] The river is not affected by the tides a few miles above Tintern.

And passing even into my purer mind
With tranquil restoration—feelings too
Of unremembered pleasure; such, perhaps,
As may have had no trivial influence
On that best portion of a good man's life;   35
His little, nameless, unremembered acts
Of kindness and of love. Nor less, I trust,
To them I may have owed another gift,
Of aspect more sublime; that blessed mood,
In which the burthen of the mystery,   40
In which the heavy and the weary weight
Of all this unintelligible world
Is lighten'd—that serene and blessed mood,
In which the affections gently lead us on,
Until, the breath of this corporeal frame,   45
And even the motion of our human blood
Almost suspended, we are laid asleep
In body, and become a living soul:
While with an eye made quiet by the power
Of harmony, and the deep power of joy,   50
We see into the life of things.

             If this
Be but a vain belief, yet, oh! how oft,
In darkness, and amid the many shapes
Of joyless day-light; when the fretful stir   55
Unprofitable, and the fever of the world,
Have hung upon the beatings of my heart,
How oft, in spirit, have I turned to thee
O sylvan° Wye! Thou wanderer through the woods,   *wooded*
How often has my spirit turned to thee!   60

And now, with gleams of half-extinguish'd thought,
With many recognitions dim and faint,
And somewhat of a sad perplexity,
The picture of the mind revives again:
While here I stand, not only with the sense   65
Of present pleasure, but with pleasing thoughts
That in this moment there is life and food
For future years. And so I dare to hope
Though changed, no doubt, from what I was, when first

70 I came among these hills; when like a roe°   *deer*
    I bounded o'er the mountains, by the sides
    Of the deep rivers, and the lonely streams,
    Wherever nature led; more like a man
    Flying from something that he dreads, than one
75 Who sought the thing he loved. For nature then
    (The coarser pleasures of my boyish days,
    And their glad animal movements all gone by)
    To me was all in all. I cannot paint
    What then I was. The sounding cataract
80 Haunted me like a passion: the tall rock,
    The mountain, and the deep and gloomy wood,
    Their colours and their forms, were then to me
    An appetite: a feeling and a love,
    That had no need of a remoter charm,
85 By thought supplied, or any interest
    Unborrowed from the eye. That time is past,
    And all its aching joys are now no more,
    And all its dizzy raptures. Not for this
    Faint[1] I, nor mourn nor murmur: other gifts
90 Have followed, for such loss, I would believe,
    Abundant recompense. For I have learned
    To look on nature, not as in the hour
    Of thoughtless youth, but hearing oftentimes
    The still, sad music of humanity,
95 Not harsh nor grating, though of ample power
    To chasten and subdue. And I have felt
    A presence that disturbs me with the joy
    Of elevated thoughts; a sense sublime
    Of something far more deeply interfused,
100 Whose dwelling is the light of setting suns,
    And the round ocean, and the living air,
    And the blue sky, and in the mind of man,
    A motion and a spirit, that impels
    All thinking things, all objects of all thought,
105 And rolls through all things. Therefore am I still
    A lover of the meadows and the woods,
    And mountains; and of all that we behold
    From this green earth; of all the mighty world

---

1   *Faint* Lose heart; grow weak.

Of eye and ear, both what they half create,
And what perceive; well pleased to recognize   110
In nature and the language of the sense,
The anchor of my purest thoughts, the nurse,
The guide, the guardian of my heart, and soul
Of all my moral being.

                  Nor, perchance,   115
If I were not thus taught, should I the more
Suffer my genial° spirits to decay: *creative*
For thou art with me, here, upon the banks
Of this fair river; thou, my dearest Friend,[1]
My dear, dear Friend, and in thy voice I catch   120
The language of my former heart, and read
My former pleasures in the shooting lights
Of thy wild eyes. Oh! yet a little while
May I behold in thee what I was once,
My dear, dear Sister! And this prayer I make,   125
Knowing that Nature never did betray
The heart that loved her; 'tis her privilege,
Through all the years of this our life, to lead
From joy to joy: for she can so inform
The mind that is within us, so impress   130
With quietness and beauty, and so feed
With lofty thoughts, that neither evil tongues,
Rash judgments, nor the sneers of selfish men,
Nor greetings where no kindness is, nor all
The dreary intercourse of daily life,   135
Shall e'er prevail against us, or disturb
Our cheerful faith that all which we behold
Is full of blessings. Therefore let the moon
Shine on thee in thy solitary walk;
And let the misty mountain winds be free   140
To blow against thee: and in after years,
When these wild ecstasies shall be matured
Into a sober pleasure, when thy mind
Shall be a mansion for all lovely forms,
Thy memory be as a dwelling-place   145
For all sweet sounds and harmonies; Oh! then,

---

1   *my dearest Friend* I.e., Dorothy Wordsworth, the poet's sister.

If solitude, or fear, or pain, or grief,
Should be thy portion, with what healing thoughts
Of tender joy wilt thou remember me,
150   And these my exhortations! Nor, perchance,
If I should be, where I no more can hear
Thy voice, nor catch from thy wild eyes these gleams
Of past existence, wilt thou then forget
That on the banks of this delightful stream
155   We stood together; and that I, so long
A worshipper of Nature, hither came,
Unwearied in that service: rather say
With warmer love, oh! with far deeper zeal
Of holier love. Nor wilt thou then forget,
160   That after many wanderings, many years
Of absence, these steep woods and lofty cliffs,
And this green pastoral landscape, were to me
More dear, both for themselves, and for thy sake.

—1798

[The world is too much with us]

The world is too much with us; late and soon,
Getting and spending, we lay waste our powers:
Little we see in nature that is ours;
We have given our hearts away, a sordid boon!°   *gift*
5   The Sea that bares her bosom to the moon;
The Winds that will be howling at all hours
And are up-gathered now like sleeping flowers;
For this, for every thing, we are out of tune;
It moves us not. Great God! I'd rather be
10   A Pagan suckled in a creed outworn;
So might I, standing on this pleasant lea,
Have glimpses that would make me less forlorn;
Have sight of Proteus[1] coming from the sea;
Or hear old Triton[2] blow his wreathed horn.

—1807

---

1   *Proteus* Shape-changing sea god.
2   *Triton* Sea god with the head and torso of a man and the tail of a fish. He was frequently depicted blowing on a conch shell.

Samuel Taylor Coleridge
1772–1834

Coleridge wrote in a 1796 letter, "I am, and ever have been, a great reader, and have read almost everything—a library-cormorant." His own work was similarly wide-ranging and prolific; Coleridge's collected writings comprise 50 volumes and reveal his interest in a myriad of subjects from history and politics to science and literary criticism. He is chiefly remembered, however, for his significant contribution to English Romantic poetry: poems such as "The Rime of the Ancient Mariner" and "Kubla Khan" that have remained fresh and affecting for generations of readers.

The son of a school headmaster, Coleridge received a robust classical education and later briefly attended Cambridge, although he left without taking a degree. After several false starts—he joined the army, and upon his release concocted an ill-fated plan to move to America to found a communal society—he began to publish his writing. His second book of poetry was *Lyrical Ballads* (1798), a collaboration with his friend William Wordsworth; it opened with "The Rime of the Ancient Mariner," which remains Coleridge's most critically lauded single poem.

Coleridge composed little poetry during the last 35 years of his life. His most important writing from this period is the two-volume *Biographia Literaria* (1817), a work of autobiography and literary criticism in which he anatomizes both poetry and poetic production, considering not only formal elements but also the psychology of the creative process.

Frost at Midnight

The Frost performs its secret ministry,
Unhelped by any wind. The owlet's cry
Came loud—and hark, again! loud as before.
The inmates of my cottage, all at rest,
Have left me to that solitude, which suits   5
Abstruser musings: save that at my side
My cradled infant slumbers peacefully.
'Tis calm indeed! so calm, that it disturbs
And vexes meditation with its strange
And extreme silentness. Sea, hill, and wood,   10
This populous village! Sea, and hill, and wood,
With all the numberless goings-on of life,
Inaudible as dreams! the thin blue flame
Lies on my low-burnt fire, and quivers not;

15 Only that film,[1] which fluttered on the grate,
   Still flutters there, the sole unquiet thing.
   Methinks, its motion in this hush of nature
   Gives it dim sympathies with me who live,
   Making it a companionable form,
20 Whose puny flaps and freaks the idling Spirit
   By its own moods interprets, every where
   Echo or mirror seeking of itself,
   And makes a toy of Thought.

                                  But O! how oft,
25 How oft, at school, with most believing mind,
   Presageful, have I gazed upon the bars,
   To watch that fluttering *stranger*! and as oft
   With unclosed lids, already had I dreamt
   Of my sweet birth-place, and the old church-tower,
30 Whose bells, the poor man's only music, rang
   From morn to evening, all the hot Fair-day,
   So sweetly, that they stirred and haunted me
   With a wild pleasure, falling on mine ear
   Most like articulate sounds of things to come!
35 So gazed I, till the soothing things, I dreamt,
   Lulled me to sleep, and sleep prolonged my dreams!
   And so I brooded all the following morn,
   Awed by the stern preceptor's° face, mine eye   *teacher's*
   Fixed with mock study on my swimming book:
40 Save if the door half opened, and I snatched
   A hasty glance, and still my heart leaped up,
   For still I hoped to see the *stranger's* face,
   Townsman, or aunt, or sister more beloved,
   My play-mate when we both were clothed alike!

45   Dear Babe, that sleepest cradled by my side,
   Whose gentle breathings, heard in this deep calm,
   Fill up the interspersèd vacancies
   And momentary pauses of the thought!
   My babe so beautiful! it thrills my heart
50 With tender gladness, thus to look at thee,
   And think that thou shalt learn far other lore,

---

1   [Coleridge's note] In all parts of the kingdom these films are called *strangers* and sup-
     posed to portend the arrival of some absent friend.

And in far other scenes! For I was reared
In the great city, pent 'mid cloisters dim,
And saw nought lovely but the sky and stars.
But *thou*, my babe! shalt wander like a breeze   55
By lakes and sandy shores, beneath the crags
Of ancient mountain, and beneath the clouds,
Which image in their bulk both lakes and shores
And mountain crags: so shalt thou see and hear
The lovely shapes and sounds intelligible   60
Of that eternal language, which thy God
Utters, who from eternity doth teach
Himself in all, and all things in himself.
Great universal Teacher! he shall mould
Thy spirit, and by giving make it ask.   65

    Therefore all seasons shall be sweet to thee,
Whether the summer clothe the general earth
With greenness, or the redbreast sit and sing
Betwixt the tufts of snow on the bare branch
Of mossy apple-tree, while the nigh thatch   70
Smokes in the sun-thaw; whether the eave-drops fall
Heard only in the trances of the blast,
Or if the secret ministry of frost
Shall hang them up in silent icicles,
Quietly shining to the quiet Moon.   75

                                      —1798

Kubla Khan

Or, A Vision in a Dream. A Fragment[1]

In Xanadu did Kubla Khan
A stately pleasure-dome decree:
Where Alph, the sacred river, ran
Through caverns measureless to man
    Down to a sunless sea.   5

---

1   [Coleridge's note] The following fragment is here published at the request of a poet
[Lord Byron] of great and deserved celebrity, and as far as the Author's own opinions
are concerned, rather as a psychological curiosity, than on the ground of any supposed
poetic merits.
    In the summer of the year 1797, the Author, then in ill health, had retired to a lone-
ly farmhouse between Porlock and Linton, on the Exmoor confines of Somerset and

So twice five miles of fertile ground
With walls and towers were girdled round:
And there were gardens bright with sinuous rills,°   *brooks*
Where blossomed many an incense-bearing tree;
10 And here were forests ancient as the hills,
Enfolding sunny spots of greenery.

But oh! that deep romantic chasm which slanted
Down the green hill athwart a cedarn cover!
A savage place! as holy and enchanted
15 As e'er beneath a waning moon was haunted

Devonshire. In consequence of a slight indisposition [dysentery], an anodyne [opium]
had been prescribed, from the effects of which he fell asleep in his chair at the moment
that he was reading the following sentence, or words of the same substance, in *Purchas's
Pilgrimage*: "Here the Khan Kubla commanded a palace to be built, and a stately garden
thereunto. And thus ten miles of fertile ground were inclosed with a wall." The author
continued for about three hours in a profound sleep, at least of the external senses,
during which time he has the most vivid confidence, that he could not have composed
less than from two to three hundred lines, if that indeed can be called composition in
which all the images rose up before him as things, with a parallel production of the cor-
respondent expressions, without any sensation or consciousness of effort. On awaking
he appeared to himself to have a distinct recollection of the whole, and taking his pen,
ink, and paper, instantly and eagerly wrote down the lines that are here preserved. At
this moment he was unfortunately called out by a person on business from Porlock, and
detained by him above an hour, and on his return to his room, found to his no small
surprise and mortification, that though he still retained some vague and dim recollection of the general purpose of the vision, yet, with the exception of some eight or ten
scattered lines and images, all the rest had passed away like the images on the surface of
a stream into which a stone has been cast, but, alas! without the after restoration of the
latter!

> Then all the charm
> Is broken—all that phantom-world so fair
> Vanishes, and a thousand circlets spread,
> And each mis-shape the other. Stay awhile,
> Poor youth! who scarcely dar'st lift up thine eyes—
> The stream will soon renew its smoothness, soon
> The visions will return! And lo, he stays,
> And soon the fragments dim of lovely forms
> Come trembling back, unite, and now once more
> The pool becomes a mirror.

[from Coleridge's "The Picture, or the Lover's Resolution" (1802), 69–78]

Yet from the still surviving recollections in his mind, the Author has frequently pur-
posed to finish for himself what had been originally, as it were, given to him. Σαμερον
αδιον ασω [from Theocritus's *Idyll* 1.145]: but the tomorrow is yet to come.

As a contrast to this vision, I have annexed a fragment of a very different character
[Coleridge's poem "The Pains of Sleep," not included in this anthology], describing with
equal fidelity the dream of pain and disease.

By woman wailing for her demon-lover!
And from this chasm, with ceaseless turmoil seething,
As if this earth in fast thick pants were breathing,
A mighty fountain momently was forced:
Amid whose swift half-intermitted burst   20
Huge fragments vaulted like rebounding hail,
Or chaffy grain beneath the thresher's flail:
And 'mid these dancing rocks at once and ever
It flung up momently the sacred river.
Five miles meandering with a mazy° motion   *labyrinthine*   25
Through wood and dale the sacred river ran,
Then reached the caverns measureless to man,
And sank in tumult to a lifeless ocean:
And 'mid this tumult Kubla heard from far
Ancestral voices prophesying war!   30
    The shadow of the dome of pleasure
    Floated midway on the waves;
    Where was heard the mingled measure
    From the fountain and the caves.
It was a miracle of rare device,   35
A sunny pleasure-dome with caves of ice!
    A damsel with a dulcimer
    In a vision once I saw:
    It was an Abyssinian maid,
    And on her dulcimer she played,   40
    Singing of Mount Abora.
    Could I revive within me
    Her symphony and song,
    To such a deep delight 'twould win me,
That with music loud and long,   45
I would build that dome in air,
That sunny dome! those caves of ice!
And all who heard should see them there,
And all should cry, Beware! Beware!
His flashing eyes, his floating hair!   50
Weave a circle round him thrice,
And close your eyes with holy dread,
For he on honey-dew hath fed,
And drunk the milk of Paradise.

—1816 (written 1798)

Percy Bysshe Shelley
1792–1822

Although he was born into wealth and privilege, Percy Bysshe Shelley opposed the powerful, especially the Tory government and press whom he believed were responsible for the oppression of the working classes. He was called "Mad Shelley" at Oxford not only for his political radicalism but also for his vocal atheism and his intense interest in science. These intellectual passions underwrite a body of remarkable visionary poetry characterized by an elegance and complexity that is at once very wonderful and very difficult.

Shelley, heir to the estate and title of his baronet father and grandfather, attended Eton College, and was still a student there when he published *Zastrozzi* (1810), a Gothic romance novel. He continued to publish during his short stint at the University of Oxford, from which he and a friend were expelled for co-authoring a pamphlet entitled *The Necessity of Atheism* (1811). In 1813 Shelley published his first important work: *Queen Mab*, a poetic utopian dream-vision that vilified conventional morality and institutional religion.

In 1819–20 Shelley wrote his greatest utopian fantasy, *Prometheus Unbound*, which imagined a world grown young again as human beings unlearn historically acquired fear and hatred in favour of love, which Shelley called "the great secret" of all morality. A year later, he penned perhaps his best-known prose work, *A Defence of Poetry* (1821), which famously ends with the bold claim, "Poets are the unacknowledged legislators of the world."

Shelley's reputation was marred· by personal as well as political scandal, not least because he abandoned his wife for Mary Godwin (later Mary Shelley, the author of *Frankenstein*), whom he married when his first wife committed suicide. Although he enjoyed scant fame or immediate influence during his lifetime, he has long been recognized as one of the most important poets of the Romantic era.

Ozymandias[1]

I met a traveller from an antique land
Who said: Two vast and trunkless legs of stone
Stand in the desert ... Near them, on the sand,
Half sunk, a shattered visage lies, whose frown,

---

1   *Ozymandias* Greek name for King Ramses II of Egypt (1304–1237 BCE). First century BCE Greek historian Diodorus Siculus records the story of this monument (Ozymandias's tomb was in the shape of a male sphinx) and its inscription, which Diodorus says reads: "King of Kings am I, Ozymandias. If anyone would know how great I am and where I lie, let him surpass one of my exploits."

And wrinkled lip, and sneer of cold command,   5
Tell that its sculptor well those passions read
Which yet survive, stamped on these lifeless things,
The hand that mocked them, and the heart that fed:
And on the pedestal these words appear:
"My name is Ozymandias, king of kings: 10
Look on my works, ye Mighty, and despair!"
Nothing beside remains. Round the decay
Of that colossal wreck, boundless and bare
The lone and level sands stretch far away.

—1818

Ode to the West Wind[1]

1

O Wild West Wind, thou breath of Autumn's being,
Thou, from whose unseen presence the leaves dead
Are driven, like ghosts from an enchanter fleeing,

Yellow, and black, and pale, and hectic° red,   *feverish*
Pestilence-stricken multitudes: O thou,   5
Who chariotest to their dark wintry bed

The wingèd seeds, where they lie cold and low,
Each like a corpse within its grave, until
Thine azure sister of the Spring shall blow

Her clarion[2] o'er the dreaming earth, and fill   10
(Driving sweet buds like flocks to feed in air)
With living hues and odours plain and hill:

Wild Spirit, which art moving everywhere;
Destroyer and Preserver; hear, oh, hear!

---

1   [Shelley's note] This poem was conceived and chiefly written in a wood that skirts the
     Arno, near Florence, and on a day when that tempestuous wind, whose temperature is
     at once mild and animating, was collecting the vapours which pour down the autumnal
     rains. They began, as I foresaw, at sunset with a violent tempest of hail and rain, at-
     tended by that magnificent thunder and lightning peculiar to the Cispaline regions.
2   *clarion* High-pitched trumpet.

2

15 Thou on whose stream, 'mid the steep sky's commotion,
Loose clouds like earth's decaying leaves are shed,
Shook from the tangled boughs of Heaven and Ocean,

Angels° of rain and lightning: there are spread   *harbingers*
On the blue surface of thine aëry surge,
20 Like the bright hair uplifted from the head

Of some fierce Mænad,[1] even from the dim verge
Of the horizon to the zenith's height,
The locks of the approaching storm. Thou dirge

Of the dying year, to which this closing night
25 Will be the dome of a vast sepulchre,
Vaulted with all thy congregated might

Of vapours,° from whose solid atmosphere   *clouds*
Black rain, and fire, and hail will burst: oh, hear!

3

Thou who didst waken from his summer dreams
30 The blue Mediterranean, where he lay,
Lulled by the coil of his chrystàlline streams,[2]

Beside a pumice isle in Baiae's bay,[3]
And saw in sleep old palaces and towers
Quivering within the wave's intenser day,

35 All overgrown with azure moss and flowers
So sweet, the sense faints picturing them! Thou
For whose path the Atlantic's level powers

---

1   *Mænad* Female attendant of Bacchus, the Greek god of wine.
2   *coil ... streams* Currents of the Mediterranean, the colours of which are often different
     from the surrounding water.
3   *pumice* Porous stone made from cooled lava; *Baiae's bay* Bay west of Naples that con-
     tains the ruins of several imperial villas.

Cleave themselves into chasms, while far below
The sea-blooms and the oozy woods which wear
The sapless foliage of the ocean, know   40

Thy voice, and suddenly grow grey with fear,
And tremble and despoil themselves:[1] oh, hear!

4

If I were a dead leaf thou mightest bear;
If I were a swift cloud to fly with thee;
A wave to pant beneath thy power, and share   45

The impulse of thy strength, only less free
Than thou, O uncontrollable! If even
I were as in my boyhood, and could be

The comrade of thy wanderings over Heaven,
As then, when to outstrip thy skiey° speed   *lofty* 50
Scarce seemed a vision; I would ne'er have striven

As thus with thee in prayer in my sore need.
Oh! lift me as a wave, a leaf, a cloud!
I fall upon the thorns of life! I bleed!

A heavy weight of hours has chained and bowed   55
One too like thee: tameless, and swift, and proud.

5

Make me thy lyre,[2] even as the forest is:
What if my leaves are falling like its own!
The tumult of thy mighty harmonies

---

1   [Shelley's note] The phenomenon alluded to at the conclusion of the third stanza is
    well known to naturalists. The vegetation at the bottom of the sea, of rivers, and of
    lakes, sympathizes with that of the land in the change of seasons, and is consequently
    influenced by the winds which announce it.
2   *lyre* Aeolian harp, a stringed instrument that produces music when exposed to wind.

60 Will take from both a deep, autumnal tone,
   Sweet though in sadness. Be thou, Spirit fierce,
   My spirit! Be thou me, impetuous one!

   Drive my dead thoughts over the universe
   Like withered leaves to quicken a new birth!
65 And, by the incantation of this verse,

   Scatter, as from an unextinguished hearth
   Ashes and sparks, my words among mankind!
   Be through my lips to unawakened Earth

   The trumpet of a prophecy! O, Wind,
70 If Winter comes, can Spring be far behind?

                                        —1820

John Keats
1795–1821

John Keats has come to epitomize the popular conception of the Romantic poet as a passionate dreamer whose intense, sensuous poetry celebrates the world of the imagination over that of everyday life. Keats published only 54 poems in his short lifetime, but his work ranges across a number of poetic genres, including sonnets, odes, romances, and epics. His poetry often seeks a beauty and truth that will transcend the world of suffering, and often questions its own process of interpretation.

Keats, who died of tuberculosis at 25, often despaired of achieving the immortality he wanted for his work. In a note to his beloved, Fanny Brawne, he expresses regret that, "if I should die ... I have left no immortal work behind me—nothing to make my friends proud of my memory—but I have loved the principle of beauty in all things, and if I had had time I would have made myself remembered." Keats had scarcely a year to live when he wrote these words, but already he had completed, in an extraordinary surge of creativity, almost all the poetry on which his reputation rests, including "The Eve of St. Agnes," "La Belle Dame sans Merci," "Lamia," and his "great Odes," which remain among the highest expressions of the form in English.

Keats was also a highly skilled letter-writer, and his extensive correspondence, in which he reflects on aesthetics, the social role of the poet, and his own sense of poetic mission, reveals a nature acutely alive to the extremes of joy and heartbreak.

When I Have Fears that I May Cease to Be

When I have fears that I may cease to be
　　Before my pen has glean'd my teeming brain,
Before high piled books, in charact'ry,[1]
　　Hold like rich garners° the full-ripen'd grain;　　　　　*granaries*
When I behold, upon the night's starr'd face,　　　　　　　　5
　　Huge cloudy symbols of a high romance,
And think that I may never live to trace
　　Their shadows, with the magic hand of chance;
And when I feel, fair creature of an hour!
　　That I shall never look upon thee more,　　　　　　　　　10
Never have relish in the fairy power
　　Of unreflecting love;—then on the shore

1　*charact'ry* Symbols or letters.

Of the wide world I stand alone, and think
    Till love and fame to nothingness do sink.

—1848 (written 1818)

La Belle Dame sans Merci: A Ballad[1]

O what can ail thee, knight-at-arms,
    Alone and palely loitering?
The sedge[2] has wither'd from the lake,
    And no birds sing.

5 O what can ail thee, knight-at-arms,
    So haggard and so woe-begone?
The squirrel's granary is full,
    And the harvest's done.

I see a lily[3] on thy brow
10   With anguish moist and fever dew,
And on thy cheeks a fading rose
    Fast withereth too.

I met a lady in the meads,°   *meadows*
    Full beautiful, a fairy's child;
15 Her hair was long, her foot was light,
    And her eyes were wild.

I made a garland for her head,
    And bracelets too, and fragrant zone;°   *belt, girdle*
She look'd at me as she did love,
20   And made sweet moan.

I set her on my pacing steed,
    And nothing else saw all day long,
For sidelong would she bend, and sing
    A faery's song.

---

1   *La Belle Dame sans Merci* French: The Beautiful Lady without Pity. This original version
    of the poem, found in a journal letter to George and Georgiana Keats, was first published
    in 1848. Keats's revised version was published in 1820.
2   *sedge* Rush-like grass.
3   *lily* Flower traditionally associated with death.

She found me roots of relish sweet,   25
 And honey wild, and manna dew,[1]
And sure in language strange she said
 "I love thee true."

She took me to her elfin grot,°   *grotto*
 And there she wept, and sigh'd full sore,   30
And there I shut her wild wild eyes
 With kisses four.

And there she lulled me asleep,
 And there I dream'd—Ah! woe betide!
The latest° dream I ever dream'd   *last* 35
 On the cold hill side.

I saw pale kings, and princes too,
 Pale warriors, death pale were they all;
They cried, "La belle dame sans merci
 Hath thee in thrall!"   40

I saw their starv'd lips in the gloam°   *gloaming, twilight*
 With horrid warning gaped wide,
And I awoke and found me here
 On the cold hill's side.

And this is why I sojourn here,   45
 Alone and palely loitering,
Though the sedge is wither'd from the lake,
 And no birds sing.

—1848 (written 1819)

---

1 *manna dew* See Exodus 16, in which God provides the Israelites with a food that falls
from heaven, called manna.

Ode to a Nightingale

1

My heart aches, and a drowsy numbness pains
    My sense, as though of hemlock° I had drunk,   *poison*
    Or emptied some dull opiate to the drains
    One minute past, and Lethe-wards[1] had sunk:
5 'Tis not through envy of thy happy lot,
    But being too happy in thine happiness—
        That thou, light-winged Dryad° of the trees,   *wood-nymph*
        In some melodious plot
Of beechen green, and shadows numberless,
10   Singest of summer in full-throated ease.

2

O, for a draught of vintage! that hath been
    Cool'd a long age in the deep-delved earth,
Tasting of Flora[2] and the country green,
    Dance, and Provençal[3] song, and sunburnt mirth!
15 O for a beaker full of the warm South,
    Full of the true, the blushful Hippocrene,[4]
        With beaded bubbles winking at the brim,
        And purple-stained mouth;
That I might drink, and leave the world unseen,
20   And with thee fade away into the forest dim:

3

Fade far away, dissolve, and quite forget
    What thou among the leaves hast never known,
The weariness, the fever, and the fret
    Here, where men sit and hear each other groan;
25 Where palsy shakes a few, sad, last grey hairs,
    Where youth grows pale, and spectre-thin, and dies;
        Where but to think is to be full of sorrow
        And leaden-eyed despairs,

---

1   *Lethe-wards* In classical myth, Lethe was a river in Hades, the waters of which brought
    forgetfulness.
2   *Flora* Roman goddess of flowers.
3   *Provençal* From Provence, the region in France associated with troubadours.
4   *Hippocrene* Water from the spring on Mount Helicon, sacred to the Muses.

Where Beauty cannot keep her lustrous eyes,
    Or new Love pine at them beyond to-morrow.   30

4

Away! away! for I will fly to thee,
    Not charioted by Bacchus and his pards,[1]
But on the viewless wings of Poesy,
    Though the dull brain perplexes and retards:
Already with thee! tender is the night,   35
    And haply° the Queen-Moon is on her throne,   *perhaps*
        Cluster'd around by all her starry Fays;°   *fairies*
        But here there is no light,
Save what from heaven is with the breezes blown
    Through verdurous glooms and winding mossy ways.   40

5

I cannot see what flowers are at my feet,
    Nor what soft incense hangs upon the boughs,
But, in embalmed° darkness, guess each sweet   *fragrant, perfumed*
    Wherewith the seasonable month endows
The grass, the thicket, and the fruit-tree wild;   45
    White hawthorn, and the pastoral eglantine;
        Fast fading violets cover'd up in leaves;
        And mid-May's eldest child,
The coming musk-rose, full of dewy wine,
    The murmurous haunt of flies on summer eves.   50

6

Darkling[2] I listen; and, for many a time
    I have been half in love with easeful Death,
Call'd him soft names in many a mused rhyme,
    To take into the air my quiet breath;
Now more than ever seems it rich to die,   55
    To cease upon the midnight with no pain,
        While thou art pouring forth thy soul abroad
        In such an ecstasy!

---

1   *Bacchus and his pards* Bacchus, the Roman god of wine, rides a chariot drawn by leop-
    ards.
2   *Darkling* In the dark.

Still wouldst thou sing, and I have ears in vain—
60   To thy high requiem become a sod.

7

Thou wast not born for death, immortal Bird!
      No hungry generations tread thee down;
The voice I hear this passing night was heard
      In ancient days by emperor and clown:°   rustic
65 Perhaps the self-same song that found a path
      Through the sad heart of Ruth,[1] when, sick for home,
            She stood in tears amid the alien corn;
            The same that oft-times hath
Charm'd magic casements, opening on the foam
70   Of perilous seas, in faery lands forlorn.

8

Forlorn! the very word is like a bell
      To toll me back from thee to my sole self!
Adieu! the fancy cannot cheat so well
      As she is fam'd to do, deceiving elf.
75 Adieu! adieu! thy plaintive anthem fades
      Past the near meadows, over the still stream,
            Up the hill-side; and now 'tis buried deep
            In the next valley-glades:
Was it a vision, or a waking dream?
80   Fled is that music—Do I wake or sleep?

—1819

Ode on a Grecian Urn

1

Thou still unravish'd bride of quietness,
      Thou foster-child of silence and slow time,
Sylvan° historian, who canst thus express   woodland
      A flowery tale more sweetly than our rhyme:
5 What leaf-fring'd legend haunts about thy shape
      Of deities or mortals, or of both,

---

1   *Ruth* In the biblical story the widowed Ruth leaves her native Moab for Judah, there
    helping her mother-in-law by working in the fields at harvest time.

In Tempe or the dales of Arcady?[1]
    What men or gods are these? What maidens loth?°   *reluctant*
What mad pursuit? What struggle to escape?
    What pipes and timbrels?° What wild ecstasy?[2]   *tambourines* 10

2

Heard melodies are sweet, but those unheard
    Are sweeter; therefore, ye soft pipes, play on;
Not to the sensual ear, but, more endear'd,
    Pipe to the spirit ditties of no tone:
Fair youth, beneath the trees, thou canst not leave   15
    Thy song, nor ever can those trees be bare;
        Bold lover, never, never canst thou kiss,
Though winning near the goal—yet, do not grieve;
        She cannot fade, though thou hast not thy bliss,
        For ever wilt thou love, and she be fair!   20

3

Ah, happy, happy boughs! that cannot shed
    Your leaves, nor ever bid the Spring adieu;
And, happy melodist, unwearied,
    For ever piping songs for ever new;
More happy love! more happy, happy love!   25
    For ever warm and still to be enjoy'd,
        For ever panting, and for ever young;
All breathing human passion far above,
    That leaves a heart high-sorrowful and cloy'd,
        A burning forehead, and a parching tongue.   30

4

Who are these coming to the sacrifice?
    To what green altar, O mysterious priest,
Lead'st thou that heifer lowing at the skies,
    And all her silken flanks with garlands drest?
What little town by river or sea shore,   35
    Or mountain-built with peaceful citadel,
        Is emptied of this folk, this pious morn?

---

1   *Tempe* Valley in ancient Greece renowned for its beauty; *Arcady* Ideal region of rural life, named for a mountainous district in Greece.

2   *What pipes ... ecstasy* This side of the vase seems to depict a Dionysian ritual, in which participants sometimes attained a state of frenzy.

And, little town, thy streets for evermore
    Will silent be, and not a soul to tell
40   Why thou art desolate, can e'er return.

5

O Attic[1] shape! Fair attitude! with brede°   *interwoven design*
    Of marble men and maidens overwrought,°   *overlaid*
With forest branches and the trodden weed;
    Thou, silent form, dost tease us out of thought
45 As doth eternity: Cold Pastoral!
    When old age shall this generation waste,
        Thou shalt remain, in midst of other woe
Than ours, a friend to man, to whom thou say'st,
    "Beauty is truth, truth beauty,"—that is all
50   Ye know on earth, and all ye need to know.

                                               —1820

To Autumn

1

Season of mists and mellow fruitfulness,
    Close bosom-friend of the maturing sun;
Conspiring with him how to load and bless
    With fruit the vines that round the thatch-eves run;
5 To bend with apples the moss'd cottage-trees,
    And fill all fruit with ripeness to the core;
        To swell the gourd, and plump the hazel shells
    With a sweet kernel; to set budding more,
And still more, later flowers for the bees,
10 Until they think warm days will never cease,
        For Summer has o'er-brimm'd their clammy cells.

2

Who hath not seen thee oft amid thy store?
    Sometimes whoever seeks abroad may find
Thee sitting careless on a granary floor,
15   Thy hair soft-lifted by the winnowing wind;
Or on a half-reap'd furrow sound asleep,

---

1   *Attic* From Attica, the region around Athens.

Drows'd with the fume of poppies, while thy hook°   *scythe*
   Spares the next swath and all its twined flowers:
And sometimes like a gleaner thou dost keep
   Steady thy laden head across a brook;   20
   Or by a cyder-press, with patient look,
      Thou watchest the last oozings hours by hours.

3

Where are the songs of Spring? Ay, where are they?
   Think not of them, thou hast thy music too—
While barred clouds bloom the soft-dying day,   25
   And touch the stubble-plains with rosy hue;
Then in a wailful choir the small gnats mourn
   Among the river sallows,° borne aloft   *willows*
      Or sinking as the light wind lives or dies;
And full-grown lambs loud bleat from hilly bourn;°   *realm* 30
   Hedge-crickets sing; and now with treble soft
   The red-breast whistles from a garden-croft;°   *enclosed garden*
      And gathering swallows twitter in the skies.

                        —1820

Elizabeth Barrett Browning
1806–1861

Once considered for the position of Poet Laureate of England, Elizabeth Barrett Browning was a writer of tremendous versatility. Best known for her sonorous love poetry, she was also one of the foremost political poets of the nineteenth century.

When she was a child in Herefordshire, England, Barrett Browning's love of reading and writing was fostered by her parents. As an adolescent, she developed an unknown illness and became dependent on the opium she was prescribed, but in 1826 she published her first collection, *An Essay on Mind and Other Poems*. By the time she published her next book, *The Seraphim and Other Poems* (1838), she had begun to suffer from either bronchiectasis or tuberculosis. However, she continued to write prolifically and to maintain an active correspondence with other writers and critics; the scholar Marjorie Stone claims that "she literally wrote herself back to life."

Barrett Browning gained international recognition for her *Poems* (1844), admiration for which motivated her future husband, the poet Robert Browning, to write to her. The love poems published as *Sonnets from the Portuguese* (1850) were written during their courtship; though they were relatively unnoticed at first, before long they became her most famous work.

Barrett Browning also published several long poems, the most significant of which was the "verse-novel" *Aurora Leigh* (1856). An epic poem focused on the character of a woman writer, it encompasses Barrett Browning's convictions on desire, power, art, love, romance, race, class structures, and the subjugation of women. Although it was her most controversial work, the poem's many admirers included George Eliot and the critic John Ruskin, who called it the "greatest poem" of the century.

from *Sonnets from the Portuguese*

Sonnet 22

When our two souls stand up erect and strong,
Face to face, silent, drawing nigh and nigher,
Until the lengthening wings break into fire
At either curvèd point—what bitter wrong
5 Can the earth do to us, that we should not long
Be here contented? Think. In mounting higher,
The angels would press on us and aspire
To drop some golden orb of perfect song
Into our deep, dear silence. Let us stay

Rather on earth, Belovèd—where the unfit   10
Contrarious moods of men recoil away
And isolate pure spirits, and permit
A place to stand and love in for a day,
With darkness and the death-hour rounding it.

Sonnet 24

Let the world's sharpness like a clasping knife
Shut in upon itself and do no harm
In this close hand of Love, now soft and warm,
And let us hear no sound of human strife
After the click of the shutting. Life to life—   5
I lean upon thee, Dear, without alarm,
And feel as safe as guarded by a charm
Against the stab of worldlings, who if rife
Are weak to injure. Very whitely still
The lilies of our lives may reassure   10
Their blossoms from their roots, accessible
Alone to heavenly dews that drop not fewer;
Growing straight, out of man's reach, on the hill.
God only, who made us rich, can make us poor.

Sonnet 43

How do I love thee? Let me count the ways.
I love thee to the depth and breadth and height
My soul can reach, when feeling out of sight
For the ends of Being and ideal Grace.
I love thee to the level of everyday's   5
Most quiet need, by sun and candlelight.
I love thee freely, as men strive for Right;
I love thee purely, as they turn from Praise.
I love thee with the passion put to use
In my old griefs, and with my childhood's faith.   10
I love thee with a love I seemed to lose
With my lost saints—I love thee with the breath,
Smiles, tears, of all my life!—and, if God choose,
I shall but love thee better after death.

—1850

Edgar Allan Poe
1809–1849

Edgar Allan Poe is one of antebellum America's most famous and controversial literary figures. Dubbed "the Leader of the Cult of the Unusual" by Jules Verne, Poe continues to be regarded as a haunted and enigmatic outcast, a public image he himself cultivated following his childhood hero, the poet Lord Byron.

Contemporary reviewers often identified Poe with the manic, mentally unhinged narrators of stories such as "The Tell-Tale Heart" (1843) and "The Black Cat" (1843), attributing his preoccupation with the perverse impulses and abysmal depths of the mind to a moral defect in his character. A notorious obituary by his literary executor, which depicted him as a mad and melancholy lost soul, his "heart gnawed by anguish," his "face shrouded in gloom," did much to establish the legend of Poe as an erratic and disturbed outsider. More recently, psychoanalytic critics—not least Freud himself—have made prooftexts of his poems and tales, speculating that Poe, who famously declared the death of a beautiful woman "the most poetical topic in the world," never overcame the loss of his mother, foster mother, and young wife, whose ghosts return in works such as "Ligeia" (1838), "The Raven" (1845), and "Annabel Lee" (1849).

Of all Poe's poetic creations, "The Raven" remains the best known and most beloved. Widely reprinted and parodied in his lifetime, the poem made him famous but did little to relieve his near constant poverty. Poe offered a meticulous, if at times tongue-in-cheek, account of the poem's construction in "The Philosophy of Composition," an essay in which he rejects the Romantic notion that poetry is born of a "fine frenzy" of spontaneous creativity. The burnished formalism of "The Raven"—its incantatory metre, sonorous diction, tightly controlled rhyme scheme, and famous refrain—is a testament to Poe's belief in the primacy of method and craft over "ecstatic intuition."

The Raven

Once upon a midnight dreary, while I pondered, weak and weary,
Over many a quaint and curious volume of forgotten <u>lore</u>—
While I nodded, nearly napping, suddenly there came a tapping,
As of some one gently rapping, rapping at my chamber <u>door</u>.
5 "'Tis some visitor," I muttered, "tapping at my chamber <u>door</u>—
        Only this and nothing <u>more</u>."

Ah, distinctly I remember it was in the bleak December,
And each separate dying ember wrought its ghost upon the floor.

Eagerly I wished the morrow;—vainly I had sought to borrow
From my books surcease of sorrow—sorrow for the lost Lenore[1]—   10
For the rare and radiant maiden whom the angels name Lenore—
Nameless here for evermore.

And the silken sad uncertain rustling of each purple curtain
Thrilled me—filled me with fantastic terrors never felt before;
So that now, to still the beating of my heart, I stood repeating   15
"'Tis some visitor entreating entrance at my chamber door—
Some late visitor entreating entrance at my chamber door;—
This it is and nothing more."

Presently my soul grew stronger; hesitating then no longer;
"Sir," said I, "or Madam, truly your forgiveness I implore;   20
But the fact is I was napping, and so gently you came rapping,
And so faintly you came tapping, tapping at my chamber door,
That I scarce was sure I heard you"—here I opened wide the door;—
Darkness there and nothing more.

Deep into that darkness peering, long I stood there wondering, fearing,   25
Doubting, dreaming dreams no mortal ever dared to dream before;
But the silence was unbroken, and the stillness gave no token,
And the only word there spoken was the whispered word, "Lenore!"
This I whispered, and an echo murmured back the word "Lenore!"
Merely this and nothing more.   30

Back into the chamber turning, all my soul within me burning,
Soon again I heard a tapping somewhat louder than before.
"Surely," said I, "surely that is something at my window lattice;
Let me see, then, what thereat is, and this mystery explore—
Let my heart be still a moment and this mystery explore;—   35
'Tis the wind and nothing more!"

Open here I flung the shutter, when, with many a flirt and flutter,
In there stepped a stately raven of the saintly days of yore;
Not the least obeisance made he; not a minute stopped or stayed he;
But, with mien of lord or lady, perched above my chamber door—   40
Perched upon a bust of Pallas[2] just above my chamber door—
Perched, and sat, and nothing more.

---

1   *Lenore* Poe's poem "Lenore" (1831) dramatizes the death of a young woman mourned by
    her lover.
2   *Pallas* Pallas Athena, Greek goddess of wisdom.

Then this ebony bird beguiling my sad fancy into smiling,
By the grave and stern decorum of the countenance it wore,
45 "Though thy crest be shorn and shaven, thou," I said, "art sure no craven,
Ghastly grim and ancient raven wandering from the Nightly shore—
Tell me what thy lordly name is on the Night's Plutonian[1] shore!"
        Quoth the raven "Nevermore."

Much I marvelled this ungainly fowl to hear discourse so plainly,
50 Though its answer little meaning—little relevancy bore;
For we cannot help agreeing that no living human being
Ever yet was blessed with seeing bird above his chamber door—
Bird or beast upon the sculptured bust above his chamber door,
        With such name as "Nevermore."

55 But the raven, sitting lonely on the placid bust, spoke only
That one word, as if his soul in that one word he did outpour.
Nothing farther then he uttered—not a feather then he fluttered—
Till I scarcely more than muttered "Other friends have flown before—
On the morrow *he* will leave me, as my hopes have flown before."
60   Then the bird said "Nevermore."

Startled at the stillness broken by reply so aptly spoken,
"Doubtless," said I, "what it utters is its only stock and store
Caught from some unhappy master whom unmerciful Disaster
Followed fast and followed faster till his songs one burden[2] bore—
65 Till the dirges of his Hope that melancholy burden bore
        Of 'Never—nevermore.'"

But the raven still beguiling all my sad soul into smiling,
Straight I wheeled a cushioned seat in front of bird, and bust and door;
Then, upon the velvet sinking, I betook myself to linking
70 Fancy unto fancy, thinking what this ominous bird of yore—
What this grim, ungainly, ghastly, gaunt, and ominous bird of yore
        Meant in croaking "Nevermore."

This I sat engaged in guessing, but no syllable expressing
To the fowl whose fiery eyes now burned into my bosom's core;
75 This and more I sat divining, with my head at ease reclining
On the cushion's velvet lining that the lamplight gloated° o'er,   *refracted*
But whose velvet violet lining with the lamplight gloating o'er,
        She shall press, ah, nevermore!

---

1 *Plutonian* In Roman mythology, Pluto is god of the underworld.
2 *burden* Theme; in a poem or song, chorus or refrain.

Then, methought, the air grew denser, perfumed from an unseen censer
Swung by angels whose faint foot-falls tinkled on the tufted[1] floor.   80
"Wretch," I cried, "thy God hath lent thee—by these angels he hath
    sent thee
Respite—respite and nepenthe[2] from thy memories of Lenore!
Quaff, oh quaff this kind nepenthe and forget this lost Lenore!"
                    Quoth the raven "Nevermore."

"Prophet!" said I, "thing of evil!—prophet still, if bird or devil!—   85
Whether Tempter sent, or whether tempest tossed thee here ashore,
Desolate yet all undaunted, on this desert land enchanted—
On this home by Horror haunted—tell me truly, I implore—
Is there—*is* there balm in Gilead?[3]—tell me—tell me, I implore!"
                    Quoth the raven "Nevermore."   90

"Prophet!" said I, "thing of evil!—prophet still, if bird or devil!
By that Heaven that bends above us—by that God we both adore—
Tell this soul with sorrow laden if, within the distant Aidenn,°   *Eden*
It shall clasp a sainted maiden whom the angels name Lenore—
Clasp a rare and radiant maiden whom the angels name Lenore."   95
                    Quoth the raven "Nevermore."

"Be that word our sign of parting, bird or fiend!" I shrieked, upstarting—
"Get thee back into the tempest and the Night's Plutonian shore!
Leave no black plume as a token of that lie thy soul hath spoken!
Leave my loneliness unbroken!—quit the bust above my door!   100
Take thy beak from out my heart, and take thy form from off my door!"
                    Quoth the raven "Nevermore."

And the raven, never flitting, still is sitting, *still* is sitting
On the pallid bust of Pallas just above my chamber door;
And his eyes have all the seeming of a demon's that is dreaming,   105
And the lamp-light o'er him streaming throws his shadow on the floor;
And my soul from out that shadow that lies floating on the floor
                Shall be lifted—nevermore!
                        —1845

---

1   *tufted* I.e., carpeted.
2   *nepenthe* Drink supposed to banish sorrow by inducing forgetfulness.
3   *Is there ... Gilead* See Jeremiah 8.22: "Is there no balm in Gilead?"; *balm* Soothing oint-
    ment; *Gilead* In the Bible, the land east of the River Jordan.

Alfred, Lord Tennyson
1809–1892

More than any other poet, Alfred, Lord Tennyson gave voice to the ambitions, anxieties, and myths of the Victorian era; he was Poet Laureate for 42 years.

Born in 1809 to a privileged, somewhat eccentric family, Tennyson decided early on that poetry was his true vocation. He left the University of Cambridge without taking a degree and devoted himself to writing in a variety of poetic forms, among them dramatic monologues (such as "Ulysses," 1842), short lyrics (such as "Tears, Idle Tears," 1847), and retellings of Arthurian narratives (such as "The Lady of Shalott," 1832). The year 1850 was trebly significant for Tennyson: after a 14-year courtship, he married Emily Sellwood; he was named Poet Laureate; and he published *In Memoriam A.H.H.*, a long, reflective poem in memory of his friend Arthur Hallam that was immediately recognized as his most important work.

Tennyson's appearance conveyed a solemn sense of respectability, and his poetry often deals with issues such as the individual's responsibility to society. But both his personality and his poetry are multi-dimensional; in much of his work, anxieties over sexuality, violence, and death lie close to the surface. Perhaps because of his engagement with such concepts, Tennyson was no stranger to controversy. For example, his long poem *Maud* (1855), which ends with the tormented protagonist departing for Crimea and "the blood-red blossom of war," was attacked by several reviewers (the writer George Eliot notable among them) for allegedly expressing a "hatred of peace."

Tennyson's verse has often been praised for its "verbal music," although his reading voice was an urgent rattle. His voice may still be heard: not long before he died, he was recorded by Thomas Edison reading "The Charge of the Light Brigade" and a few other poems.

The Lady of Shalott[1]

PART 1

On either side the river lie
Long fields of barley and of rye,
That clothe the wold° and meet the sky;   *plain*
And through the field the road runs by

---

1   *The Lady of Shalott* Elaine of the Arthurian romances, who dies of love for Lancelot; she is called "the lily maid of Astolat" in Malory's *Morte Darthur* (1485). Tennyson first encountered the story, however, in a medieval Italian romance called "La Donna di Scalotta" and changed the name to Shalott for a softer sound.

To many-towered Camelot;   5
And up and down the people go,
Gazing where the lilies blow
Round an island there below,
    The island of Shalott.

Willows whiten,[1] aspens quiver,   10
Little breezes dusk° and shiver   *darken*
Through the wave that runs for ever
By the island in the river
    Flowing down to Camelot.
Four grey walls, and four grey towers,   15
Overlook a space of flowers,
And the silent isle imbowers°   *encloses*
    The Lady of Shalott.

By the margin, willow-veiled,
Slide the heavy barges trailed   20
By slow horses; and unhailed
The shallop[2] flitteth silken-sailed
    Skimming down to Camelot:
But who hath seen her wave her hand?
Or at the casement seen her stand?   25
Or is she known in all the land,
    The Lady of Shalott?

Only reapers, reaping early
In among the bearded barley,
Hear a song that echoes cheerly   30
From the river winding clearly,
    Down to towered Camelot:
And by the moon the reaper weary,
Piling sheaves in uplands airy,
Listening, whispers "'Tis the fairy   35
    Lady of Shalott."

---

1   *Willows whiten* I.e., the wind exposes the white undersides of the leaves.
2   *shallop* Light open boat for use in shallow water.

PART 2

There she weaves by night and day
A magic web with colours gay.
She has heard a whisper say,
40 A curse is on her if she stay
    To look down to Camelot.
She knows not what the curse may be,
And so she weaveth steadily,
And little other care hath she,
45   The Lady of Shalott.

And moving through a mirror clear
That hangs before her all the year,
Shadows of the world appear.
There she sees the highway near
50   Winding down to Camelot:
There the river eddy whirls,
And there the surly village-churls,
And the red cloaks of market girls,
    Pass onward from Shalott.

55 Sometimes a troop of damsels glad,
An abbot on an ambling pad,°   *horse*
Sometimes a curly shepherd-lad,
Or long-haired page in crimson clad,
    Goes by to towered Camelot;
60 And sometimes through the mirror blue
The knights come riding two and two:
She hath no loyal knight and true,
    The Lady of Shalott.

But in her web she still delights
65 To weave the mirror's magic sights,
For often through the silent nights
A funeral, with plumes and lights
    And music, went to Camelot:
Or when the moon was overhead,
70 Came two young lovers lately wed;
"I am half sick of shadows," said
    The Lady of Shalott.

PART 3

A bow-shot from her bower-eaves,
He rode between the barley-sheaves,
The sun came dazzling through the leaves,   75
And flamed upon the brazen greaves[1]
    Of bold Sir Lancelot.
A red-cross knight for ever kneeled
To a lady in his shield,
That sparkled on the yellow field,   80
    Beside remote Shalott.

The gemmy° bridle glittered free,   *brilliant*
Like to some branch of stars we see
Hung in the golden Galaxy.
The bridle bells rang merrily   85
    As he rode down to Camelot:
And from his blazoned baldric° slung   *shoulder-strap*
A mighty silver bugle hung,
And as he rode his armour rung,
    Beside remote Shalott.   90

All in the blue unclouded weather
Thick-jewelled shone the saddle-leather,
The helmet and the helmet-feather
Burned like one burning flame together,
    As he rode down to Camelot.   95
As often through the purple night,
Below the starry clusters bright,
Some bearded meteor, trailing light,
    Moves over still Shalott.

His broad clear brow in sunlight glowed;   100
On burnished hooves his war-horse trode;
From underneath his helmet flowed
His coal-black curls as on he rode,
    As he rode down to Camelot.
From the bank and from the river   105
He flashed into the crystal mirror,
"Tirra lirra," by the river
    Sang Sir Lancelot.

---

1   *greaves* Armour worn below the knee.

She left the web, she left the loom,
110 She made three paces through the room,
She saw the water-lily bloom,
She saw the helmet and the plume,
    She looked down to Camelot.
Out flew the web and floated wide;
115 The mirror cracked from side to side;
"The curse is come upon me," cried
    The Lady of Shalott.

PART 4

In the stormy east-wind straining,
The pale yellow woods were waning,
120 The broad stream in his banks complaining,
Heavily the low sky raining
    Over towered Camelot;
Down she came and found a boat
Beneath a willow left afloat,
125 And round about the prow she wrote
    The Lady of Shalott.

And down the river's dim expanse
Like some bold seer in a trance,
Seeing all his own mischance—
130 With a glassy countenance
    Did she look to Camelot.
And at the closing of the day
She loosed the chain, and down she lay;
The broad stream bore her far away,
135   The Lady of Shalott.

Lying, robed in snowy white
That loosely flew to left and right—
The leaves upon her falling light—
Through the noises of the night
140   She floated down to Camelot:
And as the boat-head wound along
The willowy hills and fields among,
They heard her singing her last song,
    The Lady of Shalott.

Heard a carol, mournful, holy,   145
Chanted loudly, chanted lowly,
Till her blood was frozen slowly,
And her eyes were darkened wholly,
    Turned to towered Camelot.
For ere she reached upon the tide   150
The first house by the water-side,
Singing in her song she died,
    The Lady of Shalott.

Under tower and balcony,
By garden-wall and gallery,   155
A gleaming shape she floated by,
Dead-pale between the houses high,
    Silent into Camelot.
Out upon the wharfs they came,
Knight and burgher, lord and dame,   160
And round the prow they read her name,
    The Lady of Shalott.

Who is this? and what is here?
And in the lighted palace near
Died the sound of royal cheer;   165
And they crossed themselves for fear,
    All the knights at Camelot:
But Lancelot mused a little space;
He said, "She has a lovely face;
God in his mercy lend her grace,   170
    The Lady of Shalott."

                      —1832 (revised 1842)

John William Waterhouse, The Lady of Shalott, *1888. The Lady of Shalott was a frequent subject for art in the nineteenth century; perhaps the most famous example is Waterhouse's painting.*

The Lotos-Eaters[1]

"Courage!" he said, and pointed toward the land,
"This mounting wave will roll us shoreward soon."
In the afternoon they came unto a land
In which it seemed always afternoon.
5 All round the coast the languid air did swoon,
Breathing like one that hath a weary dream.
Full-faced above the valley stood the moon;
And like a downward smoke, the slender stream
Along the cliff to fall and pause and fall did seem.

10 A land of streams! some, like a downward smoke,
Slow-dropping veils of thinnest lawn,° did go;   *fine fabric*

---

1   *Lotos-Eaters* In Greek mythology, the Lotus Eaters (or Lotophagi) were a race of people
    who inhabited an island near north Africa. They existed in peaceful apathy because of
    the narcotic effects of the lotus plants they ate. When Odysseus landed on the island,
    some of his men ate the lotus plants and wanted to stay on the island, rather than re-
    turn home to their families. The incident is described in Homer's *Odyssey* 9.2.

And some through wavering lights and shadows broke,
Rolling a slumbrous sheet of foam below.
They saw the gleaming river seaward flow
From the inner land: far off, three mountain-tops,   15
Three silent pinnacles of agèd snow,
Stood sunset-flushed: and, dewed with showery drops,
Up-clomb the shadowy pine above the woven copse.°   *thicket*

The charmèd sunset lingered low adown
In the red West: through mountain clefts the dale   20
Was seen far inland, and the yellow down
Bordered with palm, and many a winding vale
And meadow, set with slender galingale;[1]
A land where all things always seemed the same!
And round about the keel with faces pale,   25
Dark faces pale against that rosy flame,
The mild-eyed melancholy Lotos-eaters came.

Branches they bore of that enchanted stem,
Laden with flower and fruit, whereof they gave
To each, but whoso did receive of them,   30
And taste, to him the gushing of the wave
Far far away did seem to mourn and rave
On alien shores; and if his fellow spake,
His voice was thin, as voices from the grave;
And deep-asleep he seemed, yet all awake,   35
And music in his ears his beating heart did make.

They sat them down upon the yellow sand,
Between the sun and moon upon the shore;
And sweet it was to dream of Fatherland,
Of child, and wife, and slave; but evermore   40
Most weary seemed the sea, weary the oar,
Weary the wandering fields of barren foam.
Then some one said, "We will return no more";
And all at once they sang, "Our island home
Is far beyond the wave; we will no longer roam."   45

---

1   *galingale* Species of sedge; rush-like grass.

CHORIC SONG[1]

1

There is sweet music here that softer falls
Than petals from blown roses on the grass,
Or night-dews on still waters between walls
Of shadowy granite, in a gleaming pass;
5   Music that gentlier on the spirit lies,
Than tired eyelids upon tired eyes;
Music that brings sweet sleep down from the blissful skies.
Here are cool mosses deep,
And through the moss the ivies creep,
10   And in the stream the long-leaved flowers weep,
And from the craggy ledge the poppy hangs in sleep.

2

Why are we weighed upon with heaviness,
And utterly consumed with sharp distress,
While all things else have rest from weariness?
15   All things have rest: why should we toil alone,
We only toil, who are the first of things,
And make perpetual moan,
Still from one sorrow to another thrown:
Nor ever fold our wings,
20   And cease from wanderings,
Nor steep our brows in slumber's holy balm;
Nor harken what the inner spirit sings,
"There is no joy but calm!"
Why should we only toil, the roof and crown of things?

3

25   Lo! in the middle of the wood,
The folded leaf is wooed from out the bud
With winds upon the branch, and there
Grows green and broad, and takes no care,
Sun-steeped at noon, and in the moon
30   Nightly dew-fed; and turning yellow
Falls, and floats adown the air.
Lo! sweetened with the summer light,
The full-juiced apple, waxing over-mellow,

---

1   *Choric Song* As performed by the Chorus in an ancient Greek play.

Drops in a silent autumn night.
All its allotted length of days,   35
The flower ripens in its place,
Ripens and fades, and falls, and hath no toil,
Fast-rooted in the fruitful soil.

4

Hateful is the dark-blue sky,
Vaulted o'er the dark-blue sea.   40
Death is the end of life; ah, why
Should life all labour be?
Let us alone. Time driveth onward fast,
And in a little while our lips are dumb.
Let us alone. What is it that will last?   45
All things are taken from us, and become
Portions and parcels of the dreadful Past.
Let us alone. What pleasure can we have
To war with evil? Is there any peace
In ever climbing up the climbing wave?   50
All things have rest, and ripen toward the grave
In silence; ripen, fall and cease:
Give us long rest or death, dark death, or dreamful ease.

5

How sweet it were, hearing the downward stream,
With half-shut eyes ever to seem   55
Falling asleep in a half-dream!
To dream and dream, like yonder amber light,
Which will not leave the myrrh-bush on the height;
To hear each other's whispered speech;
Eating the Lotos day by day,   60
To watch the crisping ripples on the beach,
And tender curving lines of creamy spray;
To lend our hearts and spirits wholly
To the influence of mild-minded melancholy;
To muse and brood and live again in memory,   65
With those old faces of our infancy
Heaped over with a mound of grass,
Two handfuls of white dust,[1] shut in an urn of brass!

---

1   *white dust* I.e., cremated remains.

6

Dear is the memory of our wedded lives,
70 And dear the last embraces of our wives
And their warm tears: but all hath suffered change:
For surely now our household hearths are cold:
Our sons inherit us: our looks are strange:
And we should come like ghosts to trouble joy.
75 Or else the island princes over-bold
Have eat our substance, and the minstrel sings
Before them of the ten years' war in Troy,
And our great deeds, as half-forgotten things.
Is there confusion in the little isle?
80 Let what is broken so remain.
The Gods are hard to reconcile:
'Tis hard to settle order once again.
There *is* confusion worse than death,
Trouble on trouble, pain on pain,
85 Long labour unto agèd breath,
Sore task to hearts worn out by many wars
And eyes grown dim with gazing on the pilot-stars.

7

But, propped on beds of amaranth and moly,[1]
How sweet (while warm airs lull us, blowing lowly)
90 With half-dropped eyelid still,
Beneath a heaven dark and holy,
To watch the long bright river drawing slowly
His waters from the purple hill—
To hear the dewy echoes calling
95 From cave to cave through the thick-twinèd vine—
To watch the emerald-coloured water falling
Through many a woven acanthus[2]-wreath divine!
Only to hear and see the far-off sparkling brine,
Only to hear were sweet, stretched out beneath the pine.

---

1   *amaranth* Mythical flowers that never wilt; also a plant with medicinal and culinary
     uses; *moly* Herb with magical protective powers.
2   *acanthus* Plant native to Mediterranean shores. The Greeks and Romans esteemed the
     plant for the elegance of its leaves.

8

The Lotos blooms below the barren peak: 100
The Lotos blows by every winding creek:
All day the wind breathes low with mellower tone:
Through every hollow cave and alley lone
Round and round the spicy downs the yellow Lotos-dust is blown.
We have had enough of action, and of motion we,   105
Rolled to starboard, rolled to larboard,° when the surge was   *port*
    seething free,
Where the wallowing monster spouted his foam-fountains in the sea.
Let us swear an oath, and keep it with an equal mind,
In the hollow Lotos-land to live and lie reclined
On the hills like Gods together, careless of mankind.   110
For they lie beside their nectar, and the bolts are hurled
Far below them in the valleys, and the clouds are lightly curled
Round their golden houses, girdled with the gleaming world:
Where they smile in secret, looking over wasted lands,
Blight and famine, plague and earthquake, roaring deeps and fiery   115
    sands,
Clanging fights, and flaming towns, and sinking ships, and praying
    hands.
But they smile, they find a music centred in a doleful song
Steaming up, a lamentation and an ancient tale of wrong,
Like a tale of little meaning though the words are strong;
Chanted from an ill-used race of men that cleave the soil,   120
Sow the seed, and reap the harvest with enduring toil,
Storing yearly little dues of wheat, and wine and oil;
Till they perish and they suffer—some, 'tis whispered—down in hell
Suffer endless anguish, others in Elysian[1] valleys dwell,
Resting weary limbs at last on beds of asphodel.[2]   125
Surely, surely, slumber is more sweet than toil, the shore
Than labour in the deep mid-ocean, wind and wave and oar;
Oh rest ye, brother mariners, we will not wander more.

                       —1842 (written 1833)

---

1   *Elysian* Heavenly. According to the ancient Greeks, Elysium was the dwelling place of
    the blessed after death.
2   *asphodel* Plant said to cover the Elysian fields.

Ulysses[1]

It little profits that an idle king,
By this still hearth, among these barren crags,
Matched with an agèd wife, I mete and dole
Unequal laws unto a savage race,
5 That hoard, and sleep, and feed, and know not me.
I cannot rest from travel: I will drink
Life to the lees:° all times I have enjoyed   *dregs*
Greatly, have suffered greatly, both with those
That loved me, and alone; on shore, and when
10 Thro' scudding drifts the rainy Hyades[2]
Vexed the dim sea: I am become a name;
For always roaming with a hungry heart
Much have I seen and known; cities of men
And manners, climates, councils, governments,
15 Myself not least, but honoured of them all;
And drunk delight of battle with my peers,
Far on the ringing plains of windy Troy.
I am a part of all that I have met;
Yet all experience is an arch wherethrough
20 Gleams that untravelled world, whose margin° fades   *horizon*
For ever and for ever when I move.
How dull it is to pause, to make an end,
To rust unburnished, not to shine in use!
As though to breathe were life. Life piled on life
25 Were all too little, and of one to me
Little remains: but every hour is saved
From that eternal silence, something more,
A bringer of new things; and vile it were
For some three suns to store and hoard myself,
30 And this grey spirit yearning in desire
To follow knowledge like a sinking star,
Beyond the utmost bound of human thought.

    This is my son, mine own Telemachus,
To whom I leave the sceptre and the isle—

---

1   *Ulysses* Latin name for Odysseus, the protagonist of Homer's *Odyssey*. Here, long after
    the adventures recounted in that poem, the aged, yet restless Ulysses prepares to em-
    bark on one last voyage.
2   *Hyades* Group of stars near the constellation Taurus and associated with rainstorms.

Well-loved of me, discerning to fulfil   35
This labour, by slow prudence to make mild
A rugged people, and through soft degrees
Subdue them to the useful and the good.
Most blameless is he, centred in the sphere
Of common duties, decent not to fail   40
In offices of tenderness, and pay
Meet° adoration to my household gods,   *appropriate*
When I am gone. He works his work, I mine.

       There lies the port; the vessel puffs her sail:
There gloom the dark broad seas. My mariners,   45
Souls that have toiled, and wrought, and thought with me—
That ever with a frolic welcome took
The thunder and the sunshine, and opposed
Free hearts, free foreheads—you and I are old;
Old age hath yet his honour and his toil;   50
Death closes all: but something ere the end,
Some work of noble note, may yet be done,
Not unbecoming men that strove with Gods.
The lights begin to twinkle from the rocks:
The long day wanes: the slow moon climbs: the deep   55
Moans round with many voices. Come, my friends,
'Tis not too late to seek a newer world.
Push off, and sitting well in order smite
The sounding furrows; for my purpose holds
To sail beyond the sunset, and the baths   60
Of all the western stars, until I die.
It may be that the gulfs will wash us down:
It may be we shall touch the Happy Isles,[1]
And see the great Achilles,[2] whom we knew.
Though much is taken, much abides; and though   65
We are not now that strength which in old days
Moved earth and heaven; that which we are, we are;
One equal temper of heroic hearts,
Made weak by time and fate, but strong in will
To strive, to seek, to find, and not to yield.   70

                                      —1842 (written 1833)

---

1   *Happy Isles* Elysium, or Isles of the Blessed, where heroes enjoyed the afterlife.
2   *Achilles* Hero from Greek mythology, also the central character of Homer's *Iliad*.

The Charge of the Light Brigade[1]

1

Half a league,[2] half a league,
Half a league onward,
All in the valley of Death
    Rode the six hundred.[3]
5 "Forward, the Light Brigade!
Charge for the guns!" he said:
Into the valley of Death
    Rode the six hundred.

2

"Forward, the Light Brigade!"
10 Was there a man dismayed?
Not though the soldier knew
    Some one had blundered:
Theirs not to make reply,
Theirs not to reason why,
15 Theirs but to do and die:
Into the valley of Death
    Rode the six hundred.

3

Cannon to right of them,
Cannon to left of them,
20 Cannon in front of them
    Volleyed and thundered;
Stormed at with shot and shell,
Boldly they rode and well,

---

1 *The Charge ... Brigade* Written some weeks after a disastrous engagement during the Crimean War. At the Battle of Balaclava on 25 October 1854, the 700 cavalrymen of the Light Brigade, acting on a misinterpreted order, directly charged the Russian artillery.

2 *league* About three miles.

3 *six hundred* The initial newspaper account read by Tennyson mentioned "607 sabres," and he retained the number even when the correct number was discovered to be considerably higher because "six is much better than seven hundred ... metrically" (*Letters* 2.101).

Into the jaws of Death,
Into the mouth of Hell   25
    Rode the six hundred.

4

Flashed all their sabres bare,
Flashed as they turned in air
Sabring the gunners there,
Charging an army, while   30
    All the world wondered:
Plunged in the battery-smoke
Right through the line they broke;
Cossack and Russian
Reeled from the sabre-stroke   35
    Shattered and sundered.
Then they rode back, but not
    Not the six hundred.

5

Cannon to right of them,
Cannon to left of them,   40
Cannon behind them
    Volleyed and thundered;
Stormed at with shot and shell,
While horse and hero fell,
They that had fought so well   45
Came through the jaws of Death,
Back from the mouth of Hell,
All that was left of them,[1]
    Left of six hundred.

6

When can their glory fade?   50
O the wild charge they made!
    All the world wondered.
Honour the charge they made!
Honour the Light Brigade,
    Noble six hundred!   55

                    —1854

---

1   *All ... them* 118 men were killed and 127 wounded; after the charge, only 195 men
were still with their horses.

Roger Fenton, Cookhouse of the 8th Hussars, *1855. In the Crimean War (1853–56), waged primarily on the Crimean Peninsula in Eastern Europe, the Russian Empire fought a group of allies that included the French, British, and Ottoman Empires. The Crimean War was the first to be photographed extensively, but both the technology of the time and the demands of Victorian taste prevented photographers from shooting scenes of battle directly. This photograph depicts the 8th Hussars, a regiment of Irish cavalry, preparing a meal.*

Roger Fenton, Valley of the Shadow of Death, *1855. This image, one of the most famous photographs of the Crimean War, came to be closely associated with Tennyson's famous 1854 poem "The Charge of the Light Brigade." The valley in the photograph is not the place where the charge occurred but another valley in the vicinity—one that soldiers had begun to call "the valley of the shadow of death" (in an echo both of Tennyson's poem and of the Bible) because of the frequency with which the Russians shelled it.*

Robert Browning
1812–1889

Robert Browning was not a popular poet for much of his lifetime. His poetry, in the eyes of many of his contemporaries, was far too obscure, littered as it was with recondite historical and literary references and with dubious subject matter—husbands murdering their wives, artists frolicking with prostitutes. Fame did come, however, and scholars now credit Browning for having realized new possibilities in the dramatic monologue, a form of poetry that, like a monologue in a dramatic production, showcases the speech of a character to an implied or imaginary audience.

Browning was born to a relatively wealthy family, and his father provided him with a rich home education, an extensive personal library, and financial support that allowed him to dedicate himself to writing. He gained moderate critical attention with the dramatic poem *Paracelsus* (1835), but most found his next long narrative poem, *Sordello* (1840), to be incomprehensible. His next volume, *Dramatic Lyrics* (1842), was more successful; it included now-famous shorter poems such as "My Last Duchess" and "Porphyria's Lover."

In 1845 Browning began corresponding with the poet Elizabeth Barrett, and the following year they eloped to Italy. Although their marriage was a happy and intensely devoted one, Browning wrote little during this time, with the notable exception of the short collection *Men and Women* (1855).

After his wife's death in 1861, Browning returned to London society, where he produced several volumes that would at last make him popular among British readers. These works included his 12-part epic "murder-poem" (as Browning called it), *The Ring and the Book* (1868–69), which told the story of a 1698 Italian murder trial in the voices of multiple characters. The 1879–80 volumes of *Dramatic Idyls* brought the poet even greater fame, both in England and internationally. Browning was at the peak of his popularity during the last decade of his life.

Porphyria's Lover[1]

The rain set early in tonight,
　　The sullen wind was soon awake,
It tore the elm-tops down for spite,
　　And did its worst to vex the lake:
　　I listened with heart fit to break.　　　　5
When glided in Porphyria; straight

1　*Porphyria's Lover* The heroine's name is derived from the Greek word meaning "purple" (the word "porphyria" was not used as a label for a group of genetically based disorders until much later in the nineteenth century).

She shut the cold out and the storm,
And kneeled and made the cheerless grate
　　Blaze up, and all the cottage warm;
10　　Which done, she rose, and from her form
Withdrew the dripping cloak and shawl,
　　And laid her soiled gloves by, untied
Her hat and let the damp hair fall,
　　And, last, she sat down by my side
15　　.And called me. When no voice replied,
She put my arm about her waist,
　　And made her smooth white shoulder bare,
And all her yellow hair displaced,
　　And, stooping, made my cheek lie there
20　　And spread, o'er all, her yellow hair,
Murmuring how she loved me—she
　　Too weak, for all her heart's endeavour,
To set its struggling passion free
　　From pride, and vainer ties dissever,
25　　And give herself to me forever.
But passion sometimes would prevail,
　　Nor could tonight's gay feast restrain
A sudden thought of one so pale
　　For love of her, and all in vain:
30　　So, she was come through wind and rain.
Be sure I looked up at her eyes
　　Happy and proud; at last I knew
Porphyria worshipped me; surprise
　　Made my heart swell, and still it grew
35　　While I debated what to do.
That moment she was mine, mine, fair,
　　Perfectly pure and good: I found
A thing to do, and all her hair
　　In one long yellow string I wound
40　　Three times her little throat around
And strangled her. No pain felt she;
　　I am quite sure she felt no pain.
As a shut bud that holds a bee,
　　I warily oped her lids: again
45　　Laughed the blue eyes without a stain.
And I untightened next the tress
　　About her neck, her cheek once more
Blushed bright beneath my burning kiss:

I propped her head up as before
  Only, this time my shoulder bore,
Her head, which droops upon it still:
  The smiling rosy little head,
So glad it has its utmost will,
  That all it scorned at once is fled,
  And I, its love, am gained instead!
Porphyria's love: she guessed not how
  Her darling one wish would be heard.
And thus we sit together now,
  And all night long we have not stirred,
  And yet God has not said a word!

50

55

60

—1836

My Last Duchess[1]

Ferrara

That's my last Duchess painted on the wall,
Looking as if she were alive. I call
That piece a wonder, now: Fra Pandolf 's[2] hands
Worked busily a day, and there she stands.
Will't please you sit and look at her? I said
"Fra Pandolf " by design, for never read
Strangers like you that pictured countenance,
The depth and passion of its earnest glance,
But to myself they turned (since none puts by
The curtain I have drawn for you, but I)
And seemed as they would ask me, if they durst,
How such a glance came there; so, not the first
Are you to turn and ask thus. Sir, 'twas not
Her husband's presence only, called that spot
Of joy into the Duchess' cheek: perhaps
Fra Pandolf chanced to say "Her mantle laps
Over my lady's wrist too much," or "Paint
Must never hope to reproduce the faint
Half-flush that dies along her throat": such stuff

5

10

15

---

1   *My Last Duchess* Based on events in the life of Alfonso II, first Duke of Ferrara, Italy,
    whose first wife died in 1561 under suspicious circumstances after three years of marriage.
    Upon her death, the Duke entered into negotiations with an agent of Count Ferdinand I
    of Tyrol, whose daughter he married in 1565.
2   *Fra Pandolf* Brother Pandolf, an imaginary painter, just as "Claus of Innsbruck" (line 56)
    is an imaginary sculptor.

20 Was courtesy, she thought, and cause enough
   For calling up that spot of joy. She had
   A heart—how shall I say?—too soon made glad,
   Too easily impressed; she liked whate'er
   She looked on, and her looks went everywhere.
25 Sir, 'twas all one! My favour at her breast,[1]
   The dropping of the daylight in the West,
   The bough of cherries some officious fool
   Broke in the orchard for her, the white mule
   She rode with round the terrace—all and each
30 Would draw from her alike the approving speech,
   Or blush, at least. She thanked men—good! but thanked
   Somehow—I know not how—as if she ranked
   My gift of a nine-hundred-years-old name
   With anybody's gift. Who'd stoop to blame
35 This sort of trifling? Even had you skill
   In speech—(which I have not)—to make your will
   Quite clear to such an one, and say, "Just this
   Or that in you disgusts me; here you miss,
   Or there exceed the mark"—and if she let
40 Herself be lessoned so, nor plainly set
   Her wits to yours, forsooth, and made excuse,
   —E'en then would be some stooping; and I choose
   Never to stoop. Oh sir, she smiled, no doubt,
   Whene'er I passed her; but who passed without
45 Much the same smile? This grew; I gave commands;
   Then all smiles stopped together. There she stands
   As if alive. Will't please you rise? We'll meet
   The company below, then. I repeat,
   The Count your master's known munificence
50 Is ample warrant that no just pretence
   Of mine for dowry will be disallowed;
   Though his fair daughter's self, as I avowed
   At starting, is my object. Nay, we'll go
   Together down, sir. Notice Neptune,[2] though,
55 Taming a sea-horse, thought a rarity,
   Which Claus of Innsbruck cast in bronze for me!

—1842

---

1   *My favour at her breast* I.e., a scarf or ribbon decorated with the Duke's heraldic colours
    or armorial bearings.
2   *Neptune* Roman god of the sea, who rides in a chariot pulled by seahorses.

Emily Brontë
1818–1848

It would seem that there were two Emily Brontës: one a shy, introverted, and unremarkable young woman, and the other the strong-willed, brilliant, and legendary woman who became almost a mythic figure after her death at the age of 30. Both versions develop from the impressions her sister Charlotte gave of her in the preface to the 1850 edition of Emily's only novel, *Wuthering Heights*. For many years it was this work for which she was best known; it was not until the start of the twentieth century that her poetry began to receive serious critical attention.

The fifth of six children born to a literary-minded Anglican clergyman, Brontë grew up in a village in the moors of West Yorkshire—a landscape that is frequently reflected in her poetic imagery. Her literary talent flourished in a house of creative writers that included her sisters Charlotte (author of *Jane Eyre*) and Anne (author of *The Tenant of Wildfell Hall*). As adults, the three sisters collaborated on a volume of poetry, which they published pseudonymously as *The Poems of Currer, Ellis, and Acton Bell* (1846); though its significance is recognized today, the edition published by the sisters sold only two copies.

Wuthering Heights and much of Brontë's poetry share a bleak tone and a preoccupation with passion, loss, and death, yet her poems exhibit a degree of tenderness not evident in her novel. Many explore an existence free of the restraints of everyday life, though attainable only through imagination—a tendency that connects Brontë to her Romantic predecessors more than to her Victorian contemporaries.

Brontë died of tuberculosis in December 1848, only one year after the publication of *Wuthering Heights*. Charlotte Brontë championed her sister's poetic reputation after Emily's death, arguing that the poems evoke the stirrings of the "heart like the sound of a trumpet."

[No coward soul is mine]

No coward soul is mine
No trembler in the world's storm-troubled sphere
I see Heaven's glories shine
And Faith shines equal arming me from Fear

O God within my breast
Almighty ever-present Deity
Life, that in me hast rest
As I Undying Life, have power in Thee

5

Vain are the thousand creeds
10 That move men's hearts, unutterably vain,
Worthless as withered weeds
Or idlest froth amid the boundless main°   *sea*

To waken doubt in one
Holding so fast by thy infinity
15 So surely anchored on
The steadfast rock of Immortality.

With wide-embracing love
Thy spirit animates eternal years
Pervades and broods above,
20 Changes, sustains, dissolves, creates and rears

Though Earth and moon were gone
And suns and universes ceased to be
And thou wert left alone
Every Existence would exist in thee

25 There is not room for Death
Nor atom that his might could render void
Since thou art Being and Breath
And what thou art may never be destroyed.

—1850 (written 1846)

[Often rebuked, yet always back returning][1]

Often rebuked, yet always back returning
    To those first feelings that were born with me,
And leaving busy chase of wealth and learning
    For idle dreams of things which cannot be:

5 Today, I will seek not the shadowy region;
    Its unsustaining vastness waxes drear;
And visions rising, legion after legion,
    Bring the unreal world too strangely near.

---

1   *[Often ... returning]* The authorship of this poem has been variously credited to Emily, Charlotte, and Anne Brontë; when the poem was first printed, under the title "Stanzas," it was recorded as having been written by Emily.

I'll walk, but not in old heroic traces,
    And not in paths of high morality, 10
And not among the half-distinguished faces,
    The clouded forms of long-past history.

I'll walk where my own nature would be leading:
    It vexes me to choose another guide:
Where the grey flocks in ferny glens are feeding; 15
    Where the wild wind blows on the mountain side.

What have those lonely mountains worth revealing?
    More glory and more grief than I can tell:
The earth that wakes *one* human heart to feeling
    Can centre both the worlds of Heaven and Hell. 20

                  —1850

[I'll come when thou art saddest]

I'll come when thou art saddest,
Laid alone in the darkened room;
When the mad day's mirth has vanished
And the smile of joy is banished
From evening's chilly gloom. 5

I'll come when the heart's real feeling
Has entire, unbiased sway,
And my influence o'er thee stealing,
Grief deepening, joy congealing,
Shall bear thy soul away. 10

Listen! 'tis just the hour,
The awful time for thee:
Dost thou not feel upon thy soul
A flood of strange sensations roll,
Forerunners of a sterner power, 15
Heralds of me?

            —1902 (written 1837)

Walt Whitman
1819–1892

An essayist, journalist, school teacher, nurse, wanderer, and lover of the natural world, Walt Whitman is best known for his ground-breaking and influential work of poetry, *Leaves of Grass* (1855–92). Although it addresses universal subjects such as selfhood, nature, and the body, Whitman intended his work primarily as a contribution to the establishment of a uniquely American literature "with neither foreign spirit, nor imagery nor form, but adapted to our case, ... strengthening and intensifying the national soul."

Whitman was born to working-class parents near Hempstead, Long Island, and the family moved to Brooklyn when he was still a child. He received six years of public school education before providing himself with an informal education in a variety of subjects using publicly available resources in New York City. As a young man, he worked as a journalist and editor and became involved with the Democratic Party; this background is reflected in the frequent political focus of *Leaves of Grass*.

A provocative work in its time, *Leaves of Grass* was criticized for its informal diction, nontraditional metre, and overt references to sex and the body, but it was also recognized by a few as a literary masterwork. Whitman sent copies of the first edition to well-known writers of the day, including John Greenleaf Whittier, who is said to have thrown his copy in the fire. Ralph Waldo Emerson, however, wrote Whitman in praise of the book.

Leaves of Grass remained an amorphous work in progress, published in a sequence of editions with Whitman's own substantial changes and additions; the first edition contained 12 poems, while the last contained more than 350.

from *Song of Myself*

1

I celebrate myself, and sing myself,
And what I assume you shall assume,
For every atom belonging to me as good belongs to you.

I loafe and invite my soul,
I lean and loafe at my ease observing a spear of summer grass.

5 My tongue, every atom of my blood, form'd from this soil, this air,
Born here of parents born here from parents the same, and their
    parents the same,
I, now thirty-seven years old in perfect health begin,

Hoping to cease not till death.
Creeds and schools in abeyance,   10
Retiring back a while sufficed at what they are, but never forgotten,
I harbour for good or bad, I permit to speak at every hazard,
Nature without check with original energy.

—1855, 1881

I Hear America Singing

I hear America singing, the varied carols I hear;
Those of mechanics, each one singing his as it should be blithe and strong,
The carpenter singing his as he measures his plank or beam,
The mason singing his as he makes ready for work, or leaves off work.
The boatman singing what belongs to him in his boat, the deckhand   5
    singing on the steamboat deck,
The shoemaker singing as he sits on his bench, the hatter singing as he
    stands,
The wood-cutter's song, the ploughboy's on his way in the morning, or
    at noon intermission or at sundown,
The delicious singing of the mother, or of the young wife at work, or of
    the girl sewing or washing,
Each singing what belongs to him or her and to none else,
The day what belongs to the day—at night the party of young fellows,   10
    robust, friendly,
Singing with open mouths their strong melodious songs.

—1860

When I Heard the Learn'd Astronomer

When I heard the learn'd astronomer,
When the proofs, the figures, were ranged in columns before me,
When I was shown the charts and diagrams, to add, divide, and
    measure them,
When I sitting heard the astronomer where he lectured with much
    applause in the lecture-room,
How soon unaccountable I became tired and sick,   5
Till rising and gliding out I wander'd off by myself,
In the mystical moist night-air, and from time to time,
Look'd up in perfect silence at the stars.

—1865

Matthew Arnold
1822–1888

Though Matthew Arnold did not compose a large body of poetry, a great deal of the poetry he did write has proved to be lasting. So too has his larger legacy of edifying and intriguing prose; Arnold's influence as a leading Victorian literary and social critic continues to be felt in current scholarly debates.

As a youth Matthew Arnold was educated at Rugby School under the direct supervision of his father, Thomas Arnold, the most famous English educator of his time. Matthew won a scholarship to Balliol College, Oxford, where he would win the prestigious Newdigate Prize for poetry three years later. His experience at Oxford made a lasting impression on the young man—one of his most celebrated poems, "The Scholar Gipsy" (1853), commemorates the spiritual beauty and elevated culture that Arnold came to associate with this educational institution.

Arnold's first book of poems, *The Strayed Reveller, and Other Poems* (1849), was published under the pseudonym "A," and displayed the aloofness and nonchalance for which he had developed a reputation at Oxford. *Poems by Matthew Arnold* (1853)—the first collection to be published under his name—exhibits a distinctive combination of angst and whimsy. But by the time that book was published Arnold was already writing poetry in a deeper, more melancholic vein; his "Dover Beach," often described as the quintessential poem of the Victorian era, was not published until 1867, but dates from c. 1851. Arnold's most important long poem, *Empedocles on Etna* (1852), dramatizes the reflections of an ancient philosopher in the hours before he commits suicide.

Arnold was elected professor of poetry at Oxford in 1857. By this time, however, he was becoming successful as a literary and social critic, and was writing very little poetry. His most important critical work is *Culture and Anarchy* (1869), which is still widely considered to be a masterpiece of social analysis; in it, he argues that the middle class should be given an education in high culture.

Dover Beach

The sea is calm tonight.
The tide is full, the moon lies fair
Upon the straits—on the French coast the light
Gleams and is gone; the cliffs of England stand,
5 Glimmering and vast, out in the tranquil bay.
Come to the window, sweet is the night-air!

Only, from the long line of spray
Where the sea meets the moon-blanched land,
Listen! you hear the grating roar
Of pebbles which the waves draw back, and fling,   10
At their return, up the high strand,°   *shore*
Begin, and cease, and then again begin,
With tremulous cadence slow, and bring
The eternal note of sadness in.

Sophocles long ago   15
Heard it on the Aegaean, and it brought
Into his mind the turbid ebb and flow
Of human misery;[1] we
Find also in the sound a thought,
Hearing it by this distant northern sea.   20

The Sea of Faith
Was once, too, at the full, and round earth's shore
Lay like the folds of a bright girdle furled.
But now I only hear
Its melancholy, long, withdrawing roar,   25
Retreating, to the breath
Of the night-wind, down the vast edges drear
And naked shingles[2] of the world.

Ah, love, let us be true
To one another! for the world, which seems   30
To lie before us like a land of dreams,
So various, so beautiful, so new,
Hath really neither joy, nor love, nor light,
Nor certitude, nor peace, nor help for pain;
And we are here as on a darkling plain   35
Swept with confused alarms of struggle and flight,
Where ignorant armies clash by night.[3]   —1867

---

1   *Sophocles ... misery* See Sophocles's *Antigone* 583–91: "Blest are those whose days have
    not tasted of evil. For when a house has once been shaken by the gods, no form of ruin is
    lacking, but it spreads over the bulk of the race, just as, when the surge is driven over the
    darkness of the deep by the fierce breath of Thracian sea-winds, it rolls up the black sand
    from the depths, and the wind-beaten headlands that front the blows of the storm give
    out a mournful roar"; *Aegaean* Arm of the Mediterranean Sea near Greece.
2   *shingles* Water-worn pebbles.
3   *ignorant ... by night* Reference to Thucydides's *History of the Peloponnesian War*, in which
    the invading Athenians became confused as night fell on the battle at Epipolae. Combat-
    ants could not tell friend from foe in the moonlight.

Emily Dickinson
1830–1886

Emily Dickinson is often compared to Walt Whitman; they are the leading figures of mid-nineteenth-century American literature, and both exerted enormous influence on the writing of later generations. But whereas Whitman was an exuberantly public figure, Dickinson was intensely private. Whitman strove continually to make a mark; Dickinson remained all but unknown until after her death.

Dickinson was one of three children of Emily and Edward Norcross of Amherst, Massachusetts; her father was an officer of Amherst College and a representative in Congress. She was educated at Amherst Academy and, briefly, at nearby Mount Holyoke College; after one year at Mount Holyoke, however, she returned to Amherst, and from the age of 18 onward she again lived with her family, allowing very few people to visit her. After reaching 30, she became a recluse. Although she acknowledged the appeal of fame and public recognition, she criticized it often in her poems; in one it was "a bright but tragic thing," in another "a fickle food / Upon a shifting plate."

Dickinson's work has a deeply personal flavour to it, but her subject matter is wide-ranging—as was her knowledge of classical and English literature. Her poems often engage with religious themes, yet they also at times suggest a profound religious skepticism. The voice we hear in her poetry is often forceful and direct—yet the poems are filled with ambiguities of syntax and of punctuation.

Dickinson wrote more than 1,700 poems, but most of these did not circulate while she was alive, even in manuscript; only a handful were published during her lifetime. The majority were discovered in a trunk in her bedroom after her death. They were first published in edited versions that regularized and "corrected" many of the eccentricities of Dickinson's punctuation; only in recent decades have readers been able to read the poems as Dickinson wrote them.

249

Wild Nights—Wild Nights!
Were I with thee
Wild Nights should be
Our luxury!

5   Futile—the Winds—
To a Heart in port—

Done with the Compass—
Done with the Chart!

Rowing in Eden—
Ah, the Sea!   10
Might I but moor—Tonight—
In Thee!

                                          —1891 (written c. 1861)

288

I'm Nobody! Who are you?
Are you—Nobody—Too?
Then there's a pair of us!
Don't tell! they'd advertise—you know!

How dreary—to be—Somebody!   5
How public—like a Frog—
To tell one's name—the livelong June—
To an admiring Bog!

                                          —1891 (written c. 1861)

341

After great pain, a formal feeling comes—
The Nerves sit ceremonious, like Tombs—
The stiff Heart questions was it He, that bore,
And Yesterday, or Centuries before?

The Feet, mechanical, go round—   5
Of Ground, or Air, or Ought—
A Wooden way
Regardless grown,
A Quartz contentment, like a stone—

This is the Hour of Lead—   10
Remembered, if outlived,
As Freezing persons, recollect the Snow—
First—Chill—then Stupor—then the letting go—

                                          —1929 (written c. 1862)

465

I heard a Fly buzz—when I died—
The Stillness in the Room
Was like the Stillness in the Air—
Between the Heaves of Storm—

5   The Eyes around—had wrung them dry—
And Breaths were gathering firm
For that last Onset—when the King
Be witnessed—in the Room—

I willed my Keepsakes—Signed away
10 What portion of me be
Assignable—and then it was
There interposed a Fly—

With Blue—uncertain stumbling Buzz—
Between the light—and me—
15 And then the Windows failed—and then
I could not see to see—

—1896 (written c. 1862)

712

Because I could not stop for Death—
He kindly stopped for me—
The Carriage held but just Ourselves—
And Immortality.

5   We slowly drove—He knew no haste
And I had put away
My labour and my leisure too,
For His Civility—

We passed the School, where Children strove
10 At Recess—in the Ring—
We passed the Fields of Gazing Grain—
We passed the Setting Sun—

Or rather—He passed Us—
The Dews drew quivering and chill—
For only Gossamer,[1] my Gown—   15
My Tippet°—only Tulle—   *shawl*

We paused before a House that seemed
A Swelling of the Ground—
The Roof was scarcely visible—
The Cornice[2]—in the Ground—   20

Since then—'tis Centuries—and yet
Feels shorter than the Day
I first surmised the Horses' Heads
Were toward Eternity—

                              —1890 (written c. 1863)

754

My Life had stood—a Loaded Gun—
In Corners—till a Day
The Owner passed—identified—
And carried Me away—

And now We roam in Sovereign Woods—   5
And now We hunt the Doe—
And every time I speak for Him—
The Mountains straight reply—

And do I smile, such cordial light
Upon the Valley glow—   10
It is as a Vesuvian[3] face
Had let its pleasure through—

And when at Night—Our good Day done—
I guard My Master's Head—

---

1   *Gossamer* Fine, sheer fabric.
2   *Cornice* Decorative moulding that runs along the top of a building's exterior wall where
     it meets the roof.
3   *Vesuvian* Refers to Mount Vesuvius, a volcano in Italy.

15 'Tis better than the Eider-Duck's[1]
Deep Pillow—to have shared—

To foe of His—I'm deadly foe—
None stir the second time—
On whom I lay a Yellow Eye—
20 Or an emphatic Thumb—

Though I than He—may longer live
He longer must—than I—
For I have but the power to kill,
Without—the power to die—

—1929 (written c. 1863)

1129

Tell all the Truth but tell it slant—
Success in Circuit lies
Too bright for our infirm Delight
The Truth's superb surprise

5 As Lightning to the Children eased
With explanation kind
The Truth must dazzle gradually
Or every man be blind—

—1945 (written c. 1868)

---

1   *Eider-Duck* Duck whose down feathers are used to stuff pillows.

Christina Rossetti
1830–1894

To the late-Victorian critic Edmund Gosse, Christina Rossetti was "one of the most perfect poets of the age." Her melding of sensuous imagery and stringent form earned her the admiration and devotion of many nineteenth-century readers, and the ease of her lyric voice remains apparent in works as diverse as the sensual "Goblin Market" and the subtle religious hymns she penned throughout her career.

Rossetti was born in London in 1830. Her father, a scholar and Italian expatriate, and her mother, who had been a governess before her marriage, inculcated in each of their four children a love of language, literature, and the arts. In 1850 several of her poems were published in *The Germ*, the journal of the Pre-Raphaelite Brotherhood founded in part by her two brothers, Dante Gabriel and William Michael. Although Rossetti was not formally a member of the Brotherhood, her aesthetic sense—and especially her attention to colour and detail—link her to the movement. Other Pre-Raphaelite values were also central to Rossetti's poetic vision, including a devotion to the faithful representation of nature and, at the same time, a penchant for symbols.

Rossetti first gained attention in the literary world with her 1862 publication of *Goblin Market and Other Poems*. The vast majority of her Victorian critics praised the volume for what one reviewer called its "very decided character and originality, both in theme and treatment," and "Goblin Market" remains among her most discussed works. Few readers have believed William Michael Rossetti's insistence that his sister "did not mean anything profound" by "Goblin Market," but many have found the precise nature of its deep suggestiveness elusive.

In 1871, Rossetti was stricken with Graves's disease, a thyroid problem, which led her to retreat even further into an already quiet life. She continued, however, to publish poetry, including *Sing-Song* (1872), a children's collection; *A Pageant and Other Poems* (1881); and *Verses* (1893). In 1892 she was among those mentioned as a possible successor to Tennyson as England's Poet Laureate. She died in 1894 as a result of breast cancer.

Goblin Market

Morning and evening
Maids heard the goblins cry:
"Come buy our orchard fruits,
Come buy, come buy:

5   Apples and quinces,
    Lemons and oranges,
    Plump unpecked cherries,
    Melons and raspberries,
    Bloom-down-cheeked peaches,
10 Swart°-headed mulberries,   *dark*
    Wild free-born cranberries,
    Crabapples, dewberries,
    Pine-apples, blackberries,
    Apricots, strawberries;—
15 All ripe together
    In summer weather,—
    Morns that pass by,
    Fair eves that fly;
    Come buy, come buy:
20 Our grapes fresh from the vine,
    Pomegranates full and fine,
    Dates and sharp bullaces,
    Rare pears and greengages,
    Damsons[1] and bilberries
25 Taste them and try:
    Currants and gooseberries,
    Bright-fire-like barberries,
    Figs to fill your mouth,
    Citrons from the South,
30 Sweet to tongue and sound to eye;
    Come buy, come buy."

    Evening by evening
    Among the brookside rushes,
    Laura bowed her head to hear,
35 Lizzie veiled her blushes:
    Crouching close together
    In the cooling weather,
    With clasping arms and cautioning lips,
    With tingling cheeks and finger tips.
40 "Lie close," Laura said,
    Pricking up her golden head:
    "We must not look at goblin men,

---

1   *bullaces ... Damsons* Bullaces, greengages, and damsons are all varieties of plums.

We must not buy their fruits:
Who knows upon what soil they fed
Their hungry thirsty roots?"   45
"Come buy," call the goblins
Hobbling down the glen.
"Oh," cried Lizzie, "Laura, Laura,
You should not peep at goblin men."
Lizzie covered up her eyes,   50
Covered close lest they should look;
Laura reared her glossy head,
And whispered like the restless brook:
"Look, Lizzie, look, Lizzie,
Down the glen tramp little men.   55
One hauls a basket,
One bears a plate,
One lugs a golden dish
Of many pounds weight.
How fair the vine must grow   60
Whose grapes are so luscious;
How warm the wind must blow
Through those fruit bushes."
"No," said Lizzie: "No, no, no;
Their offers should not charm us,   65
Their evil gifts would harm us."
She thrust a dimpled finger
In each ear, shut eyes and ran:
Curious Laura chose to linger
Wondering at each merchant man.   70
One had a cat's face,
One whisked a tail,
One tramped at a rat's pace,
One crawled like a snail,
One like a wombat prowled obtuse and furry,   75
One like a ratel° tumbled hurry skurry.   *badger*
She heard a voice like voice of doves
Cooing all together:
They sounded kind and full of loves
In the pleasant weather.   80

Laura stretched her gleaming neck
Like a rush-imbedded swan,

Like a lily from the beck,°   *stream*
Like a moonlit poplar branch,
85 Like a vessel at the launch
When its last restraint is gone.

Backwards up the mossy glen
Turned and trooped the goblin men,
With their shrill repeated cry,
90 "Come buy, come buy."
When they reached where Laura was
They stood stock still upon the moss,
Leering at each other,
Brother with queer brother;
95 Signalling each other,
Brother with sly brother.
One set his basket down,
One reared his plate;
One began to weave a crown
100 Of tendrils, leaves, and rough nuts brown
(Men sell not such in any town);
One heaved the golden weight
Of dish and fruit to offer her:
"Come buy, come buy," was still their cry.
105 Laura stared but did not stir,
Longed but had no money:
The whisk-tailed merchant bade her taste
In tones as smooth as honey,
The cat-faced purr'd,
110 The rat-paced spoke a word
Of welcome, and the snail-paced even was heard;
One parrot-voiced and jolly
Cried "Pretty Goblin" still for "Pretty Polly";—
One whistled like a bird.

115 But sweet-tooth Laura spoke in haste:
"Good Folk, I have no coin;
To take were to purloin:
I have no copper in my purse,
I have no silver either,
120 And all my gold is on the furze°   *evergreen shrub*
That shakes in windy weather

Above the rusty heather."
"You have much gold upon your head,"
They answered all together:
"Buy from us with a golden curl."   125
She clipped a precious golden lock,
She dropped a tear more rare than pearl,
Then sucked their fruit globes fair or red.
Sweeter than honey from the rock,[1]
Stronger than man-rejoicing wine,   130
Clearer than water flowed that juice;
She never tasted such before,
How should it cloy with length of use?
She sucked and sucked and sucked the more
Fruits which that unknown orchard bore;   135
She sucked until her lips were sore;
Then flung the emptied rinds away
But gathered up one kernel-stone,
And knew not was it night or day
As she turned home alone.   140

Lizzie met her at the gate
Full of wise upbraidings:
"Dear, you should not stay so late,
Twilight is not good for maidens;
Should not loiter in the glen   145
In the haunts of goblin men.
Do you not remember Jeanie,
How she met them in the moonlight,
Took their gifts both choice and many,
Ate their fruits and wore their flowers   150
Plucked from bowers
Where summer ripens at all hours?
But ever in the moonlight
She pined and pined away;
Sought them by night and day,   155
Found them no more but dwindled and grew grey;
Then fell with the first snow,
While to this day no grass will grow
Where she lies low:

---

1   *honey from the rock* See Deuteronomy 32.13.

160 I planted daisies there a year ago
    That never blow.
    You should not loiter so."
    "Nay, hush," said Laura:
    "Nay, hush, my sister:
165 I ate and ate my fill,
    Yet my mouth waters still;
    Tomorrow night I will
    Buy more": and kissed her:
    "Have done with sorrow;
170 I'll bring you plums tomorrow
    Fresh on their mother twigs,
    Cherries worth getting;
    You cannot think what figs
    My teeth have met in,
175 What melons icy cold
    Piled on a dish of gold
    Too huge for me to hold,
    What peaches with a velvet nap,
    Pellucid° grapes without one seed: *translucent*
180 Odorous indeed must be the mead°   *meadow*
    Whereon they grow, and pure the wave they drink
    With lilies at the brink,
    And sugar-sweet their sap."

    Golden head by golden head,
185 Like two pigeons in one nest
    Folded in each other's wings,
    They lay down in their curtained bed:
    Like two blossoms on one stem,
    Like two flakes of new-fall'n snow,
190 Like two wands of ivory
    Tipped with gold for awful° kings.   *awe-inspiring*
    Moon and stars gazed in at them,
    Wind sang to them lullaby,
    Lumbering owls forbore to fly,
195 Not a bat flapped to and fro
    Round their rest:
    Cheek to cheek and breast to breast
    Locked together in one nest.

Early in the morning
When the first cock crowed his warning,   200
Neat like bees, as sweet and busy,
Laura rose with Lizzie:
Fetched in honey, milked the cows,
Aired and set to rights the house,
Kneaded cakes of whitest wheat,   205
Cakes for dainty mouths to eat,
Next churned butter, whipped up cream,
Fed their poultry, sat and sewed;
Talked as modest maidens should:
Lizzie with an open heart,   210
Laura in an absent dream,
One content, one sick in part;
One warbling for the mere bright day's delight,
One longing for the night.

At length slow evening came: 215
They went with pitchers to the reedy brooks;
Lizzie most placid in her look,
Laura most like a leaping flame.
They drew the gurgling water from its deep.
Lizzie plucked purple and rich golden flags,   220
Then turning homeward said: "The sunset flushes
Those furthest loftiest crags;
Come Laura, not another maiden lags.
No wilful squirrel wags,
The beasts and birds are fast asleep."   225
But Laura loitered still among the rushes,
And said the bank was steep.

And said the hour was early still,
The dew not fall'n, the wind not chill;
Listening ever, but not catching   230
The customary cry,
"Come buy, come buy,"
With its iterated jingle
Of sugar-baited words:
Not for all her watching   235
Once discerning even one goblin
Racing, whisking, tumbling, hobbling—

Let alone the herds
That used to tramp along the glen,
240 In groups or single,
Of brisk fruit-merchant men.
Till Lizzie urged, "O Laura, come;
I hear the fruit-call, but I dare not look:
You should not loiter longer at this brook:
245 Come with me home.
The stars rise, the moon bends her arc,
Each glowworm winks her spark,
Let us get home before the night grows dark:
For clouds may gather
250 Though this is summer weather,
Put out the lights and drench us thro';
Then if we lost our way what should we do?"

Laura turned cold as stone
To find her sister heard that cry alone,
255 That goblin cry,
"Come buy our fruits, come buy."
Must she then buy no more such dainty fruit?
Must she no more such succous° pasture find,   *juicy*
Gone deaf and blind?
260 Her tree of life drooped from the root:
She said not one word in her heart's sore ache;
But peering through the dimness, nought discerning,
Trudged home, her pitcher dripping all the way;
So crept to bed, and lay
265 Silent till Lizzie slept;
Then sat up in a passionate yearning,
And gnashed her teeth for baulked desire, and wept
As if her heart would break.

Day after day, night after night,
270 Laura kept watch in vain
In sullen silence of exceeding pain.
She never caught again the goblin cry,
"Come buy, come buy"—
She never spied the goblin men
275 Hawking their fruits along the glen:
But when the noon waxed bright

Her hair grew thin and grey;
She dwindled, as the fair full moon doth turn
To swift decay and burn
Her fire away.   280

One day remembering her kernel-stone
She set it by a wall that faced the south;
Dewed it with tears, hoped for a root,
Watched for a waxing shoot,
But there came none.   285
It never saw the sun,
It never felt the trickling moisture run:
While with sunk eyes and faded mouth
She dreamed of melons, as a traveller sees
False waves in desert drouth°   *drought* 290
With shade of leaf-crowned trees,
And burns the thirstier in the sandful breeze.

She no more swept the house,
Tended the fowl or cows,
Fetched honey, kneaded cakes of wheat,   295
Brought water from the brook:
But sat down listless in the chimney-nook
And would not eat.

Tender Lizzie could not bear
To watch her sister's cankerous care,   300
Yet not to share.
She night and morning
Caught the goblins' cry:
"Come buy our orchard fruits,
Come buy, come buy:"—   305
Beside the brook, along the glen,
She heard the tramp of goblin men,
The voice and stir
Poor Laura could not hear;
Longed to buy fruit to comfort her,   310
But feared to pay too dear.
She thought of Jeanie in her grave,
Who should have been a bride;
But who for joys brides hope to have

315 Fell sick and died
In her gay prime,
In earliest winter time,
With the first glazing rime,°   *hoar frost*
With the first snow-fall of crisp Winter time.

320 Till Laura dwindling
Seemed knocking at Death's door.
Then Lizzie weighed no more
Better and worse;
But put a silver penny in her purse,
325 Kissed Laura, crossed the heath with clumps of furze
At twilight, halted by the brook:
And for the first time in her life
Began to listen and look.

Laughed every goblin
330 When they spied her peeping:
Came towards her hobbling,
Flying, running, leaping,
Puffing and blowing,
Chuckling, clapping, crowing.
335 Clucking and gobbling,
Mopping and mowing,
Full of airs and graces,
Pulling wry faces,
Demure grimaces,
340 Cat-like and rat-like,
Ratel- and wombat-like,
Snail-paced in a hurry,
Parrot-voiced and whistler,
Helter skelter, hurry skurry,
345 Chattering like magpies,
Fluttering like pigeons,
Gliding like fishes,—
Hugged her and kissed her:
Squeezed and caressed her:
350 Stretched up their dishes,
Panniers, and plates:
"Look at our apples
Russet and dun,°   *dark*

Bob at our cherries,
Bite at our peaches,   355
Citrons and dates,
Grapes for the asking,
Pears red with basking
Out in the sun,
Plums on their twigs;   360
Pluck them and suck them,—
Pomegranates, figs."

Dante Gabriel Rossetti, frontispiece to Goblin Market and Other Poems,
1862. The first edition of Goblin Market *appeared with illustrations by
Christina Rossetti's brother, the Pre-Raphaelite painter and poet Dante
Gabriel Rossetti. In this frontispiece, the round inset above the drawing of
sisters Laura and Lizzie depicts the goblins carrying their fruits to market.*

"Good folk," said Lizzie,
Mindful of Jeanie:
365 "Give me much and many"—
Held out her apron,
Tossed them her penny.
"Nay, take a seat with us,
Honour and eat with us,"
370 They answered grinning:
"Our feast is but beginning.
Night yet is early,
Warm and dew-pearly,
Wakeful and starry:
375 Such fruits as these
No man can carry;
Half their bloom would fly,
Half their dew would dry,
Half their flavour would pass by.
380 Sit down and feast with us,
Be welcome guest with us,
Cheer you and rest with us."—
"Thank you," said Lizzie: "But one waits
At home alone for me:
385 So without further parleying,°   *discussion*
If you will not sell me any
Of your fruits though much and many,
Give me back my silver penny
I tossed you for a fee."—
390 They began to scratch their pates,°   *heads*
No longer wagging, purring,
But visibly demurring,
Grunting and snarling.
One called her proud,
395 Cross-grained, uncivil;
Their tones waxed loud,
Their looks were evil.
Lashing their tails
They trod and hustled her,
400 Elbowed and jostled her,
Clawed with their nails,
Barking, mewing, hissing, mocking,
Tore her gown and soiled her stocking,

Twitched her hair out by the roots,
Stamped upon her tender feet,   405
Held her hands and squeezed their fruits
Against her mouth to make her eat.

White and golden Lizzie stood,
Like a lily in a flood,—
Like a rock of blue-veined stone   410
Lashed by tides obstreperously,—
Like a beacon left alone
In a hoary roaring sea,
Sending up a golden fire,—
Like a fruit-crowned orange tree   415
White with blossoms honey-sweet
Sore beset by wasp and bee,—
Like a royal virgin town
Topped with gilded dome and spire
Close beleaguered by a fleet   420
Mad to tug her standard down.

One may lead a horse to water,
Twenty cannot make him drink.
Though the goblins cuffed and caught her,
Coaxed and fought her,   425
Bullied and besought her,
Scratched her, pinched her black as ink,
Kicked and knocked her,
Mauled and mocked her,
Lizzie uttered not a word;   430
Would not open lip from lip
Lest they should cram a mouthful in:
But laughed in heart to feel the drip
Of juice that syruped all her face,
And lodged in dimples of her chin,   435
And streaked her neck which quaked like curd.
At last the evil people,
Worn out by her resistance,
Flung back her penny, kicked their fruit
Along whichever road they took,   440
Not leaving root or stone or shoot;
Some writhed into the ground,

Some dived into the brook
With ring and ripple,
445 Some scudded on the gale without a sound,
Some vanished in the distance.

In a smart, ache, tingle,
Lizzie went her way;
Knew not was it night or day;
Sprang up the bank, tore through the furze,
450 Threaded copse and dingle,°   *dell*
And heard her penny jingle
Bouncing in her purse,—
Its bounce was music to her ear.
She ran and ran
455 As if she feared some goblin man
Dogged her with gibe or curse
Or something worse:
But not one goblin skurried after,
Nor was she pricked by fear;
460 The kind heart made her windy-paced
That urged her home quite out of breath with haste
And inward laughter.

She cried, "Laura," up the garden,
"Did you miss me?
465 Come and kiss me.
Never mind my bruises,
Hug me, kiss me, suck my juices
Squeezed from goblin fruits for you,
Goblin pulp and goblin dew.
470 Eat me, drink me, love me;
Laura, make much of me;
For your sake I have braved the glen
And had to do with goblin merchant men."

Laura started from her chair,
475 Flung her arms up in the air,
Clutched her hair:
"Lizzie, Lizzie, have you tasted
For my sake the fruit forbidden?
Must your light like mine be hidden,

Your young life like mine be wasted,   480
Undone in mine undoing,
And ruined in my ruin,
Thirsty, cankered, goblin-ridden?"—
She clung about her sister,
Kissed and kissed and kissed her: 485
Tears once again
Refreshed her shrunken eyes,
Dropping like rain
After long sultry drouth;
Shaking with aguish° fear, and pain,   *feverish* 490
She kissed and kissed her with a hungry mouth.

Her lips began to scorch,
That juice was wormwood to her tongue,
She loathed the feast:
Writhing as one possessed she leaped and sung,   495
Rent all her robe, and wrung
Her hands in lamentable haste,
And beat her breast.
Her locks streamed like the torch
Borne by a racer at full speed,   500
Or like the mane of horses in their flight,
Or like an eagle when she stems the light
Straight toward the sun,
Or like a caged thing freed,
Or like a flying flag when armies run.   505

Swift fire spread through her veins, knocked at her heart,
Met the fire smouldering there
And overbore its lesser flame;
She gorged on bitterness without a name:
Ah! fool, to choose such part   510
Of soul-consuming care!
Sense failed in the mortal strife:
Like the watchtower of a town
Which an earthquake shatters down,
Like a lightning-stricken mast,   515
Like a wind-uprooted tree
Spun about,
Like a foam-topped waterspout

Cast down headlong in the sea,
520 She fell at last;
Pleasure past and anguish past,
Is it death or is it life?

Life out of death.
That night long Lizzie watched by her,
525 Counted her pulse's flagging stir,
Felt for her breath,
Held water to her lips, and cooled her face
With tears and fanning leaves.
But when the first birds chirped about their eaves,
530 And early reapers plodded to the place
Of golden sheaves,
And dew-wet grass
Bowed in the morning winds so brisk to pass,
And new buds with new day
535 Opened of cup-like lilies on the stream,
Laura awoke as from a dream,
Laughed in the innocent old way,
Hugged Lizzie but not twice or thrice;
Her gleaming locks showed not one thread of grey,
540 Her breath was sweet as May,
And light danced in her eyes.

Days, weeks, months, years
Afterwards, when both were wives
With children of their own;
545 Their mother-hearts beset with fears,
Their lives bound up in tender lives;
Laura would call the little ones
And tell them of her early prime,
Those pleasant days long gone
550 Of not-returning time:
Would talk about the haunted glen,
The wicked quaint fruit-merchant men,
Their fruits like honey to the throat
But poison in the blood;
555 (Men sell not such in any town):
Would tell them how her sister stood
In deadly peril to do her good,

And win the fiery antidote:
Then joining hands to little hands
Would bid them cling together,—   560
"For there is no friend like a sister
In calm or stormy weather;
To cheer one on the tedious way,
To fetch one if one goes astray,
To lift one if one totters down,   565
To strengthen whilst one stands."

—1862 (written 1859)

Lizzie protecting Laura

Laurence Housman, illustration from Goblin Market, *1893. A very popular edition of* Goblin Market, *released about three decades after the poem was first published, featured art nouveau illustrations by the writer and artist Laurence Housman.*

Cobwebs

It is a land with neither night nor day,
    Nor heat nor cold, nor any wind, nor rain,
    Nor hills nor valleys; but one even plain
Stretches thro' long unbroken miles away:
5 While thro' the sluggish air a twilight grey
    Broodeth; no moons or seasons wax and wane,
    No ebb and flow are there along the main,°   *open ocean*
    No bud-time no leaf-falling there for aye:°—   *forever*
    No ripple on the sea, no shifting sand,
10   No beat of wings to stir the stagnant space,
    No pulse of life thro' all the loveless land:
And loveless sea; no trace of days before,
    No guarded home, no toil-won resting place
    No future hope, no fear for evermore.

—1896 (written 1855)

In an Artist's Studio

One face looks out from all his canvasses,
    One selfsame figure sits or walks or leans;
    We found her hidden just behind those screens,
That mirror gave back all her loveliness.
5 A queen in opal or in ruby dress,
    A nameless girl in freshest summer greens,
    A saint, an angel—every canvass means
The same one meaning, neither more nor less.
He feeds upon her face by day and night,
10 And she with true kind eyes looks back on him
Fair as the moon and joyful as the light:
Not wan with waiting, not with sorrow dim;
Not as she is, but was when hope shone bright;
Not as she is, but as she fills his dream.

—1896 (written 1856)

Thomas Hardy
1840–1928

Novelist, dramatist, essayist, and poet, Thomas Hardy produced a prodigious body of work in the course of his long life. His writing—highly original and yet intimately connected with centuries-old traditions—is as important to the history of the novel in English as it is to that of English poetry, and as central to early twentieth-century literature as it is to that of the Victorian era.

Hardy was born outside Dorchester, surrounded by the south English landscape that would figure prominently in many of his works. Though he began a career as an architect, he left the profession in order to write. In 22 years, he produced 11 novels and 3 collections of short stories, but he turned his energies to poetry in 1895 after his novel *Jude the Obscure* was attacked by critics for its overt sexual content. (The controversy around the novel, ironically, ensured its large readership.)

Hardy's poetic work is rooted in the physical details of place—especially of natural settings—and often contemplates human suffering, disappointment, and the loss of love. He frequently returns to traditional poetic forms, such as the ballad, approaching rhythm and rhyme with precision and sensitivity. In later years, Hardy's critics judged him a superlative writer in both prose and poetry, and he was awarded honorary doctorates, fellowships, and the gold medal of the Royal Society of Literature.

After his death, Hardy's heart was removed and placed in the grave of his first wife, close to the land of his youth. His remains were then buried in Poets' Corner of Westminster Abbey where he was mourned by contemporaries including Rudyard Kipling, W.B. Yeats, and George Bernard Shaw. He was described by the British intellectual Leonard Woolf as "one of the few people who have left upon me the personal impression of greatness."

The Darkling[1] Thrush

I leant upon a coppice gate[2]
    When Frost was spectre-grey,
And Winter's dregs made desolate
    The weakening eye of day.
The tangled bine[3]-stems scored the sky   5
    Like strings of broken lyres,

---

1   *Darkling* In the dark.
2   *coppice gate* Gate leading to a thicket or small forest.
3   *bine* Hop, a climbing plant.

And all mankind that haunted nigh
    Had sought their household fires.

    The land's sharp features seemed to be
10   The Century's corpse outleant,[1]
    His crypt the cloudy canopy,
      The wind his death-lament.
    The ancient pulse of germ and birth
      Was shrunken hard and dry,
15 And every spirit upon earth
      Seemed fervourless as I.

    At once a voice arose among
      The bleak twigs overhead
    In a full-hearted evensong
20   Of joy illimited;
    An aged thrush, frail, gaunt, and small,
      In blast-beruffled plume,
    Had chosen thus to fling his soul
      Upon the growing gloom.

25 So little cause for carolings
      Of such ecstatic sound
    Was written on terrestrial things
      Afar or nigh around,
    That I could think there trembled through
30   His happy good-night air
    Some blessed Hope, whereof he knew
      And I was unaware.

                —1901 (written 31 December 1900)

---

1   *The Century's corpse outleant* I.e., as if the century were leaning out of its coffin.

The Convergence of the Twain

(Lines on the Loss of the "Titanic"[1])

1

In a solitude of the sea
Deep from human vanity,
And the Pride of Life that planned her, stilly couches she.

2

Steel chambers, late the pyres
Of her salamandrine fires,[2]   5
Cold currents thrid,° and turn to rhythmic tidal lyres.   *thread*

3

Over the mirrors meant
To glass the opulent
The sea-worm crawls—grotesque, slimed, dumb, indifferent.

4

Jewels in joy designed   10
To ravish the sensuous mind
Lie lightless, all their sparkles bleared and black and blind.

5

Dim moon-eyed fishes near
Gaze at the gilded gear
And query: "What does this vaingloriousness down here?" ...   15

6

Well: while was fashioning
This creature of cleaving wing,
The Immanent Will[3] that stirs and urges everything

---

1   *the "Titanic"* At the time the largest ship ever built, the ocean liner *Titanic* had been
    described as unsinkable, but on its maiden voyage in 1912 it collided with an iceberg;
    over 1,400 people drowned when it sank.
2   *salamandrine fires* According to mythology, salamanders are able to survive any heat.
3   *The Immanent Will* The force that pervades and determines human existence.

7

Prepared a sinister mate
20   For her—so gaily great—
A Shape of Ice, for the time far and dissociate.

8

And as the smart ship grew
In stature, grace, and hue,
In shadowy silent distance grew the Iceberg too.

9

25   Alien they seemed to be:
No mortal eye could see
The intimate welding of their later history,

10

Or sign that they were bent
By paths coincident
30 On being anon twin halves of one august event,

11

Till the Spinner of the Years
Said "Now!" And each one hears,
And consummation comes, and jars two hemispheres.

—1914

During Wind and Rain

They sing their dearest songs—
He, she, all of them—yea,
Treble and tenor and bass,
    And one to play;
5   With the candles mooning each face....
    Ah, no; the years O!
How the sick leaves reel down in throngs!

They clear the creeping moss—
Elders and juniors—aye,
10 Making the pathways neat
    And the garden gay;

And they build a shady seat....
    Ah, no; the years, the years;
See, the white storm-birds wing across.

They are blithely breakfasting all— 15
Men and maidens—yea,
Under the summer tree,
    With a glimpse of the bay,
While pet fowl come to the knee....
    Ah, no; the years O! 20
And the rotten rose is ript from the wall.

They change to a high new house,
He, she, all of them—aye,
Clocks and carpets and chairs
    On the lawn all day, 25
And brightest things that are theirs....
    Ah, no; the years, the years;
Down their carved names the rain-drop ploughs.

            —1917

Gerard Manley Hopkins
1844–1889

Although Gerard Manley Hopkins lived and worked during the Victorian period, his poems were not published until 1919, when they were released by his literary executor and gained him posthumous fame. That some critics treated Hopkins as a modernist poet is not only a matter of this timing; indeed, the close observations and fine descriptions found in his poetry do resemble the singular sensory images of modernist literature. As the reviewer Arthur Clutton-Brock wrote in 1919, Hopkins's "poems are crowded with objects sharply cut, and with sounds no less sharp and clashing."

Hopkins was educated at Oxford, where the poet and cultural critic Matthew Arnold (1822–88) was one of his teachers. In 1866, Hopkins entered the Roman Catholic Church, eventually becoming a Jesuit priest and, later, a professor of classics at University College in Dublin. He burned his early efforts at poetry (imitations of Keats written during the 1860s), but went on to write poems in his own distinctive style—syntactically disjunctive, highly alliterative, and densely rhyming—that often aim to celebrate the spiritual and the divine. His few poetry submissions to journals were rejected; uncertain about the quality of his work, and struggling with the fear that a religious life was incompatible with any attempt at artistic fame, he soon stopped trying to publish his poems.

Much of Hopkins's historical importance as a poet comes from his experimentation with metre and form. He devised a precursor to free verse that he called "sprung rhythm," a style of metre in which only the number of stressed syllables in each line is fixed, while the number of unstressed syllables can vary; Hopkins included frequent stress marks in his own verse to clarify the intended rhythm. He also used invented compound words (such as "piece-bright" and "blue-bleak") to link an object's striking characteristics. Such compounds represent an attempt to convey "inscape," a term Hopkins coined to refer to the dynamic, individual design or essence specific to each object in the world.

God's Grandeur

The world is charged with the grándeur of God.
    It will flame out, like shining from shook foil;[1]

---

1   [Hopkins's note] I mean foil in its sense of leaf or tinsel.... Shaken goldfoil gives off broad glares like sheet lightning and also, and this is true of nothing else, owing to its zigzag dints and creasings and network of small many cornered facets, a sort of fork lightning too.

It gathers to a greatness, like the ooze of oil
Crushed.[1] Why do men then now not reck° his rod?   *regard*
Génerátions have trod, have trod, have trod;   5
   And all is seared with trade; bleared, smeared, with toil;
   And wears man's smudge and shares man's smell: the soil
Is bare now, nor can foot feel, being shod.

Ánd, for° all this, náture is never spent;   *despite*
   There lives the dearest freshness deep down things;   10
And though the last lights off the black West went
   Oh, morning, at the brown brink eastward, springs—
Because the Holy Ghost óver the bent
   World broods with warm breast and with ah! bright wings.
                              —1918 (written 1877)

The Windhover[2]

To Christ Our Lord

I caught this morning morning's minion, king-
   dom of daylight's dauphin,[3] dapple-dáwn-drawn Falcon,
      in his riding
Of the rólling level úndernéath him steady air, and striding
High there, how he rung upon the rein of a wimpling° wing   *rippling*
In his écstasy! then off, off forth on swing,   5
   As a skate's heel sweeps smooth on a bow-bend: the hurl and gliding
   Rebuffed the bíg wind. My heart in hiding
Stírred for a bird,—the achieve of, the mástery of the thing!

Brute beauty and valour and act, oh, air, pride, plúme, here
   Buckle! AND the fire that breaks from thee then, a billion   10
Tímes told lovelier, more dangerous, O my chevalier!°   *horseman*

   No wŏnder of it: shéer plód makes plóugh down síllion°   *furrows*
Shíne, and blue-bleak embers, ah my dear,
   Fall, gáll themsélves, and gásh gŏld-vermílion.
                              —1918 (written 1877)

---

1   *oil / Crushed* I.e., as olive oil.
2   *Windhover* Another name for a kestrel, a small falcon that appears to hover in the
    wind.
3   *dauphin* Title of the eldest son of the king of France—the heir.

A.E. Housman
1859–1936

Although he is best remembered as a poet, most of Alfred Edward Housman's life was dedicated to his scholarly work, the translation of classical texts. His definitive edition of Manilius's *Astronomica* represents his greatest achievement in translation, although he also worked on Propertius, Ovid, Juvenal, and other classical authors. Poetry, for Housman, served as an emotional outlet and was something he worked at sporadically. As he once said: "I have seldom written poetry unless I was rather out of health, and the experience, though pleasurable, was generally agitating and exhausting."

Housman published his major poetic work at his own expense in 1896; originally written under the title *The Poems of Terence Hearsay* for the character of a young man that appears in the poems, it was published as *A Shropshire Lad*. The volume, which displays the influence of both English ballads and classical poetry, exhibits nostalgia for earlier times. Although *A Shropshire Lad* did not generate much immediate interest, it became increasingly popular during World War I, perhaps because its themes of loss and early death resonated more strongly in that era. Housman also published *Last Poems* in 1922, and a final collection, *More Poems*, was published posthumously in 1936.

Terence, This Is Stupid Stuff

"Terence, this is stupid stuff:
You eat your victuals fast enough;
There can't be much amiss, 'tis clear,
5 To see the rate you drink your beer.
But oh, good Lord, the verse you make,
It gives a chap the belly-ache.
The cow, the old cow, she is dead;
It sleeps well, the hornèd head:
10 We poor lads, 'tis our turn now
To hear such tunes as killed the cow.
Pretty friendship 'tis to rhyme
Your friends to death before their time
Moping melancholy mad:
15 Come, pipe a tune to dance to, lad."

Why, if 'tis dancing you would be,
There's brisker pipes than poetry.

Say, for what were hop-yards[1] meant,
Or why was Burton built on Trent?[2]
Oh many a peer[3] of England brews   20
Livelier liquor than the Muse,[4]
And malt does more than Milton can
To justify God's ways to man.[5]
Ale, man, ale's the stuff to drink
For fellows whom it hurts to think: 25
Look into the pewter pot°   *mug*
To see the world as the world's not.
And faith, 'tis pleasant till 'tis past:
The mischief is that 'twill not last.
Oh I have been to Ludlow[6] fair   30
And left my necktie God knows where,
And carried half-way home, or near,
Pints and quarts of Ludlow beer:
Then the world seemed none so bad,
And I myself a sterling lad;   35
And down in lovely muck I've lain,
Happy till I woke again.
Then I saw the morning sky:
Heigho, the tale was all a lie;
The world, it was the old world yet,   40
I was I, my things were wet,
And nothing now remained to do
But begin the game anew.

Therefore, since the world has still
Much good, but much less good than ill,   45
And while the sun and moon endure
Luck's a chance, but trouble's sure,
I'd face it as a wise man would,

---

1   *hop-yards* Areas of land upon which hops are grown.
2   *Burton ... Trent* Burton-on-Trent, a town in East Staffordshire, is the historical centre
     of the British brewing industry. Brewing was first begun there by Benedictine monks in
     the eleventh century.
3   *peer* Member of the British nobility. Brewers were among those raised to the peerage,
     and were thus referred to as "beer barons."
4   *Muse* One of nine Greek goddesses of arts and learning; here, the source of poetic
     inspiration.
5   *Milton ... man* See John Milton's *Paradise Lost* (1667), 1.26.
6   *Ludlow* Market town in Shropshire.

And train for ill and not for good.
50 'Tis true the stuff I bring for sale
Is not so brisk a brew as ale:
Out of a stem that scored the hand
I wrung it in a weary land.
But take it: if the smack is sour,
55 The better for the embittered hour;
It should do good to heart and head
When your soul is in my soul's stead;
And I will friend you, if I may,
In the dark and cloudy day.

60   There was a king reigned in the East:
There, when kings will sit to feast,
They get their fill before they think
With poisoned meat and poisoned drink.
He gathered all that springs to birth
65 From the many-venomed earth;
First a little, thence to more,
He sampled all her killing store;
And easy, smiling, seasoned sound,
Sate the king when healths went round.
70 They put arsenic in his meat
And stared aghast to watch him eat;
They poured strychnine in his cup
And shook to see him drink it up:
They shook, they stared as white's their shirt:
75 Them it was their poison hurt.
—I tell the tale that I heard told.
Mithridates, he died old.[1]

—1896

---

1   *There was ... died old* According to Pliny's *Natural History*, Mithridates, king of Pontus
     from approximately 114 to 63 BCE, gradually built up a tolerance to all known poisons
     by ingesting a small amount of each daily, starting in childhood.

W.B. Yeats
1865–1939

William Butler Yeats was born in Sandymount, Dublin, of Anglo-Irish parentage. He spent his early years moving between London and Sligo, a small town in the west of Ireland where his maternal grandparents lived. In London, the family moved in artistic circles that included William Morris, Bernard Shaw, and Oscar Wilde.

His early work is imbued with what he saw as the mystery and beauty of Irish myth and landscape. When Yeats's father saw his son's first poem, he declared that Yeats had "given tongue to the sea-cliffs." The early poems also contain some of the most memorable love poetry in English. In 1899, Yeats was involved in the foundation of the Irish National Theatre; he would become its director and write more than 20 plays that were performed there. But he also continued to write poetry, developing a more dramatic, collo-quial, and compact voice. Beginning with the volume *Responsibilities* (1914), he began to explore increasingly complex themes and poetic forms as he sought to give voice to the "blood-dimmed tide" of modern experience.

Yeats was deeply interested in the occult and explored the symbolic worlds of astrology, Theosophism, the tarot, and alchemy. He developed his own system of symbols and conception of history; the poems "Leda and the Swan" and "The Second Coming" are both, for example, influenced by his idea that civilizations are born cyclically, through violent, mystical, and sexual encounters.

Yeats was a formative influence on modern poetry and on the cultural and political history of Ireland; T.S. Eliot described him as "part of the consciousness of an age which cannot be understood without him." Yeats worked all his life to foster an Irish national literature, and in 1923 he was the first writer from Ireland to receive the Nobel Prize.

Easter 1916[1]

I have met them at close of day
Coming with vivid faces
From counter or desk among grey
Eighteenth-century houses.
I have passed with a nod of the head   5
Or polite meaningless words,

---

1   *Easter 1916* On Easter Monday, 24 April 1916, Irish nationalists instigated an unsuc-cessful rebellion against the British government (which was then at war with Ger-many); the Easter Rebellion lasted until 29 April. Many of the Irish nationalist leaders were executed that May.

Or have lingered awhile and said
Polite meaningless words,
And thought before I had done
10 Of a mocking tale or a gibe
To please a companion
Around the fire at the club,
Being certain that they and I
But lived where motley° is worn: *jester's costume*
15 All changed, changed utterly:
A terrible beauty is born.

That woman's days were spent
In ignorant good-will,
Her nights in argument
20 Until her voice grew shrill.[1]
What voice more sweet than hers
When, young and beautiful,
She rode to harriers?[2]
This man had kept a school
25 And rode our wingèd horse;[3]
This other his helper and friend[4]
Was coming into his force;
He might have won fame in the end,
So sensitive his nature seemed,
30 So daring and sweet his thought.
This other man I had dreamed
A drunken, vainglorious lout.[5]
He had done most bitter wrong
To some who are near my heart,

---

1   *That woman's ... shrill* Countess Markiewicz, née Constance Gore-Booth (1868–
     1927), played a central role in the Easter Rebellion; she was arrested and sentenced to
     death (though the death sentence was later commuted). Yeats later wrote a poem about
     her and her Irish-nationalist sister, "In Memory of Eva Gore-Booth and Con Markie-
     wicz" (1929).

2   *rode to harriers* Went hunting with hounds.

3   *This man ... wingèd horse* Pádraic Pearse (1879–1916) founded St. Enda's School near
     Dublin. He was a leader in the effort to revive the Gaelic language, and wrote both Irish
     and English poetry; *wingèd horse* Refers to Pegasus, the horse of the Muses.

4   *This other his helper and friend* Thomas MacDonagh (1878–1916), an Irish poet and
     playwright who also taught school.

5   *vainglorious lout* Major John MacBride (1865–1916), estranged husband of Irish na-
     tionalist Maud Gonne; their separation just two years after marriage was due in part to
     his drinking bouts.

Yet I number him in the song;   35
He, too, has resigned his part
In the casual comedy;
He, too, has been changed in his turn,
Transformed utterly:
A terrible beauty is born.   40

Hearts with one purpose alone
Through summer and winter seem
Enchanted to a stone
To trouble the living stream.
The horse that comes from the road,   45
The rider, the birds that range
From cloud to tumbling cloud,
Minute by minute they change;
A shadow of cloud on the stream
Changes minute by minute;   50
A horse-hoof slides on the brim,
And a horse plashes within it;
The long-legged moor-hens dive,
And hens to moor-cocks call;
Minute by minute they live: 55
The stone's in the midst of all.

Too long a sacrifice
Can make a stone of the heart.
O when may it suffice?
That is Heaven's part, our part   60
To murmur name upon name,
As a mother names her child
When sleep at last has come
On limbs that had run wild.
What is it but nightfall?   65
No, no, not night but death;
Was it needless death after all?
For England may keep faith
For all that is done and said.[1]
We know their dream; enough   70
To know they dreamed and are dead;

---

1   *For England ... said* England had originally granted Ireland Home Rule in 1913, but
     then postponed it due to World War I, promising to institute it after the war.

And what if excess of love
Bewildered them till they died?
I write it out in a verse—
75 MacDonagh and MacBride
And Connolly and Pearse[1]
Now and in time to be,
Wherever green is worn,
Are changed, changed utterly:
80 A terrible beauty is born.

—1916

The Second Coming[2]

Turning and turning in the widening gyre[3]
The falcon cannot hear the falconer;
Things fall apart; the centre cannot hold;
Mere anarchy is loosed upon the world,
5   The blood-dimmed tide is loosed, and everywhere
The ceremony of innocence is drowned;
The best lack all conviction, while the worst
Are full of passionate intensity.

Surely some revelation is at hand;
10 Surely the Second Coming is at hand.
The Second Coming! Hardly are those words out
When a vast image out of *Spiritus Mundi*[4]
Troubles my sight: somewhere in sands of the desert
A shape with lion body and the head of a man,[5]
15 A gaze blank and pitiless as the sun,
Is moving its slow thighs, while all about it
Reel shadows of the indignant desert birds.
The darkness drops again; but now I know
That twenty centuries of stony sleep

---

1   *Connolly* James Connolly (1868–1916), Irish socialist; *MacDonagh ... Pearse* All four
    men were executed for their involvement in the Easter Rebellion of 1916.
2   *The Second Coming* The return of Christ, as predicted in the New Testament. See Reve-
    lation 1.7: "Behold, he cometh with clouds; and every eye shall see him."
3   *gyre* Spiral formed from concentric circles.
4   *Spiritus Mundi* Latin: Spirit of the World; universal spirit that houses the images of
    civilization's past memories and provides divine inspiration for the poet. The human
    race is a connected whole in the *spiritus mundi*.
5   *shape ... man* The Egyptian Sphinx.

Were vexed to nightmare by a rocking cradle,[1]   20
And what rough beast, its hour come round at last,
Slouches towards Bethlehem to be born?

—1920

Leda and the Swan[2]

A sudden blow: the great wings beating still
Above the staggering girl, her thighs caressed
By the dark webs, her nape caught in his bill,
He holds her helpless breast upon his breast.

How can those terrified vague fingers push   5
The feathered glory from her loosening thighs?
And how can body, laid in that white rush,
But feel the strange heart beating where it lies?

A shudder in the loins engenders there
The broken wall, the burning roof and tower   10
And Agamemnon dead.[3]
                                        Being so caught up,
So mastered by the brute blood of the air,
Did she put on his knowledge with his power
Before the indifferent beak could let her drop?   15

—1924

Sailing to Byzantium[4]

1

That is no country for old men. The young
In one another's arms, birds in the trees

---

1 *rocking cradle* Cradle of the Christ Child.
2 *Leda and the Swan* In Greek mythology, Leda was visited by Zeus in the form of a swan, who in some versions of the story seduced her and in other versions raped her. From this union she bore two eggs, one becoming the twins Castor and Pollux, the other Helen (whose abduction later initiated the Trojan War).
3 *broken wall ... Agamemnon dead* Events of the Trojan War.
4 *Byzantium* Ancient city eventually renamed Constantinople (now Istanbul), capital of the Eastern Roman Empire. In *A Vision*, Yeats envisioned Byzantium as a centre for artists: "The painter, the mosaic worker, the worker in gold and silver, the illuminator of sacred books were almost impersonal, almost perhaps without the consciousness of individual design, absorbed in their subject matter and that the vision of a whole people."

—Those dying generations—at their song,
The salmon-falls, the mackerel-crowded seas,
5 Fish, flesh, or fowl, commend all summer long
Whatever is begotten, born, and dies.
Caught in that sensual music all neglect
Monuments of unageing intellect.

2

An aged man is but a paltry thing,
10 A tattered coat upon a stick, unless
Soul clap its hands and sing, and louder sing
For every tatter in its mortal dress,
Nor is there singing school but studying
Monuments of its own magnificence;
15 And therefore I have sailed the seas and come
To the holy city of Byzantium.

3\

O sages standing in God's holy fire
As in the gold mosaic of a wall,
Come from the holy fire, perne in a gyre,[1]
20 And be the singing-masters of my soul.
Consume my heart away; sick with desire
And fastened to a dying animal
It knows not what it is; and gather me
Into the artifice of eternity.

4

25 Once out of nature I shall never take
My bodily form from any natural thing,
But such a form as Grecian goldsmiths make
Of hammered gold and gold enamelling
To keep a drowsy Emperor awake;
30 Or set upon a golden bough to sing[2]
To lords and ladies of Byzantium
Of what is past, or passing, or to come.

—1927

---

1   *perne in a gyre* Rotate in a spiral; the literal definition of "perne" is "bobbin."
2   [Yeats's note] I have read somewhere that in the Emperor's palace at Byzantium was a tree made of gold and silver, and artificial birds that sang.

Paul Laurence Dunbar
1872–1906

Born in Dayton, Ohio, to parents who had both been slaves in the American South, Paul Laurence Dunbar is considered the first African American poet to have been read widely in both white and African American communities. His second book of poetry, *Majors and Minors* (1896), brought him to national attention, particularly because of that collection's "minors," poems composed in African American dialect. (The "majors" were more traditional poems influenced by the Romantic tradition and by Dunbar's contemporaries.) Though Dunbar's traditional poetic works were more numerous, it was the dialect poems that caught the public's imagination—to a degree that troubled both Dunbar and some of his critics.

Though known primarily as a poet, Dunbar worked in a wide variety of genres. In addition to poetry, he founded a newspaper and wrote short stories, novels, song lyrics, a libretto for an operetta, and the lyrics to the first all-black musical on Broadway, *In Dahomey* (1902). Gavin Jones has characterized Dunbar as "a wily manipulator of the conventions, a subtle overturner of racist stereotypes, a sensitive renderer of the multiple facets of Black consciousness at the turn of the twentieth century."

We Wear the Mask

We wear the mask that grins and lies,
It hides our cheeks and shades our eyes,—
This debt we pay to human guile;
With torn and bleeding hearts we smile,
And mouth with myriad subtleties.   5

Why should the world be over-wise,
In counting all our tears and sighs?
Nay, let them only see us, while
    We wear the mask.

We smile, but, O great Christ, our cries   10
To thee from tortured souls arise.
We sing, but oh the clay is vile
Beneath our feet, and long the mile;
But let the world dream otherwise,
    We wear the mask!   15

—1895

Robert Frost
1874–1963

Though Robert Frost's career spanned the modernist period and displays modernist influences, his work is not so easily categorized. Unlike many of his contemporaries, Frost insisted on observing rules of traditional verse—he relied on regular metre and rhyme in crafting his work—and famously said that "writing free verse is like playing tennis with the net down." A merging of traditional form with colloquial speech is the hallmark of Frost's style.

Born in San Francisco in 1874, Frost moved to New England at the age of 11. He began writing poetry while still in high school; he attended both Dartmouth College and Harvard University but never completed a degree. In 1912, Frost and his family relocated to England, a move that would prove to be a turning point in his career. While in London, he published *A Boy's Will* (1913) and *North of Boston* (1914), two full-length collections that earned Frost critical acclaim and attracted the attention of well-known poets such as Ezra Pound. By the time of Frost's return to the United States in 1915, he was established as a serious poet. Over the following decades, his reputation would grow even further with the publication of four Pulitzer Prize-winning collections: *New Hampshire: A Poem with Notes and Grace Notes* (1924), *Collected Poems* (1931), *A Further Range* (1937), and *A Witness Tree* (1943).

When Frost died in 1963, President John F. Kennedy said that the poet's death left "a vacancy in the American spirit." His epitaph reads: "I Had A Lover's Quarrel With The World."

The Road Not Taken

Two roads diverged in a yellow wood,
And sorry I could not travel both
And be one traveller, long I stood
And looked down one as far as I could
5 To where it bent in the undergrowth;

Then took the other, as just as fair,
And having perhaps the better claim,
Because it was grassy and wanted wear;
Though as for that, the passing there
10 Had worn them really about the same,

And both that morning equally lay
In leaves no step had trodden black.
Oh, I kept the first for another day!
Yet knowing how way leads on to way,
I doubted if I should ever come back.   15

I shall be telling this with a sigh
Somewhere ages and ages hence:
Two roads diverged in a wood, and I—
I took the one less travelled by,
And that has made all the difference.   20

—1916

Stopping by Woods on a Snowy Evening

Whose woods these are I think I know.
His house is in the village, though;
He will not see me stopping here
To watch his woods fill up with snow.

My little horse must think it queer   5
To stop without a farmhouse near
Between the woods and frozen lake
The darkest evening of the year.

He gives his harness bells a shake
To ask if there is some mistake.   10
The only other sound's the sweep
Of easy wind and downy flake.

The woods are lovely, dark, and deep,
But I have promises to keep,
And miles to go before I sleep,   15
And miles to go before I sleep.

—1923

Design

I found a dimpled spider, fat and white,
On a white heal-all,[1] holding up a moth
Like a white piece of rigid satin cloth—
Assorted characters of death and blight
5 Mixed ready to begin the morning right,
Like the ingredients of a witches' broth—
A snow-drop spider, a flower like a froth,
And dead wings carried like a paper kite.

What had that flower to do with being white,
10 The wayside blue and innocent heal-all?
What brought the kindred spider to that height,
Then steered the white moth thither in the night?
What but design of darkness to appall?—
If design govern in a thing so small.

—1936

---

1   *heal-all* Wildflower that is usually purple or blue; completely white ones are rare.

Wallace Stevens

1879–1955

"Life," Wallace Stevens wrote, "consists of propositions about life." His work reflects this idea insofar as it examines the relationship between the human understanding of reality—an ever-shifting product of perception and imagination—and reality itself. Although he was strongly influenced by Romanticism's emphases on nature and poetic imagination, Stevens was modernist in his concern with the role of poetry in the spiritually disillusioned world of the twentieth century.

Stevens was born in Pennsylvania and attended Harvard, where he edited the *Harvard Monthly* but left before completing a degree. After a brief and unsatisfying period as a journalist, Stevens became a lawyer. He would spend the rest of his life working in insurance firms, eventually becoming vice president of the Hartford Accident and Indemnity Company. But he also continued to write, and in his thirties he began to publish plays and some of the individual poems that would appear in his first collection, *Harmonium* (1923).

Harmonium contains some of what would become Stevens's best-known work, though its initial critical reception was lukewarm. With later volumes such as *Ideas of Order* (1935) and *The Man with the Blue Guitar* (1937), he attracted more attention, but some critics found his work too abstract and difficult, and he was disparaged for not engaging directly with the political concerns of his time. Stevens received much more profound and favourable recognition, however, toward the end of his career, when he won two National Book Awards: one for *The Auroras of Autumn* (1951), and another for his *Collected Poems* (1954), which was also awarded the Pulitzer Prize.

Thirteen Ways of Looking at a Blackbird

I

Among twenty snowy mountains,
The only moving thing
Was the eye of the blackbird.

II

I was of three minds,
Like a tree   5
In which there are three blackbirds.

III

The blackbird whirled in the autumn winds.
It was a small part of the pantomime.

IV

A man and a woman
10 Are one.
A man and a woman and a blackbird
Are one.

V

I do not know which to prefer,
The beauty of inflections
15 Or the beauty of innuendoes,
The blackbird whistling
Or just after.

VI

Icicles filled the long window
With barbaric glass.
20 The shadow of the blackbird
Crossed it, to and fro.
The mood
Traced in the shadow
An indecipherable cause.

VII

25 O thin men of Haddam,[1]
Why do you imagine golden birds?
Do you not see how the blackbird
Walks around the feet
Of the women about you?

VIII

30 I know noble accents
And lucid, inescapable rhythms;
But I know, too,
That the blackbird is involved
In what I know.

---

1   *Haddam* Town in Connecticut.

IX

When the blackbird flew out of sight,   35
It marked the edge
Of one of many circles.

X

At the sight of blackbirds
Flying in a green light,
Even the bawds° of euphony°   *brothel operators / pleasant sound*   40
Would cry out sharply.

XI

He rode over Connecticut
In a glass coach.
Once, a fear pierced him,
In that he mistook   45
The shadow of his equipage[1]
For blackbirds.

XII

The river is moving.
The blackbird must be flying.

XIII

It was evening all afternoon.   50
It was snowing
And it was going to snow.
The blackbird sat
In the cedar-limbs.

—1917

---

1   *equipage* Horses and carriage.

Anecdote of the Jar

I placed a jar in Tennessee,
And round it was, upon a hill.
It made the slovenly wilderness
Surround that hill.

5 The wilderness rose up to it,
And sprawled around, no longer wild.
The jar was round upon the ground
And tall and of a port in air.

It took dominion everywhere.
10 The jar was grey and bare.
It did not give of bird or bush,
Like nothing else in Tennessee.

—1917

William Carlos Williams
1883–1963

A major poet of the twentieth century, William Carlos Williams was also a working medical doctor who spent most of his life in his birthplace, Rutherford, New Jersey. As a poet, his primary allegiance was to American culture, and he strove to capture quintessentially American ideas and experiences in colloquial language: "not the speech of English country people ... but language modified by ... the American environment." Although he is most remembered for his poetry, it comprised only half of his more than 40 published works, which also included critical prose, short stories, novels, plays, and letters.

Of Williams's many friends in the artistic and literary avant-gardes of New York and Europe, the most significant to his career was undoubtedly fellow poet Ezra Pound, a leader in the imagist movement in which Williams became a major participant. Williams's early style was profoundly shaped by imagism's quest to capture impressions through precise, concentrated language, and this influence remains in the direct and unornamented spirit of his later work. However, he also continued to evolve as a poet, experimenting with form and idiom throughout his career.

Perhaps because of his work's deceptively easy style, critics did not begin to count Williams among the best poets of his era until the last decades of his life. The rise of his reputation began with the publication of the first book of *Paterson* (1946–63), a long poem that explores the city of Paterson (near Rutherford) from diverse angles, in both poetry and prose. Despite failing health, Williams continued writing until his death in 1963, and was posthumously awarded the Pulitzer Prize for his final collection, *Pictures from Brueghel and Other Poems* (1962).

The Red Wheelbarrow

so much depends
upon

a red wheel
barrow

glazed with rain   5
water

beside the white
chickens

—1923

Spring and All

By the road to the contagious hospital
under the surge of the blue
mottled clouds driven from the
northeast—a cold wind. Beyond, the
5 waste of broad, muddy fields
brown with dried weeds, standing and fallen

patches of standing water
the scattering of tall trees

All along the road the reddish
10 purplish, forked, upstanding, twiggy
stuff of bushes and small trees
with dead, brown leaves under them
leafless vines—

Lifeless in appearance, sluggish
15 dazed spring approaches—

They enter the new world naked,
cold, uncertain of all
save that they enter. All about them
the cold, familiar wind—

20 Now the grass, tomorrow
the stiff curl of wildcarrot leaf

One by one objects are defined—
It quickens: clarity, outline of leaf

But now the stark dignity of
25 entrance—Still, the profound change
has come upon them: rooted they
grip down and begin to awaken

—1923

This Is Just to Say

I have eaten
the plums
that were in
the icebox

and which   5
you were probably
saving
for breakfast

Forgive me
they were delicious   10
so sweet
and so cold   —1934

Landscape with the Fall of Icarus[1]

According to Brueghel
when Icarus fell
it was spring

a farmer was ploughing
his field   5
the whole pageantry

of the year was
awake tingling
near

the edge of the sea   10
concerned
with itself

sweating in the sun
that melted
the wings' wax   15

unsignificantly
off the coast
there was

a splash quite unnoticed
this was   20
Icarus drowning
                                                —1962

---

1   *Landscape ... of Icarus* Painting (c. 1555) by Pieter Brueghel the Elder based on an ancient Greek story. Wearing wings made by his father Daedalus, Icarus flew too close to the
sun; the wax on the wings melted, and Icarus fell to his death. In Brueghel's painting, an
ordinary farmer ploughing on a hill dominates the foreground, while Icarus's drowning
body appears very small in the ocean below, next to a much larger ship.

Ezra Pound
1885–1972

A modernist poet, editor, and critic, Ezra Pound promoted novelty and formal experimentation in poetry, contributing to the rise of free verse and strongly influencing the development of the twentieth-century literary avant-garde. Pound's early views were unequivocal: "no good poetry is ever written in a manner twenty years old, for to write in such a manner shows conclusively that the writer thinks from books, convention and cliché, and not from life."

Born in Indiana, in 1908 Pound moved to Europe, where he became the centre of a literary circle that included established writers such as W.B. Yeats, as well as talented new writers such as T.S. Eliot and James Joyce, whose work Pound promoted. His first collection of poetry, *Personae* (1909), a mix of traditional and newer forms of expression, was well-received by critics; his next books, however, lost critical favour due to their non-traditional nature.

In 1924 Pound moved to Italy, where he became involved in fascist politics and, during World War II, broadcast fascist and anti-Semitic propaganda for the Italian government. During the American occupation of Italy, he was arrested for treason and imprisoned in a US military camp, where he suffered a mental breakdown; declared unfit for trial, he spent the following decade in an American psychiatric hospital. Despite the controversy surrounding his politics, Pound was awarded the Bollingen Prize in 1948 for his *Pisan Cantos* (1924–48), a self-contained section of his major work, the unfinished long poem *The Cantos* (1917–69).

Pound was a leading force behind the poetic movement known as imagism. Partly drawn from tenets of classical Chinese and Japanese poetry—of which Pound was a translator—imagism departs from the elaborate style and regular metre of Victorian poetry, instead advocating the clear, precise, and economical use of language for what Pound called "the direct treatment of the 'thing'."

The River-Merchant's Wife: A Letter[1]

While my hair was still cut straight across my forehead
I played about the front gate, pulling flowers.
You came by on bamboo stilts, playing horse,
You walked about my seat, playing with blue plums.
5 And we went on living in the village of Chōkan:[2]
Two small people, without dislike or suspicion.

---

1   *The River-Merchant's ... Letter* Pound's adaptation of a poem by the Chinese poet Li Po (701–62 CE), whose name is given in its Japanese form ("Rihaku") at the end of the poem.
2   *Chōkan* Suburb of Nanking.

At fourteen I married My Lord you.
I never laughed, being bashful.
Lowering my head, I looked at the wall.
Called to, a thousand times, I never looked back.   10

At fifteen I stopped scowling,
I desired my dust to be mingled with yours
Forever and forever and forever.
Why should I climb the look out?

At sixteen you departed,   15
You went into far Ku-tō-en,[1] by the river of swirling eddies,
And you have been gone five months.
The monkeys make sorrowful noise overhead.

You dragged your feet when you went out.
By the gate now, the moss is grown, the different mosses,   20
Too deep to clear them away!
The leaves fall early this autumn, in wind.
The paired butterflies are already yellow with August
Over the grass in the West garden;
They hurt me. I grow older.   25
If you are coming down through the narrows of the river Kiang,
Please let me know beforehand,
And I will come out to meet you
          As far as Chō-fū-Sa.[2]

                                                        Rihaku
                                                        —1915

In a Station of the Metro

The apparition of these faces in the crowd;
Petals on a wet, black bough.
                              —1916 (earlier version published 1913)

---

1   *Ku-tō-en* Chang Jiang, a Chinese river, also called the Yangtze Kiang in Japanese.
2   *Chō-fū-Sa* Chang-feng Sha, a beach located in Anhui several hundred miles upriver.

Marianne Moore
1887–1972

Born in Kirkwood, Missouri, Marianne Moore was raised by her mother in the home of her grandfather, a Presbyterian pastor. Her family moved to Pennsylvania, where she received her BA from Bryn Mawr College and subsequently became a teacher at a boarding school for Native American children. In 1918, she moved with her mother to New York City, where she was soon noticed in literary circles. Some of her work was published in the journal *Dial*, which she eventually edited from 1925 until 1929.

Moore is known for poems grounded in the observation of nature, and for her deft experimentation with form and metre. She is also famous for revising her work long after publication; for instance, "Poetry," 29 lines long in 1921, is reduced to three lines in the final version published in 1967. Moore's revisions have not always been well-received, but her modest attitude toward writing suggests her rationale for revisiting works: "I'm a happy hack as a writer.... I never knew anyone with a passion for words who had as much difficulty in saying things as I do. I seldom say them in a manner I like."

Moore's *Collected Poems* (1951) was awarded the National Book Award, the Pulitzer Prize, and the Bollingen Prize. The poet James Dickey has written in praise of her style that "every poem of hers lifts us towards our own discovery-prone lives. It does not state, in effect, that I am more intelligent than you, more creative because I found this item and used it and you didn't. It seems to say, rather, I found this, and what did you find? Or, a better, what can you find?"

Poetry

I, too, dislike it: there are things that are important beyond all this fiddle.
    Reading it, however, with a perfect contempt for it, one discovers in
    it after all, a place for the genuine.
        Hands that can grasp, eyes
5   that can dilate, hair that can rise
            if it must, these things are important not because a

high-sounding interpretation can be put upon them but because they are
    useful. When they become so derivative as to become unintelligible,
    the same thing may be said for all of us, that we
10   do not admire what
        we cannot understand: the bat
            holding on upside down or in quest of something to

eat, elephants pushing, a wild horse taking a roll, a tireless wolf under
   a tree, the immovable critic twitching his skin like a horse that feels
      a flea, the base-
   ball fan, the statistician—   15
      nor is it valid
         to discriminate against "business documents and

schoolbooks":[1] all these phenomena are important. One must make
   a distinction
   however: when dragged into prominence by half poets, the result
      is not poetry,
   nor till the poets among us can be   20
      "literalists of
      the imagination"[2]—above
         insolence and triviality and can present

for inspection, "imaginary gardens with real toads in them,"[3] shall we have
   it. In the meantime, if you demand on the one hand,   25
   the raw material of poetry in
      all its rawness and
      that which is on the other hand
         genuine, then you are interested in poetry.

                                                    —1921

Poetry (Revised version)

I, too, dislike it.
   Reading it, however, with a perfect contempt for it, one discovers in
   it, after all, a place for the genuine.

                                                    —1967

---

1   *business documents and schoolbooks* Moore's note quotes from the *Diaries of Tolstoy* (1917),
    in which Tolstoy considers the boundary between poetry and prose: "Poetry is verse:
    prose is not verse. Or else poetry is everything with the exception of business documents
    and schoolbooks."
2   *literalists of the imagination* In *Ideas of Good and Evil* (1903), W.B. Yeats calls William
    Blake "a too literal realist of imagination as others are of nature."
3   *imaginary gardens ... in them* No source has been found for this phrase; despite the quo-
    tation marks, it is generally thought to be Moore's.

T.S. Eliot
1888–1965

No twentieth-century writer did more to shape the direction of modern poetry and criticism than T.S. Eliot. In poems such as "The Love Song of J. Alfred Prufrock" (1915) and *The Waste Land* (1922), Eliot founded a radical new poetical idiom to express the alienation and the "chaotic, irregular, fragmentary" experience of the modern mind, which he considered disconnected from any meaningful sense of tradition. Eliot's many essays and reviews, notably "'Tradition and the Individual Talent" (1919) and "The Metaphysical Poets" (1921), were scarcely less influential. Such writings not only provided a theoretical foundation for New Criticism, one of the most prominent critical schools of the early to mid-twentieth century; they also introduced new terms and concepts—"objective correlative," "the dissociation of sensibility," the ideal development of the poet as a "continual extinction of personality"—that have enriched the study of modern literature, not least by illuminating Eliot's own complex poetics.

Eliot's poetry is challenging, but in his reckoning it could hardly be otherwise, for he believed that "poets in our civilization, as it exists at present, must be *difficult*. Our civilization comprehends great variety and complexity, and this variety and complexity, playing upon a refined sensibility, must produce various and complex results." Among the most striking of these results is the absence—particularly in his early poetry—of fluid transitions: images are precise but often jarring and incongruous, arrestingly juxtaposed to suggest broader patterns of meaning. At once colloquial and erudite, fragmentary and unified, much of Eliot's poetry relies on ironies, tensions, and paradoxes. These qualities are ideally suited to the rigorous methodology of close reading championed by the New Critics, who focused not on the mind of the poet or the external conditions of the text's creation but on the details of the text itself.

Eliot's thought and technique evolved over his career, particularly following his conversion to Anglo-Catholicism, when—as in "Journey of the Magi" (1927) and *Four Quartets* (1943)—he began to explore more religious themes. Although his poetic output was relatively modest, his body of work occupies the very centre of literary modernism. As Northrop Frye remarked, "a thorough knowledge of Eliot is compulsory for anyone interested in contemporary literature. Whether he is liked or disliked is of no importance, but he must be read."

The Love Song of J. Alfred Prufrock[1]

S'io credesse che mia risposta fosse
A persona che mai tornasse al mondo,
Questa fiamma staria senza piu scosse.
Ma perciocche giammai di questo fondo
Non torno viva alcun, s'i'odo il vero,   5
Senza tema d'infamia ti rispondo.[2]

Let us go then, you and I,
When the evening is spread out against the sky
Like a patient etherized upon a table;
Let us go, through certain half-deserted streets,   10
The muttering retreats
Of restless nights in one-night cheap hotels
And sawdust restaurants with oyster-shells:
Streets that follow like a tedious argument
Of insidious intent   15
To lead you to an overwhelming question …
Oh, do not ask, "What is it?"
Let us go and make our visit.

In the room the women come and go
Talking of Michelangelo.   20

The yellow fog that rubs its back upon the window-panes,
The yellow smoke that rubs its muzzle on the window-panes
Licked its tongue into the corners of the evening,
Lingered upon the pools that stand in drains,
Let fall upon its back the soot that falls from chimneys,   25
Slipped by the terrace, made a sudden leap,
And seeing that it was a soft October night,
Curled once about the house, and fell asleep.

And indeed there will be time
For the yellow smoke that slides along the street,   30

---

1   *J. Alfred Prufrock* The name is likely taken from the The Prufrock-Littau Company, a
     furniture dealer located in St. Louis, Eliot's birthplace.
2   *S'io credesse … ti rispondo* Italian: "If I thought that my reply were given to anyone who
     might return to the world, this flame would stand forever still; but since never from this
     deep place has anyone ever returned alive, if what I hear is true, without fear of infamy
     I answer thee," Dante's *Inferno* 27.61–66; Guido da Montefeltro's speech as he burns in
     Hell.

Rubbing its back upon the window panes;
There will be time, there will be time[1]
To prepare a face to meet the faces that you meet
There will be time to murder and create,
35 And time for all the works and days[2] of hands
That lift and drop a question on your plate;
Time for you and time for me,
And time yet for a hundred indecisions,
And for a hundred visions and revisions,
40 Before the taking of a toast and tea.

In the room the women come and go
Talking of Michelangelo.

And indeed there will be time
To wonder, "Do I dare?" and, "Do I dare?"
45 Time to turn back and descend the stair,
With a bald spot in the middle of my hair—
(They will say: "How his hair is growing thin!")
My morning coat,[3] my collar mounting firmly to the chin,
My necktie rich and modest, but asserted by a simple pin—
50 (They will say: "But how his arms and legs are thin!")
Do I dare
Disturb the universe?
In a minute there is time
For decisions and revisions which a minute will reverse.

55 For I have known them all already, known them all—
Have known the evenings, mornings, afternoons,
I have measured out my life with coffee spoons;
I know the voices dying with a dying fall[4]
Beneath the music from a farther room.
60   So how should I presume?

And I have known the eyes already, known them all—
The eyes that fix you in a formulated phrase,

---

1   *there will be time* See Ecclesiastes 3.1–8. "To everything there is a season, and a time to
    every purpose under heaven: A time to be born, and a time to die; a time to plant, and
    a time to pluck up that which is planted; a time to kill, and a time to heal...."
2   *works and days* Title of a poem by eighth-century BCE Greek poet Hesiod.
3   *morning coat* Formal coat with tails.
4   *with a dying fall* In Shakespeare's *Twelfth Night* 1.1.1–15 Duke Orsino commands,
    "That strain again, it had a dying fall."

And when I am formulated, sprawling on a pin,
When I am pinned and wriggling on the wall,
Then how should I begin   65
To spit out all the butt-ends of my days and ways?
    And how should I presume?

And I have known the arms already, known them all—
Arms that are braceleted and white and bare
(But in the lamplight, downed with light brown hair!)   70
Is it perfume from a dress
That makes me so digress?
Arms that lie along a table, or wrap about a shawl.
    And should I then presume?
    And how should I begin?   75

    *   *   *

Shall I say, I have gone at dusk through narrow streets
And watched the smoke that rises from the pipes
Of lonely men in shirt-sleeves, leaning out of windows? ...[1]

I should have been a pair of ragged claws
Scuttling across the floors of silent seas.[2]   80

    *   *   *

And the afternoon, the evening, sleeps so peacefully!
Smoothed by long fingers,
Asleep ... tired ... or it malingers,
Stretched on the floor, here beside you and me.
Should I, after tea and cakes and ices,   85
Have the strength to force the moment to its crisis?
But though I have wept and fasted, wept and prayed,
Though I have seen my head (grown slightly bald) brought in
    upon a platter,[3]
I am no prophet[4]—and here's no great matter;

---

1   ... The ellipsis here makes note of a 38 line insertion written by Eliot, entitled *Pru-frock's Pervigilium*. The subtitle and 33 of the lines were later removed.

2   *I should ... seas* See Shakespeare's *Hamlet* 2.2, in which Hamlet tells Polonius, "for you yourself, sir, should be old as I am, if like a crab you could go backwards."

3   *brought in upon a platter* Reference to Matthew 14.1–12, in which the prophet John the Baptist is beheaded at the command of Herod, and his head presented to Salomé upon a platter.

4   *I am no prophet* See Amos 7.14. When commanded by King Amiziah not to proph-esize, the Judean Amos answered; "I was no prophet, neither was I a prophet's son; but I was a herdsman, and a farmer of sycamore fruit."

90 I have seen the moment of my greatness flicker,
   And I have seen the eternal Footman hold my coat, and snicker,
   And in short, I was afraid.

   And would it have been worth it, after all,
   After the cups, the marmalade, the tea,
95 Among the porcelain, among some talk of you and me,
   Would it have been worth while,
   To have bitten off the matter with a smile,
   To have squeezed the universe into a ball[1]
   To roll it toward some overwhelming question,
100 To say: "I am Lazarus,[2] come from the dead,
   Come back to tell you all, I shall tell you all"—
   If one, settling a pillow by her head,
       Should say: "That is not what I meant at all;
       That is not it, at all."

105 And would it have been worth it, after all,
   Would it have been worth while,
   After the sunsets and the dooryards and the sprinkled streets,[3]
   After the novels, after the teacups, after the skirts that trail along
       the floor—
   And this, and so much more?—
110 It is impossible to say just what I mean!
   But as if a magic lantern[4] threw the nerves in patterns on a screen:
   Would it have been worth while
   If one, settling a pillow or throwing off a shawl,
   And turning toward the window, should say:
115   "That is not it at all,
       That is not what I meant, at all."
               *   *   *

   No! I am not Prince Hamlet, nor was meant to be;
   Am an attendant lord, one that will do
   To swell a progress,[5] start a scene or two,
120 Advise the prince; no doubt, an easy tool,

---

1   *squeezed ... ball* See Andrew Marvell's "To His Coy Mistress," 41–42: "Let us roll our
    strength and all / Our sweetness up into one ball."
2   *Lazarus* Raised from the dead by Jesus in John 11.1–44.
3   *sprinkled streets* Streets sprayed with water to keep dust down.
4   *magic lantern* In Victorian times, a device used to project images painted on glass onto
    a blank screen or wall.
5   *progress* Journey made by royalty through the country.

Deferential, glad to be of use,
Politic, cautious, and meticulous;
Full of high sentence,[1] but a bit obtuse;
At times, indeed, almost ridiculous—
Almost, at times, the Fool.   125

I grow old ... I grow old ...
I shall wear the bottoms of my trousers rolled.

Shall I part my hair behind? Do I dare to eat a peach?
I shall wear white flannel trousers, and walk upon the beach.
I have heard the mermaids singing,[2] each to each.   130

I do not think that they will sing to me.

I have seen them riding seaward on the waves
Combing the white hair of the waves blown back
When the wind blows the water white and black.

We have lingered in the chambers of the sea   135
By sea-girls wreathed with seaweed red and brown
Till human voices wake us, and we drown.

—1915, 1917

Journey of the Magi[3]

"A cold coming we had of it,
Just the worst time of the year
For a journey, and such a long journey:
The ways deep and the weather sharp,
The very dead of winter."[4]   5
And the camels galled, sore-footed, refractory,
Lying down in the melting snow.
There were times we regretted
The summer palaces on slopes, the terraces,
And the silken girls bringing sherbet.   10

---

1   *high sentence* Serious, elevated sentiments or opinions.
2   *I have ... singing* See John Donne's "Song": "Teach me to hear the mermaids singing."
3   *Magi* Three wise men who journeyed to Bethlehem to honour Jesus at his birth (see Matthew 2.1–12).
4   *A cold ... winter* Adapted from a sermon given by Anglican preacher Lancelot Andrews on Christmas Day, 1622.

Then the camel men cursing and grumbling
And running away, and wanting their liquor and women,
And the night-fires going out, and the lack of shelters,
And the cities hostile and the towns unfriendly
15 And the villages dirty and charging high prices:
A hard time we had of it.
At the end we preferred to travel all night,
Sleeping in snatches,
With the voices singing in our ears, saying
20 That this was all folly.

Then at dawn we came down to a temperate valley,
Wet, below the snow line, smelling of vegetation;
With a running stream and a water-mill beating the darkness,
And three trees[1] on the low sky,
25 And an old white horse[2] galloped away in the meadow.
Then we came to a tavern with vine-leaves over the lintel,°   *doorframe*
Six hands at an open door dicing for pieces of silver,[3]
And feet kicking the empty wine-skins.
But there was no information, and so we continued
30 And arrived at evening, not a moment too soon
Finding the place; it was (you may say) satisfactory.

All this was a long time ago, I remember,
And I would do it again, but set down
This set down
35 This: were we led all that way for
Birth or Death? There was a Birth, certainly,
We had evidence and no doubt. I had seen birth and death,
But had thought they were different; this Birth was
Hard and bitter agony for us, like Death, our death.
40 We returned to our places, these Kingdoms,
But no longer at ease here, in the old dispensation,
With an alien people clutching their gods.
I should be glad of another death.

—1927

---

1   *three trees* Suggests the three crosses on Calvary, on which Christ and two criminals
    were crucified (see Luke 23.32–43).
2   *white horse* Ridden by Christ in Revelation 6.2 and 19.11–14.
3   *dicing … silver* Allusion to Judas's betrayal of Jesus for 30 pieces of silver, and to the
    soldiers who played dice for the robes of Christ at his crucifixion (Matthew 26.14 and
    27.35).

Edna St. Vincent Millay

1892–1950

Edna St. Vincent Millay wrote the iconic line "My candle burns at both ends" in her poem "First Fig" (1920)—a poem that inspired the imaginations of an emerging generation of sexually liberated American women. This American poet and playwright embodied the spirit of romantic rebellion characteristic of the 1920s and, throughout her career, remained a powerful presence in American public consciousness.

Millay demonstrated a talent for writing poetry at an early age, her first published poem appearing in a children's magazine when she was 14. Following her graduation from Vassar College, Millay published her first book, *Renascence and Other Poems* (1917), and moved to Greenwich Village in New York. Over the next few years her growing reputation as a poet was matched by her reputation as a freethinker in the realm of sexual politics. Two of her most significant verse collections date from this period: *A Few Figs from Thistles* (1920) and *The Harp-Weaver and Other Poems* (1923), which won the Pulitzer Prize for poetry.

Although Millay's fame was earned primarily during the early years of her career, she remained active and innovative well into the 1940s, and her work became more politically and emotionally intense. The 52 sonnets in her collection *Fatal Interview* (1931) were widely admired for their mastery of the form; the sequence draws on centuries of poetic tradition, but was reviewed as expressing "the thoughts of a new age."

[I, being born a woman and distressed]

I, being born a woman and distressed
By all the needs and notions of my kind,
Am urged by your propinquity° to find   *proximity*
Your person fair, and feel a certain zest
To bear your body's weight upon my breast: 5
So subtly is the fume of life designed,
To clarify the pulse and cloud the mind,
And leave me once again undone, possessed.
Think not for this, however, the poor treason
Of my stout blood against my staggering brain,   10
I shall remember you with love, or season
My scorn with pity,—let me make it plain:
I find this frenzy insufficient reason
For conversation when we meet again.

—1923

[What lips my lips have kissed, and where, and why]

What lips my lips have kissed, and where, and why,
I have forgotten, and what arms have lain
Under my head till morning; but the rain
Is full of ghosts tonight, that tap and sigh
5   Upon the glass and listen for reply,
And in my heart there stirs a quiet pain
For unremembered lads that not again
Will turn to me at midnight with a cry.
Thus in winter stands the lonely tree,
10   Nor knows what birds have vanished one by one,
Yet knows its boughs more silent than before:
I cannot say what loves have come and gone;
I only know that summer sang in me
A little while, that in me sings no more.

—1923

Wilfred Owen
1893–1918

One of 16 World War I poets commemorated in Westminster Abbey's Poet's Corner, Wilfred Owen is best remembered for poems such as "Anthem for Doomed Youth" and "Dulce et Decorum Est" (1920), in which he offers searing indictments of those who would send young men to war.

Owen began to experiment with poetry as a teenager. He spent the years prior to the war working as a lay assistant to the vicar of Dunsden, and later as a private tutor in Bordeaux, France. In 1915, he enlisted in the army and was commissioned as second lieutenant in the Manchester Regiment. The trauma he experienced on the front haunted Owen, who once spent days trapped in a dugout with the remains of a fellow officer. Diagnosed with shell shock in 1917, the poet was sent to recuperate at Craiglockhart War Hospital near Edinburgh. His biographer Jon Stallworthy suggests that the nightmares that are a symptom of shellshock were "a principal factor in the liberation and organization of [Owen's work....] The realities of battle, banished from his waking mind, [...] erupt into his dreams and into his poems."

At the War Hospital, he met fellow patient and recently published poet Siegfried Sassoon, who became a mentor to Owen. Up to this point, Owen's style had reflected his admiration of Romantic poets such as John Keats and Percy Shelley, but with Sassoon's encouragement, he abandoned Romantic poetics for a colloquial style similar to Sassoon's. Almost all of his best-known work was composed in the year before he was discharged from the War Hospital and sent back to France in August 1918.

Owen was killed in action one week before the end of the war.

Anthem for Doomed Youth

What passing-bells for these who die as cattle?
Only the monstrous anger of the guns.
Only the stuttering rifles' rapid rattle
Can patter out their hasty orisons.°   *prayers*
No mockeries for them from prayers or bells,   5
Nor any voice of mourning save the choirs,—
The shrill, demented choirs of wailing shells;
And bugles calling for them from sad shires.

What candles may be held to speed them all?
Not in the hands of boys, but in their eyes   10
Shall shine the holy glimmers of good-byes.

The pallor of girls' brows shall be their pall;[1]
Their flowers the tenderness of silent minds,
And each slow dusk a drawing-down of blinds.

—1920

Dulce et Decorum Est[2]

Bent double, like old beggars under sacks,
Knock-kneed, coughing like hags, we cursed through sludge,
Till on the haunting flares we turned our backs,
And towards our distant rest began to trudge.
5 Men marched asleep. Many had lost their boots,
But limped on, blood-shod. All went lame, all blind;
Drunk with fatigue; deaf even to the hoots
Of gas-shells dropping softly behind.
Gas! GAS! Quick, boys!—An ecstasy of fumbling,
10 Fitting the clumsy helmets just in time,
But someone still was yelling out and stumbling
And flound'ring like a man in fire or lime—
Dim, through the misty panes[3] and thick green light,
As under a green sea, I saw him drowning.

15 In all my dreams before my helpless sight
He plunges at me, guttering, choking, drowning.

If in some smothering dreams, you too could pace
Behind the wagon that we flung him in,
And watch the white eyes writhing in his face,
20 His hanging face, like a devil's sick of sin;
If you could hear, at every jolt, the blood
Come gargling from the froth-corrupted lungs,
Bitter as the cud
Of vile, incurable sores on innocent tongues,—
25 My friend, you would not tell with such high zest
To children ardent for some desperate glory,
The old Lie: Dulce et decorum est
Pro patria mori.

—1920

---

1   *pall* Cloth spread over a coffin, hearse, or tomb.
2   *Dulce et Decorum Est* Owen's poem takes its title from a famous line from the Roman
    poet Horace's *Odes* (3.2): "*Dulce et decorum est pro patria mori*" (Latin: "Sweet and fitting
    it is to die for one's country").
3   *panes* Visors of gas masks.

E.E. Cummings
1894–1962

Edward Estlin Cummings is best known for his avant-garde poetry, in which he experiments with syntax, grammar, and punctuation. Cummings's work found an unusually large popular audience; according to poet and critic Randall Jarrell, "No one else has ever made avant-garde, experimental poems so attractive to the general and the specific reader."

Cummings grew up in an intellectual home in Cambridge, Massachusetts, and attended Harvard University, where several of his poems were published in the anthology *Eight Harvard Poets* (1917). Upon graduating from university during World War I, Cummings went to France to be an ambulance driver, but instead was put into an internment camp for "suspicious" foreigners. He fictionalized this experience in the prose work *The Enormous Room* (1922), which was much admired by other young writers.

This was followed in 1923 by his first book of poetry, *Tulips and Chimneys*, showcasing his facility with typographical experimentation and invented language. The characteristic poem "[In Just-]," for example, describes a children's world using vibrant and playful terms such as "mud- / luscious," "balloonMan," and "puddle-wonderful." Cummings continued to write prolifically for the next several decades, producing 15 books of poems ranging from lyrical love poetry to cynical criticism of the modern world.

In 1931, Cummings visited the Soviet Union. He had been hoping to find that communism had created an ideal society, but was disillusioned by his experience, and wrote a travelogue, *Eimi* (1933), strongly critical of the Soviet regime.

[in Just-]

in Just-
spring   when the world is mud-
luscious the little
lame balloonman

whistles   far   and wee

and eddieandbill come
running from marbles and
piracies and it's
spring

5

10 when the world is puddle-wonderful

the queer
old balloonman whistles
far   and   wee
and bettyandisbel come dancing

15 from hop-scotch and jump-rope and

it's
spring
and

        the

20   goat-footed

balloonMan   whistles
far
and
wee

—1923

[(ponder,darling,these busted statues]

(ponder,darling,these busted statues
of yon motheaten forum[1] be aware
notice what hath remained
—the stone cringes
5 clinging to the stone,how obsolete

lips utter their extant smile . . . .
remark

a few deleted of texture
or meaning monuments and dolls

10 resist Them Greediest Paws of careful
time all of which is extremely
unimportant)whereas Life

matters if or

when the your-and my-
15 idle vertical worthless

---

1   *forum* Public space in an ancient Roman city.

self unite in a peculiarly
momentary

partnership(to instigate
constructive
                    Horizontal   20
business . . . . even so,let us make haste
—consider well this ruined aqueduct

lady,
which used to lead something into somewhere)

                                                              —1926

[somewhere i have never travelled,gladly beyond]

somewhere i have never travelled,gladly beyond
any experience,your eyes have their silence:
in your most frail gesture are things which enclose me,
or which i cannot touch because they are too near

your slightest look easily will unclose me   5
though i have closed myself as fingers,
you open always petal by petal myself as Spring opens
(touching skilfully,mysteriously)her first rose

or if your wish be to close me,i and
my life will shut very beautifully,suddenly,   10
as when the heart of this flower imagines
the snow carefully everywhere descending;

nothing which we are to perceive in this world equals
the power of your intense fragility:whose texture
compels me with the colour of its countries,   15
rendering death and forever with each breathing

(i do not know what it is about you that closes
and opens;only something in me understands
the voice of your eyes is deeper than all roses)
nobody,not even the rain,has such small hands   20

                                                              —1931

anyone lived in a pretty how town

anyone lived in a pretty how town
(with up so floating many bells down)
spring summer autumn winter
he sang his didn't he danced his did.

5 Women and men(both little and small)
cared for anyone not at all
they sowed their isn't they reaped their same
sun moon stars rain

children guessed(but only a few
10 and down they forgot as up they grew
autumn winter spring summer)
that noone loved him more by more

when by now and tree by leaf
she laughed his joy she cried his grief
15 bird by snow and stir by still
anyone's any was all to her

someones married their everyones
laughed their cryings and did their dance
(sleep wake hope and then)they
20 said their nevers they slept their dream

stars rain sun moon
(and only the snow can begin to explain
how children are apt to forget to remember
with up so floating many bells down)

25 one day anyone died i guess
(and noone stooped to kiss his face)
busy folk buried them side by side
little by little and was by was

all by all and deep by deep
30 and more by more they dream their sleep
noone and anyone earth by april
wish by spirit and if by yes.

Women and men(both dong and ding)
summer autumn winter spring
reaped their sowing and went their came   35
sun moon stars rain

—1940

[l(a]

l(a

le
af
fa

ll   5

s)
one
l

iness

—1958

Langston Hughes
1902–1967

In his first autobiography, *The Big Sea* (1940), Langston Hughes wrote, "my best poems were all written when I felt the worst. When I was happy, I didn't write anything." His career produced many lyric poems that have the sadness but also the vitality of jazz, blues, and bebop, and that participate in an African American tradition of struggle for positive social change. Hughes contributed to American letters not only as a poet but also as a playwright, journalist, short story writer, novelist, historian, and translator.

In the early 1920s Hughes worked odd jobs—including a stint on an American freighter travelling the African coastline—as he began to publish his work in magazines. His first poetry collection, *Weary Blues* (1926), established him as a major figure in the Harlem Renaissance, a movement of African American writers, artists, and musicians that flourished in the 1920s and 1930s. Even more than some of his Harlem Renaissance contemporaries, Hughes celebrated black working-class culture and experience in his writing.

Hughes became a Marxist in the 1930s, and he spent time in Haiti, Cuba, and the USSR learning about alternatives to American politics and economics. He also began to address contemporary urban politics more directly in his work, pronouncing his faith in Marxism in poems such as "Goodbye Christ" (1932): "And nobody's gonna sell ME / To a king, or a general, / Or a millionaire." Hughes abandoned communism after World War II but continued to write on political themes; his last work, for example, *The Panther and the Lash* (1967), was a collection of poetry focused on the civil rights movement.

The Negro Speaks of Rivers

(To W.E.B. Du Bois)[1]

I've known rivers:
I've known rivers ancient as the world and older than the flow of human
    blood in human veins.
My soul has grown deep like the rivers.

---

1   *W.E.B. Du Bois* American activist (1868–1963) and one of the founders of the NAACP (National Association for the Advancement of Colored People).

I bathed in the Euphrates when dawns were young.   5
I built my hut near the Congo and it lulled me to sleep.
I looked upon the Nile and raised the pyramids above it.
I heard the singing of the Mississippi when Abe Lincoln went down
    to New Orleans,[1] and I've seen its muddy bosom turn all golden
    in the sunset.

I've known rivers:
Ancient, dusky rivers.   10

My soul has grown deep like the rivers.

                                   —1926

Harlem (2)

What happens to a dream deferred?

    Does it dry up
    like a raisin in the sun?
    Or fester like a sore—
    And then run?
    Does it stink like rotten meat?   5
    Or crust and sugar over—
    like a syrupy sweet?
    Maybe it just sags
    like a heavy load.   10

    Or does it explode?

                                      —1951

---

1   *when Abe ... New Orleans* In 1831, Lincoln travelled down the Mississippi to New Orleans, where he witnessed the brutality of the slave market there. Some biographers suggest that this experience consolidated his opinion against slavery.

Stevie Smith

1902–1971

Stevie Smith's poetry is deceptively simple. Its plain language, playful rhymes, odd syntax, and repetitive, singsong rhythms convey a child-like sensibility—one accentuated by the bizarre "doodles" of men, women, and animals that she included with her writing. Beneath her poetry's light-hearted and humorous surface, however, is a serious engagement with such concepts as loneliness, religion, suicide, and death. As poet Peter Porter suggests, Smith was not the "naive writer" she appeared to be; on the contrary, "her unshockable eye and brilliant ear enabled her to cover almost all the unmentionable topics."

Smith lived most of her life in London, where she worked as a secretary. Her first published work was a novel entitled *Novel on Yellow Paper* (1936); its commercial success enabled her to publish her first volume of poems, *A Good Time Was Had By All* (1937). Smith would go on to write seven more poetry collections, as well as short stories, essays, literary reviews, and two more novels.

Skilled at performing her own verse, Smith was a popular figure at poetry readings in the 1960s. Although she had a large and admiring readership, for most of her career she did not receive a great deal of approval from critics, who were put off by the atypical, apparently frivolous tone of her work. However, she had gained respect as a serious poet by the time her *Selected Poems* was published in 1962, and in the last years of her life she received the Queen's Gold Medal for Poetry (1969).

Not Waving but Drowning

Nobody heard him, the dead man,
But still he lay moaning:
I was much further out than you thought
And not waving but drowning.

5 Poor chap, he always loved larking
And now he's dead
It must have been too cold for him his heart gave way,
They said.

Oh, no no no, it was too cold always
10 (Still the dead one lay moaning)
I was much too far out all my life
And not waving but drowning.

—1957

Earle Birney
1904–1995

A mountain climber, travel writer, and political activist as well as an important Canadian poet, Earle Birney was as adventurous in his work as he was in his life. He experimented with compound nouns (e.g., "seajet"), syntax and sound, and unconventional punctuation, and he frequently changed his style during his long career. As the critic George Woodcock writes, Birney possessed an "openness to the new and the unorthodox" that enabled him to create "the special voice and form appropriate to each situation."

Raised in Alberta and British Columbia, Birney attended university in Vancouver and Toronto; he lived for brief periods in England and in Utah before returning to Canada to teach at the University of British Columbia—and to publish poetry. He was an immediate success: his first collection, *David and Other Poems* (1942), won a Governor General's Award. He spent the next several decades writing prolifically and teaching, and in 1965 established Canada's first Creative Writing program.

Birney addressed many topics and adopted many different poetic styles over his long career. His work often engages with the issues of the day—Birney was a Marxist when young, and always remained strongly on the left politically—and it engages experimentally with several poetic movements, including sound poetry and concrete poetry.

Vancouver Lights

About me the night   moonless   wimples¹ the mountains
wraps ocean   land   air   and mounting
sucks at the stars   The city   throbbing below
webs the sable peninsula   The golden
strands overleap the seajet   by bridge and buoy
vault the shears of the inlet   climb the woods   5
toward me   falter   and halt   Across to the firefly
haze of a ship on the gulf's erased horizon
roll the lambent° spokes of a lighthouse   *radiant*

Through the feckless years we have come to the time
when to look on this quilt of lamps is a troubling delight   10
Welling from Europe's bog   through Africa flowing

---

1   *wimples* I.e., covers; a wimple is the head covering traditionally worn by nuns.

and Asia   drowning the lonely lumes[1] on the oceans
tiding up over Halifax   now to this winking
15 outpost comes flooding the primal ink

On this mountain's brutish forehead with terror of space
I stir   of the changeless night and the stark ranges
of nothing   pulsing down from beyond and between
the fragile planets   We are a spark beleaguered
20 by darkness   this twinkle we make in a corner of emptiness
how shall we utter our fear that the black Experimentress
will never in the range of her microscope find it?   Our Phoebus[2]
himself is a bubble that dries on Her slide   while the Nubian[3]
wears for an evening's whim a necklace of nebulae

25 Yet we must speak   we the unique glowworms
Out of the waters and rocks of our little world
we conjured these flames   hooped these sparks
by our will   From blankness and cold we fashioned stars
to our size   and signalled Aldebaran[4]
30 This must we say   whoever may be to hear us
if murk devour   and none weave again in gossamer:

These rays were ours
we made and unmade them   Not the shudder of continents
doused us   the moon's passion   nor crash of comets
35 In the fathomless heat of our dwarfdom   our dream's combustion
we contrived the power   the blast that snuffed us
No one bound Prometheus[5]   Himself he chained
and consumed his own bright liver   O stranger
Plutonian   descendant   or beast in the stretching night—
40 there was light.

—1948

---

1   *lumes* Variant form of "leams," meaning lights or rays.
2   *Phoebus* Epithet of Apollo, god of the sun; here, the sun itself.
3   *Nubian* Inhabitant of the African region of Nubia.
4   *Aldebaran* Red star of the first magnitude, in the constellation of Taurus.
5   *Prometheus* In Greek myth, the Titan who stole fire from Heaven to give to humankind; for this, his punishment was to be chained to a rock while an eagle devoured his liver each day.

The Bear on the Delhi Road

Unreal   tall as a myth
by the road the Himalayan bear
is beating the brilliant air
with his crooked arms
About him two men   bare   5
spindly as locusts   leap

One pulls on a ring
in the great soft nose   His mate
flicks   flicks with a stick
up at the rolling eyes   10

They have not led him here
down from the fabulous hills
to this bald alien plain
and the clamorous world   to kill
but simply to teach him to dance   15

They are peaceful both   these spare
men of Kashmir   and the bear
alive is their living   too
If   far on the Delhi way
around him galvanic they dance   20
it is merely to wear   wear
from his shaggy body the tranced
wish forever to stay
only an ambling bear
four-footed in berries   25

It is no more joyous for them
in this hot dust to prance
out of reach of the praying claws
sharpened to paw for ants
in the shadows of deodars[1]   30
It is not easy to free
myth from reality
or rear this fellow up
to lurch   lurch with them
in the tranced dancing of men   35

—1973

---

1   *deodars* Indian cedars.

John Betjeman
1906–1984

▮▮▮▮ Poet Laureate of England from 1972 until his death, Sir John Betjeman was a public figure who frequently appeared on radio and television programs and regularly published articles in books and magazines. Known for using light verse with serious purpose, he approached his work with a sense of humour. As he once said, "I don't think I am any good. If I thought I was any good, I wouldn't be."

Born in London, Betjeman published his first book of poems in 1931. During the early thirties he also worked as the assistant editor of *The Architectural Review*, where he developed a lifelong passion for architecture that would provide the subject matter for some of his poems as well as several prose books and documentaries. He continued to write and publish poetry while working for the British Representative in Dublin as a Press Officer, for the Ministry of Information on film propaganda during World War II, and for various newspapers and magazines as a freelance journalist.

Betjeman's *Collected Poems* (1958) was well-received by the public and critics alike, and with its publication he became what literary critic Ralph J. Mills describes as "a phenomenon in contemporary English literature, a truly popular poet." Betjeman was awarded the Queen's Gold Medal for poetry in 1960, and was knighted in 1969.

In Westminster Abbey[1]

Let me take this other glove off
   As the *vox humana*[2] swells,
And the beauteous fields of Eden
   Bask beneath the Abbey bells.
5 Here, where England's statesmen lie,
   Listen to a lady's cry.

Gracious Lord, oh bomb the Germans.[3]
   Spare their women for Thy Sake,
And if that is not too easy
10   We will pardon Thy Mistake.

---

1   *Westminster Abbey* Important central London church where coronations are held and where many influential political figures, scientists, and intellectuals are buried.

2   *vox humana* Set of pipes in a pipe organ, so named because their sound resembles that of a human voice.

3   *bomb the Germans* This poem was published during World War II (1939–45).

But, gracious Lord, whate'er shall be,
Don't let anyone bomb me.

Keep our Empire undismembered
    Guide our Forces by Thy Hand,
Gallant blacks from far Jamaica,   15
    Honduras and Togoland;[1]
Protect them Lord in all their fights,
And, even more, protect the whites.

Think of what our Nation stands for,
    Books from Boots[2] and country lanes,   20
Free speech, free passes, class distinction,
    Democracy and proper drains.
Lord, put beneath Thy special care
One-eighty-nine Cadogan Square.

Although dear Lord I am a sinner,   25
    I have done no major crime;
Now I'll come to Evening Service
    Whensoever I have the time.
So, Lord, reserve for me a crown,
And do not let my shares go down.   30

I will labour for Thy Kingdom,
    Help our lads to win the war,
Send white feathers to the cowards[3]
    Join the Women's Army Corps,
Then wash the Steps around Thy Throne   35
In the Eternal Safety Zone.

Now I feel a little better,
    What a treat to hear Thy Word
Where the bones of leading statesmen,
    Have so often been interred.   40
And now, dear Lord, I cannot wait
Because I have a luncheon date.

                                    —1940

---

1   *Togoland* Area of western Africa once divided into French Togoland (now the Republic
    of Togo) and British Togoland (now part of Ghana).
2   *Boots* British chain of for-profit libraries that rented books to customers.
3   *Send white ... cowards* Reference to the practice of giving out white feathers (symbolizing
    cowardice) to men not in military uniform as a means of shaming them into enlisting.
    This occurred during both world wars.

W.H. Auden

1907–1973

W.H. Auden's poetry documents the changing political, social, and psychological landscape of his time, describing society's material troubles and seeking a clear understanding of human existence. His work often couples contemporary speech with more traditional, structured verse forms.

Born in York, England, Wystan Hugh Auden spent his childhood in Birmingham. He won a scholarship to study natural science at Oxford, but a developing passion for poetry soon led him to transfer to English. At university, he became the central member of a cohort of writers known as the "Oxford Group," and soon after graduation he published his first major volume, *Poems* (1930).

In the thirties, Auden travelled extensively and worked variously as a schoolmaster, a university lecturer, a writer of nonfiction and experimental drama, and a verse commentator on documentary films. Though he was gay, in 1935 he entered into a marriage of convenience with Erika Mann, daughter of the German novelist Thomas Mann, to enable her escape from Nazi Germany. During the Spanish Civil War (1936–39), Auden volunteered as a propaganda writer on the side of the left—an experience that left him somewhat disillusioned with socialist politics.

In 1939, Auden moved to New York, where he settled for most of his later life. A year later he published *Another Time* (1940), which includes some of his best-known poems, such as "Musée des Beaux Arts" and "September 1, 1939." From then on, his work began to take on more subjective overtones, often with religious themes (he had abandoned Anglicanism as a youth, but returned to it in 1941). While his earlier poetry had examined concrete social ills, his later poetry developed a more complex worldview, often casting social problems in terms of personal responsibility.

With *The Collected Poetry* (1945), Auden began revising his earlier work, a task that included rewriting and even suppressing some of his most left-wing poems. When he was awarded the National Medal for Literature in 1967, the committee declared that Auden's work, "branded by the moral and ideological fires of our age, breathes with eloquence, perception, and intellectual power."

Funeral Blues[1]

Stop all the clocks, cut off the telephone,
Prevent the dog from barking with a juicy bone,
Silence the pianos and with muffled drum
Bring out the coffin, let the mourners come.

Let aeroplanes circle moaning overhead   5
Scribbling on the sky the message He is Dead,
Put crêpe bows[2] round the white necks of the public doves,
Let the traffic policemen wear black cotton gloves.

He was my North, my South, my East and West,
My working week and my Sunday rest,   10
My noon, my midnight, my talk, my song;
I thought that love would last forever: I was wrong.

The stars are not wanted now; put out every one;
Pack up the moon and dismantle the sun;
Pour away the ocean and sweep up the wood;   15
For nothing now can ever come to any good.

                                                —1936, 1940

Musée des Beaux Arts

About suffering they were never wrong,
The Old Masters: how well they understood
Its human position; how it takes place
While someone else is eating or opening a window or just walking
        dully along;
How, when the aged are reverently, passionately waiting   5
For the miraculous birth, there always must be
Children who did not specially want it to happen, skating
On a pond at the edge of the wood:

---

1   *Funeral Blues* This poem first appeared in *The Ascent of F6* (1936), a play co-written by
     Auden and Christopher Isherwood. A revised version with the present title later appeared
     in Auden's 1940 collection *Another Time*. The original 1936 version has five stanzas and
     is considerably more satirical.
2   *crêpe bows* Black crêpe, a woven fabric with a wrinkled surface, is often associated with
     mourning.

They never forgot
10 That even the dreadful martyrdom must run its course
Anyhow in a corner, some untidy spot
Where the dogs go on with their doggy life and the torturer's horse
Scratches its innocent behind on a tree.

In Brueghel's *Icarus*[1] for instance: how everything turns away
15 Quite leisurely from the disaster; the ploughman may
Have heard the splash, the forsaken cry,
But for him it was not an important failure; the sun shone
As it had to on the white legs disappearing into the green
Water; and the expensive delicate ship that must have seen
20 Something amazing, a boy falling out of the sky,
Had somewhere to get to and sailed calmly on.

—1940

September 1, 1939[2]

I sit in one of the dives
On Fifty-second Street
Uncertain and afraid
As the clever hopes expire
5 Of a low dishonest decade:
Waves of anger and fear
Circulate over the bright
And darkened lands of the earth,
Obsessing our private lives;
10 The unmentionable odour of death
Offends the September night.

Accurate scholarship can
Unearth the whole offence

---

1   *Brueghel's Icarus* The reference is to *Landscape with the Fall of Icarus* (c. 1555), a painting
     by Pieter Brueghel the Elder. It references an ancient Greek story in which Daedalus and
     his son Icarus tried to escape from Crete, where they were imprisoned, using wings of
     feathers and wax. Icarus flew too high, the wax melted, and he drowned. In Brueghel's
     painting, an ordinary farmer ploughing on a hill dominates the foreground, while Icarus's
     drowning body appears very small in the ocean below, next to a much larger ship.
2   *September 1, 1939* Date of Hitler's invasion of Poland; France and Britain declared war
     on Germany two days later. Auden had left England to take up residence in the United
     States the previous January.

From Luther[1] until now
That has driven a culture mad,   15

Find what occurred at Linz,[2]
What huge imago[3] made
A psychopathic god:
I and the public know
What all schoolchildren learn,   20
Those to whom evil is done
Do evil in return.   ·

Exiled Thucydides[4] knew
All that a speech can say
About Democracy,   25
And what dictators do,
The elderly rubbish they talk
To an apathetic grave;
Analysed all in his book,
The enlightenment driven away,   30
The habit-forming pain,
Mismanagement and grief:
We must suffer them all again.

Into this neutral air
Where blind skyscrapers use   35
Their full height to proclaim
The strength of Collective Man,
Each language pours its vain
Competitive excuse:

---

1   *Luther* Martin Luther (1483–1546), the German religious leader whose attacks on eccle-
    siastical corruption began the Protestant Reformation in Europe. Luther's writings grew
    markedly more anti-Semitic as he aged; in his book *Mein Kampf*, Hitler ranks Martin
    Luther as a great German cultural hero.
2   *Linz* Capital of upper Austria where Hitler grew up.
3   *imago* Psychoanalytic term for an idealized image of a person; imagos are formed in
    childhood and influence adult behaviour.
4   *Thucydides* Athenian historian (c. 460–c. 395 BCE) whose failure as a naval commander
    led to his 20-year exile, during which time he wrote *The History of the Peloponnesian
    War*. In his *History*, Thucydides records Pericles's funeral oration for the dead Athenian
    soldiers, which outlines the dangers and benefits of democracy. Elected 16 times to the
    position of general, Pericles instituted many democratic reforms while retaining a signifi-
    cant degree of personal power.

40 But who can live for long
    In an euphoric dream;
    Out of the mirror they stare,
    Imperialism's face
    And the international wrong.

45 Faces along the bar
    Cling to their average day:
    The lights must never go out,
    The music must always play,
    All the conventions conspire
50 To make this fort assume
    The furniture of home;
    Lest we should see where we are,
    Lost in a haunted wood,
    Children afraid of the night
55 Who have never been happy or good.

    The windiest militant trash
    Important Persons shout
    Is not so crude as our wish:
    What mad Nijinsky[1] wrote
60 About Diaghilev
    Is true of the normal heart;
    For the error bred in the bone
    Of each woman and each man
    Craves what it cannot have,
65 Not universal love
    But to be loved alone.

    From the conservative dark
    Into the ethical life
    The dense commuters come,
70 Repeating their morning vow;
    "I *will* be true to the wife,
    I'll concentrate more on my work,"

---

1   *Nijinsky* Vaslav Nijinsky (1890–1950), Russian ballet dancer and choreographer, worked
    with the Russian ballet producer Sergei Diaghilev (1872–1929) until their falling out in
    1913. In 1917 Nijinsky's mental instability forced him into permanent retirement. In his
    diary, published in 1937, Nijinsky wrote: "Some politicians are hypocrites like Diaghilev,
    who does not want universal love, but to be loved alone. I want universal love."

And helpless governors wake
To resume their compulsory game:
Who can release them now,   75
Who can reach the deaf,
Who can speak for the dumb?

Defenceless under the night
Our world in stupor lies;
Yet, dotted everywhere,   80
Ironic points of light
Flash out wherever the Just
Exchange their messages:
May I, composed like them
Of Eros[1] and of dust,   85
Beleaguered by the same
Negation and despair,
Show an affirming flame.

—1940

The Unknown Citizen

(To JS/07/M/378
This Marble Monument
Is Erected by the State)

He was found by the Bureau of Statistics to be
One against whom there was no official complaint,
And all the reports on his conduct agree
That, in the modern sense of an old-fashioned word, he was a saint,
For in everything he did he served the Greater Community.   5
Except for the War till the day he retired
He worked in a factory and never got fired,
But satisfied his employers, Fudge Motors Inc.
Yet he wasn't a scab[2] or odd in his views,
For his Union reports that he paid his dues,   10
(Our report on his Union shows it was sound)
And our Social Psychology workers found

---

1   *Eros* In contrast to the New Testament *agape*, or Christian love, *eros* represents earthly, or
     sexual love. In Greek myth, the winged Eros, son of Aphrodite, is the god of love.
2   *scab* Someone who works during a strike or refuses to join a union.

That he was popular with his mates and liked a drink.
The Press are convinced that he bought a paper every day
15 And that his reactions to advertisements were normal in every way.
Policies taken out in his name prove that he was fully insured,
And his Health-card shows he was once in hospital but left it cured.
Both Producers Research and High-Grade Living declare
He was fully sensible to the advantages of the Instalment Plan
20 And had everything necessary to the Modern Man,
A phonograph, a radio, a car and a frigidaire.
Our researchers into Public Opinion are content
That he held the proper opinions for the time of year;
When there was peace, he was for peace; when there was war, he
    went.
25 He was married and added five children to the population,
Which our Eugenist[1] says was the right number for a parent of his
    generation.
And our teachers report that he never interfered with their education.
Was he free? Was he happy? The question is absurd:
Had anything been wrong, we should certainly have heard.

—1940

---

1   *Eugenist* Scientist who studies the development of physically or mentally improved hu-
    man beings through selective breeding. Eugenics has played a key role in legitimizing
    racist ideologies such as Nazism.

George Oppen
1908–1984

George Oppen contributed to literary and political spheres not only as a poet but also as an activist, publisher, and mentor. A deeply philosophical poet, he explored ethical questions, the nature of truth, and his own humanity through his exacting words.

Oppen was born in New Rochelle, New York, and raised in affluence. After being expelled from a military academy, he attended Oregon State University at Corvallis, where he met his wife, Mary Colby. While travelling the country, the couple befriended Louis Zukofsky and other poets who became Oppen's writing peers; they dedicated their "objectivist" poetry to communicating clear, impartial perceptions of the actual world. The Oppens began to publish their colleagues' poems, co-founding first To Publishers in France in 1931 and then Objectivist Press in the United States, which printed Oppen's first collection, *Discrete Series* (1934).

After 1934 Oppen and his wife turned their attention to activism, helping those struggling through the Great Depression, and both joined the Communist Party. Oppen eventually distanced himself from the Party, and he fought in Europe during World War II, for which service he received a Purple Heart. However, the Oppens still fell under scrutiny during the anti-Communist fervour following the war, and in 1950 they went into exile in Mexico City.

In 1958 Oppen returned to the United States and resumed writing, publishing first *The Materials* (1962) then *This in Which* (1965). He received lifetime achievement awards from the American Academy and Institute of Arts and Letters and the National Endowment for the Arts, as well as the Pulitzer Prize for the celebrated collection *Of Being Numerous* (1968). He was later diagnosed with Alzheimer's disease and, with the help of Mary, he published one last collection, *Primitive* (1978), before his death.

Psalm

Veritas sequitur ... [1]

In the small beauty of the forest
The wild deer bedding down—
That they are there!

---

1   *Veritas sequitur* Latin: truth follows. The complete expression is *"veritas sequitur esse"* ("truth follows the existence of things").

Their eyes
5   Effortless, the soft lips
Nuzzle and the alien small teeth
Tear at the grass

The roots of it
Dangle from their mouths
10   Scattering earth in the strange woods.
They who are there.

Their paths
Nibbled thru the fields, the leaves that shade them
Hang in the distances
15   Of sun

The small nouns
Crying faith
In this in which the wild deer
Startle, and stare out.

—1963

The Forms of Love

Parked in the fields
All night
So many years ago,
We saw
5   A lake beside us
When the moon rose.
I remember

Leaving that ancient car
Together. I remember
10   Standing in the white grass
Beside it. We groped
Our way together
Downhill in the bright
Incredible light

Beginning to wonder   15
Whether it could be lake
Or fog
We saw, our heads
Ringing under the stars we walked
To where it would have wet our feet   20
Had it been water

—1964

Latitude, Longitude

       climbed from the road and found
over the flowers at the mountain's
rough top a bee yellow
and heavy as

       pollen in the mountainous   5
air thin legs crookedly
a-dangle if we could

find all
the gale's evidence what message
is there for us in these   10
glassy bottles the Encyclopedist

was wrong was wrong many things
too foolish
to sing
may be said this matter-   15
of-fact defines

poetry

—1975

Theodore Roethke
1908–1963

■■■■■ Known for his introspective verse, Theodore Roethke was both praised and criticized for his focus on the self. Some critics saw his personal exploration as a means to valuable insight into the human body and the unconscious mind, but others considered his scope too limited and irrelevant to the political and social concerns of the day. Despite the inward focus of his poetry, Roethke read widely, and his style was strongly influenced by the poets he admired, such as William Blake, T.S. Eliot, and W.B. Yeats. He also formed literary friendships with fellow poets W.H. Auden, Dylan Thomas, and William Carlos Williams.

Born in Michigan into a German-American family, Roethke had ambivalent childhood memories of his horticulturalist father that centred on the family's extensive greenhouses. Images of growth, decay, and death recur in his poetry, especially in what he referred to as the "greenhouse poems" included in *The Lost Son and Other Poems* (1948). By contrast, joyful love is the subject of "I Knew a Woman" from *Words for the Wind* (1958), published after his marriage to Beatrice O'Connell. *Words for the Wind* marked a new direction for Roethke, who frequently returned to love poetry in his later work.

Roethke taught at Michigan State College and was very dedicated to his teaching; however, he was dismissed after the first of what became a series of mental breakdowns and psychiatric hospitalizations. He then taught at the University of Washington where, although he was often unwell, he was valued for both his teaching and his writing. Roethke's honours include the Pulitzer Prize, two National Book Awards, and the Shelley Memorial Award.

My Papa's Waltz

The whiskey on your breath
Could make a small boy dizzy;
But I hung on like death:
Such waltzing was not easy.

5 We romped until the pans
Slid from the kitchen shelf;
My mother's countenance
Could not unfrown itself.

The hand that held my wrist
Was battered on one knuckle;   10
At every step you missed
My right ear scraped a buckle.

You beat time on my head
With a palm caked hard by dirt,
Then waltzed me off to bed   15
Still clinging to your shirt.

—1948

Root Cellar

Nothing would sleep in that cellar, dank as a ditch,
Bulbs broke out of boxes hunting for chinks in the dark,
Shoots dangled and drooped,
Lolling obscenely from mildewed crates,
Hung down long yellow evil necks, like tropical snakes.   5
And what a congress of stinks!—
Roots ripe as old bait,
Pulpy stems, rank, silo-rich,
Leaf-mould, manure, lime, piled against slippery planks.
Nothing would give up life: 10
Even the dirt kept breathing a small breath.

—1948

I Knew a Woman

I knew a woman, lovely in her bones,
When small birds sighed, she would sigh back at them;
Ah, when she moved, she moved more ways than one:
The shapes a bright container can contain!
Of her choice virtues only gods should speak,   5
Or English poets who grew up on Greek
(I'd have them sing in chorus, cheek to cheek).

How well her wishes went! She stroked my chin,
She taught me Turn, and Counter-turn, and Stand;[1]
10 She taught me Touch, that undulant white skin;
I nibbled meekly from her proffered hand;
She was the sickle; I, poor I, the rake,
Coming behind her for her pretty sake
(But what prodigious mowing we did make).

15 Love likes a gander, and adores a goose:
Her full lips pursed, the errant note to seize;
She played it quick, she played it light and loose;
My eyes, they dazzled at her flowing knees;
Her several parts could keep a pure repose,
20 Or one hip quiver with a mobile nose
(She moved in circles, and those circles moved).

Let seed be grass, and grass turn into hay:
I'm martyr to a motion not my own;
What's freedom for? To know eternity.
25 I swear she cast a shadow white as stone.
But who would count eternity in days?
These old bones live to learn her wanton ways:
(I measure time by how a body sways).

—1958

---

1   *Turn, and Counter-turn, and Stand* Allusion to *strophe*, *antistrophe*, and *epode*, the three
parts of a typical Greek ode.

Dorothy Livesay
1909–1996

In a career spanning six decades, Dorothy Livesay produced an extensive body of work that is remarkable not only for its diversity but also for its commitment to her aesthetic and ethical ideals. Chief among these was the conviction that a poem should not be an esoteric literary artifact frozen on the page but rather an accessible expression of "living speech," a popular, vital form of communication. Regardless of her subject—which included life in rural Ontario, her experience living and teaching in Africa, social injustice, class struggle, and women's rights—Livesay's poetry retains its characteristic clarity of image, forthrightness of language, and musicality.

Over the course of her writing life, Livesay experimented with an array of poetic forms, from imagist love lyrics and Georgian pastorals to socially conscious "documentary poetry" that bears witness to historical events. Although certain critics have looked askance on her more politically motivated, polemical work, Livesay rejected the notion that art should be wholly separate from activism or ideological causes. Having seen police brutality, labour unrest, and civil disobedience as a student in Europe, as well as the effects of the Depression on the working poor as a social worker in North America, Livesay felt obligated to distance herself from what she came to regard as the "decadence in modern bourgeois poetry." Many of the resulting poems were published in the Governor General's Award-winning collections *Day and Night* (1944) and *Poems for People* (1947), which together established Livesay as one of the most important Canadian poets of her generation.

Green Rain

I remember long veils of green rain
Feathered like the shawl of my grandmother—
Green from the half-green of the spring trees
Waving in the valley.

I remember the road   5
Like the one which leads to my grandmother's house,
A warm house, with green carpets,
Geraniums, a trilling canary
And shining horse-hair chairs;
And the silence, full of the rain's falling   10
Was like my grandmother's parlour

Alive with herself and her voice, rising and falling—
Rain and wind intermingled.

I remember on that day
15   I was thinking only of my love
And of my love's house.
But now I remember the day
As I remember my grandmother.
I remember the rain as the feathery fringe of her shawl.

—1932

The Three Emilys[1]

These women crying in my head
Walk alone, uncomforted:
The Emilys, these three
Cry to be set free—
5   And others whom I will not name
Each different, each the same.

Yet they had liberty!
Their kingdom was the sky:
They batted clouds with easy hand,
10   Found a mountain for their stand;
From wandering lonely they could catch
The inner magic of a heath—
A lake their palette, any tree
Their brush could be.

15   And still they cry to me
As in reproach—
I, born to hear their inner storm
Of separate man in woman's form,
I yet possess another kingdom, barred
20   To them, these three, this Emily.
I move as mother in a frame,

---

1   *The Three Emilys* Emily Brontë (1818–48), English poet and novelist; Emily Dickinson (1830–86), American poet; and Emily Carr (1871–1945), Canadian artist and writer.

My arteries
Flow the immemorial way
Towards the child, the man;
And only for brief span   25
Am I an Emily on mountain snows
And one of these.

And so the whole that I possess
Is still much less—
They move triumphant through my head: 30
I am the one
Uncomforted.

                                                —1953

Elizabeth Bishop
1911–1979

Although respected by her contemporaries and honoured with a host of prestigious appointments, prizes, awards, and fellowships, Elizabeth Bishop came to be recognized only posthumously as a major American poet on the strength of a small but scrupulously crafted body of work. That she published just 101 poems in a cluster of slender volumes is a testament to the pains she took with her art. According to the poet Robert Lowell, with whom she shared a close friendship, she was "an unerring Muse" who made "the casual perfect."

Born in Massachusetts, Bishop was raised there and in Nova Scotia, and during her adult life she travelled extensively. She lived in Brazil from 1951 to 1966, for most of that time with architect Lota de Macedo Soares. In 1956 she received the Pulitzer Prize for a collection of poetry, *Poems: North & South/A Cold Spring*; thereafter she was frequently a recipient of honours and awards.

As one who spent much of her life roving from country to country, Bishop explained her "passion for accuracy" in the following terms: "since we do float on an unknown sea I think we should examine the floating things that come our way very carefully; who knows what might depend on it?" Some of Bishop's poems, such as "First Death in Nova Scotia," draw on elements of her personal life. But she remained wary of confessional poetry, believing that a poem that luxuriates in the feelings of the poet must be of diminished significance to other readers. She made a discipline of reticence and discretion, striving never to fall into sentimental self-pity or intrude too much of herself in order that the particular might serve to illuminate and bear the weight of the universal.

First Death in Nova Scotia

In the cold, cold parlour
my mother laid out Arthur
beneath the chromographs:
Edward, Prince of Wales,
with Princess Alexandra,
and King George with Queen Mary.[1]

---

1   *chromographs* Coloured prints; *Edward, Prince ... Queen Mary* Members of the British royal family. Edward VII was Prince of Wales when he married Alexandra of Denmark in 1863. They became king and queen consort in 1901 and were succeeded by King George V and Mary of Teck in 1910.

Below them on the table
stood a stuffed loon
shot and stuffed by Uncle
Arthur, Arthur's father.   10

Since Uncle Arthur fired
a bullet into him,
he hadn't said a word.
He kept his own counsel
on his white, frozen lake,   15
the marble-topped table.
His breast was deep and white,
cold and caressable;
his eyes were red glass,
much to be desired.   20

"Come," said my mother,
"Come and say good-bye
to your little cousin Arthur."
I was lifted up and given
one lily of the valley   25
to put in Arthur's hand.
Arthur's coffin was
a little frosted cake,
and the red-eyed loon eyed it
from his white, frozen lake.   30

Arthur was very small.
He was all white, like a doll
that hadn't been painted yet.
Jack Frost had started to paint him
the way he always painted   35
the Maple Leaf (Forever).[1]
He had just begun on his hair,
a few red strokes, and then
Jack Frost had dropped the brush
and left him white, forever.   40

---

1   *the Maple Leaf (Forever)* Reference to "The Maple Leaf Forever" (1867), an unofficial
    Canadian anthem.

The gracious royal couples
were warm in red and ermine;
their feet were well wrapped up
in the ladies' ermine trains.
45 They invited Arthur to be
the smallest page at court.
But how could Arthur go,
clutching his tiny lily,
with his eyes shut up so tight
50 and the roads deep in snow?

—1962

One Art

The art of losing isn't hard to master;
so many things seem filled with the intent
to be lost that their loss is no disaster.

Lose something every day. Accept the fluster
5 of lost door keys, the hour badly spent.
The art of losing isn't hard to master.

Then practice losing farther, losing faster:
places, and names, and where it was you meant
to travel. None of these will bring disaster.

10 I lost my mother's watch. And look! my last, or
next-to-last, of three loved houses went.
The art of losing isn't hard to master.

I lost two cities, lovely ones. And, vaster,
some realms I owned, two rivers, a continent.
15 I miss them, but it wasn't a disaster.

—Even losing you (the joking voice, a gesture
I love) I shan't have lied. It's evident
the art of losing's not too hard to master
though it may look like (*Write* it!) like disaster.

—1976

Douglas LePan
1914–1998

Over the course of his long career, Douglas LePan was a soldier, diplomat, economist, civil servant, administrator, professor of English, and college principal. He is, however, chiefly remembered for the small yet distinguished body of literature that he produced as one of just a handful of Canadian writers to have been honoured with the Governor General's Award for fiction as well as poetry. The Toronto-born LePan was regarded during much of his life as a quintessentially Canadian writer; many of his poems ruminate on the Canadian landscape and its formative influence on the national psyche. But LePan also aspired to a borderless writing in his fiction and poetry, which is rich in allusions to classical and European writers. Though he believed that there would "always be a place for books that are redolent of a particular region or a particular aspect of Canadian life and experience," he also argued that there would likewise be a place "for writing which is more stripped and bare and absolute, for writing marked by little or nothing on the surface to distinguish it as Canadian and which will ultimately reveal its origin by imparting a spirit that is both adventurous and responsible and by being able to pass everywhere as true."

The poetry of *The Net and the Sword* (1953) is based primarily on LePan's experiences as a gunner in Italy during World War II—as is his one novel, *The Deserter* (1964). Though he published a volume of gay love poems in the 1990s (*Far Voyages*), it was not until after his death that critics began to appreciate the degree to which his earlier work is also infused with strong homoerotic elements.

LePan's early poetry is characteristically measured, decorous, and studded with self-consciously ornate language. Much of his later work is quite different in style—less formal, less elevated in its diction, and more direct.

A Country without a Mythology

No monuments or landmarks guide the stranger
Going among this savage people, masks
Taciturn or babbling out an alien jargon
And moody as barbaric skies are moody.

Berries must be his food. Hurriedly   5
He shakes the bushes, plucks pickerel from the river,
Forgetting every grace and ceremony,
Feeds like an Indian, and is on his way.

And yet, for all his haste, time is worth nothing.
10 The abbey clock, the dial in the garden,
Fade like saint's days and festivals.
Months, years, are here unbroken virgin forests.

There is no law—even no atmosphere
To smooth the anger of the flagrant sun.
15 November skies sting, sting like icicles.
The land is open to all violent weathers.

Passion is not more quick. Lightnings in August
Stagger, rocks split, tongues in the forest hiss,
As fire drinks up the lovely sea-dream coolness.
20 This is the land the passionate man must travel.

Sometimes—perhaps at the tentative fall of twilight—
A belief will settle that waiting around the bend
Are sanctities of childhood, that melting birds
Will sing him into a limpid gracious Presence.

25 The hills will fall in folds, the wilderness
Will be a garment innocent and lustrous
To wear upon a birthday, under a light
That curls and smiles, a golden-haired Archangel.

And now the channel opens. But nothing alters,
30 Mile after mile of tangled struggling roots,
Wild-rice, stumps, weeds, that clutch at the canoe,
Wild birds hysterical in tangled trees.

And not a sign, no emblem in the sky
Or boughs to friend him as he goes; for who
35 Will stop where, clumsily constructed, daubed
With war-paint, teeters some lust-red manitou?[1]

—1948

---

1 *manitou* Algonquin term for a spirit, deity, or other manifestation of the supernatural.

Aubade[1]

Your name on my lips. Every night
as my eyes close. And the sweetness
of your body, as though you were with me.

Your name on my lips. Every morning,
waking, that one word on my lips.   5
I remember everything, everything.

But this morning there was nothing.
Then before I could think how strange it was
I was murmuring other words,

"Deeper than death or the dark,"   10
as though your mouth were on mine.
I love you that deeply, that deeply.

—1982

The Haystack

It doesn't take a Hiroshima[2] to burn a man to a crisp.
A haystack will do. And what could be more bucolic
than that? And you get tired of sleeping in cellars or slit-trenches,
so why not behind a haystack that has simmered all day
in the warmth of an Italian September sun? But at night   5
the jackals are ready to spring, the German eighty-eights,
with their high muzzle-velocities and their low trajectories,
so that the haystack ignites like a torch and a gunner is burnt
to a crisp. How far back was that? thirty years? forty years?
He doesn't remember. He only remembers the stench   10
of fear, his own fear, and a grey army blanket, and a young
sunburned back alive on the banks of the Volturno,[3]
then burning, burning. By dire subtleties such as these
he was being prepared for the carbonization of cities.

—1987

---

1   *Aubade* Poem or song about lovers parting at dawn.
2   *Hiroshima* Japanese city that was the first city ever subjected to a nuclear attack. The
     United States dropped an atomic bomb on Hiroshima on 6 August 1945, killing ap-
     proximately 130,000 people and levelling 90 per cent of the city.
3   *Volturno* River in south-central Italy, the bank of which formed the Volturno line, a Ger-
     man defensive position in World War II .

Randall Jarrell
1914–1965

Randall Jarrell was a literary critic with exacting standards, and his entertaining and perceptive writing on twentieth-century American poetry was extremely influential. He was also an important poet in his own right, addressing subjects such as childhood and women's domestic lives—and, most famously, World War II—with simultaneous tenderness and unflinching honesty. In addition to criticism and poetry, Jarrell also authored a novel, children's books, translations, essays, and reviews.

Jarrell earned his BA (1935) and MA (1937) from Vanderbilt University in his hometown of Nashville, Tennessee. His first book of poems, *Blood for a Stranger*, was published in 1942, the same year that he enlisted in the military. His next two books, *Little Friend, Little Friend* (1945) and *Losses* (1948), drew on his experiences of the Second World War as a navigation tower operator. Together, these texts established his reputation as a skilled and sensitive poet—a reputation that grew with the publication of *The Woman at the Washington Zoo* (1960), which received the National Book Award. Jarrell also taught English and Creative Writing at a number of American universities and served as American Poet Laureate from 1956 to 1958.

The Death of the Ball Turret Gunner[1]

From my mother's sleep I fell into the State,
And I hunched in its belly till my wet fur froze.
Six miles from earth, loosed from its dream of life,
I woke to black flak° and the nightmare fighters.   *anti-aircraft fire*
5 When I died they washed me out of the turret with a hose.

—1945

---

1   *Ball Turret Gunner* Mounted on B-17 or B-24 planes, the Sperry ball turret was a one-person gun turret that required a short crew member to curl into the fetal position in order to aim and shoot.

Dylan Thomas
1914–1953

Dylan Thomas was a raucous fixture in the taverns of London's Soho-Fitzrovia district, and he haunted the rural hills and seashores of Wales. Influenced by a romantic sensibility, he sought to articulate his sense that life and death were rolled together in nature's driving "green fuse."

Thomas was born in Swansea, Wales, and his youth and childhood there would be a recurring subject in his poetry. His father was a teacher at Swansea Grammar School, which Thomas attended and where he was far from a prize pupil; as a teenager, he regularly cut classes to work on his own poetry. His first published work, "And Death Shall Have No Dominion" (1933), was printed in a literary magazine when he was only 18.

When Thomas's *18 Poems* was published the following year, the strange and disturbing power of his verse woke up London's literary establishment. The cool, controlled style of T.S. Eliot, which conditioned poetic attitudes well into the 1950s, appeared subdued next to what one critic called Thomas's "belligerent syntax." While fresh and vital, Thomas's poems are also complex, built of dense interlocking images, and tightly structured: "Do Not Go Gentle into That Good Night" (1951), for example, adopts the restrictive form of a villanelle.

Despite his heavy drinking and a turbulent marriage, Thomas continued to publish poems—as well as short stories and radio plays—until the end of his life. Constant money troubles were lessened when he began making recordings of his poetry and touring to give public readings, which were enormously popular in Europe, and even more so in the United States. He was 39 when he died in New York of problems related to alcoholism.

The Force That Through the Green Fuse Drives the Flower

The force that through the green fuse drives the flower
Drives my green age; that blasts the roots of trees
Is my destroyer.
And I am dumb to tell the crooked rose
My youth is bent by the same wintry fever.   5

The force that drives the water through the rocks
Drives my red blood; that dries the mouthing streams
Turns mine to wax.

And I am dumb to mouth unto my veins
10 How at the mountain spring the same mouth sucks.

The hand that whirls the water in the pool[1]
Stirs the quicksand; that ropes the blowing wind
Hauls my shroud sail.
And I am dumb to tell the hanging man
15 How of my clay is made the hangman's lime.[2]

The lips of time leech to the fountain head;
Love drips and gathers, but the fallen blood
Shall calm her sores.
And I am dumb to tell a weather's wind
20 How time has ticked a heaven round the stars.

And I am dumb to tell the lover's tomb
How at my sheet goes the same crooked worm.

—1933

Fern Hill

Now as I was young and easy under the apple boughs
About the lilting house and happy as the grass was green,
    The night above the dingle° starry,   *wooded dell*
        Time let me hail and climb
5   Golden in the heydays of his eyes,
And honoured among wagons I was prince of the apple towns
And once below a time I lordly had the trees and leaves
        Trail with daisies and barley
        Down the rivers of the windfall light.

10 And as I was green and carefree, famous among the barns
About the happy yard and singing as the farm was home,
    In the sun that is young once only,
        Time let me play and be
        Golden in the mercy of his means,

---

1   *The hand … the pool* In John 5.4, an angel goes to a pool in Bethesda and imbues it
    with healing properties by stirring the water.
2   *lime* Mineral used to speed up decomposition.

And green and golden I was huntsman and herdsman, the calves   15
Sang to my horn, the foxes on the hills barked clear and cold,
    And the sabbath rang slowly
      In the pebbles of the holy streams.

All the sun long it was running, it was lovely, the hay
Fields high as the house, the tunes from the chimneys, it was air   20
    And playing, lovely and watery
      And fire green as grass.
    And nightly under the simple stars
As I rode to sleep the owls were bearing the farm away,
All the moon long I heard, blessed among stables, the   25
    nightjars°   *nocturnal birds*
    Flying with the ricks° and the horses   *haystacks*
      Flashing into the dark.

And then to awake, and the farm, like a wanderer white
With the dew, come back, the cock on his shoulder: it was all
    Shining, it was Adam and maiden,   30
      The sky gathered again
    And the sun grew round that very day.
So it must have been after the birth of the simple light
In the first, spinning place, the spellbound horses walking warm
    Out of the whinnying green stable   35
      On to the fields of praise.

And honoured among foxes and pheasants by the gay house
Under the new made clouds and happy as the heart was long,
    In the sun born over and over,
      I ran my heedless ways,   40
    My wishes raced through the house high hay
And nothing I cared, at my sky blue trades,° that time   *occupations*
    allows
In all his tuneful turning so few and such morning songs
    Before the children green and golden
      Follow him out of grace,   45

Nothing I cared, in the lamb white days, that time would take me
Up to the swallow thronged loft by the shadow of my hand,
    In the moon that is always rising,
      Nor that riding to sleep

50   I should hear him fly with the high fields
And wake to the farm forever fled from the childless land.
Oh as I was young and easy in the mercy of his means,
      Time held me green and dying
   Though I sang in my chains like the sea.

—1946

Do Not Go Gentle into That Good Night

Do not go gentle into that good night,
Old age should burn and rave at close of day;
Rage, rage against the dying of the light.

Though wise men at their end know dark is right,
5 Because their words had forked no lightning they
Do not go gentle into that good night.

Good men, the last wave by, crying how bright
Their frail deeds might have danced in a green bay,
Rage, rage against the dying of the light.

10 Wild men who caught and sang the sun in flight,
And learn, too late, they grieved it on its way,
Do not go gentle into that good night.

Grave men, near death, who see with blinding sight
Blind eyes could blaze like meteors and be gay,
15 Rage, rage against the dying of the light.

And you, my father, there on the sad height,
Curse, bless, me now with your fierce tears, I pray.
Do not go gentle into that good night.
Rage, rage against the dying of the light.

—1951

P.K. Page
1916–2010

Although she was also a visual artist of no small talent and an accomplished writer of fiction and non-fiction, P.K. Page is best known as a visionary poet with a gift for fusing the physical and the metaphysical through an elaborate system of evocative imagery.

After emigrating from her native England at a young age, Page grew up on the Canadian prairies, eventually settling in Montreal. Over the course of her long career, she explored a vast intellectual terrain, from ancient philosophy and mysticism to modern psychology and neuroscience, in a style that became increasingly spare and transparent. For this reason, and because Page was a significant part of the movement to modernize Canadian poetry, she is known as a modernist poet, though her frequent use of densely patterned imagery also affiliates her with Symbolism.

Following the publication of her Governor General's Award-winning collection *The Metal and the Flower* (1954), Page lapsed into a 13-year poetic silence while accompanying her husband to Australia, Brazil, Mexico, and Guatemala on his political and diplomatic appointments. Whereas the early poems have been described as aloof portraits that observe and ruminate in a spirit of analytical detachment, the work she wrote after her return to Canada is often regarded as an attempt to move beyond aesthetic portraiture, to transcend what she called the "tyranny of subjectivity" for a more compassionate, expansive, even mystical vision of the world.

Page continued to write until her death at the age of 93. In 1998 she was made a Companion of the Order of Canada, and in 2003 her collection *Planet Earth: Poems Selected and New* was shortlisted for the Griffin Prize.

The Stenographers

After the brief bivouac[1] of Sunday,
their eyes, in the forced march of Monday to Saturday,
hoist the white flag, flutter in the snow-storm of paper,
haul it down and crack in the mid-sun of temper.

In the pause between the first draft and the carbon   5
they glimpse the smooth hours when they were children—
the ride in the ice-cart, the ice-man's name,
the end of the route and the long walk home;

---

1   *bivouac* Military camp made without covered shelters.

remember the sea where floats at high tide
10 were sea marrows growing on the scatter-green vine
or spools of grey toffee, or wasps' nests on water;
remember the sand and the leaves of the country.

Bell rings and they go and the voice draws their pencil
like a sled across snow; when its runners are frozen
15 rope snaps and the voice then is pulling no burden
but runs like a dog on the winter of paper.

Their climates are winter and summer—no wind
for the kites of their hearts—no wind for a flight;
a breeze at the most, to tumble them over
20 and leave them like rubbish—the boy-friends of blood.

In the inch of the noon as they move they are stagnant.
The terrible calm of the noon is their anguish;
the lip of the counter, the shapes of the straws
like icicles breaking their tongues, are invaders.

25 Their beds are their oceans—salt water of weeping
the waves that they know—the tide before sleep;
and fighting to drown they assemble their sheep
in columns and watch them leap desks for their fences
and stare at them with their own mirror-worn faces.

30 In the felt of the morning the calico-minded,
sufficiently starched, insert papers, hit keys,
efficient and sure as their adding machines;
yet they weep in the vault, they are taut as net curtains
stretched upon frames. In their eyes I have seen
35 the pin men of madness in marathon trim
race round the track of the stadium pupil.

—1946

Stories of Snow

Those in the vegetable rain retain
an area behind their sprouting eyes
held soft and rounded with the dream of snow
precious and reminiscent as those globes—
souvenir of some never nether land—   5
which hold their snowstorms circular, complete,
high in a tall and teakwood cabinet.

In countries where the leaves are large as hands
where flowers protrude their fleshy chins
and call their colours   10
an imaginary snowstorm sometimes falls
among the lilies.
And in the early morning one will waken
to think the glowing linen of his pillow
a northern drift, will find himself mistaken   15
and lie back weeping.
And there the story shifts from head to head,
of how, in Holland, from their feather beds
hunters arise and part the flakes and go
forth to the frozen lakes in search of swans—   20
the snow light falling white along their guns,
their breath in plumes.
While tethered in the wind like sleeping gulls
ice boats await the raising of their wings
to skim the electric ice at such a speed   25
they leap jet strips of naked water,
and how these flying, sailing hunters feel
air in their mouths as terrible as ether.
And on the story runs that even drinks
in that white landscape dare to be no colour;   30
how, flasked and water clear, the liquor slips
silver against the hunters' moving hips.
And of the swan in death these dreamers tell
of its last flight and how it falls, a plummet,
pierced by the freezing bullet   35
and how three feathers, loosened by the shot,
descend like snow upon it.

While hunters plunge their fingers in its down
deep as a drift, and dive their hands
40   up to the neck of the wrist
in that warm metamorphosis of snow
as gentle as the sort that woodsmen know
who, lost in the white circle, fall at last
and dream their way to death.

45   And stories of this kind are often told
in countries where great flowers bar the roads
with reds and blues which seal the route to snow
as if, in telling, raconteurs unlock
the colour with its complement and go
50   through to the area behind the eyes
where silent, unrefractive whiteness lies.

—1946

Al Purdy
1918–2000

Al Purdy was a staunch Canadian nationalist whose love of country was an overwhelming presence in his poetic works. Purdy wrote realistically about Canada's geography and regional history, drawing on material ranging from the lives of the long-dead Dorset Inuit to his own formative experiences train-hopping across the country, to his great love for the rock-strewn, formidable landscape of Eastern Ontario where he spent much of his life. His rough, sometimes self-deprecating poetic persona is distinctly Canadian, too, as is the colloquial style he evolved over the course of his career to reflect everyday Canadian speech. Of his writing, Purdy's friend and collaborator Doug Beardsley said, "He spoke to us, for us, he gave articulation to our lives as Canadians. He consciously set out to map this country with poetry and he did that."

Born in 1918, Purdy dropped out of school and, during his youth, spent time travelling across the country. He served in the Royal Canadian Air Force during World War II, and went on to become a cab driver and a mattress factory employee. In 1944 he published his first collection of poetry, *The Enchanted Echo*; he would later decry his early works, claiming that it was not until 1965 that he was truly a poet. That year he won his first Governor General's Award for *The Cariboo Horses*, and in 1986 he would receive another for *The Collected Poems of Al Purdy, 1956–1986*. Over the course of his career, Purdy published over 30 volumes of poetry and championed the work of other Canadian poets in his work as an editor and anthologist.

Trees at the Arctic Circle

(*Salix Cordifolia*—Ground Willow)

They are 18 inches long
or even less
crawling under rocks
grovelling among the lichens
bending and curling to escape   5
making themselves small
finding new ways to hide
Coward trees
I am angry to see them
like this   10
not proud of what they are

bowing to weather instead
careful of themselves
worried about the sky
15   afraid of exposing their limbs
like a Victorian married couple

I call to mind great Douglas Firs
I see tall maples waving green
and oaks like gods in autumn gold
20   the whole horizon jungle dark
and I crouched under that continual night
But these
even the dwarf shrubs of Ontario
mock them
25   Coward trees

And yet—and yet—
their seed pods glow
like delicate grey earrings
their leaves are veined and intricate
30   like tiny parkas
They have about three months
to ensure the species does not die
and that's how they spend their time
unbothered by any human opinion
35   just digging in here and now
sending their roots down down down
And you know it occurs to me
      about 2 feet under
those roots must touch permafrost
40   ice that remains ice forever
and they use it for their nourishment
they use death to remain alive

I see that I've been carried away
in my scorn of the dwarf trees
45   most foolish in my judgments
To take away the dignity
      of any living thing
even tho it cannot understand
      the scornful words

is to make life itself trivial 50
and yourself the Pontifex Maximus°   *High Priest*
    of nullity
I have been stupid in a poem
I will not alter the poem
but let the stupidity remain permanent 55
as the trees are
in a poem
the dwarf trees of Baffin Island

Pangnirtung[1]

—1967

Lament for the Dorsets[2]

(Eskimos extinct in the 14th century AD)

Animal bones and some mossy tent rings
scrapers and spearheads carved ivory swans
all that remains of the Dorset giants
who drove the Vikings back to their long ships[3]
talked to spirits of earth and water 5
—a picture of terrifying old men
so large they broke the backs of bears
so small they lurk behind bone rafters
in the brain of modern hunters
among good thoughts and warm things 10
and come out at night
to spit on the stars

The big men with clever fingers
who had no dogs and hauled their sleds
over the frozen northern oceans 15
awkward giants
            killers of seal
they couldn't compete with little men

---

1   *Pangnirtung* Hamlet on Baffin Island.
2   *Dorsets* Dorset people lived in the central and eastern Canadian Arctic until about 500 years ago.
3   *drove the ... long ships* In the late tenth century, Norse people briefly established temporary settlements in North America.

who came from the west with dogs
20 Or else in a warm climatic cycle
the seals went back to cold waters
and the puzzled Dorsets scratched their heads
with hairy thumbs around 1350 A.D.
—couldn't figure it out
25 went around saying to each other plaintively
      "What's wrong? What happened?
        Where are the seals gone?"
And died

Twentieth-century people
30 apartment dwellers
executives of neon death
warmakers with things that explode
—they have never imagined us in their future
how could we imagine them in the past
35 squatting among the moving glaciers
six hundred years ago
with glowing lamps?
As remote or nearly
as the trilobites and swamps
40 when coal became
or the last great reptile hissed
at a mammal the size of a mouse
that squeaked and fled

Did they ever realize at all
45 what was happening to them?
Some old hunter with one lame leg
a bear had chewed
sitting in a caribou-skin tent
—the last Dorset?
50 Let's say his name was Kudluk
and watch him sitting there
carving 2-inch ivory swans
for a dead grand-daughter
taking them out of his mind
55 the places in his mind
where pictures are
He selects a sharp stone tool

to gouge a parallel pattern of lines
on both sides of the swan
holding it with his left hand   60
bearing down and transmitting
his body's weight
from brain to arm and right hand
and one of his thoughts
turns to ivory   65
The carving is laid aside
in beginning darkness
at the end of hunger
and after a while wind
blows down the tent and snow   70
begins to cover him

After 600 years
the ivory thought
is still warm

—1968

Gwen Harwood

1920–1995

Gwen Harwood spent her childhood in Brisbane and most of her adult life in Tasmania, where she moved with her husband in 1945. In addition to publishing under her own name, Harwood is known for publishing in a series of fictional personae—a means not only of getting more work published more quickly, but also, in the case of her male personae, of garnering more serious critical attention from a literary establishment that she felt dismissed her as a "poet-housewife." Despite the sexism she encountered, Harwood earned a reputation as one of the best Australian poets of her generation and received numerous honours during her lifetime, including the Robert Frost Medallion (1977), the Patrick White Literary Award (1978), and the Order of Australia.

Before Harwood became a poet, she had considered a career in music, and she continued to develop both talents as a librettist; her poetry, too, often addresses music as a theme and displays the influence of contemporary composers in its experimentation with syntax and metre. Her work was also shaped by another passion, philosophy; Harwood's poetic preoccupation with the limits of language is informed by this interest. While much of her work explores universal themes such as growth, aging, memory, and death, some of her best-known poems address women's experiences of motherhood and domesticity through a feminist lens.

In the Park

She sits in the park. Her clothes are out of date.
Two children whine and bicker, tug her skirt.
A third draws aimless patterns in the dirt.
Someone she loved once passes by—too late

5 to feign indifference to that casual nod.
"How nice," et cetera. "Time holds great surprises."
From his neat head unquestionably rises
a small balloon ... "but for the grace of God ..."

They stand a while in flickering light, rehearsing
10 the children's names and birthdays. "It's so sweet
to hear their chatter, watch them grow and thrive,"
she says to his departing smile. Then, nursing
the youngest child, sits staring at her feet.
To the wind she says, "They have eaten me alive."

—1963

Howard Nemerov
1920–1991

Howard Nemerov combined a distinguished academic career with a writing career in both poetry and prose. His prose works—including three novels written early in his life, as well as short stories and several collections of essays—were praised, but he was best known for his 13 volumes of poetry. In these volumes he approached subjects such as death, morality, spirituality, and the importance of language in a style that is sometimes witty and sometimes serious. He often made use of traditional metrical structures and of rhyme, but strove for, as he phrased it, "simplicity and the appearance of ease" even when employing technically challenging and restrictive forms.

After graduating from Harvard University, Nemerov spent World War II as a fighter pilot. Upon his return to the United States, he began a university teaching career and published his first book of poems, *The Image and the Law* (1947). In his early work, critics noted the influence of modernist poets such as T.S. Eliot and W.H. Auden; beginning with the publication of *The Salt Garden* (1955), Nemerov's growing interest in nature and landscape led to comparisons with the poet Robert Frost (1874–1963).

In 1978, Nemerov was awarded both the Pulitzer Prize and the National Book Award for *The Collected Poems of Howard Nemerov* (1977). Ten years later, he served as Poet Laureate for the United States (1988–90). James Billington, in his announcement of the appointment, praised the range of Nemerov's writing, which, in Billington's words, extended "from the profound to the poignant to the comic."

The Vacuum

The house is so quiet now
The vacuum cleaner sulks in the corner closet,
Its bag limp as a stopped lung, its mouth
Grinning into the floor, maybe at my
Slovenly life, my dog-dead youth.   5

I've lived this way long enough,
But when my old woman died her soul
Went into that vacuum cleaner, and I can't bear
To see the bag swell like a belly, eating the dust
And the woolen mice, and begin to howl   10

Because there is old filth everywhere
She used to crawl, in the corner and under the stair.
I know now how life is cheap as dirt,
And still the hungry, angry heart
15 Hangs on and howls, biting at air.

—1955

A Way of Life

It's been going on a long time.
For instance, these two guys, not saying much, who slog
Through sun and sand, fleeing the scene of their crime,
Till one turns, without a word, and smacks
5 His buddy flat with the flat of an axe,
Which cuts down on the dialogue
Some, but it is viewed rather as normal than sad
By me, as I wait for the next ad.

It seems to me it's been quite a while
10 Since the last vision of blonde loveliness
Vanished, her shampoo and shower and general style
Replaced by this lean young lunk-
head parading along with a gun in his back to confess
How yestereve, being drunk
15 And in a state of existential despair,
He beat up his grandma and pawned her invalid chair.

But here at last is a pale beauty
Smoking a filter beside a mountain stream,
Brief interlude, before the conflict of love and duty
20 Gets moving again, as sheriff and posse expound,
Between jail and saloon, the American Dream
Where Justice, after considerable horsing around,
Turns out to be Mercy; when the villain is knocked off,
A kindly uncle offers syrup for my cough.

25 And now these clean-cut athletic types
In global hats are having a nervous debate
As they stand between their individual rocket ships
Which have landed, appropriately, on some rocks

Somewhere in Space, in an atmosphere of hate
Where one tells the other to pull up his socks   30
And get going, he doesn't say where; they fade,
And an angel food cake flutters in the void.

I used to leave now and again;
No more. A lot of violence in American life
These days, mobsters and cops all over the scene.   35
But there's a lot of love, too, mixed with the strife,
And kitchen-kindness, like a bedtime story
With rich food and a more kissable depilatory.
Still, I keep my weapons handy, sitting here
Smoking and shaving and drinking the dry beer.   40

—1967

Philip Larkin
1922–1985

██████ Holding fast to the principle that poetry is to be read rather than studied, the British poet Philip Larkin rejected what he considered the modernist critical dogma that a poem's complexity is a measure of its worthiness. In his hostility toward the poetic avant-garde, Larkin is often identified with "the Movement," a group of British writers who shunned "the aberration of modernism" and the ostentatious "culture-mongering" of poets such as T.S. Eliot and Ezra Pound, whom Larkin believed had made a virtue of obscurity and perverted a native English tradition of plain-style lyric poetry.

"There's not much to say about my work," he once observed. "When you've read a poem, that's it, it's all quite clear what it means." In stark and deliberate contrast to the modernist pursuit of impersonality, Larkin typically adopts an intimate, lucidly colloquial tone in which—in the guise of his poetic persona—he often addresses the reader directly.

Three slender volumes—*The Less Deceived* (1955), *The Whitsun Weddings* (1964), and *High Windows* (1974)—established Larkin as one of the foremost poets of his generation. Many of the poems in these collections examine the experiences of loneliness, disappointment, and despair. But while Larkin's work often suggests the futility of struggle against time's "endless extinction," many of the poems also poignantly register the momentary beauties of the world. As Larkin phrased it, echoing Keats, "One of the jobs of the poem is to make the beautiful seem true and the true beautiful," even if "the disguise can usually be penetrated."

Church Going

Once I am sure there's nothing going on
I step inside, letting the door thud shut.
Another church: matting, seats, and stone,
And little books; sprawlings of flowers, cut
5 For Sunday, brownish now; some brass and stuff
Up at the holy end; the small neat organ;
And a tense, musty, unignorable silence,
Brewed God knows how long. Hatless, I take off
My cycle-clips in awkward reverence,

10 Move forward, run my hand around the font.[1]
From where I stand, the roof looks almost new—

---

1   *font* Baptismal receptacle.

Cleaned, or restored? Someone would know: I don't.
Mounting the lectern, I peruse a few
Hectoring large-scale verses, and pronounce
"Here endeth" much more loudly than I'd meant.   15
The echoes snigger briefly. Back at the door
I sign the book, donate an Irish sixpence,
Reflect the place was not worth stopping for.

Yet stop I did: in fact I often do,
And always end much at a loss like this,   20
Wondering what to look for; wondering, too,
When churches fall completely out of use
What we shall turn them into, if we shall keep
A few cathedrals chronically on show,
Their parchment, plate and pyx[1] in locked cases,   25
And let the rest rent-free to rain and sheep.
Shall we avoid them as unlucky places?

Or, after dark, will dubious women come
To make their children touch a particular stone;
Pick simples° for a cancer; or on some   *medicinal herbs* 30
Advised night see walking a dead one?
Power of some sort or other will go on
In games, in riddles, seemingly at random;
But superstition, like belief, must die,
And what remains when disbelief has gone?   35
Grass, weedy pavement, brambles, buttress, sky,

A shape less recognisable each week,
A purpose more obscure. I wonder who
Will be the last, the very last, to seek
This place for what it was; one of the crew   40
That tap and jot and know what rood-lofts° were?   *church galleries*
Some ruin-bibber,[2] randy for antique,
Or Christmas-addict, counting on a whiff
Of gown-and-bands and organ-pipes and myrrh?
Or will he be my representative,   45

---

1   *pyx* Vessel in which the bread of the Eucharist is kept.
2   *bibber* Someone who compulsively drinks a specific drink.

Bored, uninformed, knowing the ghostly silt
Dispersed, yet tending to this cross of ground
Through suburb scrub because it held unspilt
So long and equably what since is found
50 Only in separation—marriage, and birth,
And death, and thoughts of these—for which was built
This special shell? For, though I've no idea
What this accoutred frowsty° barn is worth,   *stuffy*
It pleases me to stand in silence here;

55 A serious house on serious earth it is,
In whose blent air all our compulsions meet,
Are recognised, and robed as destinies.
And that much never can be obsolete,
Since someone will forever be surprising
60 A hunger in himself to be more serious,
And gravitating with it to this ground,
Which, he once heard, was proper to grow wise in,
If only that so many dead lie round.

—1954

Talking in Bed

Talking in bed ought to be easiest,
Lying together there goes back so far,
An emblem of two people being honest.

Yet more and more time passes silently.
5 Outside, the wind's incomplete unrest
Builds and disperses clouds about the sky,

And dark towns heap up on the horizon.
None of this cares for us. Nothing shows why
At this unique distance from isolation

10 It becomes still more difficult to find
Words at once true and kind,
Or not untrue and not unkind.

—1960

This Be the Verse

They fuck you up, your mum and dad.
    They may not mean to, but they do.
They fill you with the faults they had
    And add some extra, just for you.

But they were fucked up in their turn   5
    By fools in old-style hats and coats,
Who half the time were soppy-stern
    And half at one another's throats.

Man hands on misery to man.
    It deepens like a coastal shelf.   10
Get out as early as you can,
    And don't have any kids yourself.

                      —1971

The Old Fools

What do they think has happened, the old fools,
To make them like this? Do they somehow suppose
It's more grown-up when your mouth hangs open and drools
And you keep on pissing yourself, and can't remember
Who called this morning? Or that, if they only chose,   5
They could alter things back to when they danced all night,
Or went to their wedding, or sloped arms some September?
Or do they fancy there's really been no change,
And they've always behaved as if they were crippled or tight,
Or sat through days of thin continuous dreaming   10
Watching light move? If they don't (and they can't), it's strange;
        Why aren't they screaming?

At death, you break up: the bits that were you
Start speeding away from each other for ever
With no one to see. It's only oblivion, true: 15
We had it before, but then it was going to end,
And was all the time merging with a unique endeavour
To bring to bloom the million-petalled flower
Of being here. Next time you can't pretend

20 There'll be anything else. And these are the first signs:
   Not knowing how, not hearing who, the power
   Of choosing gone. Their looks show that they're for it:
   Ash hair, toad hands, prune face dried into lines—
                  How can they ignore it?

25 Perhaps being old is having lighted rooms
   Inside your head, and people in them, acting.
   People you know, yet can't quite name; each looms
   Like a deep loss restored, from known doors turning,
   Setting down a lamp, smiling from a stair, extracting
30 A known book from the shelves; or sometimes only
   The rooms themselves, chairs and a fire burning,
   The blown bush at the window, or the sun's
   Faint friendliness on the wall some lonely
   Rain-ceased midsummer evening. That is where they live:
35 Not here and now, but where all happened once.
                  This is why they give

   An air of baffled absence, trying to be there
   Yet being here. For the rooms grow farther, leaving
   Incompetent cold, the constant wear and tear
40 Of taken breath, and them crouching below
   Extinction's alp, the old fools, never perceiving
   How near it is. This must be what keeps them quiet:
   The peak that stays in view wherever we go
   For them is rising ground. Can they never tell
45 What is dragging them back, and how it will end?
   Not at night? Not when the strangers come? Never, throughout
   The whole hideous inverted childhood? Well,
                  We shall find out.

                                              —1973

Allen Ginsberg
1926–1997

Along with writers Jack Kerouac and William S. Burroughs, Allen Ginsberg was one of the most prominent writers of the 1950s "Beat Generation," remembered for their literary rebellion against middle-class values and formalist poetry.

Ginsberg is perhaps best known for his poem "Howl," first delivered at a poetry reading in San Francisco in 1955 and published the following year. Drawing on influences from Jewish liturgy to William Blake, the long poem condemns American society's repressive attitudes toward homosexuality, drug use, and mental illness, presenting the demonic god Moloch as an embodiment of America's obsession with money and order. Because the poem makes explicit references to drug use and homosexuality at a time when both were illegal, the publishers of "Howl" were charged with distributing obscene literature, and Ginsberg's poem became the centrepiece of a landmark obscenity trial in the United States. The publishers and the poem ultimately triumphed.

After the Beat era, Ginsberg continued to write until his death, publishing letters and essays as well as poetry. His interest in religion and philosophy, especially Hindu and Buddhist thought, provided an increasingly important focus in his later work. Like "Howl," his post-Beat poems are often politically motivated; *Wichita Vortex Sutra* (1966), for example, censures the Vietnam War, against which Ginsberg was an effective and dedicated activist.

A Supermarket in California

What thoughts I have of you tonight, Walt Whitman,[1] for I walked down the sidestreets under the trees with a headache self-conscious looking at the full moon.

In my hungry fatigue, and shopping for images, I went into the neon fruit supermarket, dreaming of your enumerations!

What peaches and what penumbras![2] Whole families shopping at night! Aisles full of husbands! Wives in the avocados, babies in the tomatoes!—and you, García Lorca,[3] what were you doing down by the watermelons?

5

---

1   *Walt Whitman* American poet (1819–92), one of Ginsberg's major influences. "A Supermarket in California" was written in 1955, 100 years after Whitman published the first edition of his collection *Leaves of Grass*.
2   *penumbras* Partially shaded regions at the edges of a shadow.
3   *García Lorca* Federico García Lorca (1899–1936), Spanish poet and dramatist.

I saw you, Walt Whitman, childless, lonely old grubber, poking among
10 the meats in the refrigerator and eyeing the grocery boys.[1]

I heard you asking questions of each: Who killed the pork chops? What
price bananas? Are you my Angel?

I wandered in and out of the brilliant stacks of cans following you, and
followed in my imagination by the store detective. We strode down the
15 open corridors together in our solitary fancy tasting artichokes, possessing
every frozen delicacy, and never passing the cashier.

Where are we going, Walt Whitman? The doors close in an hour.
Which way does your beard point tonight?

(I touch your book and dream of our odyssey in the supermarket and
20 feel absurd.)

Will we walk all night through solitary streets? The trees add shade to
shade, lights out in the houses, we'll both be lonely.

Will we stroll dreaming of the lost America of love past blue
automobiles in driveways, home to our silent cottage?

25 Ah, dear father, greybeard, lonely old courage-teacher, what America
did you have when Charon[2] quit poling his ferry and you got out on a
smoking bank and stood watching the boat disappear on the black waters of
Lethe?[3]

—1956 (written 1955)

---

1   *I saw you ... grocery boys* Although the full nature of his sexuality is still debated, most
    scholars believe that Whitman was gay.
2   *Charon* In Greek mythology, the boatman who ferried the souls of the dead across the
    river Styx to Hades.
3   *Lethe* River in Hades, the waters of which brought forgetfulness.

John Ashbery
b. 1927

John Ashbery's admiration for avant-garde music, surrealism, and American abstract expressionist painting has strongly influenced his poetry. The resulting style is experimental, complex, and often difficult. "My poetry imitates or reproduces the way knowledge or awareness come to me, which is by fits and starts and by indirection…," Ashbery has said; "[m]y poetry is disjunct, but then so is life." Ashbery is considered a leading figure in the "New York School" of poets whose work shared affinities with the city's avant-garde art scene during the 1950s and 1960s.

Ashbery was born in Rochester, New York, and attended Harvard and Columbia Universities. He then spent a decade in Paris working as a newspaper editor and art critic while also composing poetry. The collection *Some Trees* (1956) first brought him critical attention; it was followed by the experimental *The Tennis Court Oath* (1962). His reputation grew steadily after this point, and Ashbery has since become widely acknowledged as one of the most important American poets of his era. Of his more than 20 volumes of poetry, the most highly regarded is perhaps *Self-Portrait in a Convex Mirror* (1975), which won three major American literary awards, including the Pulitzer Prize.

As critical admiration for Ashbery has increased, a minority of critics have continued to find fault with the inaccessibility of his approach. For Ashbery, however, difficulty of interpretation is a sign that a poem has something new and profound to show its audience; as he says, "a poem that communicates something that's already known by the reader is not really communicating anything to him, and in fact shows a lack of respect for him."

Civilization and Its Discontents

A people chained to aurora[1]
I alone disarming you

Millions of facts of distributed light

Helping myself with some big boxes
Up the steps, then turning to no neighbourhood: 5
The child's psalm, slightly sung
In the hall rushing into the small room.

---

1   *aurora* Roman goddess personifying the dawn; also another name for the Northern and Southern Lights.

Such fire! leading away from destruction.
Somewhere in the outer ether I glimpsed you
10 Coming at me, the solo barrier did it this time,
Guessing us staying, true to be at the blue mark
Of the threshold. Tired of planning it again and again,
The cool boy distant, and the soaked-up
Afterthought, like so much rain, or roof.

15 The miracle took you in beside him.
Leaves rushed the window, there was clear water and the sound of a lock.
Now I never see you much any more.
The summers are much colder than they used to be
In that other time, when you and I were young.
20 I miss the human truth of your smile,
The halfhearted gaze of your palms,
And all things together, but there is no comic reign
Only the facts you put to me. You must not, then,
Be very surprised if I am alone: it is all for you,
25 The night, and the stars, and the way we used to be.

There is no longer any use in harping on
The incredible principle of daylong silence, the dark sunlight
As only the grass is beginning to know it,

The wreath of the north pole,
30 Festoons for the late return, the shy pensioners
Agasp on the lamplit air. What is agreeable
Is to hold your hand. The gravel
Underfoot. The time is for coming close. Useless
Verbs shooting the other words far away.

35 I had already swallowed the poison
And could only gaze into the distance at my life
Like a saint's with each day distinct.
No heaviness in the upland pastures. Nothing
In the forest. Only life under the huge trees
40 Like a coat that has grown too big, moving far away,
Cutting swamps for men like lapdogs, holding its own,
Performing once again, for you and for me.

—1963

The Improvement

Is that where it happens?
Only yesterday when I came back, I had this
diaphanous disaffection for this room, for spaces,
for the whole sky and whatever lies beyond.
I felt the eggplant, then the rhubarb.
Nothing seems strong enough for
this life to manage, that sees beyond
into particles forming some kind of entity—
so we get dressed kindly, crazy at the moment.
A life of afterwords begins.

We never live long enough in our lives
to know what today is like.
Shards, smiling beaches,
abandon us somehow even as we converse with them.
And the leopard is transparent, like iced tea.

I wake up, my face pressed
in the dewy mess of a dream. It mattered,
because of the dream, and because dreams are by nature sad
even when there's a lot of exclaiming and beating
as there was in this one. I want the openness
of the dream turned inside out, exploded
into pieces of meaning by its own unasked questions,
beyond the calculations of heaven. Then the larkspur[1]
would don its own disproportionate weight,
and trees return to the starting gate.
See, our lips bend.

—1994

---

1   *larkspur*   Plant with spikes of flowers.

Thom Gunn

1929–2004

As diverse in subject matter as in style, the poetry of Thom Gunn is difficult to classify. His friend and fellow poet Clive Wilmer described it as "contained energy," an attempt to reconcile passion and intellect, lyricism and argument, by harnessing the flow of experience through traditional verse forms.

The son of London journalists, Gunn spent much of his life in California, where he studied at Stanford and later taught at Berkeley. Gunn is often identified with "the Movement," a group of British poets who turned away from avant-gardism in favour of a more "native English" tradition of plain-style lyric poetry. Yet he always preferred to be understood as an Anglo-American writer, and his influences ranged from seventeenth-century English poets such as John Donne to the American modernist verse of Wallace Stevens and William Carlos Williams.

From his first collection, *Fighting Words* (1954), to his last, *Boss Cupid* (2000), Gunn experimented with styles and techniques. His early poetry, much of it concerned with the existential struggle for self-definition, is characterized by tightly controlled schemes of rhyme and metre. He later experimented with free verse and with varying degrees of formal regularity in the attempt to represent his liberating experiences with LSD and the utopian counterculture in 1960s San Francisco, where he lived until his death. Gunn changed tone again with *The Man with Night Sweats* (1992), which established him as a poet-chronicler and elegist of the AIDS epidemic that claimed many of his friends in the 1980s.

While many have seen Gunn's as a poetry of "tensions," Gunn himself preferred the word "continuities." His life and work, he said, "insists on continuities—between America and England, between free verse and metre, between vision and everyday consciousness."

Tamer and Hawk

I thought I was so tough,
But gentled at your hands,
Cannot be quick enough
To fly for you and show
5   That when I go I go
At your commands.

Even in flight above
I am no longer free:

You seeled[1] me with your love,
I am blind to other birds—   10
The habit of your words
Has hooded me.

As formerly, I wheel
I hover and I twist,
But only want the feel,   15
In my possessive thought,
Of catcher and of caught
Upon your wrist.

You but half civilize,
Taming me in this way.   20
Through having only eyes
For you I fear to lose,
I lose to keep, and choose
Tamer as prey.

                                        —1953

To His Cynical Mistress

And love is then no more than a compromise?
An impermanent treaty waiting to be signed
            By the two enemies?
—While the calculating Cupid feigning impartial blind
Drafts it, promising peace, both leaders wise   5
To his antics sign but secretly double their spies.

On each side is the ignorant animal nation
Jostling friendly in streets, enjoying in good faith
            This celebration
Forgetting their enmity with cheers and drunken breath   10
But for them there has not been yet amalgamation:
The leaders calmly plot assassination.

                                        —1958

---

1   *seeled* Part of the taming process in falconry, seeling requires the tamer to stitch up the
     eyes of the hawk.

The Hug

It was your birthday, we had drunk and dined
        Half of the night with our old friend
                Who'd showed us in the end
        To a bed I reached in one drunk stride.
                Already I lay snug,
        And drowsy with the wine dozed on one side.

I dozed, I slept. My sleep broke on a hug,
                Suddenly, from behind,
In which the full lengths of our bodies pressed:
                Your instep to my heel,
        My shoulder-blades against your chest.
        It was not sex, but I could feel
        The whole strength of your body set,
                Or braced, to mine,
                And locking me to you
        As if we were still twenty-two
        When our grand passion had not yet
                Become familial.
        My quick sleep had deleted all
        Of intervening time and place.
                I only knew
The stay of your secure firm dry embrace.

—1992

Adrienne Rich

1929–2012

Adrienne Rich was born in Baltimore, Maryland. Over her long career, she published more than sixteen volumes of poetry and five volumes of critical prose, most recently *Tonight No Poetry Will Serve: Poems 2007-2010, A Human Eye: Essays on Art in Society,* and *Later Poems: Selected and New 1971-2012,* published posthumously. She edited Muriel Rukeyser's *Selected Poems* for the Library of America. Among numerous other recognitions, Rich was the 2006 recipient of the National Book Foundation's Medal for Distinguished Contribution to American Letters. Her poetry and essays have been widely translated and published internationally.[1]

Aunt Jennifer's Tigers

Aunt Jennifer's tigers prance across a screen,
Bright topaz denizens of a world of green.
They do not fear the men beneath the tree;
They pace in sleek chivalric certainty.

Aunt Jennifer's fingers fluttering through her wool   5
Find even the ivory needle hard to pull.
The massive weight of Uncle's wedding band
Sits heavily upon Aunt Jennifer's hand.

When Aunt is dead, her terrified hands will lie
Still ringed with ordeals she was mastered by.   10
The tigers in the panel that she made
Will go on prancing, proud and unafraid.

—1951

---

1   Editors' note: This author biography was provided by the rights holders of Adrienne Rich's poetry, and is included at their request. Its relative brevity in no way reflects the editors' views as to the importance of Rich's work.

Living in Sin

She had thought the studio would keep itself;
no dust upon the furniture of love.
Half heresy, to wish the taps less vocal,
the panes relieved of grime. A plate of pears,
5   a piano with a Persian shawl, a cat
stalking the picturesque amusing mouse
had risen at his urging.
Not that at five each separate stair would writhe
under the milkman's tramp; that morning light
10   so coldly would delineate the scraps
of last night's cheese and three sepulchral bottles;
that on the kitchen shelf among the saucers
a pair of beetle-eyes would fix her own—
envoy from some black village in the mouldings ...
15   Meanwhile, he, with a yawn,
sounded a dozen notes upon the keyboard,
declared it out of tune, shrugged at the mirror,
rubbed at his beard, went out for cigarettes;
while she, jeered by the minor demons,
20   pulled back the sheets and made the bed and found
a towel to dust the table-top,
and let the coffee-pot boil over on the stove.
By evening she was back in love again,
though not so wholly but throughout the night
25   she woke sometimes to feel the daylight coming
like a relentless milkman up the stairs.

—1955

Diving into the Wreck

First having read the book of myths,
and loaded the camera,
and checked the edge of the knife-blade,
I put on
5   the body-armour of black rubber
the absurd slippers
the grave and awkward mask.
I am having to do this

not like Cousteau[1] with his
assiduous team   10
aboard the sun-flooded schooner
but here alone.

There is a ladder.
The ladder is always there
hanging innocently   15
close to the side of the schooner.
We know what it is for,
we who have used it.
Otherwise
it's a piece of maritime floss   20
some sundry equipment.

I go down.
Rung after rung and still
the oxygen immerses me
the blue light   25
the clear atoms
of our human air.
I go down.
My flippers cripple me,
I crawl like an insect down the ladder   30
and there is no one
to tell me when the ocean
will begin.

First the air is blue and then
it is bluer and then green and then   35
black I am blacking out and yet
my mask is powerful
it pumps my blood with power
the sea is another story
the sea is not a question of power   40
I have to learn alone
to turn my body without force
in the deep element.

---

1   *Cousteau* Jacques Cousteau (1910–97), well-known oceanographer and undersea ex-
     plorer.

And now: it is easy to forget
45 what I came for
among so many who have always
lived here
swaying their crenellated fans
between the reefs
50 and besides
you breathe differently down here.

I came to explore the wreck.
The words are purposes.
The words are maps.
55 I came to see the damage that was done
and the treasures that prevail.
I stroke the beam of my lamp
slowly along the flank
of something more permanent
60 than fish or weed

the thing I came for:
the wreck and not the story of the wreck
the thing itself and not the myth
the drowned face always staring
65 toward the sun
the evidence of damage
worn by salt and sway into this threadbare beauty
the ribs of the disaster
curving their assertion
70 among the tentative haunters.

This is the place.
And I am here, the mermaid whose dark hair
streams black, the merman in his armoured body
We circle silently
75 about the wreck
we dive into the hold.
I am she: I am he

whose drowned face sleeps with open eyes
whose breasts still bear the stress

whose silver, copper, vermeil[1] cargo lies   80
obscurely inside barrels
half-wedged and left to rot
we are the half-destroyed instruments
that once held to a course
the water-eaten log   85
the fouled compass

We are, I am, you are
by cowardice or courage
the one who find our way
back to this scene   90
carrying a knife, a camera
a book of myths
in which
our names do not appear.

—1973

---

1   *vermeil* Gold plate over silver.

Ted Hughes
1930–1998

With bold metaphors and forceful rhythms, poet Ted Hughes paints grim, often violent, visions of human existence. At the same time, he celebrates the power of nature and attempts to reunite humanity with the natural world. Hughes's first volume of poetry, *The Hawk in the Rain* (1957), received critical praise for its strong, earthy language and intense natural imagery. He further established his reputation as a major new poet with his second book, *Lupercal* (1960), and he continued to write prolifically, producing many volumes of poetry as well as verse for children, radio plays, and translations.

In 1956 Hughes married the American poet Sylvia Plath (1932–63); the couple separated in 1962, and Plath committed suicide less than a year later. Hughes put his own poetry on hold to focus on editing and publishing his wife's poems and journals, and the editorial decisions he made as her executor received intense criticism from some of her admirers. Hughes would say very little regarding his relationship with Plath until his 1998 publication of *Birthday Letters*, a series of poems addressed to her.

Wodwo (1967), Hughes's return to poetry after Plath's death, signalled a change in direction from his earlier work. A marked interest in anthropology—and especially in occult, mythic, and folktale sources—began to colour his writing. Several of his volumes were produced in collaboration with visual artists, such as photographer Fay Godwin, with whom he created *Remains of Elmet* (1979), an exploration of the history and landscape of his native West Yorkshire from ancient to industrial times.

Hughes was Britain's Poet Laureate from 1984 until his death in 1998. British poet and critic Dick Davis has offered this explanation for the continuing appeal of Hughes's poetry: "He brings back to our suburban, centrally-heated and, above all, *safe* lives reports from an authentic frontier of reality and the imagination."

The Thought-Fox

I imagine this midnight moment's forest:
Something else is alive
Beside the clock's loneliness
And this blank page where my fingers move.

5 Through the window I see no star:
Something more near
Though deeper within darkness
Is entering the loneliness:

Cold, delicately as the dark snow
A fox's nose touches twig, leaf;   10
Two eyes serve a movement, that now
And again now, and now, and now

Sets neat prints into the snow
Between trees, and warily a lame
Shadow lags by stump and in hollow   15
Of a body that is bold to come

Across clearings, an eye,
A widening deepening greenness,
Brilliantly, concentratedly,
Coming about its own business   20

Till, with a sudden sharp hot stink of fox,
It enters the dark hole of the head.
The window is starless still; the clock ticks,
The page is printed.

—1957

Pike[1]

Pike, three inches long, perfect
Pike in all parts, green tigering the gold.
Killers from the egg: the malevolent aged grin.
They dance on the surface among the flies.

Or move, stunned by their own grandeur,   5
Over a bed of emerald, silhouette
Of submarine delicacy and horror.
A hundred feet long in their world.

In ponds, under the heat-struck lily pads—
Gloom of their stillness: 10
Logged on last year's black leaves, watching upwards.
Or hung in an amber cavern of weeds

---

1   *Pike* Family of freshwater fish, some species of which can grow longer than two metres.
     Considered unusually aggressive predators, they eat other fish, amphibians, small mam-
     mals, birds, and sometimes each other.

The jaws' hooked clamp and fangs
Not to be changed at this date;
15 A life subdued to its instrument;
The gills kneading quietly, and the pectorals.

Three we kept behind glass,
Jungled in weed: three inches, four,
And four and a half: fed fry to them—
20 Suddenly there were two. Finally one.

With a sag belly and the grin it was born with.
And indeed they spare nobody.
Two, six pounds each, over two feet long,
High and dry and dead in the willow-herb—

25 One jammed past its gills down the other's gullet:
The outside eye stared: as a vice locks—
The same iron in this eye
Though its film shrank in death.

A pond I fished, fifty yards across,
30 Whose lilies and muscular tench[1]
Had outlasted every visible stone
Of the monastery that planted them—

Stilled legendary depth:
It was as deep as England. It held
35 Pike too immense to stir, so immense and old
That past nightfall I dared not cast

But silently cast and fished
With the hair frozen on my head
For what might move, for what eye might move.
40 The still splashes on the dark pond,

Owls hushing the floating woods
Frail on my ear against the dream
Darkness beneath night's darkness had freed,
That rose slowly towards me, watching.

—1959

---

1   *tench* Fish similar to carp.

Hawk Roosting

I sit in the top of the wood, my eyes closed.
Inaction, no falsifying dream
Between my hooked head and hooked feet:
Or in sleep rehearse perfect kills and eat.

The convenience of the high trees!   5
The air's buoyancy and the sun's ray
Are of advantage to me;
And the earth's face upward for my inspection.

My feet are locked upon the rough bark.
It took the whole of Creation   10
To produce my foot, my each feather:
Now I hold Creation in my foot

Or fly up, and revolve it all slowly—
I kill where I please because it is all mine.
There is no sophistry in my body: 15
My manners are tearing off heads—

The allotment of death.
For the one path of my flight is direct
Through the bones of the living.
No arguments assert my right: 20

The sun is behind me.
Nothing has changed since I began.
My eye has permitted no change.
I am going to keep things like this.

—1960

Heptonstall Old Church[1]

A great bird landed here.

Its song drew men out of rock,
Living men out of bog and heather.

---

1   *Heptonstall Old Church* The town of Heptonstall was three miles from Hughes's child-
     hood home of Mytholmroyd, in West Yorkshire. The ruins of the "old church" (dating
     from the thirteenth century) stand beside the present church, constructed in 1854. The
     bodies of Sylvia Plath (1932–63) and of Hughes's parents are buried in its churchyard.

Its song put a light in the valleys
5   And harness on the long moors.

Its song brought a crystal from space
And set it in men's heads.

Then the bird died.

Its giant bones
10   Blackened and became a mystery.

The crystal in men's heads
Blackened and fell to pieces.

The valleys went out.
The moorland broke loose.

—1979

Heptonstall Old Church, 1970s.

Derek Walcott
b. 1930

In 1992, Derek Walcott became the first Caribbean writer to receive the Nobel Prize in Literature. Throughout his career, he has grappled with the central issues of twentieth- and twenty-first-century Caribbean writing: the use of the English language versus that of Creole; the effects of a history of slavery and colonization on the region; and the deep-seated ambivalence toward English culture that results from that history.

Walcott's personal background reflects the cultural complexities of the Caribbean. A descendant both of Europeans and of former slaves, he was born into an English-speaking family on the predominantly French Creole-speaking island of St. Lucia, and has lived there or in Trinidad for most of his life. In his Nobel acceptance speech he expressed his wish that the people of the Caribbean would move beyond their painful history, claiming that "[we] make too much of that long groan which underlines the past." He proffered instead a vision of Caribbean poetry as a route to rebuilding and celebrating Caribbean culture: "the fate of poetry is to fall in love with the world, in spite of History."

Some Caribbean intellectuals have criticized Walcott's attitude toward the colonial past, arguing for an unequivocal return to African traditions or for a turning away from the English language in favour of Creole. In response to criticism of his decision to write in English, Walcott has argued that the language is shaped by those who use it.

Walcott's more than 20 books of poetry include the epic *Omeros* (1990), which merges Homer's *Odyssey* with the history of St. Lucia, and the T.S. Eliot Prize-winning collection *White Egrets* (2011). Walcott is also a prolific playwright whose work has been instrumental to the development of indigenous theatre in Trinidad.

A Far Cry from Africa

A wind is ruffling the tawny pelt
Of Africa. Kikuyu,[1] quick as flies,
Batten upon[2] the bloodstreams of the veldt.°   *open country*
Corpses are scattered through a paradise.
Only the worm, colonel of carrion, cries: 5
"Waste no compassion on these separate dead!"

---

1   *Kikuyu* Bantu-speaking people of Kenya who fought against British colonial settlers as part of the eight-year Mau Mau uprising of the 1950s.
2   *Batten upon* Thrive on; revel in.

Statistics justify and scholars seize
The salients of colonial policy.
What is that to the white child hacked in bed?
10 To savages, expendable as Jews?

Threshed out by beaters, the long rushes break
In a white dust of ibises[1] whose cries
Have wheeled since civilization's dawn
From the parched river or beast-teeming plain.
15 The violence of beast on beast is read
As natural law, but upright man
Seeks his divinity by inflicting pain.
Delirious as these worried beasts, his wars
Dance to the tightened carcass of a drum,
20 While he calls courage still that native dread
Of the white peace contracted by the dead.

Again brutish necessity wipes its hands
Upon the napkin of a dirty cause, again
A waste of our compassion, as with Spain,[2]
25 The gorilla wrestles with the superman.
I who am poisoned with the blood of both,
Where shall I turn, divided to the vein?
I who have cursed
The drunken officer of British rule, how choose
30 Between this Africa and the English tongue I love?
Betray them both, or give back what they give?
How can I face such slaughter and be cool?
How can I turn from Africa and live?

—1962

---

1   *ibises* Long-legged, stork-like birds that inhabit lakes and swamps.
2   *Spain* I.e., the Spanish Civil War (1936–39). Many foreign volunteers participated in the Civil War, perceiving it as a way to resist the international rise of fascism. After brutality on both sides, the war ended with the establishment of a dictatorship supported by the German Nazis and the Italian Fascists.

Ruins of a Great House

though our longest sun sets at right declensions and makes but winter arches, it cannot be long before we lie down in darkness, and have our light in ashes ...[1]

—BROWNE, *Urn Burial*

Stones only, the disjecta membra[2] of this Great House,
Whose moth-like girls are mixed with candledust,
Remain to file the lizard's dragonish claws.
The mouths of those gate cherubs shriek with stain;
Axle and coach wheel silted under the muck   5
Of cattle droppings.
               Three crows flap for the trees
And settle, creaking the eucalyptus boughs.
A smell of dead limes quickens in the nose
The leprosy of empire.   10
          "Farewell, green fields,
           Farewell, ye happy groves!"[3]
Marble like Greece, like Faulkner's South[4] in stone,
Deciduous beauty prospered and is gone,
But where the lawn breaks in a rash of trees   15
A spade below dead leaves will ring the bone
Of some dead animal or human thing
Fallen from evil days, from evil times.

It seems that the original crops were limes
Grown in the silt that clogs the river's skirt;   20
The imperious rakes[5] are gone, their bright girls gone,
The river flows, obliterating hurt.
I climbed a wall with the grille ironwork
Of exiled craftsmen protecting that great house
From guilt, perhaps, but not from the worm's rent   25
Nor from the padded cavalry of the mouse.

---

1   *though our ... ashes* From English essayist Thomas Browne's *Hydriotaphia: Urne-Buriall* (1658).

2   *disjecta membra* Latin: scattered remains.

3   *"Farewell, green ... happy groves!"* See William Blake's poem "Night" (1789): "Farewell, green fields and happy groves."

4   *Faulkner's South* The American South as depicted in the fiction of William Faulkner (1897–1962).

5   *rakes* Wild young noblemen.

And when a wind shook in the limes I heard
What Kipling[1] heard, the death of a great empire, the abuse
Of ignorance by Bible and by sword.

30 A green lawn, broken by low walls of stone,
Dipped to the rivulet, and pacing, I thought next
Of men like Hawkins, Walter Raleigh, Drake,[2]
Ancestral murderers and poets, more perplexed
In memory now by every ulcerous crime.
35 The world's green age then was a rotting lime
Whose stench became the charnel° galleon's text.   *mortuary*
The rot remains with us, the men are gone.
But, as dead ash is lifted in a wind
That fans the blackening ember of the mind,
40 My eyes burned from the ashen prose of Donne.[3]

Ablaze with rage I thought,
Some slave is rotting in this manorial lake,
But still the coal of my compassion fought
That Albion° too was once   *England*
45 A colony like ours, "part of the continent, piece of the main,"[4]
Nook-shotten, rook o'erblown, deranged
By foaming channels and the vain expense
Of bitter faction.
                    All in compassion ends
50 So differently from what the heart arranged:
"as well as if a manor of thy friend's ..."

—1962

---

1   *Kipling* Rudyard Kipling (1865–1936), English novelist and short story writer whose works often interrogated British imperialism.
2   *Hawkins* John Hawkins, sixteenth-century British slave trader who brought slaves from Africa to West Indian plantations; *Walter Raleigh* English explorer and poet (1552–1618); *Drake* Sir Francis Drake (1543–96), British explorer and military commander who became the first Englishman to sail around the world.
3   *Donne* English poet and minister John Donne (1572–1631).
4   *part of ... main* From John Donne's *Devotions upon Emergent Occasions*, Meditation 17 (1624): "No man is an island, entire of itself; every man is a piece of the continent, a part of the main. If a clod be washed away by the sea, Europe is the less, as well as if a promontory were, as well as if a manor of thy friend's or of thine own were...."

from *Midsummer*

52

I heard them marching the leaf-wet roads of my head,
the sucked vowels of a syntax trampled to mud,
a division of dictions, one troop black, barefooted,
the other in redcoats bright as their sovereign's blood;
their feet scuffled like rain, the bare soles with the shod.   5
One fought for a queen, the other was chained in her service,
but both, in bitterness, travelled the same road.
Our occupation and the Army of Occupation
are born enemies, but what mortar can size
the broken stones of the barracks of Brimstone Hill[1]   10
to the gaping brick of Belfast? Have we changed sides
to the mustached sergeants and the horsy gentry
because we serve English, like a two-headed sentry
guarding its borders? No language is neutral;
the green oak of English is a murmurous cathedral   15
where some took umbrage, some peace, but every shade, all,
helped widen its shadow. I used to haunt the arches
of the British barracks of Vigie.[2] There were leaves there,
bright, rotting like revers or epaulettes,[3] and the stenches
of history and piss. Leaves piled like the dropped aitches   20
of soldiers from rival shires, from the brimstone trenches
of Agincourt to the gas of the Somme.[4] On Poppy Day[5]
our schools bought red paper flowers. They were for Flanders.

---

1   *Brimstone Hill* Eighteenth-century fortress built by slaves on the island of Saint Kitts,
     in the Caribbean. First settled by the British in the early seventeenth century, Saint Kitts
     became a British colony in 1783 and gained independence as part of the Federation of
     Saint Kitts and Nevis in 1983.
2   *barracks of Vigie* On the island of St. Lucia in the Caribbean.
3   *revers* Reversed edges of a coat, vest, etc.; *epaulettes* Ornamental shoulder pieces on
     military uniforms.
4   *Agincourt* Site of Henry V's famous victory over the French in 1415; *Somme* Site of a
     World War I battle in France, which began on 1 July 1916 and lasted five months.
5   *Poppy Day* Remembrance Day (in Britain and the Commonwealth) or Veteran's Day
     (in the US), when poppies are worn to commemorate those killed in World Wars I and
     II. (See John McCrae's 1915 poem "In Flanders Fields.")

I saw Hotspur[1] cursing the smoke through which a popinjay
25 minced from the battle. Those raging commanders from
Thersites[2] to Percy, their rant is our model.
I pinned the poppy to my blazer. It bled like a vowel.

—1984

Central America

Helicopters are cutlassing the wild bananas.
Between a nicotine thumb and forefinger
brittle faces crumble like tobacco leaves.
Children waddle in vests, their legs bowed,
5 little shrimps curled under their navels.
The old men's teeth are stumps in a charred forest.
Their skins grate like the iguana's.
Their gaze like slate stones.
Women squat by the river's consolations
10 where children wade up to their knees,
and a stick stirs up a twinkling of butterflies.
Up there, in the blue acres
of forest, flies circle their fathers.
In spring, in the upper provinces
15 of the Empire, yellow tanagers
float up through the bare branches.
There is no distinction in these distances.

—1987

---

1 *Hotspur* Nickname of Sir Henry Percy (1366–1403), an English nobleman who led an uprising against King Henry IV and who figures as the hot-headed rival to Prince Hal in Shakespeare's *I Henry IV*. In a speech in *I Henry IV* 1.3.28–68, he expresses anger about a "popinjay" (frivolous, foppish man) making disrespectful small talk as bodies are carried off the battlefield.

2 *Thersites* Cowardly soldier of Greek legend who appears in Homer's *Iliad* and Shakespeare's *Troilus and Cressida*. In the *Iliad*, he complains about the incompetence of his rulers; in Shakespeare's play, he delivers cynical commentary about the foolishness of war.

Sylvia Plath

1932–1963

Sylvia Plath's early life was, outwardly, one of upper middle-class privilege. The daughter of a Boston University professor and his wife, Plath was an excellent student both in school and later at Smith, a prestigious liberal arts college for women, where she became a prolific writer of poems and short stories. Inwardly, however, she had been profoundly affected by the death of her father when she was eight, and became deeply conflicted over the roles young women in the 1950s were expected to fulfill. Following her third year at Smith she was awarded a guest editorship at the young women's magazine *Mademoiselle*; the experience was a disappointment, however, and Plath fell into a deep depression. She attempted suicide that August, and spent many months thereafter in psychiatric care.

Plath recovered, and in 1955 was awarded a scholarship to Cambridge University, where her talents as a writer began to be more widely recognized—and where she met and soon married the British poet Ted Hughes. The couple both published well-received volumes of poetry (Plath's *The Colossus* appeared in 1960) and they had two children together, but their relationship was sometimes strained and Plath continued to suffer from depression. In 1962, following Plath's discovery that Hughes had been having an affair, the two separated. Between that time and Plath's suicide in February of 1963, living with the children in a bitterly cold flat in London, she wrote the extraordinary body of work on which her reputation now rests. These poems (published posthumously in 1965 in the volume *Ariel*) are spare and controlled in their form but entirely unsparing in the searing intensity with which they explore human strangeness and savagery—perhaps most memorably, the savagery of the Holocaust.

Plath's one novel, *The Bell Jar* (1963), is highly autobiographical, and, given the sensational aspects of her life, it is not surprising that her poetry is often discussed in relation to her life. But, as Catriona O'Reilly has observed, it will not do to regard Plath's work as "an extended suicide note." Her strongest poems are almost universally accorded a vital place in the history of poetry in the twentieth century.

Daddy

You do not do, you do not do
Any more, black shoe
In which I have lived like a foot
For thirty years, poor and white,
5 Barely daring to breathe or Achoo.

Daddy, I have had to kill you.
You died before I had time—
Marble-heavy, a bag full of God,
Ghastly statue with one grey toe[1]
10 Big as a Frisco seal

And a head in the freakish Atlantic
Where it pours bean green over blue
In the waters off beautiful Nauset.[2]
I used to pray to recover you.
15 Ach, du.[3]

In the German tongue, in the Polish town[4]
Scraped flat by the roller
Of wars, wars, wars.
But the name of the town is common.
20 My Polack friend

Says there are a dozen or two.
So I never could tell where you
Put your foot, your root,
I never could talk to you.
25 The tongue stuck in my jaw.

It stuck in a barb wire snare
Ich, ich, ich, ich,[5]

---

1 *Ghastly ... grey toe* Plath's father, Otto Plath (1885–1940), died from complications due to untreated diabetes. Before he died, his toe became gangrenous and his leg was amputated.

2 *Nauset* Beach in Orleans, Massachusetts.

3 *Ach, du.* German: Oh, you.

4 *Polish town* Otto Plath emigrated to the US from the Polish town of Grabow.

5 *Ich, ich, ich, ich* German: I, I, I, I.

I could hardly speak.
I thought every German was you.
And the language obscene

An engine, an engine
Chuffing me off like a Jew.
A Jew to Dachau, Auschwitz, Belsen.[1]
I began to talk like a Jew.
I think I may well be a Jew.

The snows of the Tyrol,[2] the clear beer of Vienna
Are not very pure or true.
With my gypsy ancestress and my weird luck
And my Taroc° pack and my Taroc pack   *Tarot*
I may be a bit of a Jew.

I have always been scared of *you*,
With your Luftwaffe,[3] your gobbledygoo.
And your neat moustache
And your Aryan eye, bright blue.
Panzer-man,[4] panzer-man, O You—

Not God but a swastika
So black no sky could squeak through.
Every woman adores a Fascist,
The boot in the face, the brute
Brute heart of a brute like you.

You stand at the blackboard,[5] daddy,
In the picture I have of you,
A cleft in your chin instead of your foot
But no less a devil for that, no not
Any less the black man who

30

35

40

45

50

55

---

1   *Dachau, Auschwitz, Belsen* Sites of Nazi concentration camps during World War II.
2   *Tyrol* State in Austria.
3   *Luftwaffe* German air force during World War II.
4   *Panzer-man* "Panzers" were German armoured divisions, notably those equipped with
     tanks.
5   *You ... blackboard* Otto Plath taught biology and German at Boston University.

Bit my pretty red heart in two.
I was ten when they buried you.
At twenty I tried to die
And get back, back, back to you.
60 I thought even the bones would do.

But they pulled me out of the sack,
And they stuck me together with glue.
And then I knew what to do.
I made a model of you,
65 A man in black with a Meinkampf[1] look

And a love of the rack and the screw.
And I said I do, I do.
So daddy, I'm finally through.
The black telephone's off at the root,
70 The voices just can't worm through.

If I've killed one man, I've killed two—
The vampire who said he was you
And drank my blood for a year,
Seven years, if you want to know.
75 Daddy, you can lie back now.

There's a stake in your fat black heart
And the villagers never liked you.
They are dancing and stamping on you.
They always *knew* it was you.
80 Daddy, daddy, you bastard, I'm through.

—1965 (written 1962)

Lady Lazarus[2]

I have done it again.
One year in every ten
I manage it—

---

1 *Meinkampf* Adolf Hitler's book *Mein Kampf* (1924) outlines his political philosophy.
2 *Lazarus* Man brought back to life by Jesus after being dead for four days. See John 11.1–44.

A sort of walking miracle, my skin
Bright as a Nazi lampshade,[1]   5
My right foot

A paperweight,
My featureless, fine
Jew linen.

Peel off the napkin   10
O my enemy.
Do I terrify?—

The nose, the eye pits, the full set of teeth?
The sour breath
Will vanish in a day.   15

Soon, soon the flesh
The grave cave ate will be
At home on me

And I a smiling woman.
I am only thirty.   20
And like the cat I have nine times to die.

This is Number Three.
What a trash
To annihilate each decade.

What a million filaments.   25
The peanut-crunching crowd
Shoves in to see

Them unwrap me hand and foot—
The big strip tease.
Gentlemen, ladies   30

---

1   *Nazi lampshade* Some Nazi officials allegedly created leather souvenirs, such as lamp-
    shades, using the skin of concentration camp victims.

These are my hands
My knees.
I may be skin and bone,

Nevertheless, I am the same, identical woman.
35   The first time it happened I was ten.
It was an accident.

The second time I meant
To last it out and not come back at all.
I rocked shut

40   As a seashell.
They had to call and call
And pick the worms off me like sticky pearls.

Dying
Is an art, like everything else.
45   I do it exceptionally well.

I do it so it feels like hell.
I do it so it feels real.
I guess you could say I've a call.

It's easy enough to do it in a cell.
50   It's easy enough to do it and stay put.
It's the theatrical

Comeback in broad day
To the same place, the same face, the same brute
Amused shout:

55   "A miracle!"
That knocks me out.
There is a charge

For the eyeing of my scars, there is a charge
For the hearing of my heart—
60   It really goes.

And there is a charge, a very large charge
For a word or a touch
Or a bit of blood

Or a piece of my hair or my clothes.
So, so, Herr[1] Doktor.   65
So, Herr Enemy.

I am your opus,
I am your valuable,
The pure gold baby

That melts to a shriek.   70
I turn and burn.
Do not think I underestimate your great concern.

Ash, ash—
You poke and stir.
Flesh, bone, there is nothing there—   75

A cake of soap,[2]
A wedding ring,
A gold filling.

Herr God, Herr Lucifer
Beware   80
Beware.

Out of the ash
I rise with my red hair
And I eat men like air.

—1965 (written 1962)

---

1   *Herr* German: Sir, Lord, Mister.
2   *cake of soap* During and after the war, it was widely believed that the bodies of the dead
     from concentration camps were used to mass produce soap; historians have not found
     evidence to substantiate this rumour.

Adrian Henri
1932–2000

An artist, poet, teacher, and musician, Adrian Henri rose to prominence as one of the "Liverpool Poets" in the 1960s. Known for making poetry accessible to young and working-class audiences, this group of popular poets frequently performed their works to music before crowds of people in busy cafés and other bohemian haunts.

In 1967 Henri and fellow Liverpool Poets Roger McGough and Brian Patten were published together in the anthology *The Mersey Sound*—a collection named after the local music movement that produced The Beatles and spurred the "British invasion" of American popular music. Since its publication, *The Mersey Sound* has sold more than half a million copies, making it one of the best selling anthologies of poetry in the UK.

Henri's involvement in performance poetry eventually led to the founding of The Liverpool Scene, a poetry rock group. Henri was also a prolific painter, a passion that fellow band member Mike Evans notes was apparent in his poetry: "He wrote what he saw, as much as what he felt, though what he described was often expressed with such passion that even the most simplistic listings of people or places were lit with an emotional glow."

Mrs. Albion You've Got a Lovely Daughter[1]
(for Allen Ginsberg)[2]

Albion's most lovely daughter sat on the banks of the
    Mersey[3] dangling her landing stage in the water.

The daughters of Albion
    arriving by underground at Central Station
5   eating hot ecclescakes at the Pierhead[4]
    writing "Billy Blake is fab" on a wall in Mathew St.[5]

---

1   *Mrs. Albion … Lovely Daughter* Reference to the song "Mrs. Brown, You've Got a Lovely Daughter," popularized by the British pop band Herman's Hermits in 1963; *Albion* Ancient name for the island of Britain.

2   *Allen Ginsberg* American beat poet (1926–97).

3   *Mersey* River that runs through North West England.

4   *ecclescakes* Small flat pastries filled with currants, named after the English town Eccles; *Pierhead* Located by the riverside in Liverpool.

5   *Billy Blake* English poet William Blake (1757–1827); *Mathew St.* Street in Liverpool famous for the Cavern Club, where the Beatles frequently played.

taking off their navyblue schooldrawers and
putting on nylon panties ready for the night

The daughters of Albion
    see the moonlight beating down on them in Bebington[1]   10
    throw away their chewinggum ready for the goodnight kiss
sleep in the dinnertime sunlight with old men
    looking up their skirts in St. Johns Gardens
comb their darkblonde hair in suburban bedrooms
powder their delicate little nipples/wondering if tonight will be the night   15
their bodies pressed into dresses or sweaters
lavender at The Cavern or pink at The Sink[2]

The daughters of Albion
    wondering how to explain why they didn't go home

The daughters of Albion   20
    taking the dawn ferry to tomorrow
    worrying about what happened
    worrying about what hasn't happened
    lacing up blue sneakers over brown ankles
    fastening up brown stockings to blue suspenderbelts°   *garter belts* 25

Beautiful boys with bright red guitars
in the spaces between the stars

Reelin' an' a-rockin'
Wishin' an' a-hopin'
Kissin' an' a-prayin'   30
Lovin' an' a-layin'

Mrs. Albion you've got a lovely daughter.

         —1967

---

1   *Bebington* Small town close to Liverpool.
2   *The Sink* Popular Liverpool nightclub that opened in the 1960s.

Lucille Clifton
1936–2010

Lucille Clifton consciously broke from poetic conventions in her work, which celebrates family life, the female body, biblical characters (often envisioned as Caribbean or African), and African American history, including the history of her own family. She addressed these subjects in personal, evocative, and straightforward language. Clifton tidily expressed her impatience with conventional images of the poet with a few comments in her final interview: "There's a way you're supposed to look if you're an American poet. There's a way you're supposed to sound.... And I think it's hogwash."

Born Thelma Lucille Sayles, Clifton grew up in Buffalo, New York; her working-class parents exposed their large family to an abundance of literature. She attended university and teacher's college, but dropped out to work on her writing. A few years later, she gave birth to the first of her six children; although she claimed that at home she was "wife and mama mostly," she also said that her experience as a mother was an important source of poetic inspiration. When Clifton published her first poetry collection, *Good Times*, in 1969, it was named by *The New York Times* as one of the year's ten best books.

Clifton received the National Book Award for *Blessing the Boats: New and Selected Poems, 1988–2000* (2000), and was posthumously awarded the Frost Medal in 2010. In addition to writing more than ten poetry books for adults, Clifton was also a prolific author of children's literature that often addressed difficult subjects such as death, history, and abuse.

Miss Rosie

when i watch you
wrapped up like garbage
sitting, surrounded by the smell
of too old potato peels
5   or
when i watch you
in your old man's shoes
with the little toe cut out
sitting, waiting for your mind
10   like next week's grocery
i say
when i watch you
you wet brown bag of a woman

who used to be the best looking gal in georgia
used to be called the Georgia Rose   15
i stand up
through your destruction
i stand up

—1969

The Lost Baby Poem

the time i dropped your almost body down
down to meet the waters under the city
and run one with the sewage to the sea
what did i know about waters rushing back
what did i know about drowning   5
or being drowned

you would have been born into winter
in the year of the disconnected gas
and no car   we would have made the thin
walk over genesee hill into the canada wind   10
to watch you slip like ice into strangers' hands
you would have fallen naked as snow into winter
if you were here i could tell you these
and some other things

if i am ever less than a mountain   15
for your definite brothers and sisters
let the rivers pour over my head
let the sea take me for a spiller
of seas   let black men call me stranger
always   for your never named sake   20

—1987

Roger McGough

b. 1937

High-spirited and conversational in tone, the work of British contemporary poet Roger McGough has earned international praise. A prolific writer with more than 50 books to his credit, he has twice won the Signal Award for excellence in children's poetry, and is a Fellow of the Royal Society of Literature.

McGough began publishing poetry together with Adrian Henri and Brian Patten in the 1960s. The three became known as the "Liverpool Poets"; their work is anthologized in the popular collection *The Mersey Sound* (1967), which has sold over half a million copies. The Liverpool Poets were credited with making poetry accessible to middle- and working-class audiences, challenging the perception that this form of expression belonged exclusively to the educated and the wealthy. McGough has said that he wrote with a popular audience in mind: "If I'd written a serious poem I'd always end up making it funny, to prove to this imagined reader or listener, which would have been a fellow Liverpudlian, that I'm not better than you."

McGough is known for his comedic edge and his playful approach to language. Though his work is often lighthearted, it can also be ambiguous and melancholy. He comments: "People always seem to say I'm whimsical and anti-establishment. Sarcastic. I don't think I'm any of these things really. A bit of whimsy, maybe; sentimental, yes, I'd own up to that."

Comeclose and Sleepnow

it is afterwards
and you talk on tiptoe
happy to be part
of the darkness
5 lips becoming limp
a prelude to tiredness.
Comeclose and Sleepnow
for in the morning
when a policeman
10 disguised as the sun
creeps into the room
and your mother
disguised as birds
calls from the trees
15 you will put on a dress of guilt

and shoes with broken high ideals
and refusing coffee
run
alltheway
home.

—1967 [20]

Les Murray
b. 1938

Les Murray's humble upbringing as the son of a dairy farmer in rural New South Wales has long been a point of pride and a source of inspiration for him. In recognition both of his contribution to Australia's literary landscape and of the central part he has played in various cultural debates, Murray is today widely recognized not only as "the Bard of Bunyah"—the bush territory of his childhood—but also as Australia's national poet.

Although pointedly local in its celebration of Australia's rural heartland, Murray's poetry seeks more broadly to give, he says, "utterance and form to hitherto unexpressed elements of Australian mind and character." As he conceives it, Australia's essential nature abides in the outback: it is fundamentally pastoral, tribal, traditional, hardy, and uncompromised by the elitism and affectation of urban culture. This is the Australia—"part imaginary and part historical"—that Murray summons in collections such as *Poems against Economics* (1972) and the verse novel *The Boys Who Stole the Funeral* (1980). For Murray, despite the degrading legacy of colonialism, the rise of machine culture, and the sterility of modern city life, this indigenous Australia may be sought and recovered; to do so he looks to aboriginal history, to folklore, to pioneer and wartime experiences, and to the land itself.

A self-described "subhuman redneck," Murray has frequently attracted controversy with his outspoken condemnation of the forms of liberalism, feminism, and intellectual pretension he associates with urban Australia. Many have taken issue with Murray's politics; few have denied his ability to write with what a reviewer in *The New Republic* has described as "great linguistic power and moral energy."

Pigs

Us all on sore cement was we.
Not warmed then with glares. Not glutting mush
under that pole the lightning's tied to.
No farrow°-shit in milk to make us randy.   *young pig*
5 Us back in cool god-shit. We ate crisp.
We nosed up good rank in the tunnelled bush.
Us all fuckers then. And Big, huh? Tusked
the balls-biting dog and gutsed him wet.
Us shoved down the soft cement of rivers.
10 Us snored the earth hollow, filled farrow, grunted.
Never stopped growing. We sloughed, we soughed°   *sighed*

and balked no weird till the high ridgebacks was us
with weight-buried hooves. Or bristly, with milk.
Us never knowed like slitting nor hose-biff[1] then.
Nor the terrible sheet-cutting screams up ahead.   15
The burnt water kicking. This gone-already feeling
here in no place with our heads on upside down.

                                                        —1992

The Shield-Scales of Heraldry[2]

Surmounting my government's high evasions
stands a barbecue of crosses and birds
tended by a kangaroo and emu[3]
but in our courts, above the judge,
a lion and a unicorn still keep   5
their smaller offspring, plus a harp,
in an open prison looped with mottoes.[4]

Coats of arms, plaster Rorschach blots,
crowned stone moths, they encrust Europe.
As God was dismissed from churches   10
they fluttered in and cling to the walls,
abstract comic-pages held by scrolled beasts,
or wear on the flagstones underfoot.
They pertain to an earlier Antichrist,[5]

the one before police. Mafiose citadels   15
made them, states of one attended family
islanded in furrows.[6] The oldest
are the simplest. A cross, some coins,
a stripe, a roof tree, a spur rowel,

---

1   *biff* Blow or punch.
2   *Heraldry* Symbols and images appearing on coats of arms.
3   *barbeque ... emu* The Australian coat of arms depicts a shield decorated with crosses and
     birds, held up by a kangaroo and an emu.
4   *lion ... mottoes* In the contemporary coat of arms of the United Kingdom, a lion and a
     unicorn hold up a shield bearing a depiction of a harp and smaller lions; the shield is sur-
     rounded by a garter with a motto written on it.
5   *Antichrist* See 2 John 1.7.
6   *Mafiose citadels ... in furrows* Refers to the medieval origin of heraldry; initially a means
     of identifying friends and enemies on the battlefield, coats of arms evolved into inherited
     family symbols; *Mafiose* I.e., of organized crime.

20 bowstaves, a hollow-gutted lion,[1]
    and all in lucid target colours.

    The rhyming of name with name,
    marriages quarter and cube them
    till they are sacred campaign maps
25 or anatomy inside dissected mantling,
    glyphs minutely clear through their one
    rule, that colour must abut either
    gold or silver, the non-weapon metals.

    The New World doesn't blazon well—[2]
30 the new world ran away from blazonry
    or was sent away in chains by it—
    but exceptions shine: the spread eagle
    with the fireworks display on its belly
    and in the thinks-balloon above its head.[3]
35 And when as a half-autistic

    kid in scrub paddocks vert and or
    I grooved on the *cloisons*[4] of pedigree
    it was a vivid writing of system
    that hypnotised me, beyond the obvious
40 euphemism of force. It was eight hundred
    years of cubist art and Europe's dreamings:
    the Cup, the Rose, the Ship, the Antlers.

    High courage, bestial snobbery,
    neither now merits ungrace from us.
45 They could no longer hang me,
    throttling, for a rabbit sejant.°   *sitting upright*
    Like everyone, I would now be lord
    or lady myself, and pardon me
    or myself loose the coronet-necked hounds.

                                                          —1994

---

1   *cross ... lion* Symbols commonly seen on the shields of coats of arms.
2   *doesn't blazon well* I.e., doesn't take to heraldry.
3   *exceptions ... head* The front of the Great Seal of the United States, used as the country's
    official coat of arms, shows an eagle. In front of the eagle is a shield with red and white
    stripes and a blue portion; above the eagle is a circle containing thirteen stars.
4   *vert* Shade of green used in heraldry; *cloisons* French: partitions. Also refers to the *cloi-
    sonné* technique, sometimes used to make heraldic emblems; in *cloisonné*, thin metal strips
    are used to create distinct areas, called *cloisons*, that are each filled with coloured enamel.

The Early Dark

As the woman leaves the nursery, driving into early dark,
potholes in the lane make plants nudge and the wire-caged

fowls cluck like crockery, in the back of the station wagon.
A symphony is ending, too, over the brilliant city-plan

of the dashboard, and clapping pours like heavy rain   5
for minutes, outdoing the hoarse intake of asphalt

till her son giggles *I like that best, the applause part.*
He's getting older; now he has to win odd exchanges.

She's still partly back in the huge wind-wrangled steel shed
with its pastels and parterres[1] of seedlings, level by table   10

and the shy nurseryman, his eyes like a gatecrasher's fork
at a smorgasbord, spiking and circling. Now each object

in the headlights is unique, except the constant supplying
of trees, apparitional along verges, in near pastures. An owl

wrenches sideways off the road's hobnail; a refrigerator, shot   15
for children to breathe in it, guards someone's parcels; a boot.

A turn past this rollicking prewar bridge marks an end to tar.
Now for the hills, balancing on the tyres' running-shoes.

These road-ripples, Mum, they're sound-waves, did you know?
is also a surrender, to soothe. She recalls a suitor she told   20

about beauty's hardships, and her lovers, married and not,
whom he'd know. It felt kinder, confiding in an unattractive man.

                                                        —1999

---

1   *parterres* Ornamental gardens in which flowerboxes are arranged symmetrically on a level
     surface.

Margaret Atwood

b. 1939

In a career spanning half a century and virtually all genres, Margaret Atwood has risen to become one of Canada's most visible and versatile literary figures. Her work, which is as frequently found on best-seller lists as on academic syllabi, has been translated into over 35 languages. But despite her international appeal, Atwood remains a self-consciously Canadian writer.

Atwood writes within and across many traditional forms and categories. Although best known for novels such as *The Handmaid's Tale* (1985) and *Oryx and Crake* (2003), she initially established her reputation as a poet. Her first major collection, *The Circle Game* (1966) is concerned with national identity, particularly as it relates to Canada's natural landscape. Atwood explored similar themes in *The Animals in That Country* (1968) and *The Journals of Susanna Moodie* (1970), in which stark, precise, tightly controlled poems explore the artificial constructs that we attempt to impose on the uncontrollable, mysterious natural forces that inhabit and surround us.

The poems in her many collections range widely; national and feminist concerns are among the subjects she touches on, as are mythology, environmentalism, and old age and death. Regardless of their subject, her poems engage consistently with language itself; in Atwood's view, fiction "is the guardian of the moral and ethical sense" of a society, while "poetry is the heart of the language, the activity through which language is renewed and kept alive."

Death of a Young Son by Drowning[1]

He, who navigated with success
the dangerous river of his own birth
once more set forth

on a voyage of discovery
5   into the land I floated on
but could not touch to claim.

---

1   *Death of ... Drowning* From *The Journals of Susanna Moodie* (1970), a collection Atwood based on the life and work of Susanna Moodie, author of the 1852 pioneer memoir *Roughing It in the Bush*. Moodie's son drowned in the Moira River in Upper Canada, where the family had settled.

His feet slid on the bank,
the currents took him;
he swirled with ice and trees in the swollen water

and plunged into distant regions,   10
his head a bathysphere;[1]
through his eyes' thin glass bubbles
he looked out, reckless adventurer
on a landscape stranger than Uranus
we have all been to and some remember.   15

There was an accident; the air locked,
he was hung in the river like a heart.
They retrieved the swamped body,

cairn of my plans and future charts,
with poles and hooks   20
from among the nudging logs.

It was spring, the sun kept shining, the new grass
leapt to solidity;
my hands glistened with details.

After the long trip I was tired of waves.   25
My foot hit rock. The dreamed sails
collapsed, ragged.

   I planted him in this country
   like a flag.

             —1970

[you fit into me]

you fit into me
like a hook into an eye

a fish hook
an open eye

             —1971

---

1 *bathysphere* Spherical diving-bell for deep-sea observation.

Variation on the Word *Sleep*

I would like to watch you sleeping,
which may not happen.
I would like to watch you,
sleeping. I would like to sleep
5 with you, to enter
your sleep as its smooth dark wave
slides over my head

and walk with you through that lucent°   *shining*
wavering forest of bluegreen leaves
10 with its watery sun & three moons
towards the cave where you must descend,
towards your worst fear
I would like to give you the silver
branch, the small white flower, the one
15 word that will protect you
from the grief at the centre
of your dream, from the grief
at the centre. I would like to follow
you up the long stairway
20 again & become
the boat that would row you back
carefully, a flame
in two cupped hands
to where your body lies
25 beside me, and you enter
it as easily as breathing in

I would like to be the air
that inhabits you for a moment
only. I would like to be that unnoticed
30 & that necessary.

—1981

The Door

The door swings open,
you look in.
It's dark in there,
most likely spiders:
nothing you want.   5
You feel scared.
The door swings closed.

The full moon shines,
it's full of delicious juice;
you buy a purse,   10
the dance is nice.
The door opens
and swings closed so quickly
you don't notice.

The sun comes out,   15
you have swift breakfasts
with your husband, who is still thin;
you wash the dishes,
you love your children,
you read a book,   20
you go to the movies.
It rains moderately.

The door swings open,
you look in:
why does this keep happening now?   25
Is there a secret?
The door swings closed.

The snow falls,
you clear the walk while breathing heavily;
it's not as easy as once.   30
Your children telephone sometimes.
The roof needs fixing.
You keep yourself busy.
The spring arrives.

35 The door swings open:
    it's dark in there,
    with many steps going down.
    But what is that shining?
    Is it water?
40 The door swings closed.

    The dog has died.
    This happened before.
    You got another;
    not this time though.
45 Where is your husband?
    You gave up the garden.
    It became too much.
    At night there are blankets;
    nonetheless you are wakeful.

50 The door swings open:
    O god of hinges,
    god of long voyages,
    you have kept faith.
    It's dark in there.
55 You confide yourself to the darkness.
    You step in.
    The door swings closed.

—2007

Seamus Heaney
b. 1939

Born to farmers in County Derry, just outside Belfast, Seamus Heaney grew up in a Roman Catholic household in a predominantly Protestant part of Northern Ireland. He remained unmarked in childhood by the strife that would later affect the region; instead, he experienced a community that lived in harmony, regardless of religious affiliation. Heaney frequently draws on his roots for poetic inspiration, and many of his poems recall his childhood or draw on the activities of rural life—such as digging potatoes or churning milk—to comment on universal issues.

Much of Heaney's poetry concerns the political and sectarian violence that rocked Northern Ireland during the second half of the twentieth century. He has been criticized both for his allegedly ambivalent attitude toward the conflict and for his decision to leave Northern Ireland for the relatively stable Republic of Ireland in 1972. Heaney did not, however, forget the political turmoil of his birthplace, and in the decade following his move he wrote some of his most political works, including *North* (1975) and *Field Work* (1979).

The death of Heaney's mother in 1984 was the occasion for some of his most poignant poetry, published in *The Haw Lantern* (1987). When questioned about his memorializing of lost friends and family, Heaney responded: "The elegiac Heaney? There's nothing else." Heaney's poems addressing the past often comment indirectly on the present; among the best-known examples of this approach are his "bog poems" about the preserved bodies of ancient sacrificial victims discovered in the peat bogs of Denmark.

Heaney has combined writing with an academic career that has included guest lectureships at Harvard and Oxford. He has also written translations from ancient and medieval languages, among them a critically acclaimed translation of *Beowulf* (2000). In 1995, Heaney was awarded the Nobel Prize in Literature; the committee cited his "works of lyrical beauty and ethical depth, which exalt everyday miracles and the living past."

Digging

Between my finger and my thumb
The squat pen rests; as snug as a gun. [rhyme]

Under my window a clean rasping sound
When the spade sinks into gravelly ground:
My father, digging. I look down   5

Till his straining rump among the flowerbeds
Bends low, comes up twenty years away
Stooping in rhythm through potato drills[1]
Where he was digging.

10 The coarse boot nestled on the lug, the shaft
Against the inside knee was levered firmly.
He rooted out tall tops, buried the bright edge deep
To scatter new potatoes that we picked
Loving their cool hardness in our hands.

15 By God, the old man could handle a spade,
Just like his old man.

My grandfather could cut more turf[2] in a day
Than any other man on Toner's bog.
Once I carried him milk in a bottle
20 Corked sloppily with paper. He straightened up
To drink it, then fell to right away
Nicking and slicing neatly, heaving sods
Over his shoulder, digging down and down
For the good turf. Digging.

25 The cold smell of potato mould, the squelch and slap
Of soggy peat, the curt cuts of an edge
Through living roots awaken in my head.
But I've no spade to follow men like them.

Between my finger and my thumb
30 The squat pen rests.
I'll dig with it.

—1966

---

1   *potato drills* Rows of sown potatoes.
2   *turf* Slabs of peat.

Mid-Term Break[1]

I sat all morning in the college sick bay
Counting bells knelling classes to a close.
At two o'clock our neighbors drove me home.

In the porch I met my father crying—
He had always taken funerals in his stride—   5
And Big Jim Evans saying it was a hard blow.

The baby cooed and laughed and rocked the pram
When I came in, and I was embarrassed
By old men standing up to shake my hand

And tell me they were "sorry for my trouble,"   10
Whispers informed strangers I was the eldest,
Away at school, as my mother held my hand

In hers and coughed out angry tearless sighs.
At ten o'clock the ambulance arrived
With the corpse, stanched and bandaged by the nurses.   15

Next morning I went up into the room. Snowdrops
And candles soothed the bedside; I saw him
For the first time in six weeks. Paler now,

Wearing a poppy bruise on his left temple,
He lay in the four foot box as in his cot.   20
No gaudy scars, the bumper knocked him clear.

A four foot box, a foot for every year.

—1966

---

1   *Mid-Term Break* While Heaney was at boarding school in 1953, his four-year-old brother
     Christopher was killed in a car accident.

The Grauballe Man[1]

As if he had been poured
in tar, he lies
on a pillow of turf
and seems to weep

5   the black river of himself.
The grain of his wrists
is like bog oak,[2]
the ball of his heel

like a basalt egg.
10 His instep has shrunk
cold as a swan's foot
or a wet swamp root.

His hips are the ridge
and purse of a mussel,
15 his spine an eel arrested
under a glisten of mud.

The head lifts,
the chin is a visor
raised above the vent
of his slashed throat

20 that has tanned and toughened.
The cured wound
opens inwards to a dark
elderberry place.

Who will say "corpse"
25 to his vivid cast?
Who will say "body"
to his opaque repose?

---

1   *Grauballe Man* Man from the third century BCE whose preserved remains were found in
    1952, in a peat bog near the village of Grauballe, Denmark.
2   *bog oak* Wood of an oak tree preserved in a peat bog.

P.V. Glob, "The First Picture of the Grauballe Man," 1965. The Grauballe Man is one of hundreds of well-preserved ancient corpses that have been discovered in peat bogs in Northern Europe. In his book The Bog People: Iron Age Man Preserved *(Mose-folket: Jernalderens Mennesker bevaret I 2000 År, 1965), the Danish archaeologist P.V. Glob argued that most of these "bog people" were victims of ritual sacrifice. The* Bog People *and the photographs it contained were a source of inspiration for a number of poems by Seamus Heaney, including "The Grauballe Man."*

And his rusted hair,
a mat unlikely
as a foetus's.   30
I first saw his twisted face

in a photograph,
a head and shoulder
out of the peat,
bruised like a forceps baby,   35

but now he lies
perfected in my memory,
down to the red horn
of his nails,

40 hung in the scales
with beauty and atrocity:
with the Dying Gaul[1]
too strictly compassed

on his shield,
45 with the actual weight
of each hooded victim,
slashed and dumped.

—1975

Cutaways

i

Children's hands in close-up
On a bomb site, picking and displaying
Small shrapnel curds for the cameramen

Who stalk their levelled village. *Ferrum*
5 and *rigor* and *frigor*[2] of mouse grey iron,
The thumb and finger of my own right hand

Closing around old hard plasticine
Given out by Miss Walls, thumbing it
To nests no bigger than an acorn cup,

10 Eggs no bigger than a grain of wheat,
Pet pigs with sausage bellies, belly-buttoned
Fingerprinted sausage women and men.

---

1   *Dying Gaul* Roman copy of a lost Greek statue (c. 230–220 BCE) depicting a Gallic (French) warrior dying in battle.
2   *Ferrum* Latin: iron; *rigor* Latin: stiffness; *frigor* Latin: cold.

ii

Or trigger-fingering a six-gun stick,
Cocking a stiff hammer-thumb above
A sawn-off kitchen chair leg; or flying round   15

A gable, the wingspan of both arms
At full stretch and a-tilt, the left hand tip
Dangerously near earth, the air-shearing right

Describing arcs—angelic potential
Fleetly, unforgettably attained: 20
Now in richochets that hosannah[1] through

The backyard canyons of Mossbawn,[2]
Now a head and shoulders dive
And skive as we hightail it up and away

iii

To land hard back on heels, like the charioteer   25
Holding his own at Delphi,[3] his six horses
And chariot gone, his left hand lopped off

A wrist protruding like a waterspout,
The reins astream in his right
Ready at any moment to curb and grapple   30

Bits long fallen away.
The cast of him on a postcard was enough
To set me straight once more between two shafts,

Another's hand on mine to guide the plough,
Each slither of the share, each stone it hit   35
Registered like a pulse in the timbered grips.

—2008

---

1   *hosannah* Exclamation of praise used in Jewish and Christian worship.
2   *Mossbawn* Farmhouse where Heaney was born.
3   *charioteer ... Delphi* Bronze statue found at the temple of Apollo at Delphi and one of the
best known surviving examples of ancient Greek sculpture (c. 475 BCE).

Billy Collins
b. 1941

William James Collins served as the Poet Laureate of the United States from 2001 to 2003. He has been called "the most popular poet in America" by *The New York Times*, in recognition of his regularly sold-out readings and record-breaking book sales.

Collins was born in New York City. He wrote his first poem before the age of ten but did not embark on a serious poetic career until his forties. Instead, he began his professional life as an academic, and he remains a professor of English, claiming that the poems he teaches provide inspiration for his own work. In addition to teaching, book touring, and writing prolifically, he appears frequently on National Public Radio and is a co-founder of the *Mid-Atlantic Review*.

In explanation of his popularity, Collins—who cites Warner Brothers cartoons as a formative influence on his artistic sensibility—says that his poetry is "suburban, it's domestic, it's middle class, and it's sort of unashamedly that." His work is criticized by some literary critics and fellow poets as being too "pedestrian, or one-note," or even too "accessible." Other critics, however, agree with Collins that his poems "are slightly underrated by the word 'accessible'"; one *New York Times* reviewer, for example, praises him for "luring his readers into the poem with humour, [then leading] them unwittingly into deeper, more serious places."

Pinup

The murkiness of the local garage is not so dense
that you cannot make out the calendar of pinup
drawings on the wall above a bench of tools.
Your ears are ringing with the sound of
5 the mechanic hammering on your exhaust pipe,
and as you look closer you notice that this month's
is not the one pushing the lawn mower, wearing
a straw hat and very short blue shorts,
her shirt tied in a knot just below her breasts.
10 Nor is it the one in the admiral's cap, bending
forward, resting her hands on a wharf piling,
glancing over the tiny anchors on her shoulders.
No, this is March, the month of great winds,
so appropriately it is the one walking her dog

along a city sidewalk on a very blustery day. 15
One hand is busy keeping her hat down on her head
and the other is grasping the little dog's leash,
so of course there is no hand left to push down
her dress which is billowing up around her waist
exposing her long stockinged legs and yes the secret 20
apparatus of her garter belt. Needless to say,
in the confusion of wind and excited dog
the leash has wrapped itself around her ankles
several times giving her a rather bridled
and helpless appearance which is added to 25
by the impossibly high heels she is teetering on.
You would like to come to her rescue,
gather up the little dog in your arms,
untangle the leash, lead her to safety,
and receive her bottomless gratitude, but 30
the mechanic is calling you over to look
at something under your car. It seems that he has
run into a problem and the job is going
to cost more than he had said and take
much longer than he had thought. 35
Well, it can't be helped, you hear yourself say
as you return to your place by the workbench,
knowing that as soon as the hammering resumes
you will slowly lift the bottom of the calendar
just enough to reveal a glimpse of what 40
the future holds in store: ah,
the red polka dot umbrella of April and her
upturned palm extended coyly into the rain.

—1993

Gwendolyn MacEwen
1941–1987

One of Canada's most accomplished poets, Gwendolyn MacEwen ventured in many of her best-known poems into what she called the "elementary world" of myth, dream, and the unconscious mind. As she explained in her essay "A Poet's Journey into the Interior" (1986), "I tend to regard poetry in much the same way as the ancients regarded the chants or hymns used in holy festivals—as a means of invoking the mysterious forces which move the world, inform our deepest and most secret thoughts, and often visit us in sleep."

MacEwen's volumes of poetry include the Governor General's Award-winning collections *The Shadow-Maker* (1969) and *Afterworlds* (1987). Margaret Atwood has praised her ability to create, "in a remarkably short time, a complete and diverse poetic universe and a powerful and unique voice, by turns playful, extravagant, melancholy, daring, and profound." MacEwen's work displays remarkable breadth of tone and style, but in its subject matter returns repeatedly to a cluster of themes, among them the nature of time and memory, alchemy and mysticism, the transcendent power of imagination, the interplay—and interdependence—of darkness and light, and the subterranean truths and terrors of dreams.

Dark Pines Under Water

This land like a mirror turns you inward
And you become a forest in a furtive lake;
The dark pines of your mind reach downward,
You dream in the green of your time,
5   Your memory is a row of sinking pines.

Explorer, you tell yourself this is not what you came for
Although it is good here, and green;
You had meant to move with a kind of largeness,
You had planned a heavy grace, an anguished dream.

10 But the dark pines of your mind dip deeper
And you are sinking, sinking, sleeper
In an elementary world;
There is something down there and you want it told.

—1969

The Discovery

do not imagine that the exploration
ends, that she has yielded all her mystery
or that the map you hold
cancels further discovery

I tell you her uncovering takes years,   5
takes centuries, and when you find her naked
look again,
admit there is something else you cannot name,
a veil, a coating just above the flesh
which you cannot remove by your mere wish   10

when you see the land naked, look again
(burn your maps, that is not what I mean),
I mean the moment when it seems most plain
is the moment when you must begin again

—1969

Don McKay
b. 1942

Don McKay is a prolific Canadian poet whose work reflects a conviction that poetry is crucial to society and to private life; "poetry comes about," he writes, "because language is not able to represent raw experience, yet it must."

Born in Owen Sound and raised in Cornwall, Ontario, McKay spent a self-described "all-Canadian boyhood" camping on the Precambrian Shield and canoeing remote northern lakes. His poetry often focuses on nature and its cycles of death and loss, birth and resurgence.

McKay is renowned for his technique of defamiliarization—of inviting readers to see as new and surprising the most common objects and materials, such as tools and rocks. For McKay, these things have secret "other lives" to which we can be privy if poetic attention is paid to them. Such an approach, he asserts, may grant us deeper access to reality; defamiliarization allows us to circumvent "the mind's categories to glimpse some thing's autonomy—its rawness, its *duende* [soul], its alien being."

McKay has taught creative writing for over 25 years and is a co-founder of the Canadian poetry press Brick Books. His work has been awarded some of Canada's most prestigious prizes, including the Griffin Poetry Prize for *Strike/Slip* (2007) and Governor General's Awards for *Night Field* (1991) and *Another Gravity* (2000). In 2008, McKay was appointed a Member of the Order of Canada for his service to the country as a poet and as a generous mentor to young and aspiring writers.

Some Functions of a Leaf

To whisper. To applaud the wind
and hide the Hermit thrush.
To catch the light
and work the humble spell of photosynthesis
5   (excuse me sir, if I might have one word)
by which it's changed to wood.
To wait
willing to feed
            and be food.

10 To die with style:
as the tree retreats inside itself,
shutting off the valves at its
extremities
            to starve in technicolour, then

having served two hours in a children's leaf pile, slowly   15
stir its vitamins into the earth.

To be the artist of mortality.

—1987

Meditation on a Geode

To find one, even among souvenirs of Banff[1] from acrylic to zinc, is to
realize that rock, ordinary limestone, composes in its own medium and
has other lives. This one sits by the telephone, an impacted hollow whole
note, formed, says my old geology textbook, from the modification and
enlargement of an original void. O : every time I look inside, that twinge of   5
tabu. And something more familiar: impossible words forming a lump in
my throat, the petrified ovary of the unspoken.

I have been trying to respond to the spaces in your letter, its rests and lapses,
and the slight halo effect of words spoken in an art gallery. Thanks especially
for the potato salad recipe with the missing mystery ingredient. You've   10
been breathing the spiked air of solitude and I'm feeling jealous. Echoless.
Probably I should get more exercise, once upon a time, once upon a time.
Meanwhile the geode by the phone. Astounded.

Once upon a time there was a little animal who lived and died, got buried
in the silt and gradually decayed to nothing, which filled up with water. And   15
on the inner surface of the hole a shell of jellied silica dividing the water
inside, which is quite salty, from the fresher water outside in the limestone:
a tiny ocean in an egg. In which a subtle and irresistible idea, osmosis,
unclenches outward against the rock, widening the hole and seeping
through the silica until the salts inside and outside balance. And everything   20
(slow gong) crystallizes: : animal, emptiness, ocean, gland: ode of the earth.

—1991

---

1   *Banff* Banff National Park is a popular tourist destination in Canada, located in the
Rocky Mountains.

Meditation on Shovels

How well they love us, palm and instep, lifeline
running with the grain as we
stab   pry   heave
our grunts and curses are their music.
5 What a (stab) fucking life, you dig these
(pry) dumb holes in the ground and (heave) fill
them up again until they (stab)
dig a fucking hole for you:
                                  beautiful,
10 they love it, hum it as they stand,
disembodied backbones.
waiting for you to get back to work.

But in the Book of Symbols, after Shoes
(Van Gogh, Heidegger,[1] and Cinderella)
15 they do not appear.
Of course not.
                They're still out there
humming
patiently pointing down.

                                                    —1991

Song for the Song of the Wood Thrush

For the following few seconds, while the ear
inhales the evening
only the offhand is acceptable. Poetry
clatters. The old contraption pumping
5 iambs in my chest is going to take a break
and sing a little something. What? Not much. There's
a sorrow that's so old and silver it's no longer
sorry. There's a place
between desire and memory, some back porch
10 we can neither wish for nor recall.

                                                    —1997

---

1   *Van Gogh, Heidegger* Vincent van Gogh's painting *A Pair of Shoes* (1886) is discussed by
philosopher Martin Heidegger in his essay "The Origin of the Work of Art" (1963), in
which Heidegger draws a distinction between everyday objects and art objects. One of
Heidegger's concerns was the everyday relationship between human beings and things.

Roy Miki

b. 1942

Often preferring the free association of sound and rhythm to more traditional literary conventions, Roy Miki attempts to practise a way of thinking and creative writing that shares some of the anti-authoritarian goals of his activism. He often makes use of wordplay and multiple poetic voices to create poems that are complex, unstable, and challenging.

Miki was born on a sugar beet farm near Winnipeg, Manitoba. His parents had been forcibly relocated from the West Coast by the Canadian government, which during World War II dispossessed, transported, and interned thousands of Canadians of Japanese descent in contradiction of their rights as citizens. In the 1980s, Miki was among the leaders of the Japanese Canadian Redress Movement that eventually obtained an apology, compensation, and preventative measures from the federal government.

Miki committed many years to this issue and wrote, co-wrote, and contributed to several books on the subject, including *Redress: Inside the Japanese Canadian Call for Justice* (2004); he has also been very active as a poet and as a literary scholar. His activism and his poetic work often overlap; his poetry collection *Saving Face* (1991), for example, includes a section called "redress." Much of his work is concerned with the politics of origins and identity—and, more recently, with consumerism and globalization.

Considered a poet of the prairies but also aligned with the poetry of the West Coast, Miki has published scholarly work on other Canadian poets such as George Bowering and bpNichol, and has edited the collected poems of Roy Kiyooka. Miki earned a Governor General's Award for *Surrender* (2001), his third book of poems, and in 2006 received the Order of Canada.

attractive

the distaste for turmoil
embroiled oceanic slips

like wandering on tarmac
looking for insularity
finding dry grass   5

the promise of unbridled
recompense—risen dough
in the non-chalence forms

bleached by similitude
10 the probate will[1] runs on
neutral—gravity's weal

it's the sonic boom of
a lingual disequilibrium

the disinherited tracts of
15 murmur's master stroke

two syllables making out
in the compact rumble seat

tease of would you take
a turn if you had a choice

20 rather the brain child of
sea wagers than intervals

raucous vibes in the sunder
down of lyric i am ambushed

let's get serious a poetic
25 *text has to resonate*

                  has

to transport emotion to an
island called identity

what you want is the death
30 *of continuity the death of*
narration

            death itself

you're a cancer

          on the
35 body of real literature

---

1   *probate will* Will that has been validated by a court; a term from inheritance law used here in a pun on "will" in the sense of "volition."

you're a wart

    on the
backside of texts erotique

you're the clad maw

     of iron hick crescendo   40

babble brain

     yeah like self
reliance is a liberal habit

the lame leap freight cars
the careen of nomadic lobes   45
the lubricants rescue the wheels

             —2001

on the sublime

a poem does not beg for forgiveness. it's not like real life.
not a case of relationships gone awry. its social
innuendoes are not a matter of secrets told in privacy.

once the consideration of intent is or was misplaced.
once it was a misdemeanour to forego the forlorn.   5

memory is a stranger. a maverick sound that crowds out
noise. the ease of its deployment is dependent on the size
of the ache.

when it drops into a sullied lap.

i hesitate to use the first person in this instance. a binge   10
of bebop is no ticket to oblivion. the causal routes are
dogged with yelping signatures with nowhere to sign.

the sojourner notwithstanding.

'we' listened at the fork in the road. 'i've heard that
15   before.' the clause was held in perpetuity.

cacophonous airwaves are all the rage. the rollycoaster
on overdrive dallies then engages in tumult. fear is driven
deeper into the social debt of syntax controls and
formations that giggle on freeway billboards.

20   if its hem is showing.

'i wander by the corner store, gazing at the figures
winking back.' the encounter has ripple effects that
accumulate and announce the dispatch. the few who are
deaf to tonal variations listen to the heat waves instead.

25   the transportation wins approval.

when logic fails, logic hails a cab. 'we' cruise the early
morning city streets. the headlines as headlights, a
concept dying on the dashboard.

—2001

make it new

i have altered my tactics to reflect the new era

5   already the magnolia broken by high winds
             heals itself
the truncated branches already
speak to me.

the hallucinated cartoons spread their wings
10   no less eagles than the amber destination
of wanton discourses—
                    discards

          say what you will
the mountain ranges
15   once so populated with fleeting images
             look more attractive

histoires statistics documents
daily polls headlines make the blood rush

the earth is not heavy
with the weight of centuries   20
nor do bodies
of multitudes tread muted on fleet denizens

in the declension[1] of plumed echoes
or is it contractual fumes
the sunset clause[2] expires   25

—2001

---

1   *declension* Decay; also a grammatical term for a list of the forms a word can take according
     to its case, gender, and other factors.
2   *sunset clause* Provision attached to a piece of legislation that causes the legislation to
     expire on a predetermined date.

Sharon Olds
b. 1942

Sharon Olds's poems are notable for their intimate portrayals of taboo subjects such as family abuse, sexuality, violence, and the human body; she is often compared to an earlier generation of confessional poets such as Sylvia Plath and Anne Sexton. Olds herself describes her work as "apparently personal." Whether autobiographical or not, her poetry boldly examines many of life's fundamental experiences. Poet Tony Hoagland praises Olds's "empathetic insight" and describes her work as "an extended, meticulous, passionate, often deeply meditative testament about the 'central meanings'; skilled dramatic expressions of the most archetypal templates, obstructions and liberations of one human life."

Born in San Francisco, Olds studied at Stanford University, and she completed a PhD in English at Columbia University in 1972. Her first collection, *Satan Says* (1980), received the San Francisco Poetry Center Award, while her next, *The Dead and the Living* (1983), received the National Book Critics Circle Award. She is also a recipient of the T.S. Eliot Prize, for which she has been shortlisted multiple times: after being shortlisted for *The Father* (1992), a themed collection about an alcoholic father's death from cancer, and for *One Secret Thing* (2008), which addresses parenthood, sexuality, and past traumas, she won for *Stag's Leap* (2012), a volume centred on her experience of divorce.

The One Girl at the Boys Party

When I take my girl to the swimming party
I set her down among the boys. They tower and
bristle, she stands there smooth and sleek,
her math scores unfolding in the air around her.
5 They will strip to their suits, her body hard and
indivisible as a prime number,
they'll plunge in the deep end, she'll subtract
her height from ten feet, divide it into
hundreds of gallons of water, the numbers
10 bouncing in her mind like molecules of chlorine
in the bright blue pool. When they climb out,
her ponytail will hang its pencil lead
down her back, her narrow silk suit
with hamburgers and french fries printed on it

will glisten in the brilliant air, and they will   15
see her sweet face, solemn and
sealed, a factor of one, and she will
see their eyes, two each,
their legs, two each, and the curves of their sexes,
one each, and in her head she'll be doing her   20
wild multiplying, as the drops
sparkle and fall to the power of a thousand from her body.

—1983

Sex without Love

How do they do it, the ones who make love
without love? Beautiful as dancers,
gliding over each other like ice-skaters
over the ice, fingers hooked
inside each other's bodies, faces   5
red as steak, wine, wet as the
children at birth whose mothers are going to
give them away. How do they come to the
come to the   come to the   God   come to the
still waters,[1] and not love   10
the one who came there with them, light
rising slowly as steam off their joined
skin? These are the true religious,
the purists, the pros, the ones who will not
accept a false Messiah, love the   15
priest instead of the God. They do not
mistake the lover for their own pleasure,
they are like great runners: they know they are alone
with the road surface, the cold, the wind,
the fit of their shoes, their over-all cardio-   20
vascular health—just factors, like the partner
in the bed, and not the truth, which is the
single body alone in the universe
against its own best time.

—1984

---

1   *still waters* See Psalm 23.2: "he leadeth me beside the still waters."

Michael Ondaatje
b. 1943

Michael Ondaatje was born in 1943 in Ceylon (now Sri Lanka). His parents separated when he was two, and in 1949 his mother moved to London, where she ran a boarding school. When Ondaatje was ten he joined his mother in England. Before Ondaatje's first return to Sri Lanka in 1978, his childhood home rarely figured in his work. "Letters & Other Worlds" (1973), one of his best-known poems, is one notable exception; here he draws on his early experiences as he comes to terms with his father's death.

Ondaatje followed his older brother, Christopher, to Canada in 1962. At the University of Toronto, where he completed his BA, he began to make a name for himself as a poet, and was also introduced to Coach House Press, where he worked as an editor for several years. He cemented his reputation as a poet with *The Collected Works of Billy the Kid* (1970) and as a novelist with *In the Skin of a Lion* (1987); his more recent publications include the poetry collection *The Story* (2006) and the novel *The Cat's Table* (2011).

Many of Ondaatje's books of poetry resemble novels in their extended development of character and plot. His novels, on the other hand, are frequently described as poetic; they are often written in highly figurative language, flowing from one vivid image to the next rather than developing along any linear plot line. Ondaatje's awards include the Booker Prize, the Giller Prize, four Governor General's Awards, and the Order of Canada.

Letters & Other Worlds

"for there was no more darkness for him and, no doubt like Adam before the fall, he could see in the dark"[1]

My father's body was a globe of fear
His body was a town we never knew
He hid that he had been where we were going
His letters were a room he seldom lived in
5   In them the logic of his love could grow

My father's body was a town of fear
He was the only witness to its fear dance
He hid where he had been that we might lose him
His letters were a room his body scared

---

1   *for ... dark* Ondaatje is quoting a translation of Alfred Jarry's novel *La Dragonne* (1943) that is cited in Roger Shattuck's *The Banquet Years* (1955).

He came to death with his mind drowning.   10
On the last day he enclosed himself
in a room with two bottles of gin, later
fell the length of his body
so that brain blood moved
to new compartments   15
that never knew the wash of fluid
and he died in minutes of a new equilibrium.

His early life was a terrifying comedy
and my mother divorced him again and again.
He would rush into tunnels magnetized   20
by the white eye of trains
and once, gaining instant fame,
managed to stop a Perahara[1] in Ceylon
—the whole procession of elephants dancers
local dignitaries—by falling   25
dead drunk onto the street.

As a semi-official, and semi-white at that,
the act was seen as a crucial
turning point in the Home Rule Movement
and led to Ceylon's independence in 1948.   30

(My mother had done her share too—
her driving so bad
she was stoned by villagers
whenever her car was recognized)
For 14 years of marriage   35
each of them claimed he or she
was the injured party.
Once on the Colombo docks
saying goodbye to a recently married couple
my father, jealous   40
at my mother's articulate emotion,
dove into the waters of the harbour
and swam after the ship waving farewell.
My mother pretending no affiliation
mingled with the crowd back to the hotel.   45

---

1   *Perahara* Procession (originally of a religious nature) of praise or thanksgiving.

Once again he made the papers
though this time my mother
with a note to the editor
corrected the report—saying he was drunk
50 rather than broken hearted at the parting of friends.
The married couple received both editions
of *The Ceylon Times* when their ship reached Aden.

And then in his last years
he was the silent drinker,
55 the man who once a week
disappeared into his room with bottles
and stayed there until he was drunk
and until he was sober.

There speeches, head dreams, apologies,
60 the gentle letters, were composed.
With the clarity of architects
he would write of the row of blue flowers
his new wife had planted,
the plans for electricity in the house,
65 how my half-sister fell near a snake
and it had awakened and not touched her.
Letters in a clear hand of the most complete empathy
his heart widening and widening and widening
to all manner of change in his children and friends
70 while he himself edged
into the terrible acute hatred
of his own privacy
till he balanced and fell
the length of his body
75 the blood screaming in
the empty reservoir of bones
the blood searching in his head without metaphor

—1973

The Cinnamon Peeler[1]

If I were a cinnamon peeler
I would ride your bed
and leave the yellow bark dust
on your pillow.

Your breasts and shoulders would reek   5
you could never walk through markets
without the profession of my fingers
floating over you. The blind would
stumble certain of whom they approached
though you might bathe   10
under rain gutters, monsoon.

Here on the upper thigh
at this smooth pasture
neighbour to your hair
or the crease   15
that cuts your back. This ankle.
You will be known among strangers
as the cinnamon peeler's wife.

I could hardly glance at you
before marriage   20
never touch you
—your keen nosed mother, your rough brothers.
I buried my hands
in saffron, disguised them
over smoking tar,   25
helped the honey gatherers ...

When we swam once
I touched you in water
and our bodies remained free,
you could hold me and be blind of smell.   30
You climbed the bank and said

       this is how you touch other women

---

1   *Cinnamon Peeler* Cinnamon harvester; the spice is made from the inner bark of the
cinnamon tree.

the grass cutter's wife, the lime burners daughter.
And you searched your arms
35 for the missing perfume
                  and knew

            what good is it
to be the lime burner's daughter
left with no trace
40 as if not spoken to in the act of love
as if wounded without the pleasure of a scar.

You touched
your belly to my hands
in the dry air and said
45 I am the cinnamon
peeler's wife. Smell me.

                                       —1982

To a Sad Daughter

All night long the hockey pictures
gaze down at you
sleeping in your tracksuit.
Belligerent goalies are your ideal.

5 Threats of being traded
cuts and wounds
—all this pleases you.
O my god! you say at breakfast
reading the sports page over the Alpen[1]
10 as another player breaks his ankle
or assaults the coach.

When I thought of daughters
I wasn't expecting this
but I like this more.
15 I like all your faults
even your purple moods
when you retreat from everyone

---

1   *Alpen* Brand of muesli breakfast cereal.

to sit in bed under a quilt.
And when I say "like"
I mean of course "love"   20
but that embarrasses you.
You who feel superior to black and white movies
(coaxed for hours to see *Casablanca*)[1]
though you were moved
by *Creature from the Black Lagoon*.[2]   25

One day I'll come swimming
beside your ship or someone will
and if you hear the siren[3]
listen to it. For if you close your ears
only nothing happens. You will never change.   30

I don't care if you risk
your life to angry goalies
creatures with webbed feet.
You can enter their caves and castles
their glass laboratories. Just   35
don't be fooled by anyone but yourself.

This is the first lecture I've given you.
You're "sweet sixteen" you said.
I'd rather be your closest friend
than your father. I'm not good at advice   40
you know that, but ride
the ceremonies
until they grow dark.

Sometimes you are so busy
discovering your friends   45
I ache with loss
—but that is greed.
And some times I've gone
into *my* purple world
and lost you.   50

---

1   *Casablanca* Widely acclaimed 1942 classic film.
2   *Creature from the Black Lagoon* 1954 monster movie that typifies the "B movies" of the
    1950s.
3   *siren* In Greek mythology, creatures whose singing enchanted sailors, causing them to
    steer their ships into the rocks.

One afternoon I stepped
into your room. You were sitting
at the desk where I now write this.
Forsythia outside the window
55   and sun spilled over you
like a thick yellow miracle
as if another planet
was coaxing you out of the house
—all those possible worlds!—
60   and you, meanwhile, busy with mathematics.

I cannot look at forsythia now
without loss, or joy for you.
You step delicately
into the wild world
65   and your real prize will be
the frantic search.
Want everything. If you break
break going out not in.
How you live your life I don't care
70   but I'll sell my arms for you,
hold your secrets forever.

If I speak of death
which you fear now, greatly,
it is without answers,
75   except that each
one we know is
in our blood.
Don't recall graves.
Memory is permanent.
80   Remember the afternoon's
yellow suburban annunciation.
Your goalie
in his frightening mask
dreams perhaps
85   of gentleness.

—1984

Eavan Boland
b. 1944

Eavan Boland has developed the concept of "dailiness," a focus on the ordinary minutiae of life, as a theme throughout her work. Beginning her career at a time when, she says, "nobody thought a suburb could be a visionary place for a poet" and "nobody thought a daily moment could be [poetic]," she was inspired by "a great tenderheartedness toward these things that were denied their visionary life." Her work also draws deeply on the past: she weaves scenes of the everyday together with re-imagined figures and motifs from mythology, and she examines Irish history with particular attention to its legacy of women's oppression. Boland does not shy away from the harsh realities of women's lives—past or present; domestic violence and anorexia are among the subjects addressed in her poems.

Born in 1944, Boland grew up in London and Ireland. She attended Trinity College in Dublin, and has since taught there and at other universities, including Bowdoin College and Stanford University. Since her first collection, *23 Poems* (1962), Boland has published ten volumes of poetry, among them *In a Time of Violence* (1994), which won the Lannan Award and was shortlisted for the T.S. Eliot Award. Her anthology *New Collected Poems* (2008), containing previously unpublished works as well as a selection of her early poems, has cemented her place as a leading contemporary Irish writer. In her collection of essays *A Journey with Two Maps: Becoming a Woman Poet* (2011), Boland reflects on her identity as a woman and a poet, and on the construction of those identities by others.

Night Feed

This is dawn.
Believe me
This is your season, little daughter.
The moment daisies open,
The hour mercurial rainwater   5
Makes a mirror for sparrows.
It's time we drowned our sorrows.

I tiptoe in.
I lift you up
Wriggling   10
In your rosy, zipped sleeper.
Yes, this is the hour

For the early bird and me
When finder is keeper.

15 I crook the bottle.
How you suckle!
This is the best I can be,
Housewife
To this nursery
20 Where you hold on,
Dear life.

A slit of milk.
The last suck.
And now your eyes are open,
25 Birth-coloured and offended.
Earth wakes.
You go back to sleep.
The feed is ended.

Worms turn.
30 Stars go in.
Even the moon is losing face.
Poplars stilt for dawn
And we begin
The long fall from grace.
35 I tuck you in.

—1982

Against Love Poetry

We were married in summer, thirty years ago. I have loved you deeply from that moment to this. I have loved other things as well. Among them the idea of women's freedom. Why do I put these words side by side? Because I am a woman. Because marriage is not freedom. Therefore, every word here is written against love poetry. Love poetry can do no justice to this. Here, 5 instead, is a remembered story from a faraway history: A great king lost a war and was paraded in chains through the city of his enemy. They taunted him. They brought his wife and children to him—he showed no emotion. They brought his former courtiers—he showed no emotion. They brought his old servant—only then did he break down and weep.[1] I did not find my 10 womanhood in the servitudes of custom. But I saw my humanity look back at me there. It is to mark the contradictions of a daily love that I have written this. Against love poetry.

—2001

---

1   *a remembered ... and weep* From Herodotus, *The Histories* 3.14. The defeated king explains, "my private sorrows were too great for tears, but the troubles of my companion deserved them."

bpNichol
1944–1988

As George Bowering wrote, bpNichol "did not sound like the rest of the poets of his time." One of Canada's most important avant-garde poets, he experimented not only with lyric and narrative poetry but also with the visual and auditory aspects of language. The range of his work encompassed both concrete poetry—a visual form in which the words form an image that contributes to the poem's meaning—and sound poetry, a spoken form that engages with the sounds of speech, usually independent of actual words.

Barrie Phillip Nichol was born in Vancouver, British Columbia. His first collection, *bp* (1967), challenged the notion of the book: it was published in the form of a box containing a book, a collection of loose visual poems, a record, and a flipbook, with a "Statement" printed on the back of the box. In 1970, Nichol won the Governor General's Award for four volumes published that year: *Still Water, The true eventual story of Billie the Kid, Beach Head,* and *The Cosmic Chief.* His experiments with form and genre were continued in works such as *The Captain Poetry Poems* (1971), a convergence of pop art, concrete and lyric poetry, and myth. Of his more than 30 books and filmed or recorded performances, perhaps the most impressive is *The Martyrology* (1972–92), a "life-long" poem spanning nine books in six volumes.

Nichol often worked collaboratively; he was a member of the famed sound poetry group The Four Horsemen and a co-founder of *grOnk*, a magazine with a focus on concrete poetry. With a fellow member of The Four Horsemen, he produced theoretical writing under the pseudonym "Toronto Research Group." He was also a writer for Jim Henson's television show *Fraggle Rock* (1983–87).

Blues

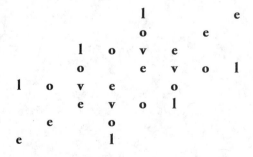

—1966

[dear Captain Poetry]

dear Captain Poetry,
your poetry is trite.
you cannot write a sonnet
tho you've tried to every night
since i've known you.   5
we're thru!!
              madame X

dear madame X

          Look how the sun leaps now upon our faces
          Stomps & boots our eyes into our skulls   10
          Drives all thot to weird & foreign places
          Till the world reels & the kicked mind dulls,
          Drags our hands up across our eyes
          Sends all white hurling into black
          Makes the inner cranium our skies   15
          And turns all looks sent forward burning back.
          And you, my lady, who should be gentler, kind,
          Have yet the fiery aspect of the sun
          Sending words to burn into my mind
          Destroying all my feelings one by one;   20
                  You who should have tiptoed thru my halls
                  Have slammed my doors & smashed me into walls.

                              love
                              Cap Poetry
                              —1970

Craig Raine
b. 1944

Craig Raine began what has been called the "Martian school" of poetry alongside Christopher Reid in the late 1970s. This style is aptly named after Raine's collection *A Martian Sends a Postcard Home* (1979), which—with his first book, *The Onion, Memory* (1978)—established his place as a leader in the movement. The goal of Martian poetry is to view the world with new eyes, even from the perspective of an alien. This is accomplished through unusual and surprising metaphors that, according to poet James Fenton, encourage readers "to become strangers in our familiar world."

Raine's early work created something of a sensation and, for a brief time, inspired many imitators, but the fashion for Martian poetry in the British literary world was short-lived. Raine himself, however, has continued to produce a body of interesting work. He applied his characteristic Martian style to a book-length narrative in *History: The Home Movie* (1994), a semi-autobiographical verse-novel about his family history set among the wars of twentieth-century Europe. Another long poem, *A la recherche du temps perdu* (2000), elegizes a lover who died of AIDS. In addition to more than ten books of poetry, Raine has also published two novels, a translated drama, two opera librettos, and several scholarly works.

An outspoken critic as well as a poet, Raine has taught at Oxford University for much of his career. He also spent ten years as poetry editor at the influential publishing house Faber & Faber, and in 1999 became the editor of his own arts journal, *Areté*.

A Martian Sends a Postcard Home

Caxtons[1] are mechanical birds with many wings
and some are treasured for their markings—

they cause the eyes to melt
or the body to shriek without pain.

5   I have never seen one fly, but
sometimes they perch on the hand.

Mist is when the sky is tired of flight
and rests its soft machine on ground:

---

1   *Caxtons* William Caxton (1422–91) introduced the printing press to England.

then the world is dim and bookish
like engravings under tissue paper.   10

Rain is when the earth is television.
It has the property of making colours darker.

Model T[1] is a room with the lock inside—
a key is turned to free the world

for movement, so quick there is a film   15
to watch for anything missed.

But time is tied to the wrist
or kept in a box, ticking with impatience.

In homes, a haunted apparatus sleeps,
that snores when you pick it up.   20

If the ghost cries, they carry it
to their lips and soothe it to sleep

with sounds. And yet, they wake it up
deliberately, by tickling with a finger.

Only the young are allowed to suffer   25
openly. Adults go to a punishment room

with water but nothing to eat.
They lock the door and suffer the noises

alone. No one is exempt
and everyone's pain has a different smell.   30

At night, when all the colours die,
they hide in pairs

and read about themselves—
in colour, with their eyelids shut.

—1979

---

1   *Model T* Early model of the automobile, produced by the Ford Motor Company; the
     Model T was the first car to enjoy mass popularity.

Tom Wayman
b. 1945

Tom Wayman's poetry depicts the challenges of daily life and work with
humour and honesty, addressing the commonplace in colloquial, conversational language. In his work, Wayman writes, he strives to "provide an
accurate depiction of our common everyday life" and to help us "consider
how our jobs shape us"—a consideration which requires that we recognize
the relative "state of unfreedom" in which most of us lead our working lives.
Much of his writing relates to working-class employment such as factory
labour and construction, but some of his best-known poems are about the
everyday experience of the university.

Born in Ontario in 1945 and raised in British Columbia, Wayman holds
a BA from the University of British Columbia and an MFA from the University of California. His first collection, *Waiting for Wayman*, was published in
1973; it has been followed by more than a dozen volumes of poetry, as well
as by short fiction, critical essays, drama, and a novel.

Wayman has edited several anthologies, often with a focus on work writing, and has been a teacher and a writer-in-residence at many Canadian
universities. Among other awards, he has received the Canadian Authors' Association Poetry Award and the A.J.M. Smith Prize for distinguished achievement in Canadian poetry. His poetry collection *My Father's Cup* (2002) was
shortlisted for the Governor General's Award.

Did I Miss Anything?

*Question frequently asked by
students after missing a class*

Nothing. When we realized you weren't here
we sat with our hands folded on our desks
in silence, for the full two hours

       Everything. I gave an exam worth
5   40 per cent of the grade for this term
       and assigned some reading due today
       on which I'm about to hand out a quiz
       worth 50 per cent

Nothing. None of the content of this course
has value or meaning   10
Take as many days off as you like:
any activities we undertake as a class
I assure you will not matter either to you or me
and are without purpose

      Everything. A few minutes after we began last time   15
      a shaft of light descended and an angel
      or other heavenly being appeared
      and revealed to us what each woman or man must do
      to attain divine wisdom in this life and
      the hereafter   20
      This is the last time the class will meet
      before we disperse to bring this good news to all people on earth

Nothing. When you are not present
how could something significant occur?

      Everything. Contained in this classroom   25
      is a microcosm of human existence
      assembled for you to query and examine and ponder
      This is not the only place such an opportunity has been gathered

      but it was one place

      And you weren't here   30

                      —1994

Robert Bringhurst
b. 1946

Robert Bringhurst spent ten years studying a variety of subjects—including physics, architecture, linguistics, and philosophy—at multiple universities before completing a BA in Comparative Literature from Indiana University. Since then he has published more than 15 collections of poetry and more than ten works of prose, including a canonical text on book design and typography, *Elements of Typographical Design* (1992).

Kate Kellaway of *The Observer* has commented that Bringhurst "has the curiosity of a scientist.... His writing is at once lyrical and spartan. And yet he is witty. And while he has no taste for lamentation, many a poem catches, calmly, at the heart." Interested in escaping what he calls "the prison of time" and "the prison of personality" through his work, Bringhurst tends not to focus on self-exploration but rather to explore larger topics: nature, timeless philosophical questions, mythology and literature (including the literature of the Bible, ancient Greek literature, and North American indigenous oral literature). He is well known for his work as a translator of Haida myths and narrative poems; that work has inspired controversy (he has been criticized for appropriating First Nations traditions), but it has also been widely praised for contributing to the preservation and promotion of Haida culture.

Bringhurst has received several prestigious awards for his works, including the Macmillan Poetry Prize (1975) and a Guggenheim Fellowship (1988), and was shortlisted for the prestigious Griffin Poetry Prize (2001). He lives on Quadra Island, British Columbia.

Leda and the Swan[1]

for George Faludy

Before the black beak reappeared
like a grin from in back of a drained cup,
letting her drop,
she fed at the sideboard of his thighs,
5   the lank air tightening in the sunrise,
yes. But no, she put on no knowledge

---

1   *Leda and the Swan* In Greek mythology, Leda was visited by Zeus in the form of a swan, who in some versions of the story raped her and in other versions seduced her. From their union she bore two eggs; one produced the twins Castor and Pollux, the other Helen (whose abduction later initiated the Trojan War). See W.B. Yeats's "Leda and the Swan," also included in this anthology.

with his power. And it was his power alone
that she saved of him for her daughter.
Not his knowledge.
No.   10
He was the one who put on knowledge.
He was the one who looked down out of heaven
with a dark croak, knowing more
than he had ever known before,
and knowing he knew it: 15

knowing the xylophone of her bones,
the lute of her back and the harp of her belly,
the flute of her throat,
woodwinds and drums of her muscles,
knowing the organ pipes of her veins;   20

knowing her as a man knows mountains he has hunted
naked and alone in—
knowing the fruits, the roots and the grasses,
the tastes of the streams
and the depths of the mosses,   25
knowing as he moves in the darkness he is also
resting at noon in the shade of her blood—
leaving behind him in the sheltered places
glyphs[1] meaning mineral and moonlight and mind
and possession and memory,   30
leaving on the outcrops signs meaning mountain
and sunlight and lust and rest and forgetting.

Yes. And the beak that opened to croak
of his knowing that morning creaked like a rehung
door and said nothing, felt nothing. The past   35
is past. What is known is as lean
as the day's edge and runs
one direction. The truth floats
down, out of fuel,
indigestible, like a feather. The lady   40
herself, though—whether
or not she was truth or untruth, or both, or was neither—

---

1   *glyphs* Carved figures or characters.

she dropped through the air like a looped rope,
a necklace of meaning, remembering
45 everything forward and backward—
the middle, the end, the beginning—
and lit like a fishing skiff gliding aground.

That evening, of course, while her husband, to whom
she told nothing, strode like the king
50 of Lakonia[1] through the orchestra
pit of her body, touching
this key and that string in his passing,
she lay like so much
green kindling,
55 fouled tackle and horse harness under his hands
and said nothing, felt
nothing, but only
lay thinking
not flutes, lutes and xylophones,
60 no: thinking soldiers
and soldiers and soldiers and soldiers
and daughters,
the rustle of knives in his motionless wings.

—1982

---

1   *Lakonia* Region in ancient Greece, of which Sparta was the principal city.

Marilyn Nelson
b. 1946

▬▬▬ The author of dozens of poetry collections, translations, and children's books, Marilyn Nelson is a prolific contributor to American literature. While her poetry traverses a range of subjects from marriage and motherhood to Christian spirituality, much of Nelson's work narrates American history, especially black history. Such volumes include *The Homeplace* (1990), which recounts her family history beginning with her great-great-grandmother; *Carver: A Life in Poems* (2001), about celebrated African American scientist George Washington Carver; and the sonnet crown *A Wreath for Emmett Till* (2005), about a teenager whose lynching galvanized the civil rights movement. Yet Nelson is more storyteller than political historian, creating poems that, as fellow poet Daniel Hoffman has said, "reach past feminist anguish and black rage" and "spring from her own sources." Some of Nelson's works are published as young adult books, but even these invite a broader audience; she explained that she wrote *Carver*, for example, "as I always do, striving for clarity and truthfulness, and imagining an audience of grown-ups."

Nelson is professor emerita at the University of Connecticut and also served as the state's Poet Laureate from 2001 to 2006. In 2004, she founded Soul Mountain Retreat, a writer's colony with special interest in "traditionally underrepresented racial and cultural groups." In 2012 Nelson received the Frost Medal for "distinguished lifetime achievement in poetry."

Minor Miracle

Which reminds me of another knock-on-wood
memory. I was cycling with a male friend,
through a small midwestern town. We came to a 4-way
stop and stopped, chatting. As we started again,
a rusty old pick-up truck, ignoring the stop sign,   5
hurricaned past scant inches from our front wheels.
My partner called, "Hey, that was a 4-way stop!"
The truck driver, stringy blond hair a long fringe
under his brand-name beer cap, looked back and yelled,
      "You fucking niggers!"   10
And sped off.
My friend and I looked at each other and shook our heads.
We remounted our bikes and headed out of town.
We were pedalling through a clear blue afternoon

15 between two fields of almost-ripened wheat
   bordered by cornflowers and Queen Anne's lace
   when we heard an unmuffled motor, a honk-honking.
   We stopped, closed ranks, made fists.
   It was the same truck. It pulled over.
20 A tall, very much in shape young white guy slid out:
   greasy jeans, homemade finger tattoos, probably
   a Marine Corps boot-camp footlockerful
   of martial arts techniques.

   "What did you say back there!" he shouted.
25 My friend said, "I said it was a 4-way stop.
   You went through it."
   "And what did I say?" the white guy asked.
   "You said: 'You fucking niggers.'"
   The afternoon froze.

30 "Well," said the white guy,
   shoving his hands into his pockets
   and pushing dirt around with the pointed toe of his boot,
   "I just want to say I'm sorry."
   He climbed back into his truck
35 and drove away.

                                              —1994

Brian Patten
b. 1946

███████ "When in public poetry should take off its clothes and wave to the nearest person in sight," writes Brian Patten; "it should be seen in the company of thieves and lovers rather than that of journalists and publishers." Patten shares his allegiance to a broad, popular audience with fellow "Liverpool Poets" Adrian Henri and Robert McGough, all three of whom wrote and performed in Liverpool at a time when bands such as The Beatles had brought the city to the centre of British popular culture. With their efforts to engage the public through performance, the Liverpool Poets opened the way for later performance poets such as Benjamin Zephaniah.

Patten was in his early twenties when he brought out his first solo collection, *Little Johnny's Confession* (1967), the same year he published with Henri and McGough in the bestselling anthology *The Mersey Sound*. Two years later, he followed this volume with *Notes to the Hurrying Man* (1969). His later work remains unpretentious but is often more serious in content; *Armada* (1996), for example, includes a series of poems in which the experience of his mother's death is intertwined with childhood memories, while *The Collected Love Poems* (2007) brings together his many poems about relationships. He has also authored several successful volumes of children's poetry.

Much of Patten's work, including "Somewhere Between Heaven and Woolworths, A Song," is written to be performed to music, and he remains committed to the importance of performance in bringing poetry to a popular audience.

Somewhere Between Heaven and Woolworths,[1] A Song

She keeps kingfishers in their cages
And goldfish in their bowls,
She is lovely and is afraid
Of such things as growing cold.

She's had enough men to please her,   5
Though they were more cruel than kind
And their love an act in isolation,
A form of pantomime.

---

1   *Woolworths* Department store chain popular for more than a century before going out of business in the 1990s.

She says she has forgotten
10 The feelings that she shared
At various all-night parties
Among the couples on the stairs,

For among the songs and dancing
She was once open wide,
15 A girl dressed in denim
With the boys dressed in lies.

She's eating roses on toast with tulip butter;
Praying for her mirror to stay young;
Though on its no longer gilted surface
20 This message she has scrawled:

"O somewhere between Heaven and Woolworths
I live I love I scold,
I keep kingfishers in their cages
And goldfish in their bowls."

—1967

Diane Ackerman
b. 1948

██████ Diane Ackerman's poetry and non-fiction prose display diverse interests that encompass history, biology, anthropology, astronomy, and human nature. She often uses scientific concepts and terms in her poetry; for example, her first volume, *The Planets: A Cosmic Pastoral* (1976), is, by her own description, "a collection of scientifically accurate poems based on the planets." She calls herself "a nature writer," but for her "nature includes everything." That outlook is reflected in her subject matter, which ranges from plants and non-human animals to the solar system, and from human civilization to love.

Like her poetry, Ackerman's prose often engages with the physical and the sensual. In her book of essays *A Natural History of the Senses* (1990), for example, Ackerman considers the five senses and their impact on the human experience, while *An Alchemy of Mind* (2005) discusses topics such as consciousness and emotion in relation to the human brain. Her other works of non-fiction include *The Zookeeper's Wife* (2007), winner of the Orion Book Award, and *One Hundred Names for Love* (2011), a finalist for the Pulitzer Prize. Although she writes in different genres, Ackerman explains, "I began as a poet, and I still think of myself as a poet.... I have a poet's sensibility."

Sweep Me through Your Many-Chambered Heart

Sweep me through your many-chambered heart
if you like, or leave me here, flushed
amid the sap-ooze and blossom: one more dish
in the banquet called April, or think me hard-
won all your days full of women. Weeks   5
later, till I felt your arms around
me like a shackle, heard all the sundown
wizardries the fired body speaks.
Tell me why, if it was no more than this,
the unmuddled tumble, the renegade kiss,   10
today, rapt in a still life[1] and unaware,
my paintbrush dropped like an amber hawk;
thinking I'd heard your footfall on the stair,
I listened, heartwise, for the knock.

—1978

---

1   *still life* Painting or other art image depicting arranged objects, often including fruit or flowers.

Lorna Crozier
b. 1948

One of Canada's most celebrated poets, Lorna Crozier is well known for the musical simplicity of her language and her artful way of approaching complex subjects in a style that is at once forthright and sly. According to Crozier, the poet is a conduit who must develop an alertness to the world's sensory details so as to recreate them in the "small charged world of the poem." In her view, "the poem is in the details," and though experience may resist or elude language, it is the task of the poet to "circle what can't be said until something of its smell, sound, taste, and gesture appears on the page."

Crozier was born in Swift Current, Saskatchewan. Much of her work is informed by the atmosphere and culture of small-town prairie life—notably *Inventing the Hawk* (1992), winner of a Governor General's Award; *A Saving Grace* (1996), inspired by Sinclair Ross's prairie novel *As for Me and My House* (1941); and the memoir *Small Beneath the Sky* (2009). But such localism is by no means narrow or restrictive: Crozier frequently takes up broad political, spiritual, and philosophical questions. Through her poetic retellings of scripture, for example, she interrogates a Judeo-Christian vision of the world.

Critics have approached Crozier's work from many different angles. Some focus on her intimate connection to the Canadian prairies or her concern with social injustice; others explore her fascination with the gaps in our stories and experiences, with absence, silence, loss, and all that which "can't be said."

from *The Sex Lives of Vegetables*

Carrots

Carrots are fucking
the earth. A permanent
erection, they push deeper
into the damp and dark.
5 All summer long
they try so hard to please.
Was it good for you,
was it good?

Perhaps because the earth won't answer
they keep on trying.   10
While you stroll through the garden
thinking *carrot cake,*
carrots and onions in beef stew,
carrot pudding with caramel sauce,
they are fucking their brains out   15
in the hottest part of the afternoon.

Onions

The onion loves the onion.
It hugs its many layers,
saying O, O, O,
each vowel smaller
than the last.   5

Some say it has no heart.
It doesn't need one.
It surrounds itself,
feels whole. Primordial.
First among vegetables.   10

If Eve had bitten it
instead of the apple,
how different
Paradise.

—1985

The Dark Ages of the Sea

Because we are mostly
made of water and water
calls to water
like the ocean to the river,
the river to the stream,   5
there was a time when
children fell into wells.

It was a time of farms
across the grasslands,
10   ancient lakes
that lay beneath them,
and a faith in things
invisible, be it water
never seen or something
15   trembling in the air.

We are born to fall
and children fell,
some surviving
to tell the tale,
20   pulled from the well's
dark throat,
wet and blind with terror
like a calf
torn from the womb
25   with ropes.

Others diminished into ghosts,
rode the bucket up
and when you drank
became the cold shimmer
30   in your cup, the metallic
undertaste of nails
some boy had carried
in his pocket
or the silver locket
35   that held a small girl's
dreams.

In those days people
spoke to horses,
voices soft as bearded
40   wheat; music lived
inside a stone. Not to say
it was good, that falling,
but who could stop it?

We are made
of mostly water   45
and water calls to water
through centuries of reason
children fall
light and slender
as the rain.   50

—1995

When I Come Again to My Father's House

When I come again to my father's house
I will climb wide wooden steps
to a blue door. Before I knock
I will stand under the porchlight and listen.
My father will be sitting in a plaid shirt,   5
open at the throat, playing his fiddle—
something I never heard in our other life.

Mother told me his music stopped
when I was born. He sold the fiddle
to buy a big console radio.   10
One day when I was two
I hit it with a stick,
I don't know why, Mother covering
the scratches with a crayon
so Father wouldn't see.   15
It was the beginning of things
we kept from him.

Outside my father's house
it will be the summer
before the drinking starts,   20
the jobs run out, the bitterness
festers like a sliver buried
in the thumb, too deep under the nail
to ever pull it out. The summer
before the silences, the small   25
hard moons growing in his throat.

When I come again to my father's house
the grey backdrop of the photos
my mother keeps in a shoebox
30 will fall away, the one sparse tree
multiply, branches green with rain.
My father will stand in his young man's pose
in front of a car, foot on the runningboard,
sleeves rolled up twice on each forearm.

35 I will place myself beside him.
The child in me will not budge
from this photograph,
will not leave my father's house
unless my father as he was
40 comes with me, throat swollen
with rain and laughter,
young hands full of music,
the slow, sweet song of his fiddle
leading us to my mother's
45 home.

—1995

Timothy Steele
b. 1948

Emerging at a time when free verse and experimental poetry prevailed, Timothy Steele has distinguished himself by embracing the expressive capacities of poetic constraint. He is often identified with the New Formalism that began in the 1980s—a movement in which contemporary poets have re-engaged with standard verse forms and regular poetic patterning. But Steele has been reluctant to accept this label, instead claiming kinship with a longer lineage of formal poets. He has been praised for combining colloquial language with traditional form to address everyday and personal subject matter, employing, as poet Mary Kinzie remarks, "restraint as a mechanism for the release of both wit and feeling."

Born in Burlington, Vermont, Steele obtained a BA from Stanford University and then completed a PhD in English and American Literature at Brandeis University. In 1979 he published his first collection of poems, *Uncertainties and Rest*; that was followed by several more volumes, including *Sapphics Against Anger and Other Poems* (1986), *The Color Wheel* (1994), and *Toward the Winter Solstice* (2006).

Steele has received numerous awards and honours, including a Guggenheim Fellowship and a Peter I.B. Lavan Younger Poets Award, and he has taught at several California universities. As a critic, he is the author of *Missing Measures: Modern Poetry and the Revolt Against Meter* (1990), an analysis of modernist poetry in relation to metre and formal structure; and *All the Fun's in How You Say a Thing* (1999), an educational volume designed to teach students about poetic form, which he argues "gives a poem resistant grace and power."

Sapphics[1] Against Anger

Angered, may I be near a glass of water;
May my first impulse be to think of Silence,
Its deities (who are they? do, in fact, they
        Exist? etc.).

May I recall what Aristotle says of   5
The subject: to give vent to rage is not to

---

1   *Sapphics* Stanzas in a form named after the Greek poet Sappho (late seventh–early sixth century BCE). Each stanza comprises two 11-syllable lines and one 5-syllable line.

Release it but to be increasingly prone
10   To its incursions.[1]

May I imagine being in the Inferno,
Hearing it asked: "Virgilio mio,[2] who's
That sulking with Achilles[3] there?" and hearing
          Virgil say: "Dante,

15

That fellow, at the slightest provocation,
Slammed phone receivers down, and waved his arms like
A madman. What Attila did to Europe,
          What Genghis Khan did

20   To Asia,[4] that poor dope did to his marriage."
May I, that is, put learning to good purpose,
Mindful that melancholy is a sin, though
          Stylish at present.

Better than rage is the post-dinner quiet,
The sink's warm turbulence, the streaming platters,
25   The suds rehearsing down the drain in spirals
          In the last rinsing.

For what is, after all, the good life save that
Conducted thoughtfully, and what is passion
If not the holiest of powers, sustaining
          Only if mastered.

—1986

---

1   *What Aristotle … its incursions* See Book IV of Aristotle's *Nicomachean Ethics*, in which
    he discusses the cultivation of virtue in oneself as a means to attaining the good life.
2   *Virgilio mio* Italian: my Virgil. In *Inferno*, the first part of Italian poet Dante Alighieri's
    Divine Comedy (c. 1308–21), Virgil is Dante's guide through hell.
3   *Achilles* Mythological hero of the Trojan War. In the *Divine Comedy* 1.5.64–66, Dante
    sees him being punished for the sin of lust in the second circle of hell.
4   *Attila* King of the Huns (c. 439–53) with a reputation for savagery, who expanded the
    European territory of the Hunnic Empire; *Genghis Khan* Ruler (1162–1227) who es-
    tablished a vast Mongolian Empire using tactics that included brutal pillaging and mass
    slaughter.

Agha Shahid Ali

1949–2001

Agha Shahid Ali was a Shia Muslim born in predominantly Hindu New Delhi, raised in Sunni Kashmir, and later educated in the United States, where he lived and worked for many years as an academic, poet, and translator. He drew inspiration from his diverse cultural heritage and literary influences, finding fertile ground for his imagination in both his native and adopted homelands. He was raised, he wrote, "a bilingual, bicultural (but never rootless) being," and his loyalties to English and Urdu were so deeply felt and closely joined that they "led not to confusion, but to a strange, arresting clarity."

In collections such as *The Half-Inch Himalayas* (1987), Ali often looks back on the past and dwells on the experience of living apart from one's history. But, in taking stock of what he has left behind, the poet also comes to better represent his own nature and place in the world. In *A Walk through the Yellow Pages* (1987) and *A Nostalgist's Map of America* (1991), Ali does not simply write poems about the vast and varied landscapes of the United States and the American Southwest; he writes as an American poet, working in the tradition of the American sublime.

Among Ali's most significant literary contributions are his translations of the celebrated Urdu poet Faiz Ahmed Faiz. Before Ali published *The Rebel's Silhouette* (1991), both Faiz's poetry and the *ghazal*, a Persian lyric form consisting of rhymed, thematically self-contained couplets, were little known in the West. Here as in much of his work, Ali was keen to experiment with ways to, as he phrased it, "make English behave outside its aesthetic habits."

Postcard from Kashmir

Kashmir shrinks into my mailbox,
my home a neat four by six inches.

I always loved neatness. Now I hold
the half-inch Himalayas in my hand.
This is home. And this the closest
I'll ever be to home. When I return,
the colours won't be so brilliant,
the Jhelum's[1] waters so clean,

5

---

1   *Jhelum* River originating in the Himalayas in Kashmir.

so ultramarine. My love
10 so overexposed.
And my memory will be a little
out of focus, in it
a giant negative, black
and white, still undeveloped.

—1987

The Wolf's Postscript to "Little Red Riding Hood"

First, grant me my sense of history:
I did it for posterity,
for kindergarten teachers
and a clear moral:
5   Little girls shouldn't wander off
in search of strange flowers,
and they mustn't speak to strangers.

And then grant me my generous sense of plot:
Couldn't I have gobbled her up
10 right there in the jungle?
Why did I ask her where her grandma lived?
As if I, a forest-dweller,
didn't know of the cottage
under the three oak trees
15 and the old woman lived there
all alone?
As if I couldn't have swallowed her years before?

And you may call me the Big Bad Wolf,
now my only reputation.
20 But I was no child-molester
though you'll agree she was pretty.

And the huntsman:
Was I sleeping while he snipped
my thick black fur
and filled me with garbage and stones?[1]   25
I ran with that weight and fell down,
simply so children could laugh
at the noise of the stones
cutting through my belly,
at the garbage spilling out   30
with a perfect sense of timing,
just when the tale
should have come to an end.

—1987

---

1   *And the ... stones* In the version of the Red Riding Hood story that appears in *Grimm's Fairy Tales* (1812–15), a huntsman discovers the wolf asleep and cuts its stomach open. He rescues the child and her grandmother, who are still alive inside, and they kill the wolf by filling its stomach with stones.

Anne Carson
b. 1950

Hailed by Michael Ondaatje as "the most exciting poet writing in English today," Anne Carson is known for formally experimental work that draws on a deep knowledge of literary history, from ancient Greek poetry and medieval mysticism to modernism and contemporary psychoanalysis. Her many accolades include the Griffin Prize for Poetry, the T.S. Eliot Prize for Poetry, and the Order of Canada.

Carson is a professor of classics, and her academic work and her poetry strongly influence each other. These talents most clearly overlap in her Greek translation work, including *If Not, Winter: Fragments of Sappho* (2002) and the three-play collection *An Oresteia* (2009). Captivated by the mindset of ancient Greek culture, Carson says that "what's entrancing about the Greeks is that you get little glimpses, little latches of similarity [to contemporary culture], embedded in unbelievable otherness." Her own poems often view the ancient through a contemporary lens; *Autobiography of Red: A Novel in Verse* (1998), for example, transforms the Greek story of Herakles' battle with the monster Geryon into a story of troubled love between twentieth-century men.

Carson's style is distinctive for its blending of genres, often occupying the borders between poetry and prose. Her first book of poetry, *Short Talks* (1992), is presented as a compilation of miniature lectures, while works such as *Plainwater* (1995) and *Men in the Off Hours* (2000) include poetic essays alongside more traditional lyric poetry. She is also known for her novels in free verse, such as *Autobiography of Red* and *The Beauty of the Husband: A Fictional Essay in 29 Tangos* (2001). With *Nox* (2010), Carson revives her first love—visual art—to memorialize the life of her brother through an interweaving of translation, original poetry, and photographic collage.

from *Short Talks*

On Rain

It was blacker than olives the night I left. As I
ran past the palaces, oddly joyful, it began to
rain. What a notion it is, after all—these small
shapes! I would get lost counting them. Who
5   first thought of it? How did he describe it to
the others? Out on the sea it is raining too.
It beats on no one.

On Sylvia Plath[1]

Did you see her mother on television? She said
plain, burned things. She said I thought it an
excellent poem but it hurt me. She did not say
jungle fear. She did not say jungle hatred wild
jungle weeping chop it back chop it. She said   5
self-government she said end of the road. She
did not say humming in the middle of the air[2]
what you came for chop.

On Walking Backwards

My mother forbade us to walk backwards. That
is how the dead walk, she would say. Where did
she get this idea? Perhaps from a bad translation. The dead, after all, do not walk backwards
but they do walk behind us. They have no lungs   5
and cannot call out but would love for us to
turn around. They are victims of love, many of
them.

—1992

---

1   *Sylvia Plath* (1932-63), American poet and author. The mother in her semi-autobio-
    graphical novel *The Bell Jar* (1963) and many of the mother figures in her poetry are
    portrayed with hostility.

2   *in the middle of the air* See Plath's poem "The Disquieting Muses" (1960): "I woke one
    day to see you, mother, / Floating above me in bluest air."

Dana Gioia
b. 1950

Dana Gioia is often cited as the leader of the New Formalist movement, a movement that, beginning in the 1980s, has encouraged a re-engagement with more traditional uses of rhyme, metre, and standard verse forms. Unlike some others in the movement, however, Gioia writes free as well as formal verse and employs forms of his own invention alongside traditional ones; he has said that he cannot "imagine a poet who wouldn't want to have all the possibilities of the language available, especially the powerful enchantments of metre, rhyme, and narrative."

Initially intending to study music at Stanford University, Gioia was drawn instead to the rhythms of poetry, and he eventually undertook graduate work in Comparative Literature at Harvard. Opting not to continue with an academic career, he then earned an MBA and began a business career with General Foods Corporation, where he eventually rose to the rank of vice president. He continued to write and publish in his spare time, however, and when his work began to receive critical attention he resigned from General Foods to pursue a full-time writing career.

Gioia's poetry collections include *Daily Horoscope* (1986), *The Gods of Winter* (1991), and *Pity the Beautiful* (2012). He is also a translator and librettist, and he has commanded serious attention as a critic, both for his articulation of New Formalist principles and for his 1991 essay "Can Poetry Matter?", in which he laments the isolation of the poet from mainstream culture and calls for poetry to be made "more present in American public life."

Thanks for Remembering Us

The flowers sent here by mistake,
signed with a name that no one knew,
are turning bad. What shall we do?
Our neighbour says they're not for her,
5 and no one has a birthday near.
We should thank someone for the blunder.
Is one of us having an affair?
At first we laugh, and then we wonder.

The iris was the first to die,
10 enshrouded in its sickly-sweet
and lingering perfume. The roses
fell one petal at a time,

and now the ferns are turning dry.
The room smells like a funeral,
but there they sit, too much at home,   15
accusing us of some small crime,
like love forgotten, and we can't
throw out a gift we've never owned.

—1983

Planting a Sequoia[1]

All afternoon my brothers and I have worked in the orchard,
Digging this hole, laying you into it, carefully packing the soil.
Rain blackened the horizon, but cold winds kept it over the Pacific,
And the sky above us stayed the dull grey
Of an old year coming to an end.   5

In Sicily a father plants a tree to celebrate his first son's birth—
An olive or a fig tree—a sign that the earth has one more life to bear.
I would have done the same, proudly laying new stock into my father's orchard,
A green sapling rising among the twisted apple boughs,
A promise of new fruit in other autumns.   10

But today we kneel in the cold planting you, our native giant,
Defying the practical custom of our fathers,
Wrapping in your roots a lock of hair, a piece of an infant's birth cord,
All that remains above earth of a first-born son,
A few stray atoms brought back to the elements.   15

We will give you what we can—our labour and our soil,
Water drawn from the earth when the skies fail,
Nights scented with the ocean fog, days softened by the circuit of bees.
We plant you in the corner of the grove, bathed in western light,
A slender shoot against the sunset.   20

And when our family is no more, all of his unborn brothers dead,
Every niece and nephew scattered, the house torn down,
His mother's beauty ashes in the air,
I want you to stand among strangers, all young and ephemeral to you,
Silently keeping the secret of your birth.   25

—1991

---

1   *Planting a Sequoia* Written about Gioia's first son, who died in infancy.

Roo Borson
b. 1952

Roo Borson's poetry, often meditative and sensual, has been praised by author Timothy Findley for its "compelling atmosphere of wonder." Frequent themes in her work include nature—especially the natural landscapes of North America—and the recollected past; "most of my work," she says, "uses memory and is about memory in some way."

Borson first became known for the contemplative lyrical poetry of *Landfall* (1970) and *Smoky Light of the Fields* (1980). Longer works such as *Rain* (1980) and *The Whole Night, Coming Home* (1984) marked a new interest in narrative and prose, while *Intent, or the Weight of the World* (1989) and *Water Memory* (1996) saw an increased emphasis on the personal. More recent works such as *Short Journey Upriver Toward Oishida* (2004) and *Rain; Road; An Open Boat* (2012) display the influence of Japanese poetry. Borson is also a member of the "collaborative poetry group" Pain Not Bread, which published the collection *Introduction to the Introduction to Wang Wei* in 2000.

Born Ruth Elizabeth Borson in Berkeley, California, Borson moved to Vancouver to attend the University of British Columbia, where she earned her MFA in 1977. In addition to the Griffin Poetry Prize, she has received three CBC Literary Awards and has been nominated several times for the Governor General's Literary Award, winning for *Short Journey Upriver Toward Oishida* in 2004. Borson has served as writer-in-residence at the University of Toronto and other Canadian universities.

Water Memory

Water does not remember, it moves
among reeds, nudges the little boat
(a little), effloresces[1] a shadowy fog
which forgets for us the way home
though the warm dry rooms are   5
in us. (Stretched on the examining table we
feel it when the unfamiliar hand
presses just there.) Water,
on its own, would not remember,
but herd follows herd, and memory is a shepherd   10
of the gentlest wants. Not even blood
can recall, though the live

---

1   *effloresces* Produces particles when exposed to air.

kidney shipped in its special box
wakes up one day in someone new.
No one made this world, there's no need
to feel ashamed. Be water,
find a lower place, go there.

15

—1996

Rita Dove
b. 1952

In Rita Dove's poetry, provocative images bridge the gap between the ordinary and the extraordinary. Her work traverses the space between the personal and the historical; Dove is, according to poet Brenda Shaughnessy, "a master at transforming a public or historic element—re-envisioning a spectacle and unearthing the heartfelt, wildly original private thoughts such historic moments always contain."

Born in Akron, Ohio, Dove was encouraged by her mother to develop a childhood passion for reading. She later studied Creative Writing at Miami University and the University of Iowa Writers' Workshop. After obtaining her MFA, she began to make a name for herself as a poet, first with *Yellow House on the Corner* (1980) and later with *Thomas and Beulah* (1986), a Pulitzer Prize-winning volume inspired by the life stories of her grandparents.

Dove works in a variety of genres: in addition to poetry collections, she has published verse drama and several book-length poems, from *Thomas and Beulah* to *Sonata Mulattica* (2009), a narrative based on the life of the eighteenth-century musician George Polgreen Bridgetower. Dove is also a prose fiction author, essayist, newspaper columnist, lyricist, and editor. Poet Laureate of the United States from 1993 to 1995, she remains an advocate for the public support of poetry. "Persephone, Falling" appeared in *Mother Love* (1995), a collection of poems focusing on the mother-daughter relationship.

Persephone, Falling[1]

One narcissus among the ordinary beautiful
flowers, one unlike all the others! She pulled,
stooped to pull harder—
when, sprung out of the earth
on his glittering terrible
carriage, he claimed his due.
It is finished. No one heard her.
No one! She had strayed from the herd.

---

1   *Persephone, Falling* In Greek mythology, Persephone was the daughter of Zeus and Demeter, and became the wife of Hades, god of the underworld. Because Persephone was so beautiful and desired by the male gods of Olympus, Demeter took her to Earth and kept her hidden for protection. One day as Persephone was out gathering flowers, Hades leapt from a crack in the earth and dragged her with him to the underworld.

(Remember: go straight to school.
This is important, stop fooling around!   10
Don't answer to strangers. Stick
with your playmates. Keep your eyes down.)
This is how easily the pit
opens. This is how one foot sinks into the ground.

—1988

Dionne Brand
b. 1953

■■■■ For Dionne Brand, poetry is "a philosophical mode for thinking through how one lives in the world and one's relation to other human beings." Her poetry frequently engages with issues of race (and racism), and of gender and sexuality, at times bringing acutely personal perspectives into play to explore these facets of existence.

While Brand has written acclaimed novels, short stories, non-fiction prose, and documentaries, she remains best known as a poet. Her collections include *Chronicles of a Hostile Sun* (1984), a book of poems based on her experience working for a non-government organization in Grenada; *Land to Light On* (1997), a Governor General's Award-winning volume that focuses on experiences of displacement and homelessness, linking them to histories of slavery, colonialism, and migration; and *thirsty* (2002), a book-length poem set in the city of Toronto. She received a Griffin Poetry Prize for *Ossuaries* (2011), another long poem, which the award judges praised for "fulfilling the novelistic narrative ambition of her work, [without] sacrific[ing] the tight lyrical coil of the poetic line."

Born in Trinidad, Brand immigrated to Canada in 1970. She earned a BA at the University of Toronto (1975) and, later, an MA at the Ontario Institute for Studies in Education (1989). She has held a number of prestigious university positions including Distinguished Visiting Scholar at St. Lawrence University and University Research Chair at the University of Guelph. Brand was named Poet Laureate of Toronto in 2009.

from *thirsty*

30

Spring darkness is forgiving. It doesn't descend
abruptly before you have finished work,
it approaches palely waiting for you
to get outside to witness another illumined hour

5 you feel someone brush against you,
on the street, you smell leather, the lake,
the coming leaves, the rain's immortality
pierces you, but you will be asleep when it arrives

you will lie in the groove of a lover's neck
unconscious, translucent, tendons singing,   10
and that should be enough, the circumference
of the world narrowed to your simple dreams

Days are perfect, that's the thing about them,
standing here in half darkness, I think this.
It's difficult to rise to that, but I expect it   15
I expect each molecule of my substance to imitate that

I can't of course, I can't touch syllables
tenderness, throats.
Look it's like this, I'm just like the rest,
limping across the city, flying when I can   20

32

Every smell is now a possibility, a young man
passes wreathed in cologne, that is hope;
teenagers, traceries of marijuana, that is hope too, utopia;

smog braids the city where sweet grass used to,
yesterday morning's exhaust, this day's   5
breathing by the lightness, the heaviness of the soul.

Every night the waste of the city is put out and taken away
to suburban landfills and recycling plants,
and that is the rhythm everyone would prefer in their life,

that the waste is taken out, that what may be useful   10
be saved and the rest, most of it, the ill of it,
buried.

Sometimes the city's stink is fragrant offal,
sometimes it is putrid. All depends on what wakes you up,
the angular distance of death or the elliptic of living.   15

—2002

Kim Addonizio
b. 1954

Known for her direct and empathetic depictions of love, loss, desire, and struggle, Kim Addonizio has achieved recognition for her poetry and novels, as well as for public readings in which she often blends poetry with the sounds of the blues harmonica. Her many honours include a Guggenheim Fellowship, a Pushcart Prize, and two National Endowment for the Arts Fellowships.

Born in Washington, DC, Addonizio obtained a BA and an MA from San Francisco State University, then worked as a lecturer at several colleges while she began to pursue her writing career. Her first collection, *Three West Coast Women* (1987), was a collaboration with fellow poets Laurie Duesing and Dorianne Laux. Several solo volumes followed, including *The Philosopher's Club* (1994), *Tell Me* (2000), and *Lucifer at the Starlite* (2009). As a poet, Addonizio is notable for writing both in free verse and in fixed forms (including the sonnet and a variant of the sonnet that she invented, the sonnenizio); her work displays an abiding interest in the interplay of syntax and rhythm, and a highly developed (if often unobtrusive) talent for rhyme.

With Dorianne Laux, Addonizio co-authored *The Poet's Companion: A Guide to the Pleasures of Writing Poetry* (1997); in 2009, she released *Ordinary Genius: A Guide for the Poet Within*, her own collection of writing exercises and personal insights. Addonizio has taught writing at Goddard College, at San Francisco State University, and through private workshops.

First Poem for You

I like to touch your tattoos in complete
darkness, when I can't see them. I'm sure of
where they are, know by heart the neat
lines of lightning pulsing just above
5 your nipple, can find, as if by instinct, the blue
swirls of water on your shoulder where a serpent
twists, facing a dragon. When I pull you
to me, taking you until we're spent
and quiet on the sheets, I love to kiss
10 the pictures in your skin. They'll last until
you're seared to ashes; whatever persists
or turns to pain between us, they will still
be there. Such permanence is terrifying.
So I touch them in the dark; but touch them, trying.

—1994

Sarah Arvio
b. 1954

Sarah Arvio's poetry addresses subjects that range from love and loss to dream psychology and the workings of language in a meditative, technically playful, and frequently comic style.

Born in Philadelphia, Pennsylvania, Arvio grew up in New York State and earned her MFA from Columbia University. She is fluent in French and Spanish as well as English and has worked as a freelance translator for the United Nations; she has also translated novels, stories, poems, and documentary film. For several years, she was a Lecturer in Creative Writing at Princeton.

It was not until her forties, after she began psychoanalysis, that Arvio found her voice as a poet. In 2002 she published her first book, *Visits from the Seventh*, a collection of poems written through a process she describes as the "channelling" or transcription of voices—although she does not specify whether these voices originated in the spirit realm or her own unconscious. *Visits from the Seventh* received a Rome Prize, which enabled Arvio to go to the American Academy in Rome. There she wrote her next collection, *Sono: Cantos* (2006), a volume praised by poet Robert Pinsky for raising witty wordplay "to an unusual, expressive intensity." In *Night Thoughts* (2013), Arvio engages directly with her experience of psychoanalysis in a series of poems describing her dreams, accompanied by "Notes" analyzing their meanings.

Wood

The last thing I ever wanted was to
write again about grief did you think I
would your grief this time not mine oh good

grief enough is enough in my life that is
enough was enough I had all those   5
grievances all those griefs all engraved

into the wood of my soul but would you
believe it the wood healed I grew up and
grew out and would you believe it I found

your old woody heart sprouting I thought   10
good new growth good new luxuriant green
leaves leaves on their woody stalks and I said

I'll stake my life on this old stick I'll stick
and we talked into the morning and night
15 and laughed green leaves and sometimes a flower

oh bower of good new love I would have it
I would bow to the new and the green
and wouldn't you know it you were a stick

yes I know a good stick so often and then
20 a stick in my ribs in my heart your old
dark wood your old dark gnarled stalk

sprouting havoc and now I have grief again
and now I've stood for what I never should
green leaves of morning dark leaves of night

—2009

Carol Ann Duffy
b. 1955

As Jeanette Winterson has written, Carol Ann Duffy is Britain's "favourite poet after Shakespeare." In 2009, when Duffy was appointed the first female Poet Laureate of the United Kingdom, Prime Minister Gordon Brown described her as "a truly brilliant modern poet who has stretched our imaginations by putting the whole range of human experiences into lines that capture emotions perfectly." She is also (to quote Winterson once more) "political in that she wants to change things, [and] idealistic in that she believes she—and poetry—can change things. And, of course, she's a woman, she's a Celt, and she's gay."

Duffy was born in Glasgow, Scotland, and raised in Staffordshire, England. She graduated from the University of Liverpool in 1977 with an honours degree in philosophy, and over the following decade she wrote a number of radio plays and collections of poems. Her talent with a variety of poetic forms and her reluctance to shy away from disturbing content are both evident in her first book, *Standing Female Nude* (1985), which included, for example, a first-person poem from the point of view of a burgeoning murderer and an unflinching depiction of a Holocaust scene. In 1999, Duffy published *The World's Wife*, a series of dramatic monologues written in the voices of the wives of famous historical and fictional figures. *Mean Time* (1993), a volume of poems about the emotional struggles and triumphs of adolescence, won the Whitbread Poetry Award. In 2005, Duffy received the T.S. Eliot Award for *Rapture*, a semi-autobiographical collection recounting a love story from first sight to eventual collapse. Her 2011 work *The Bees* incorporates poems on war and climate change alongside lyrics on the death of the poet's mother.

Duffy's work is extraordinary not least of all for its formal artistry; she is renowned as a master of poetic rhythm and of rhyme as much as of image and metaphor. In her discussions of poetry as well as in the poems themselves, she draws connections between sounds and their human meanings: a poem, she has said, "is the place in language [where] we are most human and we can see ourselves fully—far more than prose in fiction. A poem is able to hold so much in so little space."

Drunk

Suddenly the rain is hilarious.
The moon wobbles in the dusk.

What a laugh. Unseen frogs
belch in the damp grass.

5 The strange perfumes of darkening trees.
Cheap red wine

and the whole world a mouth.
Give me a double, a kiss.

—1993

The Good Teachers

You run round the back to be in it again.
No bigger than your thumbs, those virtuous women
size you up from the front row. Soon now,
Miss Ross will take you for double History.
5 You breathe on the glass, making a ghost of her, say
South Sea Bubble Defenestration of Prague.[1]

You love Miss Pirie. So much, you are top
of her class. So much, you need two of you
to stare out from the year, serious, passionate.
10 The River's Tale by Rudyard Kipling[2] by heart.
Her kind intelligent green eye. Her cruel blue one.
You are making a poem up for her in your head.

But not Miss Sheridan. Comment vous appelez.[3]
But not Miss Appleby. Equal to the square
15 of the other two sides. Never Miss Webb.
Dar es Salaam. Kilimanjaro.[4] Look. The good teachers
swish down the corridor in long, brown skirts,
snobbish and proud and clean and qualified.

And they've got your number. You roll the waistband
20 of your skirt over and over, all leg, all
dumb insolence, smoke-rings. You won't pass.

---

1   *South Sea ... Prague* Two unconnected historical incidents.
2   *The River's Tale* 1911 poem summarizing English history up to the end of Roman oc-
      cupation; *Rudyard Kipling* Bombay-born English novelist, poet, and short story writer
      (1865–1936).
3   *Comment vous appelez* French: what do you call.
4   *Dar es Salaam. Kilimanjaro* The largest city and the tallest mountain, respectively, in
      Tanzania.

You could do better. But there's the wall you climb
into dancing, lovebites, marriage, the Cheltenham
and Gloucester,[1] today. The day you'll be sorry one day.

—1993

Crush

The older she gets,
the more she awakes
with somebody's face strewn in her head
like petals which once made a flower.

What everyone does   5
is sit by a desk
and stare at the view, till the time
where they live reappears. Mostly in words.

Imagine a girl
turning to see   10
love stand by a window, taller,
clever, anointed with sudden light.

Yes, like an angel then,
to be truthful now.
At first a secret, erotic, mute;   15
today a language she cannot recall.

And we're all owed joy,
sooner or later.
The trick's to remember whenever
it was, or to see it coming.   20

—1998

Rapture

Thought of by you all day, I think of you.
The birds sing in the shelter of a tree.
Above the prayer of rain, unacred blue,
not paradise, goes nowhere endlessly.

---

1   *Cheltenham and Gloucester* Commercial bank in the United Kingdom.

5 How does it happen that our lives can drift
far from our selves, while we stay trapped in time,
queuing° for death? It seems nothing will shift   *lining up*
the pattern of our days, alter the rhyme
we make with loss to assonance with bliss.
10 Then love comes, like a sudden flight of birds
from earth to heaven after rain. Your kiss,
recalled, unstrings, like pearls, this chain of words.
Huge skies connect us, joining here to there.
Desire and passion on the thinking air.

—2005

Treasure

A soft ounce of your breath
in my cupped palm.
The gold weight of your head
on my numb arm.

5 Your heart's warm ruby
set in your breast.
The art of your hands,
the slim turquoise veins under your wrists.

Your mouth, the sweet, chrism[1] blessing
10 of its kiss,
the full measure of bliss pressed
to my lips.

Your fine hair, run through my fingers,
sieved.
15 Your silver smile, your jackpot laugh,
bright gifts.

Sighted amber, the 1001 nights
of your eyes.
Even the sparkling fool's gold
20 of your lies.

—2005

---

1   *chrism* Consecrated oil used for anointing in some Christian churches.

Marilyn Dumont
b. 1955

For Marilyn Dumont, poetry is a form of activism: beginning with her first collection, *A Really Good Brown Girl* (1997), she has evocatively told the neglected stories of Canadian Aboriginal experience. Her following works, *green girl dreams mountains* (2001) and *that tongued belonging* (2007), have been commended for their exploration of poverty, femininity, and the effects of colonization in Canada.

Although Dumont's commitment to Canadian Aboriginal issues has not changed, her approach to writing has developed in the course of her poetic career. *A Really Good Brown Girl*, she says, directly expresses "anger, shame, hurt, disillusionment and grief about the subjugation and mistreatment of Aboriginal peoples and traditions in Canada." Since then, however, she has found it more effective to communicate similar concepts "in different ways—through humour, through pathos, through sleight of hand, through elegance." Both approaches have attracted critical acclaim: Dumont received a Gerald Lampert Memorial Award for *A Really Good Brown Girl*, and *that tongued belonging* was chosen as Aboriginal Book of the Year by McNally Robinson and Poetry Book of the Year at the Ânskohk Aboriginal Literature Festival.

Dumont was born in northeastern Alberta in 1955 and spent her youth living in logging camps in the Alberta foothills. She is Métis and Cree, a descendant of Gabriel Dumont (a leader of Métis forces during the Northwest Rebellion of 1885), and was raised in a bilingual Cree and English household. She has been Writer-in-Residence at several institutions (among them the University of Alberta, the University of Windsor, Grant MacEwan University, and Athabasca University), and has also taught in the Aboriginal Emerging Writers Program at the Banff Centre for the Arts.

Not Just a Platform for My Dance

this land is not
just a place to set my house my car my fence

this land is not
just a plot to bury my dead my seed

this land is   5
my tongue   my eyes   my mouth
this headstrong grass and relenting willow

these flat-footed fields and applauding leaves
these frank winds and electric sky lines
10   are my prayer
they are my medicine
and they become my song
this land is not
just a platform for my dance

—1996

The White Judges

We lived in an old schoolhouse, one large room that my father converted
into two storeys with a plank staircase leading to the second floor. A single
window on the south wall created a space that was dimly lit even at midday.
All nine kids and the occasional friend slept upstairs like cadets in rows of
5   shared double beds, ate downstairs in the kitchen near the gas stove and
watched TV near the airtight heater in the adjacent room. Our floors were
worn linoleum and scatter rugs, our walls high and bare except for the
family photos whose frames were crowded with siblings waiting to come of
age, marry or leave. At supper eleven of us would stare down a pot of moose
10   stew, bannock and tea, while outside the white judges sat encircling our
house.

And they waited to judge

waited till we ate tripe
watched us inhale its wild vapour
15   sliced and steaming on our plates,
watched us welcome it into our being,
sink our teeth into its rubbery texture
chew and roll each wet and tentacled piece
swallow its gamey juices
20   until we had become it and it had become us.

Or waited till the cardboard boxes
were anonymously dropped at our door, spilling with clothes
waited till we ran swiftly away from the windows and doors
to the farthest room for fear of being seen
25   and dared one another to
'open it'
'no you open it'

'no you'
someone would open it
cautiously pulling out a shirt   30
that would be tried on
then passed around till somebody claimed it by fit
then sixteen or eighteen hands would be pulling out
skirts, pants, jackets, dresses from a box transformed now
into the Sears catalogue.   35

Or the white judges would wait till twilight
and my father and older brothers
would drag a bloodstained canvas
heavy with meat from the truck onto our lawn, and
my mother would lift and lay it in place   40
like a dead relative,
praying, coaxing and thanking it
then she'd cut the thick hair and skin back
till it lay in folds beside it like carpet

carving off firm chunks   45
until the marble bone shone out of the red-blue flesh
long into the truck-headlight-night she'd carve
talking in Cree to my father and in English to my brothers
long into the dark their voices talking us to sleep
while our bellies rested in the meat days ahead.   50

Or wait till the guitars came out
and the furniture was pushed up against the walls
and we'd polish the linoleum with our dancing
till our socks had holes.

Or wait till a fight broke out   55
and the night would settle in our bones
and we'd ache with shame
for having heard or spoken
that which sits at the edge of our light side
that which comes but we wished it hadn't   60
like 'settlement' relatives who would arrive at Christmas and
leave at Easter.

—1996

Robin Robertson

b. 1955

Poet, editor, and translator Robin Robertson was raised on the northeast coast of Scotland but has spent most of his professional life in London. He first established himself in the publishing industry as an editor and did not release a collection of his own poetry until his forties; this first book, *A Painted Field* (1997), was followed by *Slow Air* (2002), *Swithering* (2006), and *The Wrecking Light* (2010).

Robertson's work is known for its often bleak view of human relationships; for its use of natural imagery, especially imagery reflecting the landscape of Robertson's native Scotland; and for its frequent allusions to classical and Celtic mythology. Yet his work is immediate and contemporary in tone. *The New Yorker* has praised his "genius ... for finding the sensually charged moment—in a raked northern seascape, in a sexual or gustatory encounter—and depicting it in language that is simultaneously spare and ample."

Robertson is the first poet to win Britain's Forward Prize in all three categories: Best First Collection, Best Collection, and Best Single Poem. He was honoured with the E.M. Forster Award in 2004, elected a Fellow of the Royal Society of Literature in 2009, and presented with the T.S. Eliot Prize for Poetry in 2010. Robertson has also received critical praise for his work as a translator; such works include a translation of Euripides' play *Medea* (2008) and *The Deleted World* (2007), a bilingual edition of selections by the Swedish poet Tomas Tranströmer.

The Park Drunk

He opens his eyes to a hard frost,
the morning's soft amnesia of snow.

The thorned stems of gorse
are starred crystal; each bud
5   like a candied fruit, its yellow
picked out and lit
by the low pulse
of blood-orange
riding in the eastern trees.

10 What the snow has furred
to silence, uniformity,
frost amplifies, makes singular:

giving every form a sound,
an edge, as if
frost wants to know what   15
snow tries to forget.

And so he drinks for winter,
for the coming year,
to open all the beautiful tiny doors
in their craquelure[1] of frost;   20
and he drinks
like the snow falling, trying
to close the biggest door of all.

—2006

What the Horses See at Night

When the day-birds have settled
in their creaking trees,
the doors of the forest open
for the flitting
drift of deer   5
among the bright croziers[2]
of new ferns
and the legible stars;
foxes stream from the earth;
a tawny owl   10
sweeps the long meadow.
In a slink of river-light
the mink's face
is already slippery with yolk,
and the bay's   15
tiny islands are drops
of solder
under a drogue[3] moon.
The sea's a heavy sleeper,
dreaming in and out with a catch   20
in each breath, and is not disturbed

---

1   *craquelure* Texture of fine cracks found in old varnish or paint.
2   *croziers* Curled ends of new fern fronds.
3   *drogue* Funnel-shaped object dragged behind a boat or other vehicle to reduce its speed.

by that *plowt*[1]—the first
in a play of herring, a shoal
silvering open
25 the sheeted black skin of the sea.
Through the starting rain, the moon
skirrs[2] across the sky dragging
torn shreds of cloud behind.
The fox's call is red
30 and ribboned
in the snow's white shadow.
The horses watch the sea climb
and climb and walk
towards them on the hill,
35 hear the vole
crying under the alder,
our children
breathing slowly in their beds.

—2006

---

1   *plowt* Scots: splash.
2   *skirrs* Scots: scurries.

Li-Young Lee
b. 1957

When Li-Young Lee was two years old his Chinese family fled persecution in Indonesia, travelling through Hong Kong, Macau, and Japan before they reached the United States in 1964. Lee's work often focuses on his personal life, including his relationships with his wife and children; the most frequently recurring figure is his father, who had been Mao Zedong's personal physician, but in the United States became a Presbyterian minister. Lee strives to unite his examination of personal memories with a more universal exploration of selfhood and spirituality, describing himself as "an amateur mystic."

Although Lee is often pigeonholed as an immigrant writer and acknowledges the influence of Imperial-era Chinese poets such as Tu Fu and Su Tung-po, he also cites the influence of his father's Christianity on his work—and the influence of writers such as John Keats, Walt Whitman, and Cynthia Ozick. Resisting pressure to identify his poetry as "Asian," "American," or even "Asian-American," Lee says, "I want to be a global poet."

Lyrical and elegant in his handling of themes of exile, identity, and mortality, Lee has received critical acclaim since the publication of his first book, *Rose* (1986). Although his reputation rests primarily on poetry collections such as *The City in Which I Love You* (1990) and *Behind My Eyes* (2008), he has also published an American Book Award-winning prose memoir, *The Winged Seed* (1995).

Persimmons

In sixth grade Mrs. Walker
slapped the back of my head
and made me stand in the corner
for not knowing the difference
between *persimmon* and *precision*. 5
How to choose

persimmons. This is precision.
Ripe ones are soft and brown-spotted.
Sniff the bottoms. The sweet one
will be fragrant. How to eat: 10
put the knife away, lay down newspaper.
Peel the skin tenderly, not to tear the meat.
Chew the skin, suck it,

and swallow. Now, eat
15 the meat of the fruit,
so sweet,
all of it, to the heart.

Donna undresses, her stomach is white.
In the yard, dewy and shivering
20 with crickets, we lie naked,
face-up, face-down.
I teach her Chinese.
Crickets: *chiu chiu.* Dew: I've forgotten.
Naked: I've forgotten.
25 *Ni, wo:* you and me.
I part her legs,
remember to tell her
she is beautiful as the moon.

Other words
30 that got me into trouble were
fight and *fright, wren* and *yarn.*
Fight was what I did when I was frightened,
Fright was what I felt when I was fighting.
Wrens are small, plain birds,
35 yarn is what one knits with.
Wrens are soft as yarn.
My mother made birds out of yarn.
I loved to watch her tie the stuff;
a bird, a rabbit, a wee man.

40 Mrs. Walker brought a persimmon to class
and cut it up
so everyone could taste
a *Chinese apple.* Knowing
it wasn't ripe or sweet, I didn't eat
45 but watched the other faces.

My mother said every persimmon has a sun
inside, something golden, glowing,
warm as my face.

Once, in the cellar, I found two wrapped in newspaper,
50 forgotten and not yet ripe.
I took them and set both on my bedroom windowsill,

where each morning a cardinal
sang, *The sun, the sun.*

Finally understanding
he was going blind, 55
my father sat up all one night
waiting for a song, a ghost.
I gave him the persimmons,
swelled, heavy as sadness,
and sweet as love. 60

This year, in the muddy lighting
of my parents' cellar, I rummage, looking
for something I lost.
My father sits on the tired, wooden stairs,
black cane between his knees, 65
hand over hand, gripping the handle.
He's so happy that I've come home.
I ask how his eyes are, a stupid question.
All gone, he answers.

Under some blankets, I find a box. 70
Inside the box I find three scrolls.
I sit beside him and untie
three paintings by my father:
Hibiscus leaf and a white flower.
Two cats preening. 75
Two persimmons, so full they want to drop from the cloth.

He raises both hands to touch the cloth,
asks, *Which is this?*

This is persimmons, Father.

Oh, the feel of the wolftail on the silk, 80
the strength, the tense
precision in the wrist.
I painted them hundreds of times
eyes closed. These I painted blind.
Some things never leave a person: 85
scent of the hair of one you love,
the texture of persimmons,
in your palm, the ripe weight.

—1986

Benjamin Zephaniah
b. 1958

Benjamin Zephaniah is known as a writer of dub poetry, a form based on reggae rhythms that is best appreciated if the poem is read aloud. Through his insistence that poetry needs to be spoken and "performed," either live or on television, Zephaniah engages with a broad audience that might not otherwise seek out his work. He is a vegan, a Rastafarian, and a human rights activist, and much of his work is political, provoking his audiences to confront racism and other forms of injustice in Britain and across the world. His voice is sometimes humorous and hopeful, but is also expressive of anger; as he writes, "Black people do not have / Chips on their shoulders / They just have injustice on their backs."

Zephaniah was brought up in a Jamaican community in Birmingham, England. Frustrated, possibly because of his dyslexia, he left school at 13 and gained a local reputation as a poet before moving to London, where his first book, *Pen Rhythm*, was released in 1980. Since then he has published, performed, and recorded poetry for adults and children and has written novels for youth addressing subjects such as racism and violence.

Zephaniah's recordings often combine poetry with music that has its base in reggae but incorporates other influences, from jazz to hip hop; he has recorded with the reggae band The Wailers, with drummer Trevor Morais, and with singer-songwriter Sinéad O'Connor. Zephaniah holds more than a dozen honorary doctorates and in 2003 was offered the title Officer of the Order of the British Empire, which he refused.

Dis Poetry

Dis poetry is like a riddim dat drops
De tongue fires a riddim dat shoots like shots
Dis poetry is designed fe rantin
Dance hall style, big mouth chanting,
5 Dis poetry nar put yu to sleep
Preaching follow me
Like yu is blind sheep,
Dis poetry is not Party Political
Not designed fe dose who are critical.

10 Dis poetry is wid me when I gu to me bed
It gets into me dreadlocks
It lingers around me head
Dis poetry goes wid me as I pedal me bike
I've tried Shakespeare, Respect due dere

But dis is de stuff I like.   15
Dis poetry is not afraid of going ina book
Still dis poetry need ears fe hear an eyes fe hav a look
Dis poetry is Verbal Riddim, no big words involved
An if I hav a problem de riddim gets it solved,
I've tried to be more Romantic, it does nu good for me   20
So I tek a Reggae Riddim an build me poetry,
I could try be more personal
But you've heard it all before,
Pages of written words not needed
Brain has many words in store,   25
Yu could call dis poetry Dub Ranting
De tongue plays a beat
De body starts skanking,[1]
Dis poetry is quick an childish
Dis poetry is fe de wise an foolish,   30
Anybody can do it fe free,
Dis poetry is fe yu an me,
Don't stretch yu imagination
Dis poetry is fe de good of de Nation,
Chant,   35
In de morning
I chant
In de night
I chant
In de darkness   40
An under de spotlight,
I pass thru University
I pass thru Sociology
An den I got a Dread degree
In Dreadfull Ghettology.   45

Dis poetry stays wid me when I run or walk
An when I am talking to meself in poetry I talk,
Dis poetry is wid me,
Below me an above,
Dis poetry's from inside me   50
It goes to yu
WID LUV.

—1995

---

1   *skanking* Style of dancing associated with reggae music.

George Elliott Clarke
b. 1960

George Elliott Clarke is a playwright, academic, critic, and poet known for the power and lyricism of his language. His poetry draws on biblical stories, oral narratives, and music, especially jazz and the blues. He often uses linked poems as a mode of storytelling; speaking of the story-in-verse, Clarke has said that a "lyric poem—even a haiku—is always a little drama, a little story—just as every snapshot is a truncated tale. So, as soon as one compiles a bunch of lyrics, they almost always begin to comprise a narrative."

A political and cultural activist as well as a writer, Clarke frequently addresses the history and experiences of black Canadians in his work; he is especially interested in Maritimers of African descent, whom he refers to as "Africadians." Clarke's interests in black history and narrative poetry come together in works such as his verse novel *Whylah Falls* (1990), set in the 1930s in the fictional black Nova Scotian community of Whylah Falls.

Clarke himself is a seventh-generation Canadian and the descendant of black Loyalists who settled in Nova Scotia in 1783. He holds degrees from the University of Waterloo (BA), Dalhousie University (MA), and Queen's University (PhD). He was named the E.J. Pratt Professor of Canadian Literature at the University of Toronto in 2003 and Poet Laureate of Toronto in 2012. Among Clarke's many awards are numerous honorary doctorates, the Governor General's Award for his collection *Execution Poems* (2001), the Martin Luther King, Jr. Achievement Award (2004), the Pierre Elliott Trudeau Fellows Prize (2005), and the Order of Canada (2008).

from *Whylah Falls*

Blank Sonnet

The air smells of rhubarb, occasional
Roses, or first birth of blossoms, a fresh,
Undulant hurt, so body snaps and curls
Like flower. I step through snow as thin as script,
5 Watch white stars spin dizzy as drunks, and yearn
To sleep beneath a patchwork quilt of rum.
I want the slow, sure collapse of language
Washed out by alcohol. Lovely Shelley,[1]

---

1   *Shelley* The speaker's lover.

I have no use for measured, cadenced verse
If you won't read. Icarus-like,[1] I'll fall   10
Against this page of snow, tumble blackly
Across vision to drown in the white sea
That closes every poem—the white reverse
That cancels the blackness of each image.

Look Homeward, Exile

I can still see that soil crimsoned by butchered
Hog and imbrued with rye, lye, and homely
Spirituals everybody must know,
Still dream of folks who broke or cracked like shale:
Pushkin, who twisted his hands in boxing,   5
Marrocco, who ran girls like dogs and got stabbed,
Lavinia, her teeth decayed to black stumps,
Her lovemaking still in demand, spitting
Black phlegm—her pension after twenty towns,
And Toof; suckled on anger that no Baptist   10
Church could contain, who let wrinkled Eely
Seed her moist womb when she was just thirteen.
            And the tyrant sun that reared from barbed-wire
Spewed flame that charred the idiot crops
To Depression, and hurt my granddaddy   15
To bottle after bottle of sweet death,
His dreams beaten to one, tremendous pulp,
Until his heart seized, choked; his love gave out.
            But Beauty survived, secreted
In freight trains snorting in their pens, in babes   20
Whose faces were coal-black mirrors, in strange
Strummers who plucked Ghanaian banjos, hummed
Blind blues—precise, ornate, rich needlepoint,
In sermons scorched with sulphur and brimstone,
And in my love's dark, orient skin that smelled   25
Like orange peels and tasted like rum, good God!
            I remember my Creator in the old ways:
I sit in taverns and stare at my fists;

---

1   *Icarus* Ancient Greek mythological character who flew using wings made of feathers and
     wax. When Icarus flew too close to the sun, the wax melted, and he fell into the ocean
     and drowned.

I knead earth into bread, spell water into wine.
30 Still, nothing warms my wintry exile—neither
Prayers nor fine love, neither votes nor hard drink:
For nothing heals those saints felled in green beds,
Whose loves are smashed by just one word or glance
Or pain—a screw jammed in thick, straining wood.

—1990

Casualties

January 16, 1991[1]

Snow annihilates all beauty
this merciless January.
A white blitzkrieg,[2] Klan—cruel,
arsons and obliterates.

5 Piercing lies numb us to pain.
Nerves and words fail so we
can't feel agony or passion,
so we can't flinch or cry,

when we spy blurred children's
10 charred bodies protruding
from the smoking rubble
of statistics or see a man

stumbling in a blizzard
of bullets. Everything is
15 normal, absurdly normal.
We see, as if through a snow-

---

1   *January 16, 1991* Date of the beginning of the Gulf War (January–February 1991), in
which the United States and its allies expelled the Iraqi military from Kuwait, which
Iraq had invaded the previous year. The war demonstrated the power of American
military technology; there were fewer than 500 casualties on the side of the American-led
coalition, but tens of thousands of civilian casualties and as many as 100,000 casualties
among Iraqi soldiers. The war also created millions of refugees.
2   *blitzkrieg* Intensive war strategy that combines aerial bombing and mechanized ground
troops to surprise and overwhelm an enemy; the American-led coalition used this sort of
strategy in the Gulf War.

storm, darkly. Reporters
rat-a-tat-tat tactics,
stratagems. Missiles bristle
behind newspaper lines.   20

Our minds chill; we weather
the storm, huddle in dreams.
Exposed, though, a woman,
lashed by lightning, repents

of her flesh, becomes a living   25
X-ray, "collateral damage."
The first casualty of war
is language.

—1992

Jackie Kay
b. 1961

Deemed "one of the most sure-footed voices in contemporary literature" by *The Guardian*, Jackie Kay is a writer of poetry, fiction, children's books, drama, and autobiography. She began writing in her late teens, she has said, because, as a black lesbian growing up in Scotland, she found "there wasn't anybody else saying the things I wanted to say.... I started out of that sense of wanting to create some images for myself."

Born to a Nigerian father and Scottish mother, Kay was adopted and raised in Glasgow by white parents—an experience that has informed much of her writing, including poetry collections such as *The Adoption Papers* (1991) and *Fiere* (2011) as well as her 2010 prose memoir *Red Dust Road*. "I sometimes take my own experience as a diving board to jump off into the pool of my imagination," Kay has said of her work, which often delves into aspects of identity, including race, culture, and sexuality. Her novel *Trumpet* (1998), for example, concerns a biological woman who lives his life as a man, while her BBC radio play *The Lamplighter* (2007) examines the history of the Atlantic slave trade.

Kay has more than 15 publications to her credit and is the recipient of numerous awards. She won the *Guardian* Fiction Prize for *Trumpet* and the CLPE Poetry Award for her children's poetry collection *Red, Cherry Red* (2007), and in 2006 she was made a Member of the Order of the British Empire for services to literature. She teaches creative writing at Newcastle University.

In My Country

Walking by the waters
down where an honest river
shakes hands with the sea,
a woman passed round me
5   in a slow watchful circle,
as if I were a superstition;

or the worst dregs of her imagination,
so when she finally spoke
her words spliced into bars
10   of an old wheel. A segment of air.
"*Where do you come from?*"
"Here," I said. "Here. These parts."

—1991

Her

I had been told about her
How she would always, always
How she would never, never
I'd watched and listened
But I still fell for her   5
How she always, always
How she never, never

In the small brave night
Her lips, butterfly moments
I tried to catch her and she laughed   10
A loud laugh that cracked me in two
But then I had been told about her
How she would always, always
How she would never, never

We two listened to the wind   15
We two galloped a pace
We two, up and away, away, away.
And now she's gone
Like she said she would go
But then I had been told about her
How she would always, always.

—2005

High Land

I don't remember who kissed who first,
who touched who first, who anything to whom.
All I remember in the highland night—
the sheep loose outside,
the full moon smoking in the sky—   5
was that you led me and I led you.
And all of a sudden we were in a small room
in a big house with the light coming in
and your legs open; mine too.
And it was this swirling, twirling thing.   10
It's hard to fasten it down;

it is hard to remember what was what—
who was who when the wind was coming in.

—2005

Late Love

How they strut about, people in love,
How tall they grow, pleased with themselves,
Their hair, glossy, their skin shining.
They don't remember who they have been.

5 How filmic they are just for this time.
How important they've become—secret, above
The order of things, the dreary mundane.
Every church bell ringing, a fresh sign.

How dull the lot that are not in love.
10 Their clothes shabby, their skin lustreless;
How clueless they are, hair a mess; how they trudge
Up and down the streets in the rain,

remembering one kiss in a dark alley,
A touch in a changing room, if lucky, a lovely wait
15 For the phone to ring, maybe, baby.
The past with its rush of velvet, its secret hush

Already miles away, dimming now, in the late day.

—2005

Lavinia Greenlaw
b. 1962

Lavinia Greenlaw's diverse career and background have allowed her to explore in writing a wide array of subjects—from science and music to art, history, and travel. Her style is characterized by precise description and a sometimes dry humour; her several collections of poetry include *Night Photograph* (1993), *A World Where News Travelled Slowly* (1997), *Minsk* (2003), and *The Casual Perfect* (2011).

Greenlaw was born in London and her childhood experiences in a science-oriented family have provided inspiration for many of her poems. She has been a writer-in-residence for such institutions as the Science Museum and the Royal Society of Medicine, but also worked as an arts administrator after earning an MA in seventeenth-century art from the Courtauld Institute. She teaches writing at the University of East Anglia, where she has served as chair of the Poetry Society and director of the Poetry MA program.

In addition to her books of poetry, Greenlaw has authored two novels and two non-fiction books (including the acclaimed 2007 memoir *The Importance of Music to Girls*). She has also written song texts and libretti for several operas, adapted works by Virginia Woolf and Geoffrey Chaucer into radio dramas, and created documentaries for BBC radio. Her interest in audio media led to her 2011 Ted Hughes Award-winning sound work *Audio Obscura*, a composition of monologues to be listened to in a train station. Her other accolades include a Forward Prize, a Cholmondeley Award, and an Arts Council Writer's Award.

Electricity

The night you called to tell me
that the unevenness between the days
is as simple as meeting or not meeting,
I was thinking about electricity—
how at no point on a circuit   5
can power diminish or accumulate,
how you also need a lack of balance
for energy to be released. *Trust it.*
Once, being held like that,
no edge, no end and no beginning,   10
I could not tell our actions apart:
if it was you who lifted my head to the light,

if it was I who said how much I wanted
to look at your face. *Your beautiful face.*

—1993

Zombies

1980, I was returned to the city exposed
in black and white as the lights went on and on.
A back-alley neon sign, the first I'd seen,
drew us sweetly down and in to brightness:
5 a doll's parasol, a spike of green cherries,
the physic of apricot brandy, actual limes
and morning-to-night shades of rum.
Newly old enough and government-moneyed,
we knocked them back, melting the ice
10 between us and the unaccustomed looseness
of being legitimate and free. What possessed us?
Was it the kick of spirits or the invisible syrup
in which they swam that worked in our veins,
charming us into a car and forty miles east

15 to the fields of our years of boredom?
Did we not remember the curse of this place?
How Sundays drank our blood as we watched
dry paint or the dust on the television screen.
How people died bursting out of a quiet life,
20 or from being written into a small world's stories.
Who can see such things and live to tell?
How we hunted all night for noise and love,
striking out once across ploughed and frozen earth,
lurching from rut to rut until at the edge
25 we smashed our way out through a hedge, to fall
eight feet to the road. Of course, we felt nothing.
Was it not ourselves who frightened us most?
As if brightness or sweetness could save us.

—2003

Simon Armitage
b. 1963

⬛⬛⬛ Simon Armitage was born in West Yorkshire, England, and worked as a probation officer in Manchester before becoming a full-time poet; his northern English background is reflected in both the language and subject matter of his work. Named Britain's Millennium Poet in 2000, he is also known for his work as a playwright, lecturer, translator, and novelist.

In Armitage's words, poetry is "a kind of human consequence" of our existence as "a species that looks for pattern, and looks for significance, and looks for meaning in a life"—a sentiment that speaks to the search for meaning behind the commonplace that characterizes his poetry. This attention to everyday subject matter is mirrored in Armitage's language, which is strongly influenced by northern British vernacular. Often colloquial in tone, many of his poems are straightforward on the surface, but their apparent simplicity conceals multiple levels of complex, ambiguous meaning. As poet Peter McDonald suggests, Armitage's work encourages readers to realize that "[t]hings are always ... more complicated than they appear, but also than we really want them to be."

Armitage does not constrain himself to a specific mode of writing; his more than 20 published works include two novels, several works of nonfiction, and translations of Homer's *Odyssey* and of the fourteenth-century Middle English poem *Sir Gawain and the Green Knight*. He is also involved in the British television and film scene and has written an opera libretto as well as song lyrics for his rock band The Scaremongers. Armitage is a Fellow of the Royal Society of Literature and vice-president of the Poetry Society in London.

Poem

And if it snowed and snow covered the drive
he took a spade and tossed it to one side.
And always tucked his daughter up at night.
And slippered[1] her the one time that she lied.

And every week he tipped up[2] half his wage.   5
And what he didn't spend each week he saved.
And praised his wife for every meal she made.
And once, for laughing, punched her in the face.

---

1   *slippered* Spanked with a shoe.
2   *tipped up* I.e., handed over.

And for his mum he hired a private nurse.
10 And every Sunday taxied her to church.
And he blubbed when she went from bad to worse.
And twice he lifted ten quid from her purse.

Here's how they rated him when they looked back:
sometimes he did this, sometimes he did that.

—1989

Very Simply Topping Up the Brake Fluid

Yes, love, that's why the warning light comes on. Don't
panic. Fetch some universal brake fluid
and a five-eighths screwdriver from your toolkit
then prop the bonnet open. Go on, it won't

5 eat you. Now, without slicing through the fan-belt
try and slide the sharp end of the screwdriver
under the lid and push the spade connector
through its bed, go on, that's it. Now you're all right

to unscrew, no, clockwise, you see it's Russian
10 love, back to front, that's it. You see, it's empty.
Now, gently with your hand and I mean gently,
try and create a bit of space by pushing

the float-chamber sideways so there's room to pour,
gently does it, that's it. Try not to spill it, it's
15 corrosive: rusts, you know, and fill it till it's
level with the notch on the clutch reservoir.

Lovely. There's some Swarfega[1] in the office
if you want a wash and some soft roll above
the cistern° for, you know. Oh don't mind him, love,   *toilet tank*
20 he doesn't bite. Come here and sit down Prince. Prince!

Now, where's that bloody alternator? Managed?
Oh any time, love. I'll not charge you for that
because it's nothing of a job. If you want
us again we're in the book. Tell your husband.

—1989

---

1   *Swarfega* British-made hand cleaner used to remove grease.

It Could Be You[1]

We interrupt our live coverage of the War
for details of tonight's National Lottery draw:

the winning numbers are fourteen, eighteen,
thirty-nine, forty-four, eighty-two, and ninety-one.[2]

The bonus ball is number two-thousand-and-some.   5
A record jackpot pay-out will be shared between

winning ticket holders in Belfast, Aberdeen,
Milford Haven and East Acton. Now back to the action.

—2002

---

1   *It Could Be You* Slogan of the UK National Lottery.
2   *fourteen … ninety-one* The wars in which Great Britain participated during the twentieth
     century include World War I (1914–18), World War II (1939–45), the Falklands War
     (1982), and the Gulf War (1991).

Ian Iqbal Rashid
b. 1965

Multifaceted artist Ian Iqbal Rashid is a poet, screenwriter, and director. Born Iqbal Rashid in Dar es Salaam, Tanzania, to a South Asian Muslim family, he was five years old when the family was forced to flee Tanzania. They settled in Toronto, where Rashid took up the name "Ian" when his first-grade teacher told him "Iqbal" was too difficult to pronounce.

Rashid's poetry is often concerned with cultural identity, sexual orientation, and the intersections between the two. His first poetry collection, *Black Markets, White Boyfriends and Other Acts of Elision* (1991), was nominated for the Gerald Lampert Memorial Prize. *Song of Sabu* (1994), his next collection, includes poems about the Indian American film actor Sabu (1924–63), who is also the subject of Rashid's first short film, *Surviving Sabu* (1998).

Rashid worked as a writer in British television before becoming a self-taught filmmaker. His first feature-length film, *Touch of Pink* (2004), is a semi-autobiographical comedy about a gay man coming out to his traditional Muslim mother. Both *Touch of Pink* and Rashid's second film, *How She Move* (2007), premiered at the Sundance Film Festival.

Rashid currently lives in the United Kingdom and regularly travels between England and Canada.

Could Have Danced All Night

1.

I once used to dream of being held knowingly by a man
on whom I would not look.

Then this all came again, the embrace held
in the ease of a dance, held within your hands small
5 yet capable and roped with thick vein.
And when I tried, it didn't surprise me
to be able to look into eyes, yours, like mine
the rough colour of night, into your shy, pie face.

Standing together tonight I long for the anise
10 taste of Thai basil on your skin,
your pale denim thighs and ass resplendent
in strobes of evening light.

Tonight I would dance with you across an alien landscape.
We might fly. ("I'm positive.")
But this night finds our legs rooted, knotted,   15
planted painfully like a flag. ("I've tested positive.")

2.

Tonight, I watch you walking away,
wheeling your burden before you into the night.
Fists jab my thighs on either side.
Fists which mean to unclench hold
fingers which mean to interlock   5
with yours, like pieces of a puzzle
join, into a picture of two men dancing.

Tonight movement is limited:
from hand to mouth to mind.
Tobacco, caustic laughter in the lungs,   10
the careful sipping of our herbal teas,
the careful sipping of our everything-will-be-all-rights.

—1991

Christian Bök
b. 1966

Few poets, especially those to whom the term *avant-garde* has been applied, live to see their work appear on international bestseller lists; Toronto-born poet Christian Bök is a rare exception. In *Eunoia* (2001), his Griffin Prize-winning collection of poetry and prose acclaimed as much for its ingenuity and playfulness as for its discipline, Bök set himself the task of composing a series of lipograms, each using only one of the five vowels ("Chapter I" from this series is included below). In addition to this exacting requirement, Bök imposed a number of other conditions upon himself: the use of the letter *y* would be forbidden; each of the collection's five chapters would have to contain "a culinary banquet, a prurient debauch, a pastoral tableau, and a nautical voyage"; and every line or sentence of the poem would have to accent "internal rhyme through the use of syntactical parallelism."

Like the writers affiliated with the French *Oulipo* school (*Ouvroir de littérature potentielle*, or "workshop of potential literature"), Bök seeks inspiration in constraint. *Eunoia* is more than an elaborate literary stunt: the poetical tension between the strictures of form and the expansiveness of content becomes a crucible and a catalyst as Bök experiments with expression through repression, thereby revealing the plasticity of the language and the "personality" of each vowel.

Although best known for *Eunoia*, Bök is also the author of the collection *Crystallography* (1994), in which he explores the intersection of art and science by positing a relationship between words and crystal formations. In all of his work, Bök experiments with what he calls "lucid writing," a form of composition that "concerns itself with the exploratory examination of its own pattern."

Chapter I

for Dick Higgins

Writing is inhibiting. Sighing, I sit, scribbling in ink
this pidgin[1] script. I sing with nihilistic witticism,
disciplining signs with trifling gimmicks—impish
hijinks which highlight stick sigils. Isn't it glib?
5 Isn't it chic? I fit childish insights within rigid limits,
writing schtick which might instill priggish misgiv-

---

1   *pidgin* Linguistically simplified.

ings in critics blind with hindsight. I dismiss nit-
picking criticism which flirts with philistinism. I
bitch; I kibitz—griping whilst criticizing dimwits,
sniping whilst indicting nitwits, dismissing simplis-   10
tic thinking, in which philippic[1] wit is still illicit.

Pilgrims, digging in shifts, dig till midnight in mining
pits, chipping flint with picks, drilling schist with drills,
striking it rich mining zinc. Irish firms, hiring micks[2]
whilst firing Brits, bring in smiths with mining skills: 15
kilnwrights grilling brick in brickkilns, millwrights
grinding grist in gristmills. Irish tinsmiths, fiddling
with widgits, fix this rig, driving its drills which spin
whirring drillbits. I pitch in, fixing things. I rig this
winch with its wiring; I fit this drill with its piping. I   20
dig this ditch, filling bins with dirt, piling it high, sift-
ing it, till I find bright prisms twinkling with glitz.

Hiking in British districts, I picnic in virgin firths,[3]
grinning in mirth with misfit whims, smiling if I find
birch twigs, smirking if I find mint sprigs. Midspring   25
brings with it singing birds, six kinds (finch, siskin, ibis,
tit, pipit, swift), whistling shrill chirps, trilling *chirr
chirr* in high pitch. Kingbirds flit in gliding flight,
skimming limpid springs, dipping wingtips in rills
which brim with living things: krill, shrimp, brill—   30
fish with gilt fins, which swim in flitting zigs. Might
Virgil[4] find bliss implicit in this primitivism? Might
I mimic him in print if I find his writings inspiring?

Fishing till twilight, I sit, drifting in this birch skiff,
jigging kingfish with jigs, brining in fish which nip   35
this bright string (its vivid glint bristling with stick
pins). Whilst I slit this fish in its gills, knifing it, slicing
it, killing it with skill, shipwrights might trim this jib,
swinging it right, hitching it tight, riding brisk winds

---

1   *philippic* Bitter, reproachful, ranting.
2   *micks* Offensive slang: Irish people.
3   *firths* Inlets.
4   *Virgil* Roman poet (70–19 BCE). His *Eclogues* have primarily rural settings, and in his
    Georgics he describes agricultural processes.

40 which pitch this skiff, tipping it, tilting it, till this ship
in crisis flips. Rigging rips. Christ, this ship is sinking. Diving in, I swim, fighting this frigid swirl, kicking, kicking, swimming in it till I sight high cliffs,
rising, indistinct in thick mists, lit with lightning.

45 Lightning blinks, striking things in its midst with
blinding light. Whirlwinds whirl; driftwinds drift.
Spindrift is spinning in thrilling whirligigs. Which
blind spirit is whining in this whistling din? Is it
this grim lich,[1] which is writhing in its pit, lifting its
50 lid with whitish limbs, rising, vivific, with ill will in
its mind, victimizing kids timid with fright? If it is—
which blind witch is midwifing its misbirth, binding
this hissing djinni[2] with witching spiritism? Is it this
thin, sickish girl, twitching in fits, whilst writing
55 things in spirit-writing? If it isn't—it is I; it is I ...

Lightning flicks its riding whip, blitzing this night
with bright schisms. Sick with phthisis[3] in this driz-
zling mist, I limp, sniffling, spitting bilic spit, itching
livid skin (skin which is tingling with stinging pin-
60 pricks). I find this frigid drisk dispiriting; still, I fight
its chilling windchill. I climb cliffs, flinching with
skittish instincts. I might slip. I might twist this infirm wrist, crippling it, wincing whilst I bind it in its
splint, cringing whilst I gird it in its sling; still, I risk
65 climbing, sticking with it, striving till I find this rift,
in which I might fit, hiding in it till winds diminish.

Minds grim with nihilism still find first light inspiring. Mild pink in tint, its shining twilight brings bright
tidings which lift sinking spirits. With firm will, I finish
70 climbing, hiking till I find this inviting inn, in which
I might sit, dining. I thirst. I bid girls bring stiff drinks
—gin fizz which I might sip whilst finishing this rich
dish, nibbling its tidbits: ribs with wings in chili, figs

---

1 *lich* Corpse, especially a reanimated one.
2 *djinni* In Islamic mythology, a spirit with supernatural abilities.
3 *phthisis* Wasting sickness.

with kiwis in icing. I swig citric drinks with vim, tip-
ping kirsch, imbibing it till, giggling, I flirt with girl-   75
ish virgins in miniskirts: *wink, wink.* I miss living
in sin, pinching thighs, kissing lips pink with lipstick.

Slick pimps, bribing civic kingpins, distill gin in stills,
spiking drinks with illicit pills which might bring bliss.
Whiz kids in silk-knit shirts script films in which   80
slim girls might strip, jiggling tits, wiggling hips, in-
citing wild shindigs. Twin siblings in bikinis might kiss
rich bigwigs, giving this prim prig his wish, whipping
him, tickling him, licking his limp dick till, rigid,
his prick spills its jism. Shit! This ticklish victim is   85
trifling with kink. Sick minds, thriving in kinship
with pigs, might find insipid thrills in this filth. This
flick irks critics. It is swinish; it is piggish. It stinks.

Thinking within strict limits is stifling. Whilst Viking
knights fight griffins, I skirmish with this riddling   90
sphinx (this sigil—I), I print lists, filing things (kin with
kin, ilk with ilk), inscribing this distinct sign, listing
things in which its imprint is intrinsic. I find its missing links, divining its implicit tricks. I find it whilst
skindiving in Fiji; I find it whilst picnicking in Linz. I   95
find it in Inniskillin; I find it in Mississippi. I find it
whilst skiing in Minsk. (Is this intimism civilizing if
Klimt limns it, if Liszt[1] lilts it?) I sigh; I lisp. I finish writing this writ, signing it, kind sir: NIHIL, DICIT, FINI.[2]

—2001

---

1   *intimism* Genre of painting involving the impressionistic portrayal of domestic
     scenes; *Klimt* Gustav Klimt (1862–1918), Austrian artist; *limns* Portrays (here, by
     painting); *Liszt* Franz Liszt (1811–86), Hungarian composer and pianist.
2   *NIHIL, DICIT, FINI* Latin: NOTHING, HE SAYS, THE END.

Alice Oswald
b. 1966

Named one of the Poetry Book Society's "Next Generation" Poets in 2004, Alice Oswald has captured readers' attention with her bold depictions of the environment. Rejecting the sentimentalizing traditions of nature poetry, she strives to acknowledge nature as powerful, vulnerable, and alien to human beings. In her writing, she says, "I'm continually smashing down the nostalgia in my head. And I am trying to enquire of the landscape itself what it feels about itself.... There's a whole range of words that people use about landscape. Pastoral? Idyll? I can't stand them." If Oswald's overall approach is arresting, so too is her poetic style; the reader is continually surprised by small details of diction, of syntax, of rhythm, and of rhyme.

Born in Reading, Oswald read Classics at Oxford. After graduating she worked as a gardener, an occupation she has credited with providing thinking time in which her early poems could develop. In 1996, Oswald published *The Thing in the Gap-Stone Stile*, which won the Forward Poetry Prize for Best First Collection. The Devon landscape where she lives, depicted as a world of beauty and fear, features prominently both in this and in later work. In order to write the book-length poem *Dart* (for which she received the T.S. Eliot Award in 2002), Oswald researched for three years, spending time near the Dart River and interviewing the people who live and work alongside it.

Oswald's published volumes include *Woods Etc.* (2005), *A Sleepwalk on the Severn* (2009), and *Weeds and Wild Flowers* (2009), a collaboration with artist Jessica Greenman. *Memorial*, Oswald's 2011 work, draws upon her classical education, revisiting the mythological landscape of Homer's *Iliad* from the perspective of ordinary soldiers.

Wedding

From time to time our love is like a sail
and when the sail begins to alternate
from tack to tack, it's like a swallowtail
and when the swallow flies it's like a coat;
5   and if the coat is yours, it has a tear
like a wide mouth and when the mouth begins
to draw the wind, it's like a trumpeter
and when the trumpet blows, it blows like millions ...
and this, my love, when millions come and go
10   beyond the need of us, is like a trick;
and when the trick begins, it's like a toe

tip-toeing on a rope, which is like luck;
and when the luck begins, it's like a wedding,
which is like love, which is like everything.

—1996

Woods etc.

footfall, which is a means so steady
and in small sections wanders through the mind
unnoticed, because it beats constantly,
sweeping together the loose tacks of sound

I remember walking once into increasing   5
woods, my hearing like a widening wound
first your voice and then the rustling ceasing.
the last glow of rain dead in the ground

that my feet kept time with the sun's imaginary
changing position, hoping it would rise   10
suddenly from scattered parts of my body
into the upturned apses of my eyes.

no clearing in that quiet, no change at all.
in my throat the little mercury line
that regulates my speech began to fall   .   15
rapidly the endless length of my spine

—2005

Dunt[1]

a poem for a nearly dried-up river

Very small and damaged and quite dry,
a Roman water nymph[2] made of bone
tries to summon a river out of limestone.

---

1   *Dunt* Stream in the Gloucestershire County area of England.
2   *nymph* In classical mythology, a beautiful spirit associated with a natural setting.

Very eroded faded,
5   her left arm missing and both legs from the knee down,
a Roman water nymph made of bone
tries to summon a river out of limestone.

Exhausted, utterly worn down,
a Roman water nymph made of bone,
10   being the last known speaker of her language,
she tries to summon a river out of limestone.

Little distant sound of dry grass. Try again.

A Roman water nymph made of bone,
very endangered now,
15   in a largely unintelligible monotone,
she tries to summon a river out of limestone.

Little distant sound as of dry grass. Try again.

Exquisite bone figurine with upturned urn,
in her passionate self-esteem, she smiles, looking sideways.
20   She seemingly has no voice but a throat-clearing rustle
as of dry grass. Try again.

She tries leaning,
pouring pure outwardness from a grey urn.

Little slithering sounds as of a rabbit man in full night gear.
25   Who lies so low in the rickety willow herb
that a fox trots out of the woods
and over his back and away. Try again.
Very small and damaged and quite dry,
a Roman water nymph made of bone,
30   she pleads, she pleads a river out of limestone.

Little hobbling tripping of a nearly dried-up river
not really moving through the fields,
having had the gleam taken out of it
to the point where it resembles twilight.
35   Little grumbling shivering last-ditch attempt at a river
more nettles than water. Try again.

Very speechless, very broken old woman,
her left arm missing and both legs from the knee down,
she tries to summon a river out of limestone.

Little stoved-in, sucked-thin   40
low-burning glint of stones,
rough-sleeping and trembling and clinging to its rights.
Victim of Swindon.[1]
Puddle midden.°   *garbage heap*
Slum of overgreened foot-churn and pats   45
whose crayfish are cheap toolkits
made of the mud stirred up when a stone's lifted.

It's a pitiable likeness of clear running,
struggling to keep up with what's already gone:
the boat the wheel the sluice gate,   50
the two otters larricking° along. Go on.   *gallivanting*

And they say oh they say
in the days of better rainfall
it would flood through five valleys, there'd be cows and milking stools
washed over the garden walls   55
and when it froze you could skate for five miles. Yes go on.

Little loose-end shorthand unrepresented
beautiful disused route to the sea,
fish path with nearly no fish in.

—2006

---

1   *Swindon* Town in Wiltshire, England.

Karen Solie
b. 1966

The subject matter of Karen Solie's poetry spans great distances: from the rural landscapes of Saskatchewan where she was born and raised to the bars and hotels of urban Canada; from the scientific terms of physics and biology to the emotional language of disappointment and desire. Fellow poet Don McKay has described her work as "fierce writing of quickness and edge that can take on just about anything ... with candour and a trenchant humour that's the cutting edge of intelligence."

Karen Solie worked for three years as a reporter in Lethbridge, Alberta, before completing a BA from the University of Lethbridge. Her career as a published poet began when her work was included in the anthology *Breathing Fire: Canada's New Poets* (1995), and six years later she released her first collection, *Short Haul Engine*, which won the Dorothy Livesay Poetry Prize. Solie then moved from Alberta to Toronto, where she further established herself as an important voice in Canadian poetry with her next collections, *Modern and Normal* (2005) and *Pigeon* (2009). *Pigeon* won several awards, including the Trillium Award and the Griffin Poetry Prize; the Griffin judges noted Solie's ability to "pull great wisdom from the ordinary" and "to see at once into and through our daily struggle, often thwarted by our very selves, toward something like an honourable life."

Solie has taught poetry at the Banff Centre for the Arts, been writer-in-residence at several Canadian universities, and held the first International Writer's Residency at the University of St. Andrews in Scotland.

Sturgeon

Jackfish and walleye circle like clouds as he strains
the silt floor of his pool, a lost lure in his lip,
Five of Diamonds, River Runt, Lazy Ike,[1]
or a simple spoon, feeding
5 a slow disease of rust through his body's quiet armour.
Kin to caviar, he's an oily mudfish. Inedible.
Indelible. Ancient grunt of sea
in a warm prairie river, prehistory a third eye in his head.
He rests, and time passes as water and sand
10 through the long throat of him, in a hiss, as thoughts
of food. We take our guilts

---

1   *Five of Diamonds ... Lazy Ike* Popular fishing lures. "Spoon" is also a type of lure.

to his valley and dump them in,
give him quicksilver° to corrode his fins, weed killer,   *mercury*
gas oil mix, wrap him in poison arms.
Our bottom feeder,   15
sin-eater.

On an afternoon mean as a hook we hauled him
up to his nightmare of us and laughed
at his ugliness, soft sucker mouth opening,
closing on air that must have felt like ground glass,   20
left him to die with disdain
for what we could not consume.
And when he began to heave and thrash over yards of rock
to the water's edge and, unbelievably, in,
we couldn't hold him though we were teenaged   25
and bigger than everything. Could not contain
the old current he had for a mind, its pull,
and his body a muscle called river, called spawn.

—2001

Nice

> "I think I'm kind of two-faced. I'm very ingratiating. It really kind
> of annoys me. I'm just sort of a little too nice. Everything is Oooo."
> —Diane Arbus[1]

Still dark, but just. The alarm
kicks on. A voice like a nice hairdo
squeaks *People, get ready*
for another nice one. Low 20s,
soft breeze, ridge of high pressure   5
settling nicely. Songbirds swallowing, ruffling,
starting in. Does anyone curse
the winter wren, calling in Christ's name
for just one bloody minute of silence?
Of course not. They sound nice.   10
I pull away and he asks why I can't
be nicer to him. Well,
I have to work, I say, and wouldn't it be nice

---

1   *Diane Arbus* (1923-71), American photographer.

15 if someone made some money today?
Very nice, he quavers, rolling
his face to the wall. A nice face.
A nice wall. We agreed on the green
down to hue and shade straight away.
That was a very nice day.

—2003

Self-Portrait in a Series of Professional Evaluations

An excellent vocabulary, but spatial skills
are lacking. Poor in math. A bit uncoordinated,
possibly the inner ear? An eye exam
5 may be required. Not what you'd call a natural
athlete. Doesn't play well with others. Tries hard.

Fine sense of melody but a weak left hand. For God's sake
practice with a metronome. Your Chopin
is all over the place. Test scores indicate aptitude
10 for a career in the secretarial sciences. Handwriting
suggests some latent hostility. A diligent worker,
though often late. Please note:

an AC/DC t-shirt does not constitute professional
attire. You drove *how* long on the spare?
15 A good grasp of theory, though many sentence fragments
and an unusual fondness for semicolons; a tendency
toward unsubstantiated leaps. A black aura.

Needs to stroke essence of tangerine through the aura.
Should consider regular facials. Most people walk around
20 dehydrated all the time and don't even know it.
Normal. Negative. This month, avoid air travel
and dark-haired men. Focus on career goals.
Make a five-year plan.

—2005

Arundhathi Subramaniam
b. 1967

Arundhathi Subramaniam's poetry often addresses philosophical, political, or spiritual questions at the level of the local, the individual, and the everyday—an approach frequently inflected by Subramaniam's complex relationship with her home city of Mumbai. Her first two books of poetry, *On Cleaning Bookshelves* (1991) and *Where I Live* (2005), were published in English in her native India; her third collection, *Where I Live: New & Selected Poems* (2009), was published in the United Kingdom. In response to what she calls "the increasing spirit of cultural nativism … [that interprets] the use of English as a reactionary throwback to the imperial past," she has defended her choice of language, arguing that "English is Indian—period. It's as Indian as cricket and democracy."

Subramaniam's commitment to the sincere consideration of spiritual matters has found expression not only in her poetry but also in her account of the Buddha's life, *The Book of Buddha* (2005), and her biography of contemporary yogi Jaggi Vasudev, *Sadhguru* (2010). In 2003, she received the Charles Wallace Fellowship at the University of Stirling, and in 2009 was given the Raza Award for Poetry. She has worked for the National Centre for the Performing Arts in Mumbai and was for many years a member of Mumbai's Poetry Circle.

To the Welsh Critic Who Doesn't Find Me Identifiably Indian

You believe you know me,
wide-eyed Eng Lit type
from a sun-scalded colony,
reading my Keats[1]—or is it yours—
while my country detonates   5
on your television screen.

You imagine you've cracked
my deepest fantasy—
oh, to be in an Edwardian[2] vicarage,
living out my dharma[3]   10

---

1   *Keats* John Keats (1795–1821), English poet.
2   *Edwardian* Characteristic of England during King Edward VII's reign (1901–10).
3   *dharma* In various Indian religions, the inherent nature and order of the universe, and a person's actions which uphold that order.

with every sip of dandelion tea
and dreams of the weekend jumble sale ...

You may have a point.
I know nothing about silly mid-offs,[1]
I stammer through my Tamil,[2]
15 and I long for a nirvana
that is hermetic,
odour-free,
bottled in Switzerland,
money-back-guaranteed.

20 This business about language,
how much of it is mine,
how much yours,
how much from the mind,
how much from the gut,
25 how much is too little,
how much too much,
how much from the salon,
how much·from the slum,
how I say verisimilitude,
30 how I say Brihadaranyaka,[3]
how I say vaazhapazham[4]—
it's all yours to measure,
the pathology of my breath,
the halitosis of gender,
35 my homogenised plosives[5]
about as rustic
as a mouth-freshened global village.

Arbiter of identity,
remake me as you will.
40 Write me a new alphabet of danger,
a new patois to match

---

1   *mid-offs* Cricket term referring to the left side of the field.
2   *Tamil* Language spoken by the Tamil people in parts of India and Sri Lanka.
3   *Brihadaranyaka* Brihadaranyaka Upanishad, one of the Sanskrit texts that form the philosophical basis of the Hindu religion.
4   *vaazhapazham* Tamil: banana.
5   *plosives* Consonant sounds (such as *b*, *d*, and *p*), created by briefly halting airflow.

the Chola[1] bronze of my skin.
Teach me how to come of age
in a literature you've bark-scratched
into scripture.   45
Smear my consonants
with cow-dung and turmeric and godhuli.[2]
Pity me, sweating,
rancid, on the other side of the counter.
Stamp my papers,   50
lease me a new anxiety,
grant me a visa
to the country of my birth.
Teach me how to belong,
the way you do,   55
on every page of world history.

—2005

---

1   *Chola* Chola dynasty, a long-ruling Tamil dynasty that rose to power in southern India
     during the Middle Ages.
2   *godhuli* Urdu or Sanskrit: dusk; in Sanskrit, literally "the dust raised by the feet of cattle."

Rita Wong
b. 1968

Rita Wong describes the subject matter of her poetry as "scary, interrelated phenomena like social and environmental injustice, pollution, and global warming." Her poems often condemn the impact big corporations have on human rights and on the food system, but Wong also emphasizes her readers' collective responsibility to the often geographically distant people who face intolerable working conditions or the consequences of environmental damage. Environmental concerns are, for Wong, inextricable from concerns of race, class, and gender; her poetry is powerfully focused on globalization and the legacy of colonization.

A writer who makes frequent use of puns and other language play and often omits punctuation, Wong is experimental in her approach to poetry—an attitude that extends from the layout of words on the page to the writing process itself. Many of her poems include, as marginalia, Chinese characters or hand-written political or cultural statements, sometimes quotations from other thinkers that inform her work. Her long poem *sybil unrest* (2009), a collaboration with fellow Vancouver writer Larissa Lai, was composed over email.

Wong was raised in Calgary and received a PhD from Simon Fraser University, where she studied Asian North American literature. Her first book of poetry, *monkeypuzzle*, was published in 1998; her next, *forage* (2007), received the Dorothy Livesay Poetry Prize and was the winner of Canada Reads Poetry 2011. Wong is an associate professor at the Emily Carr University of Art and Design, where she teaches Critical and Cultural Studies.

opium[1]

chemical history narcopolemics
attempted genocide call it crack war
alcohol white powder suffocates
shades of deep brown earth red desert
yellow skin dependency myths who
needs the high of trying to kill the other?
racist gaze tingles on my skin induced
economic muscle flexes to displace
millions rifles fire behind the dollar
signs & still the underground pulses
suffering blue veins seek the
transformative heart as ordnance° drops
on embassies and arteries cry for kin

artillery

—2007

5

10

"Queen Victoria waged war twice... in order to ensure the free commerce of opium."
—Avital Ronell

---

1   The handwritten quotation is from American philosopher and critical theorist Avital
Ronell's *Crack Wars: Literature, Addiction, Mania* (1992). Britain conducted two
"Opium Wars" (1839–42 and 1856–60) to force the Chinese government to legalize the
importation of opium; trading opium for tea and other Chinese luxuries was important
to the British economy.

nervous organism[1]

[Handwritten marginal quotation, running around the poem:] "Some philosophers who assume that all meaning is descriptive meaning tell us that, as a poem does not describe things rationally, it must be a description of emotion. According to this, the litered core of poetry should be a cri de coeur, to use the elegant expression, the direct statement of a nervous organism confronted with something that seems to demand an emotional response, like a dog howling at the moon." —Northrop Frye

jellyfish potato/ jellypo fishtato/ glow in the pork toys/
nab your crisco while it's genetically cloudy boys/
science lab in my esophagus/ what big beakers you have
sir/ all the better to mutate you with my po monster/
5 po little jelly-kneed demonstrator/ throws flounder-crossed
tomatoes/ hafta nasty nafta[2] through mexico,
california, oregon, washington, canada/ hothoused
experiment nestled beside basketballs of lettuce,
avocado bullets/ industrial food defeats nutrition/
10 immune systems attrition/ soil vampires call/ shiny
aisles all touch and no contact/ jellypish for tato smack/
your science experiment snack yields slugfish arteries
brain murmurs tumour precipitation whack

—2007

---

1 The handwritten quotation is from Canadian literary critic Northrop Frye's *Anatomy of Criticism* (1957); *cri de coeur* French: cry of the heart.
2 *nafta* North American Free Trade Agreement, a free trade pact between the United States, Canada, and Mexico that took effect in 1994.

Rachel Zolf
b. 1968

Rachel Zolf has no qualms about defying traditional conventions in her work. Despite the "resistance to experimental writing" she sees in the literary community, she has embraced experimental poetry for its ability to challenge readers and encourage them to see things differently. "[I]n all my books," she has said, "I try to enact situations where the reader feels uncomfortable, dislocated in their own skin, and is forced to think about why they feel that way."

Zolf often makes use of found text in her work. Her collection *Neighbour Procedure* (2010), for example, addresses the Israeli-Palestinian conflict through a collage of text that originally appeared in a broad range of sources, from news reports to twentieth-century critical theory. Her Trillium Award-winning collection *Human Resources* (2007) similarly draws on eclectic material, especially language she encountered while working as a corporate copywriter. Zolf also holds what she describes as "the first collaborative MFA in creative writing," which she earned by composing original poems out of material sent to her by more than eighty other poets.

In addition to publishing several books of poetry, Zolf has worked in film and television and as poetry editor for *The Walrus*. She is an assistant professor at the University of Calgary, where her research and teaching focus on "the intersection of creative writing and contemporary theoretical practices."

from *Human Resources*[1]

[The job is to write in 'plain language.' No adjectives, adornment or surfeit]

The job is to write in 'plain language.' No adjectives, adornment or surfeit of meaning nuclear increasing[(w1269)]. All excess excised save the discrete pithy moment. Sonnet's rising eight lines, sublime orgasmic turn, dying six: perfect expenditure. Brisk stride along the green green grounds, sudden dip, ha-ha!

[New performance weightings a bit of a moving target the future liability of make this sing]

New performance weightings a bit of a moving target the future liability of make this sing.

Just to make sure we're speaking the same language we no longer have to use this caveat existing amounts grandfathered.

5 We'll have to wrap our heads around clear as mud I would like to move the goal posts.

Chunk it down into various links I'm totally medicated as I type.

---

1   *Human Resources* In a note at the end of *Human Resources* Zolf writes that, with the exception of a few poems not included in this anthology,

All [...] poems were made by the author's proprietary machine-mind™, with some assistance from WordCount™ and QueryCount™ at www.wordcount.org. The former is a searchable list of the 86,800 most frequently used words in English, while the latter is a searchable list of words most frequently queried in WordCount. [...]
WordCount values are represented in the text by the letter w [and] Query-Count by Q[...]. As QueryCount rankings shuffle every few hours to reflect recent word queries, Q values in this text will not match present QueryCount rankings. [...] Orthography and punctuation are also used as found.

[Given enough input elements, a writing machine can spew about anything]

Given enough input elements, a writing machine can spew about anything: private jets, exquisite gardens, offshore-banking havens, the Great Ephemeral Skin, how much we love our passionate[Q8992] francesca snazzy prat employees, how you breathe life into our Mission, Vision, Values, what we give you if you lose one finger[Q691] fool dance then gold on one hand and three toes on   5 one foot (25% of the premiums you've paid for years), or three fingers on one hand and four toes (50%) or two hands and two feet (75%!). Unlike poetry, it flows with ease and on the same page as BMO banker Barrett: 'a student who can divine[Q2855] pablo from swiss prostate patterns of imagery in Chaucer's *Canterbury Tales* can surely be taught the principles of double-entry accounting   10

[I don't want to trip over this in the future from where I'm sitting can you suggest massages]

I don't want to trip over this in the future from where I'm sitting can you suggest massages.

This will give you a sense of the 'new look' it seems the tail's wagging the tail this block of content has been rationalized.

We took this offline to firm up the 'one-stop shopping spot' for HR content   5
requires minor refreshing.

My head's spinning in reverse 360s just to close the loop with you.

—2007

Stephanie Bolster
b. 1969

Stephanie Bolster's body of work includes both miscellaneous collections and long poems or poem series united by a single theme; *A Page from the Wonders of Life on Earth* (2011), for example, takes zoos as its subject. Visual art, from seventeenth-century Dutch painting to contemporary photography, is a source of inspiration in works such as *Two Bowls of Milk* (1999) and "Long Exposure." Shortlisted for the 2012 CBC Poetry Prize, "Long Exposure" is part of a longer project based on the "post-disaster photographs" of Robert Polidori (b. 1951).

Bolster's first book, *White Stone: The Alice Poems* (1998) is focused on the protagonist of Lewis Carroll's children's classics *Alice's Adventures in Wonderland* (1865) and *Through the Looking-Glass* (1872), as well as on Alice Liddell, the real child after whom the character is named. In *White Stone*, Bolster explores the lives of both Alices, going so far as to create hypothetical relationships between Alice and the likes of Christopher Robin and Elvis Presley, as well as placing her in North America and in Bolster's own life. Bolster has discussed her approach in *The New Quarterly*: "by placing Alice within my own place and time, I was able to see that here and now were every bit as rich, nonsensical and distressing as both Wonderland and Victorian England." *White Stone* received several awards, including the Governor General's Award for Poetry.

Stephanie Bolster grew up in Burnaby, British Columbia, and earned an MFA from the University of British Columbia. She lives in Montreal, where she is associate professor at Concordia University.

from *White Stone*

Portrait of Alice, Annotated

Who was it strung these footnotes
from her toes and scribbled
italics on her wrists, indicating perhaps
that only slim-wristed girls
5 were allowed to enter Wonderland?

They wound her with measuring tape,
noted the resulting data on her skin, figures
for chest and waist identical. To her mouth

was taped a parchment proclamation
detailing origins of those words she spoke   10

as if they were as intimately hers
as earlobes. But the evidence proved
those words had a long history of their own,
belonged to themselves and would
outlive her. Whatever she had said   15

to end up in this predicament
was not her fault, she was exempt, thus safe.
What could be done to her now? Even her breasts
were claimed before they'd risen; some said
he'd placed his nitrate-ridden hands there.[1]   20

The critics overwrote each other
till all their words were tattooed black
upon her. Have mercy, she cried as they came
with the thousand-volumed weight of archives,
but those words were not hers either.   25

Portrait of Alice with Christopher Robin[2]

In the midst of a winter wood
she walks like old age,
bent under falling snow and the ghost
of her written self, heavy
as bundled kindling on her back.   5

At a tree's base he huddles his narrow shoulders
as if lost—his head, familiar from books
hung forward in dangerous
chilled sleep, calves downy-haired
and goose-bumped past short pants.   10

---

1   *some said ... hands there* Some biographers have suggested that Lewis Carroll might have
     been a paedophile; *nitrate* Cellulose nitrate, chemical compound used in photography.
     Lewis Carroll was a photographer and often took portraits of children, including Alice.

2   *Christopher Robin* Boy in A.A. Milne's children's stories *Winnie-the-Pooh* (1926) and *The
     House at Pooh Corner* (1928); the character is named after Milne's son.

Lewis Carroll, Alice Liddell as "The Beggar Maid," 1858. Lewis Carroll is most famous as the author of Alice's Adventures in Wonderland *(1865) and its sequel, but he was also an accomplished portrait photographer known for his images of children. Like many photographers of the time, he often portrayed his subjects in dramatic roles. Alice Liddell, the daughter of Carroll's friend Henry Liddell, posed for some of Carroll's most remarkable photographs, and the character of Alice is named after her.*

An italic fall of snowflakes
various as dreams across his face.

She watches his trembling lips
mumble of yellowed bears and bluster[1] and rain,
of being irrevocably stuck,   15
then presses her hand to his cheek.
His lashes flutter, he shows her
his eyes made of glaciers and pronounces her name.

To the magic flame he makes
with two rubbed sticks   20
she gives her pinafore[2] and white socks,
the ribbon from her fallen hair.
He fumbles with his buttons, burns
his trousers and dirty shirt.

They point to figures in the smoke—   25
lumpen bear, white rabbit, honey pot,
tea cup. Naked together, they watch with ash-stung
eyes and neither blink nor shiver.

                                                          —1998

---

1   *bluster* Word used in A.A. Milne's *The House at Pooh Corner*.
2   *pinafore* Apron worn over a dress; a white pinafore is part of Alice's iconic costume.

R. W. Gray
b. 1969

██████ "I write for the uncertainty. I write for the mythology of it," says poet, serial novelist, short story author, and screenwriter Robert W. Gray; "uncertainty doesn't cloud the truth so much as unleash it." Praised by author Douglas Glover as "an amazing young writer with a startling range and emotional penetration," Gray has published poetry in journals such as *Arc* and in anthologies such as *Seminal: The Anthology of Canada's Gay Male Poets* (2007).

Gray works in a variety of media. Almost a dozen of Gray's short screenplays have been filmed, including *alice & huck* (2008), which won awards at festivals in New Orleans, Honolulu, and Beverly Hills. In 2010 he published his first book, *Crisp*, a collection of short fiction. It was well received by critics; Mark Jarman of *The Fiddlehead* has described Gray's stories as "exuberant, cinematic tales … a startling mix of wild currents and landlocked inner lives that are playful and scary."

Gray was born and raised in the northwest coastal region of British Columbia, and he attended the University of Alberta, where he earned a PhD in Poetry and Psychoanalysis in 2003. He has served as the head of the Screenwriting Programme at the Vancouver Film School and teaches film and screenwriting at the University of New Brunswick.

How this begins

Thrums he does, thrums like waves breaking, waves falling over each other on their way to his feet, but who can blame them.

Up along the streets the maples look awkward in their new dresses, billowing in the traffic gusts. Something, everything, has to begin.

5 Later we will recall this moment, though I will not speak of his clavicles and he will not mention my bottom lip. He tries to find some way to offer me a strawberry from the musky handful he picked on his way to work and I try to find some other word for clavicle but am distracted by his full-throated approach to wearing a T-shirt.

10 There are strawberry seeds under his fingernails. Tonight, falling asleep, a hand near his face on the pillow, he will smell strawberries and the crushed green runners. The strawberries he shucked for his and another's mouth. He will remember my bottom lip.

We will not agree. He will think it was a hot day, summer finally giving in.
I will remember mostly the breeze through the open door, how spring just 15
kept hanging around.

This will be the moment he liked me the least, but I liked him the most. He
thought I was a sideways glance. I thought he was a swallow of water.

He will kiss me, outside at a table, leaning down to me as I look up,
suspicious of a man who kisses me so soon and kisses me in a café. 20

He will wonder what comes next. I will wonder what just happened.

This is how it begins. He will not know I am on my way to analysis. That I
was going to admit that I am tired of longing for longing. Tired of making
up stories about picked strawberries.

—2006

Sharon Harris
b. 1972

Sharon Harris is a Canadian artist whose work combines a range of forms and mediums, including poetry, prose, photography, sculpture, and painting. Influenced by the poet bpNichol, much of her work has a significant visual dimension and depends for its effect on the interplay of word and image. In her concrete poems, the typographical characteristics and arrangement of the words on the page become part of the overall sense-making apparatus.

Harris's first full-length poetry collection, *AVATAR* (2006), is a blended, hybrid work that mingles figures and letters to create meaning. In it, she experiments with an array of devices and ideas, from pataphysics—the fictional science of imaginary phenomena—to the limits of art and language. This latter idea is a problem to which she returns repeatedly, both throughout the collection and in her work more generally: how does one write about things and places beyond words? *AVATAR* is preoccupied with the nature and uses of the phrase "I love you," which is at once ubiquitous and elusive, full of power and void of meaning.

At once playful and thoughtful, Harris's work invites the reader/viewer to look again at familiar words and phrases and see the concepts they gesture toward in an altogether different light.

99. Where Do Poems Come From?

Moisten your finger and hold it
straight up in the air. You will notice
at once that one side of the finger is
cold. This is the direction from
5 which the poem is coming.

—2005

FIGURE L

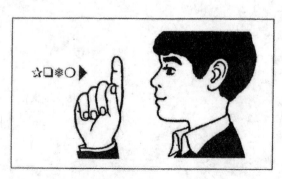

70. Why Do Poems Make Me Cry?

Reading a poem releases noxious
gases into your environment. The
brain reacts by telling your tear
ducts to produce water, to dilute the
irritating acid so the eyes are pro-   5
tected. Your other reaction is proba-
bly to rub your eyes, but this will
make the irritation a lot worse if you
have poem juices all over your
hands.   10

There are all kinds of remedies for
dealing with this irritating phenomenon, some more effective than
others. As a general rule, move your
head as far away from the poem   15
as you can, so the gas will mostly dis-
perse before it reaches your eyes. The
simplest solution might be to not

—2005

Poetry in Translation

The translation of poetry is a process about which numerous writers have commented. Many have begun with the question of whether it is even possible to translate poems. Henry Wadsworth Longfellow—canonical American poet, and also one of the many translators of Dante's *Divine Comedy*—asserted that the translator should strive "to report what the author says, not to explain what he means," and advocated paying limited attention to matters of aesthetics or poetic form. At the other end of the spectrum, poet Octavio Paz suggested that, while a "literal translation is not impossible," such work is merely "a mechanism, a string of words that help us read the text in its original language. It is a glossary rather than a translation, which is always a literary activity." The problems for the translator are, in the first place, a matter of sense, as a word's meaning in one language can only be approximated in another: as poet and translator Erin Mouré puts it, "each word in a language is affected, touched, perturbed, split by the culture in which it is used." Furthermore, most of the elements considered crucial to poetry—elements such as rhythm, rhyme, and the nuances of figurative language—may vanish once the sense of the original has been rendered. It is no surprise, therefore, that translated poems are often considered to be original creative works in and of themselves.

For students of literature, the analysis of a translated work thus invites a kind of double approach. In the first place, the translation can be examined with the same attention to the way form interacts with meaning as would serve a literary text read in the original language. In the second place, especially when the original text is accessible (or when more than one translation is provided), the student can explore how approximations have been made, and how the process of translation may reveal something about the way writers from both language backgrounds make use of words to mean more than something literal. For example, when reading two different translations of Lorca's "Romance de la Luna, Luna," one might inquire into the effect of translating the Spanish phrase "El niño la mira, mira" as either "The young boy watches her, watches" (trans. Gunn) or "The boy-child looks and looks at her" (trans. Cobb). What is the difference between a "young boy" and a "boy-child," or between "watching"—a word that may connote an extended period of observation—and simply "looking," which might be thought of as a more innocuous activity (especially as it is associated with a "child")? Even without being able to understand the original, one might ask: do the lulling sounds contained in the phrase "la mira, mira" evoke the same response as the sounds in either of the translations ("watches her, watches" or "looks and looks at her")? How much does the reader of the translated poem have to know about moon symbolism in the Spanish tradition in order to develop a critical argument about this "romance" that—at the level of interpretation—tells the tale of a child's death? If Lorca's moon symbolism is "lost in translation"—i.e., if English-speaking readers think of the moon as signifying changeability, madness, or the feminine principle, according to their own cultural context—how does this alter the way the texts created by Gunn or Cobb can be read? Though it may be the case that no translation of a poem is ever a copy of the original, poems in translation provide almost unending opportunities to examine the complexity of the way form, diction, and cultural context produce sense.

Sappho

c. 630-612 BCE–c. 570 BCE

Very little can be said with certainty about Sappho's biography. Even the birth and death dates given above are still debated, and much of what is surmised about her life is based on references made in her poetry. Much of her work itself has also been lost in the course of history; only one of Sappho's poems survives in its entirety, while the rest of her extant work is made up of fragments found in damaged sources or quoted in the work of other ancient writers.

Probably the wife of an aristocrat and mother of a daughter named Cleis, Sappho was thought to have spent much of her time teaching and studying the arts within a circle of women friends and students on the Greek island of Lesbos. Her writing frequently expresses passionate feeling toward other women; this is often interpreted as sexual love, and the word "lesbian" itself derives from its connection to Sappho as a resident of Lesbos. Speculation regarding Sappho's sexual orientation has affected her reputation and reception since ancient times.

Sappho is remembered for intimately emotional poems on subjects such as love, friendship, marriage, and spirituality—a marked difference from the political and heroic content of most of her contemporaries' writing. Her work, written to be sung to the accompaniment of a stringed instrument called a lyre, came to be greatly admired and contributed to the early development of the lyric form (so named for the instrument with which it is associated). Plato (c. 427–c. 347 BCE) called her "the tenth Muse," adding her to the ranks of the nine gods of the arts in Greek mythology.

Sappho's popularity has fluctuated over the centuries, but her work has influenced poets from her own time to the present day, and it continues to be appreciated by and translated for contemporary readers. The following translations were composed by Canadian classicist and poet Anne Carson (b. 1950) and appeared in her book *If Not, Winter: Fragments of Sappho* (2002). Carson has used square brackets to indicate some—but not all—places where the source text has been damaged and words are absent or illegible. As you will see when you turn to her translations, Carson provides extensive notes that offer both factual information and more impressionistic responses to words, stressing the extent to which translations involve attempts to capture both denotative and connotative dimensions of the original poem.

2

]
. . ανοθεν κατιου[ϲ|-
δευϱυμμεκϱητεϲιπ[.]ϱ[   ]|. ναῦον
ἄγνον ὄππ[αι ·]| χάϱιεν μὲν ἄλϲος
μαλί[αν],| βῶμοι δ' ἔ‹ν›ι θυμιάμε—
5   νοι [λι]|βανώτω‹ι›·

ἐν δ' ὔδωϱ ψῦχϱοι‹‹ϳ| κελάδει δι' ὔϲδων
μαλίνων,| βϱόδοιϲι δὲ παῖϲ ὀ χῶϱος
ἐϲκίαϲτ', αἰθυϲϲομένων δὲ φύλλων|
        κῶμα καταιϱιον·

10 ἐν δὲ λείμων| ἱππόβοτος τέθαλε
τωτ. . .(.)ϱιν|νοις ἄνθεϲιν, αἰ ‹δ'› ἄηται
μέλλιι|χα πν[έο]ιϲιν [
        [   ]

ἔνθα δὴ ϲὺ ϲυ.αν| ἔλοιϲα Κύπϱι
χϱυϲίαιϲιν ἐν κυ|λίκεϲϲιν ἄβϱως
15 ‹ὀ›μ‹με›μεί|χμενον θαλίαιϲι| νέκταϱ
        οἰνοχόειϲα

—Late 7th or early 6th century

2

]
here[1] to me from Krete to this holy temple
where is your graceful grove
of apple trees and altars smoking
    with frankincense.

And in it cold water makes a clear sound through   5
apple branches and with roses the whole place
is shadowed and down from radiant-shaking leaves
    sleep[2] comes dropping.

And in it a horse meadow has come into bloom
with spring flowers and breezes   10
like honey are blowing
    [   ]

In this place you Kypris[3] taking up
in gold cups[4] delicately
nectar mingled with festivities: 15
    pour.

---

1   [Carson's note] "here": adverb of place that means "hither, to this place" with verbs of
    motion or "here, in this place" with verbs of rest, often used as an interjection "Come on!
    Here now!" when followed by an imperative verb. Notice that the imperative verb evoked
    by this adverb, for which the whole poem with its slow weight of onomatopoeically
    accumulating clauses seems to be waiting, does not arrive until the very last word: "pour"
    (16). Arrival is the issue, for it sanctifies waiting: *attente de Dieu* [French: waiting for God].
    The poem is a hymn of the type called "kletic," that is, a calling hymn, an invocation to
    god to come from where she is to where we are. Such a hymn typically names both
    of these places, setting its invocation in between so as to measure the difference—a
    difference exploded as soon as the hymn achieves its aim. Inherent in the rationale of
    a kletic hymn, then, is an emptiness or distance that it is the function of the hymn to
    mark by an act of attention. Sappho suspends attention between adverb at the beginning
    and verb at the end: the effect is uncanny—as if creation could be seen waiting for an
    event that is already perpetually *here*. There is no clear boundary between far and near;
    there is no climactic moment of god's arrival. Sappho renders a set of conditions that
    at the beginning depend on Aphrodite's absence but by the end include her presence—
    impossible drop that saturates the world. "God can only be present in creation under the
    form of absence," says Simone Weil, in *Gravity and Grace*, translated by Arthur Willis
    (Lincoln, Nebraska, 1997), 162.

2   [Carson's note] "sleep": *kōma* is a noun used in the Hippokratic texts [Ancient Greek
    medical texts] of the lethargic state called "coma" yet not originally a medical term. This

Papyrus with a fragment of a poem by Sappho, third century BCE. *A copy of a Sappho poem was written on this papyrus a few centuries after her death. It was discovered in the early 2000s; the papyrus had been used in the wrappings surrounding an ancient Egyptian mummy.*

is the profound, weird, sexual sleep that enwraps Zeus after love with Hera (Homer *Iliad* 14.359); this is the punishing, unbreathing stupor imposed for a year on any god who breaks an oath (Hesiod *Theogony* 798); this is the trance of attention induced by listening to music of the lyre (Pindar *Pythians* 1.12); this is the deep religious stillness described by Gregory of Nazianzus in a Christian poem from the fourth century A.D. that appears to be modelled on Sappho's, for Gregory imagines himself awaiting his god in a garden:

Breezes whispered ...
lavishing beautiful sleep [*kōma*] from the tops of the trees
on my heart so very weary.
—*Patrologia graeca* 37, ed. J.P. Migne (Paris, 1862), 755ff.

Otherworldliness is intensified in Sappho's poem by the synaesthetic quality of her *kōma*—dropping from leaves set in motion by a shiver of light over the tree: Sappho's adjective *aithussomenon* ("radiant-shaking," 7) blends visual and tactile perceptions with a sound of rushing emptiness.

3   *Kypris* Epithet of Aphrodite. It refers to the island of Cyprus, where a cult dedicated to her was located and where she was said to have emerged from the sea at her birth.

4   [Carson's note] "gold cups": not mortal tableware, nor is nectar a beverage normally enjoyed by any but gods (along with ambrosia, e.g., *Odyssey* 5.92–4).

55

κατθάνοιϲα δὲ κείϲηι οὐδέ ποτα μναμοϲύνα ϲέθεν
ἔϲϲετ' οὐδὲ ποκ' ὕϲτερον· οὐ γὰρ πεδέχηιϲ βρόδων
τῶν ἐκ Πιερίαϲ, ἀλλ' ἀφάνης κὰν 'Αίδα δόμωι
φοιτάϲηιϲ πεδ' ἀμαύρων νεκύων ἐκπεποταμένα.

—Late 7th or early 6th century

55

Dead you will lie and never memory of you
will there be nor desire into the aftertime—for you do not share in the roses
of Pieria,[1] but invisible too in Hades'[2] house
you will go your way among dim shapes. Having been breathed out.[3]

---

1 *Pieria* Area in northern Greece and mythical birthplace of the Muses, nine Greek
   goddesses of knowledge and the arts.
2 *Hades* God of the underworld.
3 [Carson's note] "Dead.... Having been breathed out": a participle in the aorist tense (*kat-
   thanoisa*) begins the poem and a participle in the perfect tense (*ekpepotamena*) ends it.
   The aorist tense expresses past action as a point of fact; the perfect tense renders past
   action whose effect continues into the future; so does Sappho's poem softly exhale some
   woman from the point of death into an infinitely featureless eternity. Cognate with words
   for wings, flying, fluttering and breath, the participle *ekpepotamena*, with its splatter of
   plosives and final open vowel, sounds like the escape of a soul into nothingness.

Francesco Petrarch

1304–1374

Francesco Petrarch was born in Arezzo, Italy. He is best remembered for his *Rime sparse* (*Scattered Rhymes*, c. 1327–74), a series of 366 sonnets and other poems written about a woman named Laura, with whom Petrarch claimed to have fallen in love upon seeing her in a church in Avignon, France. He continued to add to (and rework) the collection throughout his life, though Laura herself died in 1348. The poems are not addressed to Laura; indeed, they are concerned more with Petrarch's emotional and spiritual development than they are with the object of his unrequited love. In their self-scrutiny, in the longing they express for an idealized and unattainable beauty, and in the ways in which they give poetic expression to these feelings through elaborate metaphors, paradox, and smoothly rhyming Italian verse, Petrarch's sonnets became a model for poets throughout the Renaissance.

Though known today primarily for his love poetry, Petrarch was a classical scholar, an ambassador and frequent traveller, and a cleric in the Roman Catholic Church. He was also famous in his own time for a range of scholarly writing and for his unfinished epic poem *Africa*. Although the *Rime sparse* were written in Italian, his other works were composed in Latin.

294

Soleasi nel mio cor star bella et viva,
com' alta donna in loco humile et basso:
or son fatto io per l'ultimo suo passo,
non pur mortal, ma morto, et ella è diva.

L'alma d'ogni suo ben spogliata et priva,   5
Amor de la sua luce ignudo et casso,
devrian de la pietà romper un sasso;
ma non è chi lor duol riconti o scriva:

ché piangon dentro, ov' ogni orecchia è sorda
se non la mia, cui tanta doglia ingombra   10
ch' altro che sospirar nulla m'avanza.

Veramente siam noi polvere et ombra,
veramente la voglia cieca e 'ngorda,
veramente fallace è la speranza.

—c. 1327–74

294[1]

In my heart she used to stand lovely and live,
Like a great lady in a place low and humble:
Now I am shown, by her final passing,
To be not only mortal, but dead, while she is divine.

My soul stripped of all its blessedness, deprived,   5
And love, stripped of her light, erased,
Are strong enough to break stone into pity
But none can tell or write of that pain:

They grieve within, and all ears are deaf
Except my own, blocked by grief,   10
And nothing is left me but sighs.

This is truth: we are nothing but ashes and shadow.
This is truth: the will grasps blindly.
This is truth: false are our hopes.

---

1   *294* Translation by D. LePan and M. Okun for this anthology (© Broadview Press).

Arthur Rimbaud
1854–1891

"One must be absolutely modern," wrote the French poet Arthur Rimbaud, whose career as an author of rebellious, complex, and sensually loaded verse and prose poetry was as brief as it was influential. His intense, non-traditional approach placed him among the French Symbolists, a group of poets and artists who strove not to depict objective reality but to express emotions, interior thoughts, and abstract ideas through metaphor. Rimbaud's often hallucinatory style would influence the surrealist movement of the 1920s, as well as a number of other twentieth-century artistic movements.

Rimbaud accomplished his entire poetic output in less than five years. Raised by his mother in Charleville, France, he was a high-achieving student until 1870, the year he published his first poems. The following year he sent some of his work to the Symbolist poet Paul Verlaine, who responded with an invitation to visit his home in Paris. The two poets soon became lovers, and they travelled together, leading a wild existence characterized by drinking, drug use, and violent arguments—their relationship ended when Verlaine shot Rimbaud in the wrist and was sentenced to two years in prison. Soon afterward, Rimbaud finished the only book he would publish himself, a short work of prose poetry entitled *Une saison en enfer* (*A Season in Hell*, 1873).

Around the age of 20, Rimbaud stopped writing poetry. He continued to travel extensively and eventually worked in Africa as a colonial tradesman. After this point, he showed little interest in the fate of his work, but in 1886 Verlaine edited and arranged for the publication of *Les Illuminations*, a collection of Rimbaud's prose poems.

The following poems have been translated by English poet, drama teacher, and translator Oliver Bernard (b. 1925).

À la Musique

Place de la Gare, à Charleville

Sur la place taillée en mesquines pelouses,
Square où tout est correct, les arbres et les fleurs,
Tous les bourgeois poussifs qu'étranglent les chaleurs
Portent, les jeudis soirs, leurs bêtises jalouses

—L'orchestre militaire, au milieu du jardin,   5
Balance ses schakos dans la *Valse des fifres*:
—Autour, aux premiers rangs, parade le gandin;
Le notaire pend à ses breloques à chiffres.

Des rentiers à lorgnons soulignent tous les couacs:
Les gros bureaux bouffis traînent leurs grosses dames   10
Auprès desquelles vont, officieux cornacs,
Celles dont les volants ont des airs de réclames;

Scene Set to Music

Place de la Gare, Charleville

On the square which is chopped into mean little plots of grass, the square
where all is just so, both the trees and the flowers, all the wheezy townsfolk
whom the heat chokes bring, each Thursday evening, their envious silliness.

The military band, in the middle of the gardens, swing their shakos[1] in
the *Waltz of the Fifes*: round about, near the front rows, the town dandy struts;   5
the notary hangs like a charm from his own watch chain.

Private incomes in pince-nez point out all false notes: great counting-
house desks, bloated, drag their stout spouses—close by whom, like bustling
elephant keepers, walk females whose flounces remind you of sales.

---

1   *shakos* Tall cylindrical military hats.

Sur les bancs verts, des clubs d'épiciers retraités
Qui tisonnent le sable avec leur canne à pomme,
15 Fort sérieusement discutent les traités,
Puis prisent en argent, et reprennent: « En somme!... »

Épatant sur son banc les rondeurs de ses reins,
Un bourgeois à boutons clairs, bedaine flamande,
Savoure son onnaing d'où le tabac par brins
20 Déborde—vous savez, c'est de la contrebande;—

Le long des gazons verts ricanent les voyous;
Et, rendus amoureux par le chant des trombones,
Très naïfs, et fumant des roses, les pioupious
Caressent les bébés pour enjôler les bonnes...

10   On the green benches, retired grocers' clubs, poking the sand with their knobbed walking canes, gravely discuss trade agreements and then take snuff from silver boxes, and resume: "In short!..."
     Spreading over his bench all the fat of his rump, a pale-buttoned burgher, a Flemish corporation, savours his Onnaing,[1] whence shreds of tobacco hang
15 loose—you realize, it's smuggled, of course ...
     Along the grass borders yobs[2] laugh in derision; and, melting to love at the sound of trombones, very simple, and sucking at roses, the little squaddies[3] fondle the babies to get round their nurses ...

---

1   *Onnaing* Clay pipe made in Onnaing, a municipality in Northern France renowned for its pipe manufacturing.
2   *yobs* Disruptive youths.
3   *squaddies* Soldiers.

—Moi, je suis, débraillé comme un étudiant,   25
Sous les marronniers verts les alertes fillettes:
Elles le savent bien; et tournent en riant,
Vers moi, leurs yeux tout pleins de choses indiscrètes.

Je ne dis pas un mot: je regarde toujours
La chair de leurs cous blancs brodés de mèches folles: 30
Je suis, sous le corsage et les frêles atours,
Le dos divin après la courbe des épaules.

J'ai bientôt déniché la bottine, le bas ...
—Je reconstruis les corps, brûlé de belles fièvres.
Elles me trouvent drôle et se parlent tout bas ...   35
—Et mes désirs brutaux s'accrochent à leurs lèvres.

                                   —1889 (written 1870)

As for me, I follow, dishevelled like a student under the green chestnuts,
the lively young girls—which they know very well, and they turn to me,   20
laughing, eyes which are full of indiscreet things.
    I don't say a word: I just keep on looking at the skin of their white necks
embroidered with stray locks: I go hunting, beneath bodices and thin attire,
the divine back below the curve of the shoulders.
    Soon I've discovered the boot and the stocking ...—I re-create their bodies,   25
burning with fine fevers. They find me absurd, and talk together in low voices
...—And my savage desires fasten on to their lips ...

Voyelles

A noir, E blanc, I rouge, U vert, O bleu: voyelles,
Je dirai quelque jour vos naissances latentes:
A, noir corset velu des mouches éclatantes
Qui bombinent autour des puanteurs cruelles,

5 Golfes d'ombre; E, candeurs des vapeurs et des tentes,
Lances des glaciers fiers, rois blancs, frissons d'ombelles;
I, pourpres, sang craché, rire des lèvres belles
Dans la colère ou les ivresses pénitentes;

U, cycles, vibrements divins des mers virides,
10 Paix des pâtis semés d'animaux, paix des rides
Que l'alchimie imprime aux grands fronts studieux;

Ô, suprême Clairon plein des strideurs étranges,
Silence traversés des Mondes et des Anges:
—Ô l'Oméga, rayon violet de Ses Yeux!—

—1883 (written c. 1871)

Vowels

A black, E white, I red, U green, O blue: vowels, I shall tell, one day, of your
mysterious origins: A, black velvety jacket of brilliant flies which buzz around
cruel smells,

    gulfs of shadow; E, whiteness of vapours and of tents, lances of proud
5 glaciers, white kings, shivers of cow-parsley; I, purples, spat blood, smile of
beautiful lips in anger or in the raptures of penitence;

    U, waves, divine shudderings of viridian[1] seas, the peace of pastures dotted
with animals, the calm of the furrows which alchemy prints on broad studious
foreheads;

10   O, sublime Trumpet full of strange piercing sounds, silences crossed by
Angels and by Worlds —O the Omega! the violet ray of Her Eyes!

---

1   *viridian* Blue-green.

Federico García Lorca
1898–1936

Federico García Lorca is best remembered for his modern reinterpretations of traditional Andalusian (southern Spanish) art forms, from folk ballads to puppet theatre. His passionate, often violent poems and plays were popular and acclaimed both within his native Spain and internationally.

Lorca grew up in the Andalusian countryside and in Granada but settled in Madrid as a university student. A theatrical personality, he quickly became a social success in a circle of intellectual and artistic friends that included the painter Salvador Dalí. Professional success came with his third book, *Romancero gitano* (*Gypsy Ballads*, 1928), which was popular with the public, although its incorporation of flamenco and Andalusian traditions led some critics to dismiss his work as quaint. However, Lorca would also earn modernist credibility through his engagement with surrealism, notably in his posthumously published collection *Poeta en Nueva York* (*Poet in New York*, 1940), written during an overseas trip in 1929–30.

Lorca began writing plays in the 1920s and focused increasingly on theatre toward the end of his career. As a playwright, he is best known for a trilogy of dramas about Spanish peasants beginning with the tragedy *Bodas de sangre* (*Blood Wedding*, 1933).

As political events in the 1930s led to the rise of fascism in Spain, Lorca declined an opportunity to escape to New York, saying, "I'm a poet, and no one kills poets." In the first year of the Spanish Civil War (1936–39), he was arrested and killed by the fascist forces, and was buried in a mass grave.

The following poem is accompanied by two English translations, included here both to provide additional insight into the original poem and to invite consideration of the process of translation itself.

Romance de la luna, luna   *A Conchita García Lorca*

La luna vino a la fragua
con su polisón de nardos.
El niño la mira, mira.
El niño la está mirando.
5   En el aire conmovido
mueve la luna sus brazos
y enseña, lúbrica y pura,
sus senos de duro estaño.
Huye luna, luna, luna.
10   Si vinieran los gitanos,
harían con tu corazón
collares y anillos blancos.
Niño, déjame que baile.
Cuando vengan los gitanos,
15   te encontrarán sobre el yunque
con los ojillos cerrados.
Huye luna, luna, luna,
que ya siento sus caballos.
Niño, déjame, no pises
20   mi blancor almidonado.

El jinete se acercaba
tocando el tambor del llano.
Dentro de la fragua el niño,
tiene los ojos cerrados.
25   Por el olivar venían,
bronce y sueño, los gitanos.
Las cabezas levantadas
y los ojos entornados.

Cómo canta la zumaya,
30   ¡ay, cómo canta en el árbol!
Por el cielo va la luna
con un niño de la mano.

Dentro de la fragua lloran,
dando gritos, los gitanos.
35   El aire la vela, vela.
El aire la está velando.

—1927

[The moon came to the forge]¹

The moon came to the forge²
  with her skirt of white, fragrant flowers.
  The young boy watches her, watches.
  The boy is watching her.

In the electrified air   5
  the moon moves her arms
  and points out, lecherous and pure,
  her breasts of hard tin.

Flee, moon, moon, moon.
  If the gypsies were to come,   10
  they would make with your heart
  white necklaces and rings.

Young boy, leave me to dance.
  When they come, the gypsies
  will find you upon the anvil   15
  with closed eyes.

Flee, moon, moon, moon.
  Already I sit astride horses.
  Young boy, leave me, don't step on
  my starched whiteness.   20

The horse rider approaches
  beating the drum of the plain.
  Within the forge the young man
  has closed eyes.

Through the olive grove they come,   25
  the gypsies—bronze and dreaming,
  heads lifted
  and eyes half closed.

Hark, hear the night bird—
  how it sings in the tree.   30
  Across the sky moves the moon,
  holding the young boy by the hand.

Within the forge the gypsies cry,
  are crying out.
  The air watches over her, watches.   35
  The air is watching over her.

---

1   *[The moon came to the forge]* Translated by Helen Gunn.
2   *forge* Workshop where blacksmiths melt and reshape metal.

Ballad of the Moon, Moon, Moon[1]

The moon came down to the forge in skirts
    With tuberose[2] bustle white.
The boy-child looks and looks at her,
    Keeps looking at the sight.

5 The moon then moves her arms about
    In an atmosphere astir,
And shows the hard tin of her breasts,
    Lascivious and pure.

Run away from here, oh moon, moon, moon!
10   Should the gypsies come tonight
They'd make your heart into necklaces
    And also rings of white.

Child, move and let me do my dance.
    Whenever the gypsies appear
15 They'll find you with your eyes shut tight
    Upon the anvil here.

Run away, oh moon, moon, moon, I feel
    The hoofbeats in the night!
Child, leave me alone, don't put your feet
20   Upon my starchéd white.

The approaching horseman was beating time
    Upon the drum of the plain.
Inside the forge his eyes shut tight
    The little boy remains.

25 Bronze and dream, the gypsy clan
    Came down through the olive grove,
Their heads held high up toward the sky,
    Their eyes in trance half-closed.

Oh how the screech-owl starts to sing,
30   Sings in his tree nearby!
The moon with boy-child by the hand
    Is going through the sky.

Inside the forge the gypsy clan
    Is loudly wailing, weeping;
35 The air its wake[3] is keeping, keeping,
    The air its wake is keeping.

---

1   *Ballad of the Moon, Moon, Moon* Translated by Carl W. Cobb.
2   *tuberose* Mexican plant with large white flowers similar in appearance to lilies.
3   *wake* Practice of sitting with or watching over the body of a deceased person.

Pablo Neruda

1904–1973

Chilean poet and political figure Pablo Neruda was a prolific writer whose work extended from erotic love poetry to political poems that gave voice to his commitment to communism. Adored in Chile and popular worldwide, he was also critically acclaimed; in 1971 he was awarded a Nobel Prize for "poetry that with the action of an elemental force brings alive a continent's destiny and dreams."

Neruda achieved fame at the age of 20 with his sensuous, highly figurative book *Veinte poemas de amor y una canción desesperada* (*Twenty Love Poems and a Song of Despair*, 1924). In his twenties, he joined the Chilean diplomatic service and acted as a consul in several nations; he was serving in Madrid when the Spanish Civil War (1936–39) broke out. His collection *España en el corazón* (*Spain in the Heart*, 1937) chronicles the atrocities of the war, including the execution of his friend the poet Federico García Lorca.

In 1943, Neruda joined the Chilean Communist Party and was elected to the Senate. When communism was banned in Chile, he was forced into hiding, where he completed *Canto general* (*General Song*, 1950), an epic re-examining South American history from a communist perspective; he then spent three years in exile, unable to return to Chile until 1952. In the later 1950s, he wrote several books of odes concerned with everyday life and ordinary objects.

Neruda died in 1973, in the weeks following a right-wing coup in Chile. Thousands of people defied the new dictatorship to attend his funeral.

The translation of "Exilio" included below is by Scottish poet, essayist, and linguist Alastair Reid (b. 1926); the translation of "Un Perro Ha Muerto" is by Californian writer William O'Daly (b. 1951), who has translated eight volumes of Neruda's poetry.

Exilio

Entre castillos de piedra cansada,
calles de Praga bella,
sonrisas y abedules siberianos,
Capri, fuego en el mar, aroma
5 de romero amargo
y el último, el amor,
el esencial amor se unió a mi vida
en la paz generosa,
mientras tanto,
10 entre una mano y otra mano amiga
se iba cavando un agujero oscuro
en la piedra de mi alma
y allí mi patria ardía
llamándome, esperándome, incitándome
15 a ser, a preserver, a padecer.

El destierro es redondo:
un círculo, un anillo:
le dan vuelta tus pies, cruzas la tierra,
no es tu tierra,
20 te despierta la luz, y no es tu luz,
la noche llega: faltan tus estrellas,
hallas hermanos: pero no es tu sangre.
Eres como un fantasma avergonzado
de no amar más a los que tanto te aman,
25 y aún es tan extraño que te falten
las hostiles espinas de tu patria,
el ronco desamparo de tu pueblo,
los asuntos amargos que te esperan
y que te ladrarán desde la puerta.

30 Pero con corazón irremediable
recordé cada signo innecesario
como si sólo deliciosa miel
se anidara en el árbol de mi tierra
y esperé en cada pájaro
35 el más remoto trino,
el que me despertó desde la infancia
bajo la luz mojada.

Exile

Among castles of tired stone,
streets of beautiful Prague,
smiles and Siberian birches,
Capri, fire in the sea, scent
of harsh rosemary,   5
and lastly, love,
essential love brought all my life together
in a generous peace,
meanwhile
with one hand and its friend, the other,   10
a dark hole was being dug out
in the stone of my spirit
and in it my country was burning,
calling me, waiting for me, spurring me on
to be, to preserve, to endure.   15

Exile is round in shape,
a circle, a ring.
Your feet go in circles, you cross land
and it's not your land.
Light wakes you up and it's not your light.   20
Night comes down, but your stars are missing.
You discover brothers, but they're not of your blood.
You're like an embarrassed ghost,
not loving more those who love you so much,
and it's still so strange to you that you miss   25
the hostile prickles of your own country,
the loud helplessness of your own people,
the bitter matters waiting for you
that will be snarling at you from the door.

But inevitably in my heart   30
I remembered every useless sign
as if only the sweetest honey
gathered in the tree of my own country
and I expected from every bird
the most faraway song   35
such as woke me from childhood on
in the damp light of dawn.

Me pareció mejor la tierra pobre
de mi país, el cráter, las arenas,
40 el rostro mineral de los desiertos
que la copa de luz que me brindaron.
Me sentí solo en el jardín, perdido:
fui un rústico enemigo de la estatua,
de lo que muchos siglos decidieron
45 entre abejas de plata y simetría.

Destierros! La distancia
se hace espesa,
respiramos el aire por la herida:
vivir es un precepto obligatorio.
50 Así es de injusta el alma sin raíces:
rechaza la belleza que le ofrecen:
busca su desdichado territorio:
y sólo allí el martirio o el sosiego.

—1964

It seemed better to me, the poor earth
of my country—crater, sand,
the mineral face of the deserts—   40
than the glass filled with light they toasted me with.
I felt lost and alone in the garden.
I was a rustic enemy of the statues,
of what many centuries had arrived at
among silver bees and symmetry.   45

Exiles! Distance
grows thicker.
We breathe air through a wound.
To live is a necessary obligation.
So, a spirit without roots is an injustice.   50
It rejects the beauty that is offered it.
It searches for its own unfortunate country
and only there knows martyrdom or quiet.

Un Perro Ha Muerto

Mi perro ha muerto.

Lo enterré en el jardín
junto a una vieja máquina oxidada.

Allí, no más abajo,
5 ni más arriba,
se juntará conmigo alguna vez.
Ahora él ya se fue con su pelaje,
su mala educación, su nariz fría.
Y yo, materialista que no cree
10 en el celeste cielo prometido
para ningún humano,
para este perro o para todo perro
creo en el cielo, sí, creo en un cielo
donde yo no entraré, pero él me espera
15 ondulando su cola de abanico
para que yo al llegar tenga amistades.

Ay no diré la tristeza en la tierra
de no tenerlo más por compañero
que para mí jamás fue un servidor.
20 Tuvo hacia mí amistad de un erizo
que conservaba su soberanía,
la amistad de una estrella independiente
sin más intimidad que la precisa,
sin exageraciones:
25 no se trepaba sobre mi vestuario
llenándome de pelos o de sarna,
no se frotaba contra mi rodilla
como otros perros obsesos sexuales.
No, mi perro me miraba
30 dándome la atención que necesito,
la atención necesaria
para hacer comprender a un vanidoso
que siendo perro él,
con esos ojos, más puros que los míos,

A Dog Has Died

My dog has died.

I buried him in the garden
beside a rusty old engine.

There, not too deep,
not too shallow,   5
he will greet me sometime.

He already left with his coat,
his bad manners, his cold nose.
And I, a materialist who does not believe
in the starry heaven promised   10
to a human being,
for this dog and for every dog
I believe in heaven, yes, I believe in a heaven
that I will never enter, but he waits for me
wagging his big fan of a tail   15
so I, soon to arrive, will feel welcomed.

No, I will not speak about my sadness on earth
at not having him as a companion anymore,
he never stooped to becoming my servant.
He offered me the friendship of a sea urchin   20
who always kept his sovereignty,
the friendship of an independent star
with no more intimacy than necessary,
with no exaggerations:
he never used to climb over my clothes   25
covering me with hair or with mange,
he never used to rub against my knee
like other dogs, obsessed with sex.
No, my dog used to watch me
giving me the attention I need,   30
yet only the attention necessary
to let a vain person know
that he being a dog,
with those eyes, more pure than mine,

35 perdía el tiempo, pero me miraba
con la mirada que me reservó
toda su dulce, su peluda vida,
su silenciosa vida,
cerca de mí, sin molestarme nunca,
40 y sin pedirme nada.

Ay cuántas veces quise tener cola
andando junto a él por las orillas
del mar, en el Invierno de Isla Negra,
en la gran soledad: arriba el aire
45 traspasado de pájaros glaciales
y mi perro brincando, hirsuto, lleno
de voltaje marino en movimiento:
mi perro vagabundo y olfatorio
enarbolando su cola dorada
50 frente a frente al Océano y su espuma.

Alegre, alegre, alegre
como los perros saben ser felices,
sin nada más, con el absolutismo
de la naturaleza descarada.
55 No hay adiós a mi perro que se ha muerto.
Y no hay ni hubo mentira entre nosotros.

Ya se fue y lo enterré, y eso era todo.

—1974

was wasting time, but he watched   35
with a look that reserved for me
every bit of sweetness, his shaggy life,
his silent life,
sitting nearby, never bothering me,
never asking anything of me.   40

O, how many times I wanted to have a tail
walking next to him on the seashore,
in the Isla Negra[1] winter,
in the vast solitude: above us
glacial birds pierced the air   45
and my dog frolicking, bristly hair, full
of the sea's voltage in motion:
my dog wandering and sniffing around,
brandishing his golden tail
in the face of the ocean and its spume.   50

O merry, merry, merry,
like only dogs know how to be happy
and nothing more, with an absolute
shameless nature.
There are no goodbyes for my dog who has died.   55
And there never were and are no lies between us.

He has gone and I buried him, and that was all.

---

1   *Isla Negra* Coastal area in central Chile.

Paul Celan

1920–1970

Paul Antschel, who wrote under the pseudonym Paul Celan, was born in Czernovitz, Romania, to a German-speaking Jewish family. His life and work were profoundly affected by the Holocaust. In 1941, the German allies occupied Czernovitz, and Celan and his parents were forced to live in a ghetto. Not long after, he was separated from his parents when they were sent to an internment camp, where they later died; Celan himself was sent to a forced labour camp. He wrote poetry throughout his imprisonment.

With the notable exception of "Todesfugue" ("Death Fugue," 1952)—one of his most famous poems—Celan's poetry does not usually portray the camps directly. However, he described his writing in general as a response to the trauma of the Holocaust: "Only one thing remained reachable, close and secure amid all losses: language.... But it had to go through its own lack of answers, through terrifying silence, through the thousand darknesses of murderous speech.... It gave me no words for what was happening, but went through it." Especially in his later poetry, Celan was often concerned with the ways in which language itself was affected by the events of the Holocaust—an issue complicated by the fact that he composed most of his work in German, the language of those who perpetrated the atrocities. His expressions of suffering, grief, and loss are often difficult to interpret, as his work is characterized by surreal imagery, fragmented words and syntax, and dense allusion.

Celan spent the last 20 years of his life in Paris, where in addition to writing he was a teacher of German literature and translator of poetry from several languages. His work received such prestigious European awards as the Bremen Prize for Literature (1958) and the Georg Büchner Prize (1960). Celan committed suicide in 1970.

The following poems have been translated by German-born British poet, translator, and critic Michael Hamburger (1924–2007).

Totenhemd

Was du aus Leichtem wobst,
trag ich dem Stein zu Ehren.
Wenn ich im Dunkel die Schreie
wecke, weht es sie an.

Oft, wenn ich stammeln soll,   5
wirft es vergessene Falten,
und der ich bin, verzeiht
dem, der ich war.

Aber der Haldengott
rührt seine dumpfeste Trommel,   10
und wie die Falte fiel,
runzelt der Finstre die Stirn.

—1952

Shroud

That which you wove out of light thread
I wear in honour of stone.
When in the dark I awaken
the screams, it blows on them, lightly.

Often, when I should stammer,   5
it raises forgotten crinkles
and he that I am forgives
him that I was.

But the god of the slagheaps
beats his most muted drum,   10
and just as the crinkle ran
the grim one puckers his brow.

Todesfuge

Schwarze Milch der Frühe wir trinken sie abends
wir trinken sie mittags und morgens wir trinken sie nachts
wir trinken und trinken
wir schaufeln ein Grab in den Lüften da liegt man nicht eng
5 Ein Mann wohnt im Haus der spielt mit den Schlangen der schreibt
der schreibt wenn es dunkelt nach Deutschland dein goldenes Haar
    Margarete
er schreibt es und tritt vor das Haus und es blitzen die Sterne er pfeift seine
    Rüden herbei
er pfeift seine Juden hervor läßt schaufeln ein Grab in der Erde
er befiehlt uns spielt auf nun zum Tanz

10 Schwarze Milch der Frühe wir trinken dich nachts
wir trinken dich morgens und mittags wir trinken dich abends
wir trinken und trinken
Ein Mann wohnt im Haus der spielt mit den Schlangen der schreibt
der schreibt wenn es dunkelt nach Deutschland dein goldenes Haar
    Margarete
15 Dein aschenes Haar Sulamith wir schaufeln ein Grab in den Lüften da liegt
    man nicht eng

Er ruft stecht tiefer ins Erdreich ihr einen ihr andern singet und spielt
er greift nach dem Eisen im Gurt er schwingts seine Augen sind blau
stecht tiefer die Spaten ihr einen ihr andern spielt weiter zum Tanz auf

Schwarze Milch der Frühe wir trinken dich nachts
20 wir trinken dich mittags und morgens wir trinken dich abends
wir trinken und trinken

Death Fugue[1]

Black milk of daybreak we drink it at sundown
we drink it at noon in the morning we drink it at night
we drink and we drink it
we dig a grave in the breezes there one lies unconfined
A man lives in the house he plays with the serpents he writes   5
he writes when dusk falls to Germany your golden hair Margarete[2]
he writes it and steps out of doors and the stars are flashing he whistles his
    pack out
he whistles his Jews out in earth has them dig for a grave
he commands us strike up for the dance[3]

Black milk of daybreak we drink you at night   10
we drink in the morning at noon we drink you at sundown
we drink and we drink you
A man lives in the house he plays with the serpents he writes
he writes when dusk falls to Germany your golden hair Margarete
your ashen hair Shulamith[4] we dig a grave in the breezes there one lies   15
    unconfined

He calls out jab deeper into the earth you lot you others sing now and play
he grabs at the iron in his belt he waves it his eyes are blue
jab deeper you lot with your spades you others play on for the dance

Black milk of daybreak we drink you at night
we drink you at noon in the morning we drink you at sundown   20
we drink and we drink you

---

1   *Fugue* Musical composition in which a theme is introduced and then repeated with variations.

2   *Margarete* Character in German author Johann Wolfgang von Goethe's classic play *Faust* (1808–32). In Part One of the play, Faust makes a pact with the devil; under the devil's influence, he seduces the beautiful Margarete, whose life is destroyed by their relationship.

3   *he commands ... the dance* Some Nazi concentration camps had prisoner orchestras, which were required to provide music as the other prisoners marched to and from work and were sometimes forced to play during executions or during the selection of prisoners to be gassed.

4   *Shulamith* Hebrew name of Solomon's beautiful, idealized lover in the biblical Song of Songs.

ein Mann wohnt im Haus dein goldenes Haar Margarete
dein aschenes Haar Sulamith er spielt mit den Schlangen
Er ruft spielt süßer den Tod der Tod ist ein Meister aus Deutschland
25   er ruft streicht dunkler die Geigen dann steigt ihr als Rauch in die Luft
dann habt ihr ein Grab in den Wolken da liegt man nicht eng

Schwarze Milch der Frühe wir trinken dich nachts
wir trinken dich mittags der Tod ist ein Meister aus Deutschland
wir trinken dich abends und morgens wir trinken und trinken
30   der Tod ist ein Meister aus Deutschland sein Auge ist blau
er trifft dich mit bleierner Kugel er trifft dich genau
ein Mann wohnt im Haus dein goldenes Haar Margarete
er hetzt seine Rüden auf uns er schenkt uns ein Grab in der Luft
er spielt mit den Schlangen und träumet der Tod ist ein Meister aus Deutschland

35   dein goldenes Haar Margarete
dein aschenes Haar Sulamith

—1948

a man lives in the house your golden hair Margarete
your ashen hair Shulamith he plays with the serpents
He calls out more sweetly play death death is a master from Germany
he calls out more darkly now stroke your strings then as smoke you will rise   25
     into air
then a grave you will have in the clouds there one lies unconfined

Black milk of daybreak we drink you at night
we drink you at noon death is a master from Germany
we drink you at sundown and in the morning we drink and we drink you
death is a master from Germany his eyes are blue   30
he strikes you with leaden bullets his aim is true
a man lives in the house your golden hair Margarete
he sets his pack on to us he grants us a grave in the air
he plays with the serpents and daydreams death is a master from Germany

your golden hair Margarete   35
your ashen hair Shulamith

Nicole Brossard
b. 1943

As a poet, novelist, essayist, and activist, Nicole Brossard has contributed extensively to the fields of literary criticism, feminist thought, and literature, earning recognition both in her native province of Quebec and on a larger global stage. She has received two Governor General's Awards (1974 and 1984), Quebec's Prix Athanase-David (1991), and the Canada Council for the Arts Molson Prize (2006).

Born in Montreal, Brossard attended le Collège Marguerite Bourgeoys and l'Université de Montréal. After briefly working as a teacher she began a writing career, co-founding the formalist literary magazine *La Barre du Jour* (1965–77) and publishing her first book of poetry, *Aube à la saison* (*Dawning Season*, 1965). Her abstract style and her interest in the adaptability of language soon earned her a reputation as a progressive, inventive writer; in the celebrated novel *Le désert mauve* (*Mauve Desert*, 1987), for example, she employs an unconventional form and a nonlinear narrative. While pushing boundaries within her own writing, she continued to foster literary community, founding the feminist paper *Les Têtes de pioche* (1976–79) and co-founding *La Nouvelle Barre du Jour* (1977–90). Written from a feminist, lesbian, and urban French Canadian perspective, her work calls for social transformation, putting into practice her belief that "literature is subversion, transgression, and vision."

Brossard has written over 30 books, including poetry collections such as *Mécanique jongleuse* (*Daydream Mechanics*, 1974), *Amantes* (*Lovhers*, 1980), and *Double Impression* (1984). Her many collaborative projects include the film *Some American Feminists* (1977), which she co-directed with two other Canadian filmmakers. Writing in French and English, she has translated some of her poetry herself, finding that the process enables her to further explore the potential and limits of language.

The following poems have been translated by Montreal-born writer Robert Mazjels (b. 1950) and Canadian poet Erin Mouré (b. 1955). Their 2007 translation of Brossard's *Cahier de roses & de civilisation* (*Notebook of Roses and Civilization*, 2003) was shortlisted for a Governor General's Award and for the Griffin Prize.

Geste

je ne sais le comment
le commencement des pensées quand
elles se greffent à des gestes simples
comme s'il y avait un rapport entre
5 l'intention de bouger et la manière de penser
sans trop de malheur, la voix sensuelle
et toute l'ampleur d'une science au corps

—1989

Gesture

I don't know the how
the first howl of thoughts when
they graft on to simple gestures
somehow as if there were a link between
5 the intent to move and a way of thinking
without too much grief, the sensual voice
and all the fullness of a science of the body

[tous ces mois passés]

tous ces mois passés
à regarder les palmiers par en-dessous
de la naissance des parfums de jasmin
tout ce temps passé
à chercher la zone *twilight* du bord de l'univers   5
oui par en-dessous de la naissance
quand la tête est plongée
dans une ambiance de voix
et le cœur enroulé dans ses excès de réalité

—2003

[all these months spent]

all these months spent
gazing at the palms from below
the birth of the scent of jasmine
all this time spent
seeking the twilight zone at the edge of *l'univers*   5
yes from below its birth
when the head is plunged
into a world of voices
and the heart swathed in its excesses of reality

Yehuda Amichai

1924–2000

Israeli poet Yehuda Amichai said his first collection "outraged most critics—I was attacked for using colloquial language, attacked for trying techniques no one had ever tried before." Popular audiences, however, immediately appreciated his innovative use of everyday Hebrew alongside biblical language; his biographer Nili Scharf Gold has described him as "Israel's beloved unofficial national poet."

Born in Germany, Amichai was educated in Hebrew as a child, and when he was 11 his family moved to Palestine. During World War II, he worked for the British engineering corps in Egypt, and in the following decades he would be a schoolteacher, an activist, and—although he considered himself a proponent of nonviolence—a soldier in the Israeli military in three different wars. He began to seriously write poetry at the beginning of the 1950s while attending the Hebrew University of Jerusalem.

"I try to create a kind of equality between my personal history and the history around me," Amichai said, and he is remembered both for love poetry and for poetry reflecting his first-hand experience of Israel's formation and development. Critical appreciation of his work grew to match his popularity, and, among many other awards, Amichai received the Israel Prize for Poetry in 1982.

Amichai was also successful internationally, and his poems have been translated from Hebrew into more than 35 languages. In some respects, the plainness of his style is amenable to translation, but other distinctive qualities of his writing appear only in the Hebrew originals. Translator Robert Alter acknowledges the impossibility of capturing Amichai's "sensitivity to the expressive sounds of the Hebrew words he uses," his "inventive puns," and his sophisticated allusions to "densely specific Hebrew terms and texts."

The following poem was translated by Glenda Abramson, retired professor of Hebrew and Jewish Studies at Oxford, and Tudor Parfitt, founding director of the Centre for Jewish Studies at the University of London.

תַּיָּרִים

בְּקִוּוּרֵי אֲבֵלִים הֵם עוֹרְכִים אֶצְלֵנוּ,
יוֹשְׁבִים בְּיָד וָשֵׁם, מַרְצִינִים לְיַד הַכֹּתֶל הַמַּעֲרָבִי
וְצוֹחֲקִים מֵאֲחוֹרֵי וִילוֹנוֹת כְּבֵדִים בְּחַדְרֵי מָלוֹן,
מִצְטַלְּמִים עִם מֵתִים חֲשׁוּבִים בְּקֶבֶר רָחֵל
5   וּבְקֶבֶר הֶרְצְל וּבְגִבְעַת הַתַּחְמֹשֶׁת,
בּוֹכִים עַל יְפִי גְּבוּרַת נְעָרֵינוּ
וְחוֹשְׁקִים בְּקַשִׁיחוּת נַעֲרוֹתֵינוּ
וְתוֹלִים אֶת תַּחְתּוֹנֵיהֶם
לְיִבּוּשׁ מָהִיר
10   בְּאַמְבַּטְיָה כְּחֻלָּה וְצוֹנֶנֶת.

פַּעַם יָשַׁבְתִּי עַל מַדְרֵגוֹת לְיַד שַׁעַר בִּמְצוּדַת דָּוִד, אֶת שְׁנֵי הַסַּלִּים הַכְּבֵדִין
שַׂמְתִּי לְיָדִי. עָמְדָה שָׁם קְבוּצַת תַּיָּרִים סְבִיב הַמַּדְרִיךְ וְשִׁמַּשְׁתִּי לָהֶם נְקֻדַּר
צִיּוּן. "אַתֶּם רוֹאִים אֶת הָאִישׁ הַזֶּה עִם הַסַּלִּים? קְצָת יָמִינָה מֵרֹאשׁוֹ נִמְצֵאאח
קֶשֶׁת מִן הַתְּקוּפָה הָרוֹמִית. קְצָת יָמִינָה מֵרֹאשׁוֹ". אֲבָל הוּא זָז, הוּא זָז!
15   אָמַרְתִּי בְּלִבִּי: הַגְּאֻלָּה תָּבוֹא רַק אִם יַגִּידוּ לָהֶם: אַתֶּם רוֹאִים שָׁם אֶ
הַקֶּשֶׁת מִן הַתְּקוּפָה הָרוֹמִית? לֹא חָשׁוּב: אֲבָל לְיָדָהּ, קְצָת שְׂמֹאלָה וּלְמַטָה
מִמֶּנָּה, יוֹשֵׁב אָדָם שֶׁקָּנָה פֵּרוֹת וִירָקוֹת לְבֵיתוֹ.

—1980

Tourists

Visits of condolence is all we get from them.
They squat at the Holocaust Memorial,
They put on grave faces at the Wailing Wall[1]
And they laugh behind heavy curtains
In their hotels.   5
They have their pictures taken
Together with our famous dead
At Rachel's Tomb and Herzl's[2] Tomb
And on the top of Ammunition Hill.[3]
They weep over our sweet boys   10
And lust after our tough girls
And hang up their underwear
To dry quickly
In cool, blue bathrooms.

Once I sat on the steps by a gate at David's Tower,[4] I placed my two heavy   15
baskets at my side. A group of tourists was standing around their guide and
I became their target marker. "You see that man with the baskets? Just right
of his head there's an arch from the Roman Period. Just right of his head."
"But he's moving, he's moving!" I said to myself: redemption will come only
if their guide tells them, "You see that arch from the Roman period? It's not   20
important: but next to it, left and down a bit, there sits a man who's bought
fruit and vegetables for his family."

---

1   *Wailing Wall* Jewish site of pilgrimage and prayer. Originally part of the walls surrounding
    the site of the Temple in Jerusalem, it is traditionally considered sacred as a remnant of
    that Temple.
2   *Rachel* Biblical wife of Jacob. According to tradition, the site of her tomb is just out-
    side Bethlehem; *Herzl* Theodor Herzl (1860–1904), Viennese activist, journalist, play-
    wright, and founder of the Zionist movement. His grave is in Jerusalem.
3   *Ammunition Hill* Site of a major battle in the Six-Day War (1967) between Israel and
    Jordan, Egypt, and Syria; a museum and memorial are now located there.
4   *David's Tower* Tower of David, a citadel in Jerusalem with an architectural history span-
    ning 2,000 years.

Reesom Haile

1946–2003

Eritrean poet and activist Reesom Haile argued for the importance of preserving language: "If you lose your language, it isn't just the language you lose. It's the cultural codes imbedded in that language. It's the values, the sense of community.... This is what I do not want my people to lose." Haile's poetry is composed in Tigrinya, one of Eritrea's most widely spoken languages. Although he frequently performed live—reflecting Eritrean traditions of oral poetry—he also published written work in Tigrinya and in bilingual English/Tigrinya editions.

Haile grew up in an Eritrean farming community. He left the country during the war of independence (1961–91) in which Eritrea, then a province of Ethiopia, fought to secede and form its own nation. Over the next two decades, Haile worked as a journalist, university teacher, and consultant to the United Nations and various NGOs. When he returned home in 1994—a year after Eritrea officially achieved independence—he began a career in poetry that connected social activism with a desire to revitalize and celebrate Eritrean language and culture.

Haile's first collection of poems, *waza ms qumneger ntnsae hager* (*Tragicomedies for Resurrecting a Nation*, 1997), is written in Tigrinya and won the 1998 Raimok prize, Eritrea's most prestigious literary award. His two bilingual collections, *We Have Our Voice* (2000) and *We Invented the Wheel* (2002), consolidated his international reputation as a master of lively, passionate, often witty verse informed by keenly felt political and social ideals. Amiri Baraka has praised his "spare poetic line [that] carries the weight of incisive image, narrative clarity, [and] irony plus a droll humour." A prolific writer, Haile died in 2003, having composed more than 2,000 poems.

The following poems have been translated by Charles Cantalupo (b. 1951), a poet, critic, editor, and distinguished professor at Penn State University. Cantalupo translated both *We Have Our Voice* and *We Invented the Wheel* in consultation with Haile.

ስደት

አብ ካይሮ ኤርፖርት
ዞርያ ዝለበሳ
ገለ ሓሙሳ ሱሳ
ልቢ ዝማርኻ
ልቢ ዘፍስሳ   5
ርእናዮን ናይ ኢትዮጵያ ኤክስፖርት
ንብይሩት ክሓልፉ
ናይ ሰብ ዓራት ከንጽፉ
ህይወተን ከሕልፉ
ክንደይ ከይህብትማ ክንደይ ከየዕርፉ   10
ይኹነልክን ይቕነዕክን በላ ሕለፉ
ነዚኣስ አይንደልያ አይንሃርፉ።

c. 1997–99

Knowledge

First the earth, then the plow:
So knowledge comes out of knowledge.
We know, we don't know.
We don't know we know.
We know we don't know.   5
We think
This looks like that—
This lemon, that orange—
Until we taste the bitter.

አመሪካ ኢሉኩም

ዝሞተ እንተ ሞተ
ንዑ ኮላ ንስተ
ዝብላዕ ዘይብልኩም
እንሀልኩም ማንካ
5 ዝሽመት ዘይብልኩም
እንሀልኩም ባንካ
ዘሎኩም ነጊፍኩም
ኩሉ ንዓይ አመሪካ

ናብራ ከሎኩም
10 ናብራ ተለቂሕኩም
ናብራ ከሎኩም
ናብራ ተገዚእኩም
ናብራ ከሎኩም
ናብራ ለሚንኩም
15 አነ ክጽውዕ
አቤት እንዳበልኩም
ናጽነት ሓርነት
እንታይ ክገብረልኩም

ነዚ ዘይአመንኩም
20 ብረት ክሽጠልኩም
እንተ ብህይወትኩም
እንተ ብሞትኩም
ክኸስበኩም 'የ
አፍሪቃው ያን።

c. 1997–99

Dear Africans

The overweight
God, America,
Is always late.
Don't wait.

You already know   5
What he'll state:
I regret the hearsay
Of so many dead and dying
And so much crying.

You already know   10
What he'll think:
It's dress-down Friday.
Can we have a snack?
Oh, man! Make that a big Mac
And a large Coke.   15
By the way, don't smoke.

Glossary

Accent: in poetry the natural emphasis (stress) speakers place on a syllable.

Accentual Verse: poetry in which a line is measured only by the number of accents or stresses, not by the number of syllables.

Accentual-Syllabic Verse: poetry in which a line is measured by the number of syllables and by the pattern of accented (stressed) and unaccented (unstressed) syllables. This is the most common metrical system in traditional English verse.

Aesthetes: members of a late nineteenth-century movement that valued "art for art's sake"—for its purely aesthetic qualities, as opposed to valuing art for the moral content it may convey, for the intellectual stimulation it may provide, or for a range of other qualities.

Allegory: a narrative with both a literal meaning and secondary, often symbolic meaning or meanings. Allegory frequently employs personification to give concrete embodiment to abstract concepts or entities, such as feelings or personal qualities. It may also present one set of characters or events in the guise of another, using implied parallels for the purposes of satire or political comment.

Alliteration: the grouping of words with the same initial consonant (e.g., "break, blow, burn, and make me new"). See also *assonance* and *consonance*.

Alliterative Verse: poetry that employs alliteration of stressed syllables in each line as its chief structural principle.

Allusion: a reference, often indirect or unidentified, to a person, thing, or event. A reference in one literary work to another literary work, whether to its content or its form, also constitutes an allusion.

Ambiguity: an "opening" of language created by the writer to allow for multiple meanings or differing interpretations. In literature, ambiguity may be deliberately employed by the writer to enrich meaning; this differs from any unintentional, unwanted ambiguity in non-literary prose.

Anachronism: accidentally or intentionally attributing people, things, ideas, and events to historical periods in which they do not and could not possibly belong.

Analogy: a broad term that refers to our processes of noting similarities among things or events. Specific forms of analogy in poetry include *simile* and *metaphor*.

Anapaest: a metrical foot containing two unstressed syllables followed by one stressed syllable: xx / (e.g., underneath, intervene).

Antistrophe: from Greek drama, the chorus's countermovement or reply to an initial movement (*strophe*). See *ode*.

Apostrophe: a figure of speech (a *trope*; see *figures of speech*) in which a writer directly addresses an object—or a dead or absent person—as if the imagined audience were actually listening.

Archetype: in literature and mythology, a recurring idea, symbol, motif, character, or place. To some scholars and psychologists, an archetype represents universal human thought-patterns or experiences.

Assonance: the repetition of identical or similar vowel sounds in stressed syllables in which the surrounding consonants are different: for example, "shame" and "fate"; "gale" and "cage"; or the long "i" sounds in "Beside the pumice isle...."

Atmosphere: see *tone*.

Aubade: a lyric poem that greets or laments the arrival of dawn.

Ballad: a folk song, or a poem originally recited to an audience, which tells a dramatic story based on legend or history.

Ballad Stanza: a quatrain with alternating four-stress and three-stress lines, rhyming *abcb*. A variant is "common measure," in which the alternating lines are strictly iambic, and rhyme *abab*.

Baroque: powerful and heavily ornamented in style. "Baroque" is a term from the history of visual art and of music that is sometimes also used to describe certain literary styles.

Bathos: an anticlimactic effect brought about by a writer's descent from an elevated subject or tone to the ordinary or trivial.

Black Comedy: humour based on death, horror, or any incongruously macabre subject matter.

Blank Verse: unrhymed lines written in iambic pentameter. (A form introduced to English verse by Henry Howard, Earl of Surrey, in his translation of parts of Virgil's *Aeneid* in 1547.)

Bombast: inappropriately inflated or grandiose language.

Broken Rhyme: a kind of rhyme in which a multi-syllable word is split at the end of a line and continued onto the next, to allow an end-rhyme with the split syllable.

Burlesque: satire of a particularly exaggerated sort, particularly that which ridicules its subject by emphasizing its vulgar or ridiculous aspects.

Caesura: a pause or break in a line of verse occurring where a phrase, clause, or sentence ends, and indicated in scansion by the mark ||. If it occurs in the middle of the line, it is known as a "medial" caesura.

Canon: in literature, those works that are commonly accepted as possessing authority or importance. In practice, "canonical" texts or authors are those that are discussed most frequently by scholars and taught most frequently in university courses.

Canto: a sub-section of a long (usually epic) poem.

Canzone: a short song or poem, with stanzas of equal length and an *envoy*.

Caricature: an exaggerated and simplified depiction of character; the reduction of a personality to one or two telling traits at the expense of all other nuances and contradictions.

Carpe Diem: Latin (from Horace) meaning "seize the day." The idea of enjoying the moment is a common one in Renaissance love poetry. See, for example, Marvell's "To His Coy Mistress."

Catalexis: the omission of unstressed syllables from a line of verse (such a line is referred to as "catalectic"). In iambic verse it is usually the first syllable of the line that is omitted; in trochaic, the last. For example, in the first stanza of Housman's "To an Athlete Dying Young" the third line is catalectic: i.e., it has dropped the first, unstressed syllable called for by the poem's iambic tetrameter form: "The time you won your town the race / We chaired you through the market-place; / Man and boy stood cheering by, / And home we brought you shoulder-high."

Catharsis: the arousal through the performance of a dramatic tragedy of "emotions of pity and fear" to a point where "purgation" or "purification" occurs and the feelings are released or transformed. The concept was developed by Aristotle in his *Poetics* from an ancient Greek medical concept, and adapted by him into an aesthetic principle.

Characterization: the means by which an author develops and presents a character's personality qualities and distinguishing traits. A character may be established in the story by descriptive commentary or may be developed less directly—for example, through his or her words, actions, thoughts, and interactions with other characters.

Chiasmus: a figure of speech (a scheme) that reverses word order in successive parallel clauses. If the word order is A-B-C in the first clause, it becomes C-B-A in the second: for example, Donne's line "She is all states, and all princes, I" ("The Sun Rising") incorporates this reversal.

Classical: originating in or relating to ancient Greek or Roman culture. As commonly conceived, *classical* implies a strong sense of formal order. The term *neoclassical* is often used with reference to literature of the Restoration and eighteenth century that was strongly influenced by ancient Greek and Roman models.

Conceit: an unusually elaborate metaphor or simile that extends beyond its original tenor and vehicle, sometimes becoming a "master" analogy for the entire poem (see, for example, Donne's "The Flea"). Ingenious or fanciful images and comparisons were especially popular with the *metaphysical* poets of the seventeenth century, giving rise to the term "metaphysical conceit."

Concrete Poetry: an experimental form, most popular during the 1950s and 1960s, in which the printed type itself forms a visual image of the poem's key words or ideas. See also *pattern poetry*.

Conflict: struggles between characters and opposing forces. Conflict can be internal (psychological) or external (conflict with another character, for instance, or with society or nature).

Connotation: the implied, often unspoken meaning(s) of a given word, as distinct from its *denotation*, or literal meaning. Connotations may have highly emotional undertones and are usually culturally specific.

Consonance: the pairing of words with similar initial and ending consonants, but with different vowel sounds (live/love, wander/wonder). See also *alliteration*.

Convention: aesthetic approach, technique, or practice accepted as characteristic and appropriate for a particular form. It is a convention of certain sorts of plays, for example, that the characters speak in blank verse, of other sorts of plays that characters speak in rhymed couplets, and of still other sorts of dramatic performances that characters frequently break into song to express their feelings.

Couplet: a pair of rhyming lines, usually in the same metre. If they form a complete unit of thought and are grammatically complete, the lines are known as a closed couplet. See also *heroic couplet*.

Dactyl: a metrical foot containing one strong stress followed by two weak stresses: / xx (e.g., muttering, helplessly). A minor form known as "double dactyls" makes use of this metre for humorous purposes, e.g., "Jiggery pokery" or "Higgledy Piggledy."

Denotation: see *connotation*.

Dialogue: words spoken by characters to one another. (When a character is addressing him or her self or the audience directly, the words spoken are referred to as a *soliloquy*.)

Diction: word choice. Whether the diction of a literary work (or of a literary character) is colloquial, conversational, formal, or of some other type contributes significantly to the tone of the text as well as to characterization.

Didacticism: aesthetic approach emphasizing moral instruction.

Dimeter: a poetic line containing two metrical feet.

Dirge: a song or poem that mourns someone's death. See also *elegy* and *lament*.

Dissonance: harsh, unmusical sounds or rhythms that writers may use deliberately to achieve certain effects. Also known as cacophony.

Dramatic Irony: this form of *irony* occurs when an audience has access to information not available to the character.

Dramatic Monologue: a lyric poem that takes the form of an utterance by a single person addressing a silent listener. The speaker may be an historical personage (as in some of Robert Browning's dramatic monologues), a figure drawn from myth or legend (as in some of Tennyson's), or an entirely imagined figure (as in Webster's "A Castaway").

Dub Poetry: a form of protest poetry originating in Jamaica, with its roots in dance rhythms, especially reggae, and often accompanied in performance by drums and music. See also *rap*.

Duple Foot: a duple foot of poetry has two syllables. The possible duple forms are *iamb* (in which the stress is on the second of the two syllables), *trochee* (in which the stress is on the first of the two syllables), *spondee* (in which both are stressed equally), and *pyrrhic* (in which both syllables are unstressed).

Eclogue: now generally used simply as an alternative name for a pastoral poem. In classical times and in the early modern period, however, an *eclogue* (or *idyll*) was a specific type of pastoral poem—a dialogue or dramatic monologue involving rustic characters. (The other main sub-genre of the pastoral was the *georgic*.)

Elegiac Stanza: a quatrain of iambic pentameters rhyming *abab*, often used in poems meditating on death or sorrow. The best-known example is Thomas Gray's "Elegy Written in a Country Churchyard."

Elegy: a poem which formally mourns the death of a particular person (e.g., Tennyson's "In Memoriam") or in which the poet meditates on other serious subjects (e.g., Gray's "Elegy"). See also *dirge*.

Elision: omitting or suppressing a letter or an unstressed syllable at the beginning or end of a word, so that a line of verse may conform to a given metrical scheme. For example, the three syllables at the beginning of Shakespeare's sonnet 129 are reduced to two by the omission of the first vowel: "Th' expense of spirit in a waste of shame." See also *syncope*.

Ellipsis: the omission of a word or words necessary for the complete grammatical construction of a sentence, but not necessary for our understanding of the sentence.

End-Rhyme: see *rhyme*.

End-Stopped: a line of poetry is said to be end-stopped when the end of the line coincides with a natural pause in the syntax, such as the conclusion of a sentence; e.g., in this couplet from Pope's "Essay on Criticism," both lines are end-stopped: "A little learning is a dangerous thing; / Drink deep, or taste not the Pierian spring." Compare this with *enjambment*.

Enjambment: the "running-on" of the sense from one line of poetry to the next, with no pause created by punctuation or syntax.

Envoy (Envoi): a stanza or half-stanza that forms the conclusion of certain French poetic forms, such as the *sestina* or the *ballade*. It often sums up or comments upon what has gone before.

Epic: a lengthy narrative poem, often divided into books and sub-divided into cantos. It generally celebrates heroic deeds or events, and the style tends to be lofty and grand. Examples in English include Spenser's *The Faerie Queene* and Milton's *Paradise Lost*.

Epic Simile: an elaborate simile, developed at such length that the vehicle of the comparison momentarily displaces the primary subject with which it is being compared.

Epigram: a very short poem, sometimes in closed couplet form, characterized by pointed wit.

Epigraph: a quotation placed at the beginning of a work to indicate or fore-shadow the theme.

Epiphany: a moment at which matters of significance are suddenly illumi-nated for a literary character (or for the reader), typically triggered by something small and seemingly of little import. The term first came into wide currency in connection with the fiction of James Joyce.

Epithalamion: a poem celebrating a wedding. The best-known example in English is Edmund Spenser's "Epithalamion" (1595).

Epode: the third part of an *ode*, following the *strophe* and *antistrophe*.

Ethos: the perceived character, trustworthiness, or credibility of a writer or narrator.

Eulogy: text expressing praise, especially for a distinguished person recently deceased.

Euphemism: mode of expression through which aspects of reality considered to be vulgar, crudely physical, or unpleasant are referred to indirectly rather than named explicitly. A variety of euphemisms exist for the pro-cesses of urination and defecation; *passed away* is often used as a euphe-mism for *died*.

Euphony: pleasant, musical sounds or rhythms—the opposite of *dissonance*.

Existentialism: a philosophical approach according to which the meaning of human life is derived from the actual experience of the living individual. The existential worldview, in which life is assumed to have no essential or pre-existing meanings other than those we personally choose to endow it with, can produce an *absurdist* sensibility.

Eye-Rhyme: see *rhyme*.

Feminine Rhyme: see *rhyme*.

Fiction: imagined or invented narrative. In literature, the term is usually used to refer to prose narratives (such as novels and short stories).

Figures of Speech: deliberate, highly concentrated uses of language to achieve particular purposes or effects on an audience. There are two kinds of figures: schemes and *tropes*. Schemes involve changes in word-sound and word-order, such as *alliteration* and *chiasmus*. Tropes play on our understandings of words to extend, alter, or transform meaning, as in *metaphor* and *personification*.

First-Person Narrative: narrative recounted using *I* and *me*. See also *narrative perspective*.

Fixed Forms: the term applied to a number of poetic forms and stanzaic patterns, many derived from French models, such as *ballade, rondeau, sestina, triolet*, and *villanelle*. Other "fixed forms" include the *sonnet, rhyme royal, haiku*, and *ottava rima*.

Flat Character: the opposite of a *round character*, a flat character is defined by a small number of traits and does not possess enough complexity to be psychologically realistic. "Flat character" can be a disparaging term, but need not be; flat characters serve different purposes in a fiction than round characters, and are often better suited to some types of literature, such as allegory or farcical comedy.

Foil: in literature, a character whose behaviour and/or qualities set in relief for the reader or audience those of a strongly contrasting character who plays a more central part in the story.

Foot: a unit of a line of verse that contains a particular combination of stressed and unstressed syllables. Dividing a line into metrical feet (*iambs, trochees*, etc.), then counting the number of feet per line, is part of *scansion*. See also *metre*.

Foreshadowing: the inclusion of elements in a story that hint at some later development(s) in the same story. For example, in Flannery O'Connor's "A Good Man Is Hard to Find," the old family burying ground that the family sees on their drive foreshadows the violence that follows.

Free Verse: poetry that does not follow any regular metre, line length, or rhyming scheme. In many respects, though, free verse follows the complex natural "rules" and rhythmic patterns (or cadences) of speech.

Freytag's Pyramid: a model of plot structure developed by the German novelist, playwright, and critic Gustav Freytag and introduced in his book *Die Technik des Dramas* (1863). In the pyramid, five stages of plot are identified as occurring in the following order: exposition, rising action, climax, falling action, and *dénouement*. Freytag intended his pyramid to diagram the structure of classical five-act plays, but it is also used as a tool to analyze other forms of fiction (even though many individual plays and stories do not follow the structure outlined in the pyramid).

Genre: a class or type of literary work. The concept of genre may be used with different levels of generality. At the most general, poetry, drama, and prose fiction are distinguished as separate genres. At a lower level of generality various sub-genres are frequently distinguished, such as (within the genre of prose fiction) the novel, the novella, and the short story; and, at a still lower level of generality, the mystery novel, the detective novel, the novel of manners, and so on.

Georgic: (from Virgil's *Georgics*) a poem that celebrates the natural wealth of the countryside and advises how to cultivate and live in harmony with it. Pope's *Windsor Forest* and James Thomson's *Seasons* are classed as georgics. Georgics were often said to make up, with *eclogues*, the two alliterative forms of pastoral poetry.

Ghazal: derived from Persian and Indian precedents, the ghazal presents a series of thoughts in closed couplets usually joined by a simple rhyme-scheme such as: *a/a b/a c/a d/a, ab bb cb eb fb*, etc.

Gothic: in architecture and the visual arts, a term used to describe styles prevalent from the twelfth to the fourteenth centuries, but in literature a term used to describe work with a sinister or grotesque tone that seeks to evoke a sense of terror on the part of the reader or audience. Gothic literature originated as a genre in the eighteenth century with works such as Horace Walpole's *The Castle of Otranto*. To some extent the notion of the medieval itself then carried with it associations of the dark and the grotesque, but from the beginning an element of intentional exaggeration (sometimes verging on self-parody) attached itself to the genre. The Gothic trend of youth culture that began in the late twentieth century is less clearly associated with the medieval, but shares with the various varieties of Gothic literature (from Walpole in the eighteenth century, to Bram Stoker in the early twentieth, to Stephen King and Anne Rice in the late twentieth) a fondness for the sensational and the grotesque, as well as a propensity to self-parody.

Grotesque: literature of the grotesque is characterized by a focus on extreme or distorted aspects of human characteristics. (The term can also refer particularly to a character who is odd or disturbing.) This focus can serve to comment on and challenge societal norms. The story "A Good Man Is Hard to Find" employs elements of the grotesque.

Haiku: a Japanese poetic form with three unrhymed lines of typically five, seven, and five syllables. Conventionally, it uses precise, concentrated images to suggest states of feeling.

Heptameter: a line containing seven metrical feet.

Heroic Couplet: a pair of rhymed iambic pentameters, so called because the form was much used in seventeenth- and eighteenth-century poems and plays on heroic subjects.

Hexameter: a line containing six metrical feet.

Horatian Ode: inspired by the work of the Roman poet Horace, an ode that is usually calm and meditative in tone, and homostrophic (i.e., having regular stanzas) in form. Keats's odes are English examples.

Hymn: a song whose theme is usually religious, in praise of divinity. Literary hymns may praise more secular subjects.

Hyperbole: a *figure of speech* (a *trope*) that deliberately exaggerates or inflates meaning to achieve particular effects, such as the irony in A.E. Housman's claim (from "Terence, This Is Stupid Stuff") that "malt does more than Milton can / To justify God's ways to man."

Iamb: the most common metrical foot in English verse, containing one unstressed syllable followed by a stressed syllable: x / (e.g., between, achieve).

Idyll: traditionally, a short pastoral poem that idealizes country life, conveying impressions of innocence and happiness.

Image: a representation of a sensory experience or of an object that can be known by the senses.

Imagery: the range of images in a given work. We can gain much insight into works by looking for patterns of imagery. For example, the imagery of spring (budding trees, rain, singing birds) in Kate Chopin's "The Story of an Hour" reinforces the suggestions of death and rebirth in the plot and theme.

Imagism: a poetic movement that was popular mainly in the second decade of the twentieth century. The goal of imagist poets (such as H.D. and Ezra Pound in their early work) was to represent emotions or impressions through highly concentrated imagery.

Incantation: a chant or recitation of words that are believed to have magical power. A poem can achieve an "incantatory" effect through a compelling rhyme scheme and other repetitive patterns.

Interlocking Rhyme: see *rhyme*.

Internal Rhyme: see *rhyme*.

Intertextuality: the relationships between one literary work and other literary works. A literary work may connect with other works through *allusion*, *parody*, or *satire*, or in a variety of other ways.

Irony: the use of irony draws attention to a gap between what is said and what is meant, or what appears to be true and what is true. Types of irony include verbal irony (which includes *hyberbole*, *litotes*, and *sarcasm*), *dramatic irony*, and structural irony (in which the gap between what is "said" and meant is sustained throughout an entire piece, as when an author makes use of an unreliable narrator or speaker—see Robert Browning's "My Last Duchess").

Lament: a poem that expresses profound regret or grief either because of a death, or because of the loss of a former, happier state.

Language Poetry: a movement that defies the usual lyric and narrative conventions of poetry, and that challenges the structures and codes of everyday language. Often seen as both politically and aesthetically subversive, its roots lie in the works of modernist writers such as Ezra Pound and Gertrude Stein.

Litotes: a *figure of speech* (a *trope*) in which a writer deliberately uses understatement to highlight the importance of an argument, or to convey an ironic attitude.

Lyric: a poem, usually short, expressing an individual speaker's feelings or private thoughts. Originally a song performed with accompaniment on a lyre, the lyric poem is often noted for musicality of rhyme and rhythm. The lyric genre includes a variety of forms, including the *sonnet*, the *ode*, the *elegy*, the *madrigal*, the *aubade*, the *dramatic monologue*, and the *hymn*.

Madrigal: a lyric poem, usually short and focusing on pastoral or romantic themes. A madrigal is often set to music.

Masculine Ending: a metrical line ending on a stressed syllable.

Masculine Rhyme: see *rhyme*. An alternative term is hard landing.

Melodrama: originally a term used to describe nineteenth-century plays featuring sensational story lines and a crude separation of characters into moral categories, with the pure and virtuous pitted against evil villains. Early melodramas employed background music throughout the action of the play as a means of heightening the emotional response of the audience. By extension, certain sorts of prose fictions or poems are often described as having melodramatic elements.

Metafiction: fiction that calls attention to itself as fiction. Metafiction is a means by which authors render us conscious of our status as readers, often in order to explore the relationships between fiction and reality.

Metaphor: a *figure of speech* (in this case, a *trope*) in which a comparison is made or identity is asserted between two unrelated things or actions without the use of "like" or "as."

Metaphysical Poets: a group of seventeenth-century English poets, notably Donne, Cowley, Marvell, and Herbert, who employed unusual, difficult imagery and *conceits* in order to develop intellectual and religious themes. The term was first applied to these writers to mark as far-fetched their use of philosophical and scientific ideas in a poetic context.

Metonymy: a *figure of speech* (a *trope*), meaning "change of name," in which a writer refers to an object or idea by substituting the name of another object or idea closely associated with it: for example, the substitution of "crown" for monarchy, "the press" for journalism, or "the pen" for writing. *Synecdoche* is a kind of metonymy.

Metre: the pattern of stresses, syllables, and pauses that constitutes the regular rhythm of a line of verse. The metre of a poem written in the English accentual-syllabic tradition is determined by identifying the stressed and unstressed syllables in a line of verse, and grouping them into recurring units known as feet. See *accent, accentual-syllabic, caesura, elision,* and *scansion.* For some of the better-known metres, see *iamb, trochee, dactyl, anapaest,* and *spondee.* See also *monometer, dimeter, trimeter, tetrameter, pentameter,* and *hexameter.*

Mock-Heroic: a style applying the elevated diction and vocabulary of epic poetry to low or ridiculous subjects. An example is Alexander Pope's "The Rape of the Lock."

Modernism: in the history of literature, music, and the visual arts, a movement that began in the early twentieth century, characterized by a thoroughgoing rejection of the then-dominant conventions of literary plotting and characterization, of melody and harmony, and of perspective and other naturalistic forms of visual representation. In literature (as in music and the visual arts), modernists endeavoured to represent the complexity of what seemed to them to be an increasingly fragmented world by adopting techniques of presenting story material, illuminating character, and employing imagery that emphasized (in the words of Virginia Woolf) "the spasmodic, the obscure, the fragmentary."

Monologue: an extended speech by a single speaker or character in a poem or play. Unlike a *soliloquy*, a dramatic monologue has an implied listener.

Monometer: a line containing one metrical foot.

Mood: this can describe the writer's attitude, implied or expressed, toward the subject (see *tone*); or it may refer to the atmosphere that a writer creates in a passage of description or narration.

Motif: pattern formed by the recurrence of an idea, image, action, or plot element throughout a literary work, creating new levels of meaning and strengthening structural coherence. The term is taken from music, where it describes recurring melodies or themes. See also *theme.*

Narration: the process of disclosing information, whether fictional or non-fictional.

Narrative Perspective: the point of view from which a story is narrated. A first-person narrative is recounted using *I* and *me*, whereas a third-person narrative is recounted using *he, she, they*, and so on. When a narrative is written in the third person and the narrative voice evidently "knows" all that is being done and thought, the story is typically described as being recounted by an "omniscient narrator." Second-person narratives, in which the narrative is recounted using *you*, are very rare.

Narrator: the voice (or voices) disclosing information. In fiction, the narrator is distinguished from both the author (a real, historical person) and the implied author (whom the reader imagines the author to be). Narrators can also be distinguished according to the degree to which they share the reality of the other characters in the story and the extent to which they participate in the action; according to how much information they are privy to (and how much of that information they are willing to share with the reader); and according to whether or not they are perceived by the reader as reliable or unreliable sources of information. See also *narrative perspective*.

Neoclassicism: literally the "new classicism," the aesthetic style that dominated high culture in Europe through the seventeenth and eighteenth centuries, and in some places into the nineteenth century. Its subject matter was often taken from Greek and Roman myth and history; in *style*, it valued order, reason, clarity, and moderation.

Nonsense Verse: light, humorous poetry that contradicts logic, plays with the absurd, and invents words for amusing effects. Lewis Carroll is one of the best-known practitioners of nonsense verse.

Octave: also known as "octet," the first eight lines in certain forms of sonnet—notably the *Italian/Petrarchan*, in which the octet rhymes *abbaabba*. See also *sestet* and *sonnet*.

Octosyllabic: a line of poetry with eight syllables, as in iambic tetrameter.

Ode: originally a classical poetic form, used by the Greeks and Romans to convey serious themes. English poetry has evolved three main forms of ode: the Pindaric (imitative of the odes of the Greek poet Pindar); the Horatian (modelled on the work of the Roman writer Horace); and the irregular ode. The Pindaric ode has a tripartite structure of *strophe, antistrophe,* and *epode* (meaning turn, counterturn, and stand), modelled on the songs and movements of the *Chorus* in Greek drama. The Horatian ode is more personal, reflective, and literary, and employs a pattern of repeated stanzas. The irregular ode, as its name implies, avoids a recurrent stanza pattern, and is sometimes irregular in line length also (for example, Wordsworth's "Ode: Intimations of Immortality").

Omniscient Narrator: see *narrative perspective*.

Onomatopoeia: a *figure of speech* (a scheme) in which a word "imitates" a sound, or in which the sound of a word seems to reflect its meaning.

Ottava Rima: an eight-line stanza, usually in iambic pentameter, with the rhyme scheme *abababcc*. For an example, see Yeats's "Sailing to Byzantium."

Oxymoron: a *figure of speech* (a *trope*) in which two words whose meanings seem contradictory are placed together; we see an example in Shakespeare's *Twelfth Night*, when Orsino refers to the "sweet pangs" of love.

Pantoum: linked quatrains in a poem that rhymes *abab*. The second and fourth lines of one stanza are repeated as the first and third lines of the stanza that follows. In the final stanza the pattern is reversed: the second line repeats the third line of the first stanza, the fourth and final line repeats the first line of the first stanza.

Parody: a close, usually mocking imitation of a particular literary work, or of the well-known style of a particular author, in order to expose or magnify weaknesses. Parody is a form of *satire*—that is, humour that may ridicule and scorn its object.

Pastiche: a discourse that borrows or imitates other writers' characters, forms, style, or ideas, sometimes creating something of a literary patchwork. Unlike a parody, a pastiche can be intended as a compliment to the original writer.

Pastoral: in general, pertaining to country life; in prose, drama, and poetry, a stylized type of writing that idealizes the lives and innocence of country people, particularly shepherds and shepherdesses. See also *eclogue, georgic, idyll*.

Pastoral Elegy: a poem in which the poet uses the pastoral style to lament the death of a friend, usually represented as a shepherd. Milton's "Lycidas" provides a good example of the form, including its use of such conventions as an invocation of the muse and a procession of mourners.

Pathetic Fallacy: a form of *personification* in which inanimate objects are given human emotions: for example, rain clouds "weeping." The word "fallacy" in this connection is intended to suggest the distortion of reality or the false emotion that may result from an exaggerated use of personification.

Pathos: the emotional quality of a discourse; or the ability of a discourse to appeal to our emotions. It is usually applied to the mood conveyed by images of pain, suffering, or loss that arouse feelings of pity or sorrow in the reader.

Pattern Poetry: a predecessor of modern *concrete poetry* in which the shape of the poem on the page is intended to suggest or imitate an aspect of the poem's subject. George Herbert's "Easter Wings" is an example of pattern poetry.

Pentameter: verse containing five metrical feet in a line.

Performance Poetry: poetry composed primarily for oral performance, often very theatrical in nature. See also *dub poetry* and *rap*.

Persona: the assumed identity or "speaking voice" that a writer projects in a discourse. The term "persona" literally means "mask."

Personification: a *figure of speech* (a *trope*), also known as "prosopopoeia," in which a writer refers to inanimate objects, ideas, or non-human animals as if they were human, or creates a human figure to represent an abstract entity such as Philosophy or Peace.

Phoneme: a linguistic term denoting the smallest unit of sound that it is possible to distinguish. The words *fun* and *phone* each have three phonemes, though one has three letters and one has five.

Point of View: see *narrative perspective*.

Postmodernism: in literature and the visual arts, a movement influential in the late twentieth and early twenty-first centuries. In some ways postmodernism represents a reaction to modernism, in others an extension of it. With roots in the work of French philosophers such as Jacques Derrida and Michel Foucault, it is deeply coloured by theory; indeed, it may be said to have begun at the "meta" level of theorizing rather than at the level of practice. Like modernism, postmodernism embraces difficulty and distrusts the simple and straightforward. More broadly, postmodernism is characterized by a rejection of absolute truth or value, of closed systems, of grand unified narratives.

Postmodernist fiction is characterized by a frequently ironic or playful tone in dealing with reality and illusion; by a willingness to combine different styles or forms in a single work (just as in architecture the postmodernist spirit embodies a willingness to borrow from seemingly disparate styles in designing a single structure); and by a highly attuned awareness of the problematized state of the writer, artist, or theorist as observer.

Prose Poem: a poetic discourse that uses prose formats (e.g., it may use margins and paragraphs rather than line breaks or stanzas) yet is written with the kind of attention to language, rhythm, and cadence that characterizes verse.

Prosody: the study and analysis of metre, rhythm, rhyme, stanzaic pattern, and other devices of versification.

Protagonist: the central character in a literary work.

Prothalamion: a wedding song; a term coined by the poet Edmund Spenser, adapted from *epithalamion*.

Pun: a play on words, in which a word with two or more distinct meanings, or two words with similar sounds, may create humorous ambiguities. Also known as "paranomasia."

Pyrrhic: a metrical foot containing two weak stresses.

Quantitative Metre: a metrical system used by Greek and Roman poets, in which a line of verse was measured by the "quantity," or length of sound of each syllable. A foot was measured in terms of syllables classed as long or short.

Quantity: duration of syllables in poetry. The line "There is a Garden in her face" (the first line from the poem of the same name by Thomas Campion) is characterized by the short quantities of the syllables. The last line of Thomas Hardy's "During Wind and Rain" has the same number of syllables as the line by Campion, but the quantities of the syllables are much longer—in other words, the line takes much longer to say: "Down their carved names the rain drop ploughs."

Quatrain: a four-line stanza.

Quintet: a five-line stanza. Sometimes given as "quintain."

Rap: originally coined to describe informal conversation, "rap" now usually describes a style of performance poetry in which a poet will chant rhymed verse, sometimes improvised and usually with musical accompaniment that has a heavy beat.

Realism: as a literary term, the presentation through literature of material closely resembling real life. As notions both of what constitutes "real life" and of how it may be most faithfully represented in literature have varied widely, "realism" has taken a variety of meanings. The term "naturalistic" has sometimes been used as a synonym for *realistic*; naturalism originated in the nineteenth century as a term denoting a form of realism focusing in particular on grim, unpleasant, or ugly aspects of the real.

Refrain: one or more words or lines repeated at regular points throughout a poem, often at the end of each stanza or group of stanzas. Sometimes a whole stanza may be repeated to create a refrain, like the chorus in a song.

Rhyme: the repetition of identical or similar sounds, usually in pairs and generally at the ends of metrical lines.

    End-Rhyme: a rhyming word or syllable at the end of a line.

    Eye Rhyme: rhyming that pairs words whose spellings are alike but whose pronunciations are different: for example, though/slough.

    Feminine Rhyme: a two-syllable (also known as "double") rhyme. The first syllable is stressed and the second unstressed: for example, hasty/tasty. See also *triple rhyme*.

    Interlocking Rhyme: the repetition of rhymes from one stanza to the next, creating links that add to the poem's continuity and coherence. Examples may be found in Shelley's use of *terza rima* in "Ode to the West Wind" and in Dylan Thomas's *villanelle* "Do Not Go Gentle into That Good Night."

    Internal Rhyme: the placement of rhyming words within lines so that at least two words in a line rhyme with each other.

    Masculine Rhyme: a correspondence of sound between the final stressed syllables at the end of two or more lines, as in grieve/leave, ar-rive/sur-vive.

Slant Rhyme: an imperfect or partial rhyme (also known as "near" or "half" rhyme) in which the consonant sounds of stressed syllables match but the vowel sounds do not. E.g., spoiled/spilled, taint/stint.

Triple Rhyme: a three-syllable rhyme in which the first syllable of each rhyme-word is stressed and the other two unstressed (e.g., lottery/coterie).

True Rhyme: a rhyme in which everything but the initial consonant matches perfectly in sound and spelling.

Rhyme Royal: a stanza of seven iambic pentameters, with a rhyme-scheme of *ababbcc*. This is also known as the Chaucerian stanza, as Chaucer was the first English poet to use this form. See also *septet*.

Rhythm: in speech, the arrangement of stressed and unstressed syllables creates units of sound. In song or verse, these units may be shaped into a regular rhythmic pattern, described in prosody as *metre*.

Romanticism: a major social and cultural movement, originating in Europe, that shaped much of Western artistic thought in the late eighteenth and nineteenth centuries. Opposing the ideal of controlled, rational order associated with the Enlightenment, Romanticism emphasizes the importance of spontaneous self-expression, emotion, and personal experience in producing art. In Romanticism, the "natural" is privileged over the conventional or the artificial.

Rondeau: a 15-line poem, generally octosyllabic, with only two rhymes throughout its three stanzas, and an unrhymed refrain at the end of the ninth and fifteenth lines, repeating part of the opening line.

Round Character: a complex and psychologically realistic character, often one who changes as a work progresses. The opposite of a round character is a *flat character*.

Sarcasm: a form of *irony* (usually spoken) in which the meaning is conveyed largely by the tone of voice adopted; something said sarcastically is meant to imply its opposite.

Satire: literary work designed to make fun of or seriously criticize its subject. According to many literary theories of the Renaissance and neoclassical periods, the ridicule through satire of a certain sort of behaviour may function for the reader or audience as a corrective of such behaviour.

Scansion: the formal analysis of patterns of rhythm and rhyme in poetry. Each line of accentual-syllabic verse will have a certain number of fairly regular "beats" consisting of alternating stressed and unstressed syllables. To "scan" a poem is to count the beats in each line, to mark stressed and unstressed syllables and indicate their combination into "feet," to note pauses, and to identify rhyme schemes with letters of the alphabet.

Scheme: see *figures of speech*.

Septet: a stanza containing seven lines.

Sestet: a six-line stanza. A sestet forms the second grouping of lines in an *Italian/Petrarchan sonnet*, following the octave. See *sonnet* and *sestina*.

Sestina: an elaborate unrhymed poem with six six-line stanzas and a three-line *envoy*.

Setting: the time, place, and cultural environment in which a story or work takes place.

Simile: a *figure of speech* (a *trope*) which makes an explicit comparison between a particular object and another object or idea that is similar in some (often unexpected) way. A simile always uses "like" or "as" to signal the connection. Compare with *metaphor*.

Soliloquy: in drama (or, less often, poetry), a speech in which a character, usually alone, reveals his or her thoughts, emotions, and/or motivations without being heard by other characters. The convention was frequently employed during the Elizabethan era, and many of the best-known examples are from Shakespeare; for example, Hamlet's "To be, or not to be" speech is a soliloquy. Soliloquies differ from *dramatic monologues* in that dramatic monologues address an implied listener, while the speaker of a soliloquy thinks aloud or addresses the audience.

Sonnet: a highly structured lyric poem, which normally has 14 lines of iambic pentameter. We can distinguish four major variations of the sonnet.

> **Italian/Petrarchan:** named for the fourteenth-century Italian poet Petrarch, has an octave rhyming *abbaabba*, and a sestet rhyming *cdecde*, or *cdcdcd* (other arrangements are possible here). Usually, a turn in argument takes place between the octave and sestet.

> **Miltonic:** developed by Milton and similar to the Petrarchan in rhyme scheme, but eliminating the turn after the octave, thus giving greater unity to the poem's structure of thought.

> **Shakespearean:** often called the English sonnet, this form has three quatrains and a couplet. The quatrains rhyme internally but do not interlock: *abab cdcd efef gg*. The turn may occur after the second quatrain, but is usually revealed in the final couplet. Shakespeare's sonnets are the best-known examples of this form.

> **Spenserian:** after Edmund Spenser, who developed the form in his sonnet cycle *Amoretti*. This sonnet form has three quatrains linked through interlocking rhyme, and a separately rhyming couplet: *abab bcbc cdcd ee*.

Spenserian Stanza: a nine-line stanza, with eight iambic pentameters and a concluding 12-syllable line, rhyming *ababbcbcc*.

Spondee: a metrical foot containing two strong stressed syllables: // (e.g., blind mouths).

Sprung Rhythm: a modern variation of accentual verse, created by the English poet Gerard Manley Hopkins, in which rhythms are determined largely by the number of strong stresses in a line, without regard to the number of unstressed syllables. Hopkins felt that sprung rhythm more closely approximated the natural rhythms of speech than did conventional poetry.

Stanza: any lines of verse that are grouped together in a poem and separated from other similarly structured groups by a space. In metrical poetry, stanzas share metrical and rhyming patterns; however, stanzas may also be formed on the basis of thought, as in irregular odes. Conventional stanza forms include the *tercet*, the *quatrain*, *rhyme royal*, the *Spenserian stanza*, the *ballad stanza*, and *ottava rima*.

Stock Character: a character defined by a set of characteristics that are stereotypical and/or established by literary convention; examples include the "wicked stepmother" and the "absent-minded professor."

Stress: see *accent*.

Strophe: a *stanza*. In a Pindaric *ode*, the *strophe* is the first stanza. This is followed by an *antistrophe*, which presents the same metrical pattern and rhyme scheme, and finally by an *epode*, differing in metre from the preceding stanzas. Upon completion of this "triad," the entire sequence can recur.

Style: a distinctive or specific use of language and form.

Sublime: a concept, popular in eighteenth-century England, that sought to capture the qualities of grandeur, power, and awe that may be inherent in or produced by undomesticated nature or great art. The sublime was thought of as higher and loftier than something that is merely beautiful.

Substitution: a deliberate change from the dominant pattern of stresses in a line of verse to create emphasis or variation. Thus the first line of Shakespeare's sonnet "Shall I compare thee to a summer's day?" is decidedly iambic in metre (x/x/x/x/x/), whereas the second line substitutes a trochee (/x) in the opening foot: "Thou art more lovely and more temperate."

Subtext: implied or suggested meaning of a passage of text, or of an entire work.

Surrealism: Surrealism incorporates elements of the true appearance of life and nature, combining these elements according to a logic more typical of dreams than waking life. Isolated aspects of surrealist art may create powerful illusions of reality, but the effect of the whole is usually to disturb or question our sense of reality rather than to confirm it.

Syllabic Verse: poetry in which the length of a line is measured solely by the number of syllables, regardless of accents or patterns of stress.

Syllable: vocal sound or group of sounds forming a unit of speech; a syllable may be formed with a single effort of articulation. Some syllables consist of a single phoneme (e.g., the word *I*, or the first syllable in the word *u*-ni-ty) but others may be made up of several phonemes (as with one-syllable words such as *lengths*, *splurged*, and *through*). By contrast, the much shorter words *ago*, *any*, and *open* each have two syllables.

Symbol: something that represents itself but goes beyond this in suggesting other meanings. Like metaphor, the symbol extends meaning; but while the tenor and vehicle of metaphor are bound in a specific relationship, a symbol may have a range of connotations. For example, the image of a rose may call forth associations of love, passion, transience, fragility, youth, and beauty, among others. Depending upon the context, such an image could be interpreted in a variety of ways, as in Blake's lyric, "The Sick Rose."

Syncope: in poetry, the dropping of a letter or syllable from the middle of a word, as in "trav'ller." Such a contraction allows a line to stay within a metrical scheme. See also *catalexis* and *elision*.

Synecdoche: a kind of *metonymy* in which a writer substitutes the name of a part of something to signify the whole: for example, "sail" for ship or "hand" for a member of the ship's crew.

Syntax: the ordering of words in a sentence.

Tercet: a group, or stanza, of three lines, often linked by an interlocking rhyme scheme as in *terza rima*. See also *triplet*.

Terza Rima: an arrangement of tercets interlocked by a rhyme scheme of *aba bcb cdc ded*, etc., and ending with a couplet that rhymes with the second-last line of the final tercet (for example, *efe, ff*). See, for example, Percy Shelley's "Ode to the West Wind."

Tetrameter: a line of poetry containing four metrical feet.

Theme: in general, an idea explored in a work through character, action, and/ or image. To be fully developed, however, a theme must consist of more than a single concept or idea: it should also include an argument about the idea. Thus if a poem examines the topic of jealousy, we might say the theme is that jealousy undermines love or jealousy is a manifestation of insecurity. Few, if any, literary works have single themes.

Third-Person Narrative: see *narrative perspective*.

Tone: the writer's attitude toward a given subject or audience, as expressed through an authorial persona or "voice." Tone can be projected through particular choices of wording, imagery, figures of speech, and rhythmic devices. Compare *mood*.

Tragedy: in the traditional definition originating in discussions of ancient Greek drama, a serious narrative recounting the downfall of the protagonist, usually a person of high social standing. More loosely, the term has been applied to a wide variety of literary forms in which the tone is predominantly a dark one and the narrative does not end happily.

Trimeter: verse containing three metrical feet in a line.

Triolet: a French form in which the first line appears three times in a poem of only eight lines. The first line is repeated at lines four and seven; the second line is repeated in line eight. The triolet has only two rhymes: *abaaabab*.

Triple Foot: poetic foot of three syllables. The possible varieties of triple foot are the anapest (in which two unstressed syllables are followed by a stressed syllable), the dactyl (in which a stressed syllable is followed by two unstressed syllables), and the mollossus (in which all three syllables are stressed equally). English poetry tends to use *duple* rhythms far more frequently than triple rhythms.

Triplet: a group of three lines with the same end-rhyme, much used by eighteenth-century poets to vary or punctuate the flow of couplets. See also *tercet*.

Trochee: a metrical foot containing one strong stress followed by one weak stress.

Trope: any figure of speech that plays on our understandings of words to extend, alter, or transform "literal" meaning. Common tropes include *metaphor, simile, personification, hyperbole, metonymy, oxymoron, synecdoche,* and *irony*. See also *figures of speech*.

Turn (Italian "volta"): the point in a *sonnet* where the mood or argument changes. The turn may occur between the octave and sestet, i.e., after the eighth line, or in the final couplet, depending on the kind of sonnet.

Unreliable Narrator: a narrator whose reporting or understanding of events invites questioning from the reader. Narrators may be considered unreliable if they lack sufficient intelligence or experience to understand events, or if they have some reason to misrepresent events. See also *narrative perspective*.

Vers libre (French): see *free verse*.

Verse: a general term for works of poetry, usually referring to poems that incorporate some kind of metrical structure. The term may also describe a line of poetry, though more frequently it is applied to a stanza.

Villanelle: a poem usually consisting of 19 lines, with five three-line stanzas (tercets) rhyming *aba*, and a concluding quatrain rhyming *abaa*. The first and third lines of the first tercet are repeated at fixed intervals throughout the rest of the poem. See, for example, Dylan Thomas's "Do Not Go Gentle into That Good Night."

Volta: See *turn*.

Zeugma: a *figure of speech* (*trope*) in which one word links or "yokes" two others in the same sentence, often to comic or ironic effect. For example, a verb may govern two objects, as in Pope's line "Or stain her honour, or her new brocade."

Permission Acknowledgements

Diane Ackerman. "Sweep Me through Your Many-Chambered Heart," from *Jaguar of Sweet Laughter* by Diane Ackerman, copyright © 1991 by Diane Ackerman. Used by permission of Random House, Inc. Any third party use of this material, outside of this publication, is prohibited. Interested parties must apply directly to Random House, Inc. for permission.

Kim Addonizio. "First Poem for You," from *The Philosopher's Club*. BOA Editions, Ltd., 1994. Copyright © Kim Addonizio. Reprinted by permission of the author.

Agha Shahid Ali. "Postcard from Kashmir," from *The Half-Inch Himalayas*, copyright © 1987 by Agha Shahid Ali. Published by Wesleyan University Press. Reprinted by permission of Wesleyan University Press. "The Wolf's Postscript to 'Little Red Riding Hood,'" from *A Walk Through the Yellow Pages*. SUN/gemini Press, 1987. Reprinted by permission of Iqbal Agha.

Yehuda Amichai. "Tourists," from *The Selected Poetry of Yehuda Amichai*. Translated by Chana Bloch and Stephen Mitchell, with a New Foreword by C.K. Williams. University of California Press. English translation reprinted with the permission of University of California Press via Copyright Clearance Center. Original Hebrew reprinted with the permission of Hana Amichai.

Simon Armitage. "It Could Be You," from *The Universal Home Doctor* by Simon Armitage. Faber and Faber, 2002; reprinted with the permission of Faber and Faber Ltd. "Poem," from *Kid* by Simon Armitage. Faber and Faber, 2002; reprinted with the permission of Faber and Faber Ltd. "Very Simply Topping Up the Brake Fluid," originally published in *Zoom!* by Bloodaxe Books, 1989; reprinted with the permission of Bloodaxe Books.

John Ashbery. "Civilization and Its Discontents," from *Rivers and Mountains* by John Ashbery. Copyright © 1962, 1966 by John Ashbery; reprinted by permission of Georges Borchardt, Inc., on behalf of the author. "The Improvement," from *And the Stars Were Shining* by John Ashbery. Copyright © 1994 by John Ashbery; reprinted by permission of Georges Borchardt, Inc., on behalf of the author.

Margaret Atwood. "Death of a Young Son by Drowning," from *The Journals of Susanna Moodie*. Copyright © Oxford University Press Canada, 1970; reprinted by permission of the publisher. "The Door," from *The Door* by Margaret Atwood. Copyright © 2007, O.W. Toad Ltd.; reprinted by permission of McClelland & Stewart. "Variation on the Word Sleep," from *True Stories*. Copyright © Oxford University Press Canada, 1981; reprinted by permission of the publisher. "You Fit Into Me," from *Power Politics* by Margaret Atwood, published by

by Nicole Brossard. Écrits des Forges, 1989; reprinted with the permission of Écrits des Forges.

Anne Carson. "On Walking Backwards," "On Sylvia Plath," and "On Rain," from *Short Talks*. Brick, 1992. Reprinted with the permission of United Talent Agency.

Paul Celan. "Shroud" and "Death Fugue," from *Poems of Paul Celan*, translated by Michael Hamburger. Translation copyright © 1972, 1980, 1988, 2002 by Michael Hamburger; reprinted by permission of Persea Books, Inc., New York. All rights reserved. "Totenhemd" and "Todesfuge" from *Mohn und Gedächtnis*, copyright © 1952, Deutsche Verlags-Anstalt, München, in der Verlagsgruppe Random House GmbH. Reprinted with permission.

George Elliott Clarke. "Blank Sonnet" and "Look Homeward, Exile," from *Whylah Falls*. Polestar Book Publishers, 1990; reprinted with the permission of the author. "Casualties," from *Fiery Spirits and Voices: Canadian Writers of African Descent*, edited by Ayanna Black. Harper Collins, 1992; reprinted with the permission of the author.

Lucille Clifton. "The Lost Baby Poem" and "Miss Rosie," from *The Collected Poems of Lucille Clifton*. Copyright © 1987 by Lucille Clifton. Reprinted with the permission of The Permissions Company, Inc. on behalf of BOA Editions Ltd. <www.boaeditions.org>.

Billy Collins. "Pinup," from *The Art of Drowning* by Billy Collins, copyright © 1995. Reprinted by permission of the University of Pittsburgh Press.

Lorna Crozier. "Carrots," "Onions," and "The Dark Ages of the Sea," from *The Blue Hour of the Day* by Lorna Crozier. Copyright © 2007, Lorna Crozier; reprinted by permission of McClelland & Stewart. "When I Come Again to My Father's House," from *Everything Arrives at the Light*. McClelland & Stewart, 1995; reprinted with the permission of the author.

Rita Dove. "Persephone, Falling," from *Mother Love* by Rita Dove. Copyright © 1995 by Rita Dove. Used by permission of W.W. Norton & Company, Inc.

Carol Ann Duffy. "Crush" and "Drunk," from *Mean Time*, copyright © 1993 by Carol Ann Duffy; reproduced by permission of the author c/o Rogers, Coleridge & White Ltd., London. "Treasure" and "Rapture," from *Rapture*. Picador, 2005. Reproduced by permission of Pan Macmillan.

Marilyn Dumont. "Not Just a Platform For My Dance" and "White Judges," from *A Really Good Brown Girl*. Brick Books, 1996. Reprinted with the permission of Brick Books.

T.S. Eliot. "Journey of the Magi" and "The Love Song of J. Alfred Prufrock," from *Collected Poems 1909–1962*. Harcourt Brace & Company, 1963. Reprinted with the permission of Faber and Faber Ltd.

Robert Frost. "Design," "Stopping by Woods on a Snowy Evening," and "The Road Not Taken," from *The Poetry of Robert Frost*, edited by Edward Connery Lathem. Copyright © 1923, 1969 by Henry Holt and Company; copyright © 1936, 1951 by Robert Frost; copyright © 1964 by Lesley Frost Ballantine. Reprinted by permission of Henry Holt and Company, LLC.

Ted Hughes. "Hawk Roosting," "Pike," "Heptonstall Old Church," and "The Thought-Fox," from *Collected Poems*, edited by Paul Keegan. Faber and Faber, 2003. Reprinted with the permission of Faber and Faber Ltd.

Randall Jarrell. "The Death of the Ball Turret Gunner," from *The Complete Poems* by Randall Jarrell. Copyright © 1969, renewed 1997 by Mary von S. Jarrell. Reprinted by permission of Farrar, Straus and Giroux, LLC.

Jackie Kay. "In My Country," "Her," "High Land," and "Late Love," from *Darling: New & Selected Poems*. Bloodaxe Books, 2007. Reprinted with the permission of Bloodaxe Books.

Philip Larkin. "Church Going," "The Old Fools," "This Be the Verse," and "Talking in Bed," from *The Complete Poems of Philip Larkin*, edited by Archie Burnett. Faber and Faber, 2012. Reprinted with the permission of Faber and Faber Ltd.

Li-Young Lee. "Persimmons," from *Rose*. Copyright © 1986 by Li-Young Lee. Reprinted with the permission of The Permissions Company, Inc., on behalf of BOA Editions Ltd.

Douglas LePan. "The Haystack," "Aubade," and "A Country without a Mythology," from *Weathering It: Complete Poems 1948–1987*. McClelland & Stewart, 1987. Reprinted with the permission of Don LePan.

Dorothy Livesay. "The Three Emilys," from *Archive for Our Times: Previously Uncollected and Unpublished Poems by Dorothy Livesay*, edited by Dean J. Irvine. Arsenal Pulp Press, 2002; reprinted with the permission of the publisher. "Green Rain," from *Green Pitcher*. Macmillan, 1928; reprinted with the permission of Jay Stewart, Literary Executrix for the Estate of Dorothy Livesay.

Federico García Lorca. "Romance de la Luna, Luna" by Federico García Lorca, copyright © Herederos de Federico García Lorca from *Obras Completas* (Galaxia/Gutenberg, 1996 edition). "Romance de la Luna, Luna," translated by Helen Gunn. Retrieved from <http://dan.drydog.com/helen/romance_de_la_luna.html>. Reprinted with the permission of Helen Gunn. "Ballad of the Moon, Moon, Moon" by Carl W. Cobb, copyright © Carl W. Cobb and Herederos de Federico García Lorca. All rights reserved. For information regarding rights and permissions of all of Lorca's works in Spanish or in English, please contact lorca@artslaw.co.uk or William Peter Kosmas, Esq., 8 Franklin Square, London W14 9UU, England.

Gwendolyn MacEwen. "Dark Pines under Water" and "The Discovery," from *The Shadow-Maker*. Macmillan, 1969. Reprinted with the permission of David MacKinnon.

Roger McGough. "Comeclose and Sleepnow," from *The Mersey Sound* (copyright © Roger McGough 1967) is reprinted by permission of United Agents (<www.unitedagents.co.uk>) on behalf of Roger McGough.

Don McKay. "Some Functions of a Leaf," "Meditations on Shovels," and "Song for the Song of the Wood Thrush," from *Camber* by Don McKay. Copyright © 2004 Don McKay; reprinted by permission of McClelland & Stewart. "Meditation on

Michael Ondaatje. "Letters and Other Worlds," "The Cinnamon Peeler," and "To a Sad Daughter," from *The Cinnamon Peeler* by Michael Ondaatje. Copyright © 1989 by Michael Ondaatje. Reprinted by permission of Michael Ondaatje.

George Oppen. "Psalm," from *New Collected Poems*, copyright © 1965 by George Oppen. Reprinted by permission of New Directions Publishing Corp. "The Forms of Love" and "Latitude, Longitude," from *New Collected Poems*, copyright © 1975 by George Oppen. Reprinted by permission of New Directions Publishing Corp.

Alice Oswald. "Woods etc.," from *Woods, etc.* Faber and Faber, 2008, reprinted with the permission of Faber and Faber Ltd. "Wedding," from *The Thing in the Gap-Stone Stile.* Faber and Faber, 2007, reprinted with the permission of Faber and Faber Ltd. "Dunt," from *The 2008 Rhysling Anthology*, edited by Drew Morse. Science Fiction Poetry Association, 2008. Originally published in *Agni*, No. 64 (2006). Reprinted with the permission of United Agents on behalf of Alice Oswald.

P.K. Page. "Stories of Snow" and "The Stenographers," from *The Hidden Room*. The Porcupine's Quill, 1997. Reprinted with the permission of The Porcupine's Quill.

Brian Patten. "Somewhere Between Heaven and Woolworths, A Song," from *The Mersey Sound* (poems by Roger McGough, Brian Patten, Adrian Henri). Copyright © Brian Patten, 1968. Reproduced by permission of the author c/o Rogers, Coleridge & White Ltd., London.

Sylvia Plath. "Daddy" and "Lady Lazarus," from *Collected Poems*, edited by Ted Hughes. Faber and Faber, 1981. Reprinted with the permission of Faber and Faber Ltd.

Ezra Pound. "In a Station of the Metro" and "The River-Merchant's Wife: A Letter," from *Personae*, copyright © 1926 by Ezra Pound. Reprinted by permission of New Directions Publishing Corp.

Al Purdy. "Lament for the Dorsets" and "Trees at the Arctic Circle," from *Beyond Remembering: The Collected Poems of Al Purdy*, edited by Sam Solecki. Harbour Publishing, 2000. Reprinted with the permission of Harbour Publishing, <www.harbourpublishing.com>.

Craig Raine. "A Martian Sends a Postcard Home," from *A Martian Sends a Postcard Home* by Craig Raine. Copyright © Craig Raine, 1979. Reprinted with permission.

Ian Iqbal Rashid. "Could Have Danced All Night," from *Seminal: The Anthology of Canada's Gay Male Poets*, edited by John Barton and Billeh Nickerson. Arsenal Pulp Press, 2007. Reprinted with the permission of the author.

Adrienne Rich. "Aunt Jennifer's Tigers," copyright © 2002, 1951 by Adrienne Rich; "Diving into the Wreck," copyright © 2002 by Adrienne Rich, copyright © 1973 by W.W. Norton & Company Inc.; "Living in Sin," copyright © 2002, 1955 by Adrienne Rich; from *The Fact of a Doorframe: Selected Poems 1950–2001* by Adrienne Rich. Used by permission of W.W. Norton & Company, Inc.

William Carlos Williams. "Spring and All," "The Red Wheelbarrow," and "This Is Just to Say," from *The Collected Poems: Volume 1, 1909–1939*, copyright © 1938 by New Directions Publishing Corp. Reprinted by permission of New Directions Publishing Corp. "Landscape with the Fall of Icarus," from *The Collected Poems: Volume 2, 1939–1962*, copyright © 1962 by William Carlos Williams. Reprinted by permission of New Directions Publishing Corp.

Rita Wong. "opium" and "nervous organism," from *forage*. Nightwood Editions, 2007. Reprinted with the permission of Nightwood Editions, <www.nightwood editions.com>.

Benjamin Zephaniah. "Dis Poetry," from *City Psalms*. Bloodaxe Books, 1992. Reprinted with the permission of Bloodaxe Books.

Rachel Zolf. "Human Resources" (pages 4 & 5), "Human Resources" (pages 6 & 7), and "Notes" (excerpt), from *Human Resources*. Coach House Books, 2007. Reprinted with the permission of the author and Coach House Books.

The publisher has endeavoured to contact rights holders for all copyrighted material, and would appreciate receiving any information as to errors or omissions.

Solutions to the Exeter Book riddles:
23, penis or onion (rose has also been suggested); 33, iceberg; 81, fish and river.

Index of First Lines

1980, I was returned to the city
    exposed   430
A black, E white, I red, U green, O
    blue: vowels   478
A broken Altar, Lord, thy servant
    rears   55
A cold coming we had of it   229
A great bird landed here   309
A little black thing among the
    snow   108
A noir, E blanc, I rouge, U vert, O bleu:
    voyelles   478
A people chained to aurora   295
a poem does not beg for forgiveness. it's
    not like real life   355
A soft ounce of your breath   410
A sudden blow: the great wings beating
    still   207
A sweet disorder in the dress   52
A wind is ruffling the tawny pelt   311
About me the night moonless wimples
    the mountains   243
About suffering they were never
    wrong   249
According to Brueghel   219
After great pain, a formal feeling
    comes—   171
After the brief bivouac of Sunday   275
Albion's most lovely daughter sat on the
    banks of the   324
All afternoon my brothers and I have
    worked in the orchard   397
All night long the hockey pictures   364
all these months spent   499
Among castles of tired stone   485
Among twenty snowy mountains   213
An excellent vocabulary, but spatial
    skills   446
And if it snowed and snow covered the
    drive   431

And love is then no more than a
    compromise?   299
Angered, may I be near a glass of
    water   389
Animal bones and some mossy tent
    rings   281
anyone lived in a pretty how
    town   238
As if he had been poured   342
As the woman leaves the nursery,
    driving into early dark   333
As virtuous men pass mildly away   48
Aunt Jennifer's tigers prance across a
    screen   301
Batter my heart, three personed God;
    for you   48
Because I could not stop for
    Death—   172
Because we are mostly   385
Before the black beak reappeared   376
Bent double, like old beggars under
    sacks   234
Between my finger and my thumb   339
Black milk of daybreak we drink it at
    sundown   495
By the road to the contagious
    hospital   218
Carrots are fucking   384
Caxtons are mechanical birds with
    many wings   372
chemical history narcopolemics   451
Children's hands in close-up   344
climbed from the road and found   257
Come live with me and be my love   39
"Courage!" he said, and pointed toward
    the land   148
Creature came through waves, sailed
    strangely   28
Dead you will lie and never memory of
    you   471

dear Captain Poetry   371
Death be not proud, though some have
    called thee   47
Did you see her mother on television?
    She said plain, burned things.
    She   395
Dis poetry is like a riddim dat
    drops   420
Do not go gentle into that good
    night   274
do not imagine that the
    exploration   349
Entre castillos de piedra cansada   484
First, grant me my sense of history   392
First having read the book of
    myths   302
First the earth, then the plow   505
Five years have passed; five summers,
    with the length   112
footfall, which is a means so
    steady   441
For the following few seconds, while the
    ear   352
From my mother's sleep I fell into the
    State   270
From time to time our love is like a
    sail   441
Gather ye rosebuds while ye may   53
Given enough input elements, a
    writing machine can spew about
    anything   455
Had we but world enough, and
    time   64
Half a league, half a league   156
Happy ye leaves when as those lilly
    hands   35
He opens his eyes to a hard frost   414
He was found by the Bureau of
    Statistics to be   253
He, who navigated with success   334
Helicopters are cutlassing the wild
    bananas   316
Here rests his head upon the lap of
    earth   101

here to me from Krete to this holy
    temple   469
How do I love thee? Let me count the
    ways   137
How do they do it, the ones who make
    love   359
How they strut about, people in
    love   428
How vainly men themselves amaze   61
How well they love us, palm and instep,
    lifeline   352
I am a wondrous thing, a joy to
    women   27
I can still see that soil crimsoned by
    butchered   423
I caught this morning morning's
    minion, king   199
I celebrate myself, and sing myself   166
I don't know the how   500
I don't remember who kissed who
    first   427
I don't want to trip over this in the
    future from where I'm sitting can
    you   455
I found a dimpled spider, fat and
    white   212
I had been told about her   427
i have altered my tactics to reflect the
    new era   356
I have done it again   320
I have eaten   218
I have met them at close of day   203
I hear America singing, the varied carols
    I hear   167
I heard a Fly buzz—when I died—   172
I heard them marching the leaf-wet
    roads of my head   315
I imagine this midnight moment's
    forest   306
I knew a woman, lovely in her
    bones   259
I leant upon a coppice gate   193
I like to touch your tattoos in
    complete   404

I make this song of myself, deeply
     sorrowing   26
I met a traveller from an antique
     land   122
I once used to dream of being held
     knowingly by a man   434
I placed a jar in Tennessee   216
I remember long veils of green
     rain   261
I sat all morning in the college sick
     bay   341
I sit in one of the dives   250
I sit in the top of the wood, my eyes
     closed   309
I thought I was so tough   298
I wander thro' each charter'd
     street   110
I would like to watch you sleeping   336
I, being born a woman and
     distressed   231
I, too, dislike it: there are things that
     are important beyond all this
     fiddle   222
I, too, dislike it   223
I'll come when thou art saddest   165
I'm Nobody! Who are you?   171
I've known rivers   240
If all the world and love were
     young   38
If I were a cinnamon peeler   363
In a solitude of the sea   195
in Just   235
In my heart she used to stand lovely and
     live   473
In sixth grade Mrs. Walker   417
In the cold, cold parlour   264
In the midst of a winter wood   457
In the small beauty of the forest   255
In this strange labyrinth how shall I
     turn?   51
In Xanadu did Kubla Khan   119
Is that where it happens?   297
It doesn't take a Hiroshima to burn a
     man to a crisp   269

It is a land with neither night nor
     day   192
it is afterwards   328
It little profits that an idle king   154
It was blacker than olives the night
     I left. As I ran past the palaces,
     oddly   394
It was your birthday, we had drunk and
     dined   300
It's been going on a long time   286
Jackfish and walleye circle like clouds as
     he strains   444
je ne sais le comment   500
jellyfish potato/ jellypo fishtato/ glow in
     the pork toys   452
Kashmir shrinks into my mailbox   391
l e   370
l(a   239
La luna vino a la fragua   480
Let me not to the marriage of true
     minds   43
Let me take this other glove of   246
Let the world's sharpness like a clasping
     knife   137
Little lamb, who made thee   105
Lord, who createdst man in wealth and
     store   56
Love, a child, is ever crying   50
loveless vessels   439
Madame, ye ben of al beaute shrine   29
Mark but this flea, and mark in
     this   46
Mi perro ha muerto   488
Moisten your finger and hold it   462
Morning and evening   175
My dog has died   489
My father's body was a globe of
     fear   360
My heart aches, and a drowsy numbness
     pains   130
My Life had stood—a Loaded
     Gun—   173
My mistress' eyes are nothing like the
     sun   43

My mother forbade us to walk
  backwards. That is how the dead
  walk, she   395
New performance weightings a bit of
  a moving target the future liability
  of   454
No coward soul is mine   163
No monuments or landmarks guide the
  stranger   267
No, helpless thing, I cannot harm thee
  now   102
Nobody heard him, the dead man   242
Not silent is my house; I am quiet   28
Nothing would sleep in that cellar, dank
  as a ditch   259
Nothing. When we realized you weren't
  here   374
Now as I was young and easy under the
  apple boughs   272
O Rose, thou art sick   108
O what can ail thee, knight-at-
  arms   128
O Wild West Wind, thou breath of
  Autumn's being   123
Often rebuked, yet always back
  returning   164
On either side the river lie   142
On the square which is chopped into
  mean little plots of grass, the
  square   475
Once I am sure there's nothing going
  on   288
Once upon a midnight dreary, while I
  pondered, weak and weary   138
One day I wrote her name upon the
  strand   36
One face looks out from all his
  canvasses   192
One narcissus among the ordinary
  beautiful   400
Parked in the fields   256
Pike, three inches long, perfect   307
(ponder,darling,these busted
  statues   236

Reading a poem releases noxious   463
S'io credesse che mia risposta fosse   225
Schwarze Milch der Frühe wir trinken
  sie abends   494
Season of mists and mellow
  fruitfulness   134
Shall I compare thee to a summer's
  day?   41
She had thought the studio would keep
  itself   302
She keeps kingfishers in their cages   381
She sits in the park. Her clothes are out
  of date   284
Snow annihilates all beauty   424
so much depends   217
Soleasi nel mio cor star bella et viva   473
somewhere i have never travelled,gladly
  beyond   237
Spring darkness is forgiving. It doesn't
  descend   402
Still dark, but just. The alarm   445
Stones only, the disjecta membra of this
  Great House   313
Stop all the clocks, cut off the
  telephone   249
Suddenly the rain is hilarious   407
Sur la place taillée en mesquines
  pelouses   475
Surmounting my government's high
  evasions   331
Sweep me through your many-
  chambered heart   383
Talking in bed ought to be easiest   290
Tell all the Truth but tell it
  slant—   174
Terence, this is stupid stuff   200
That is no country for old men. The
  young   207
That time of year thou mayst in me
  behold   42
That which you wove out of light
  thread   493
That's my last Duchess painted on the
  wall   161

The air smells of rhubarb, occasional   422

The apparition of these faces in the crowd   221

The art of losing isn't hard to master   266

The curfew tolls the knell of parting day   96

the distaste for turmoil   353

The door swings open   337

The flowers sent here by mistake   396

The force that through the green fuse drives the flower   271

The Frost performs its secret ministry   117

The house is so quiet now   285

The job is to write in 'plain language.' No adjectives, adornment or surfeit   454

The last thing I ever wanted was to   405

The long love that in my thought doth harbour   32

The moon came down to the forge in skirts   482

The moon came to the forge   481

The murkiness of the local garage is not so dense   346

The night you called to tell me   429

The older she gets   409

The onion loves the onion   385

The overweight   507

The rain set early in tonight   159

The sea is calm tonight   168

the time i dropped your almost body down   327

The whiskey on your breath   258

The world is charged with the grándeur of God   198

The world is too much with us; late and soon   116

There is a garden in her face   44

There is sweet music here that softer falls   150

These women crying in my head   262

They are 18 inches long   279

They flee from me that sometime did me seek   33

They fuck you up, your mum and dad   291

They sing their dearest songs—   196

This is dawn   367

this land is not   411

This land like a mirror turns you inward   348

Those in the vegetable rain retain   277

Thou ill-formed offspring of my feeble brain   59

Thou still unravish'd bride of quietness   132

Thought of by you all day, I think of you   409

Thrums he does, thrums like waves breaking, waves falling over each other   460

To find one, even among souvenirs of Banff from acrylic to zinc, is to   351

To whisper. To applaud the wind   350

tous ces mois passes   499

True ease in writing comes from art, not chance   68

Turning and turning in the widening gyre   206

'Twas mercy brought me from my Pagan land   104

Two long had loved, and now the nymph desired   66

Two roads diverged in a yellow wood   210

Tyger! Tyger! burning bright   108

Unreal tall as a myth   245

Us all on sore cement was we   330

Very small and damaged and quite dry   441

Visits of condolence is all we get from them   503

Walking by the waters   426

Was du aus Leichtem wobst   493
Water does not remember, it
    moves   398
We interrupt our live coverage of the
    War   433
We lived in an old schoolhouse,
    one large room that my father
    converted   412
We wear the mask that grins and
    lies   209
We were married in summer, thirty
    years ago. I have loved you deeply
    from   369
What dire offence from am'rous causes
    springs   71
What do they think has happened, the
    old fools   291
What happens to a dream
    deferred?   241
What lips my lips have kissed, and
    where, and why   232
What needs my Shakespeare for his
    honoured bones   57
What passing-bells for these who die as
    cattle?   233
What thoughts I have of you tonight,
    Walt Whitman, for I walked   293
When I come again to my father's
    house   387
When I consider how my light is
    spent   58
When I have fears that I may cease to
    be   127
When I heard the learn'd
    astronomer   167

When I take my girl to the swimming
    party   358
when i watch you   326
When in disgrace with fortune and
    men's eyes   42
When my mother died I was very
    young   107
When our two souls stand up erect and
    strong   136
When the day-birds have settled   415
Whenas in silks my Julia goes   53
Which reminds me of another knock-
    on-wood   379
While my hair was still cut straight
    across my forehead   220
Who was it strung these footnotes   456
Whose woods these are I think I
    know   211
Whoso list to hunt, I know where is an
    hind   34
Wild Nights—Wild Nights!   170
Writing is inhibiting. Sighing, I sit,
    scribbling in ink this pidgin script.
    I   436
Yes, love, that's why the warning light
    comes on. Don't   432
You believe you know me   447
You do not do, you do not do   318
you fit into me   335
You run round the back to be in it
    again   408
Your name on my lips. Every
    night   269

Index of Authors and Titles

À la Musique   475
Ackerman, Diane   383
Addonizio, Kim   404
["After great pain, a formal feeling
   comes"]   171
Against Love Poetry   369
Ali, Agha Shahid   391
[all these months spent]   500
Altar, The   55
Amichai, Yehuda   501
Anecdote of the Jar   216
Anthem for Doomed Youth   233
anyone lived in a pretty how
   town   238
Armitage, Simon   431
Arnold, Matthew   168
Arvio, Sarah   405
Ashbery, John   295
attractive   353
Atwood, Margaret   334
Aubade   269
Auden, W.H.   248
Aunt Jennifer's Tigers   301
Ballad of the Moon, Moon, Moon   482
Barbauld, Anna Laetitia   102
Barrett Browning, Elizabeth   136
["Batter my heart, three personed God;
   for you"] (Sonnet 14)   48
Bear on the Delhi Road, The   245
["Because I could not stop for
   Death"]   172
Betjeman, John   246
Birney, Earle   243
Bishop, Elizabeth   264
Blake, William   105
Blank Sonnet   422
Blues   370
Bök, Christian   436
Boland, Eavan   367
Bolster, Stephanie   456
Borson, Roo   398

bpNichol   370
Bradstreet, Anne   59
Brand, Dionne   402
Bringhurst, Robert   376
Brontë, Emily   163
Brossard, Nicole   498
Browning, Robert   159
Campion, Thomas   44
Carrots   384
Carson, Anne   394
Casualties   424
Caterpillar, The   102
Celan, Paul   492
Central America   316
Chapter I   436
Charge of the Light Brigade, The   156
Chaucer, Geoffrey   29
Chimney Sweeper, The   107
Chimney Sweeper, The   108
Church Going   288
Cinnamon Peeler, The   363
Civilization and Its Discontents   295
Clarke, George Elliott   422
Clifton, Lucille   326
Cobwebs   192
Coleridge, Samuel Taylor   117
Collins, Billy   346
Comeclose and Sleepnow   328
Convergence of the Twain, The   195
Could Have Danced All Night   434
Country without a Mythology, A   267
Crozier, Lorna   384
Crush   409
Cummings, E.E.   235
Cutaways   344
Daddy   318
Dark Ages of the Sea, The   385
Dark Pines Under Water   348
Darkling Thrush, The   193
["Dead you will lie and never memory
   of you"]   471

Dear Africans   507
[dear Captain Poetry]   371
["Death be not proud, though some
    have called thee"] (Sonnet 10)   47
Death Fugue   495
Death of a Young Son by
    Drowning   334
Death of the Ball Turret Gunner,
    The   270
Delight in Disorder   52
Design   212
Dickinson, Emily   170
Did I Miss Anything?   374
Digging   339
Dis Poetry   420
Discovery, The   349
Diving into the Wreck   302
Do Not Go Gentle into That Good
    Night   274
Donne, John   46
Door, The   337
Dove, Rita   400
Dover Beach   168
Drunk   407
Duffy, Carol Ann   407
Dulce et Decorum Est   234
Dumont, Marilyn   411
Dunbar, Paul Laurence   209
Dunt   441
During Wind and Rain   196
Early Dark, The   333
Easter 1916   203
Easter Wings   56
Electricity   429
Elegy Written in a Country
    Churchyard   96
Eliot, T.S.   224
Essay on Criticism, An, from   68
["Every smell is now a possibility, a
    young man"]   403
Exeter Book Riddles   27
Exile   485
Exilio   484
Far Cry from Africa, A   311
Fern Hill   272

Finch, Anne, Countess of
    Winchilsea   66
First Death in Nova Scotia   264
First Poem for You   404
Flea, The   46
Force That Through the Green Fuse
    Drives the Flower, The   271
Forms of Love, The   256
Frost at Midnight   117
Frost, Robert   210
Funeral Blues   249
García Lorca, Federico   479
Garden, The   61
Geste   499
Gesture   499
Ginsberg, Allen   293
Gioia, Dana   396
[Given enough input elements, a
    writing machine can spew about
    anything]   455
Goblin Market   175
God's Grandeur   198
Good Teachers, The   408
Grauballe Man, The   342
Gray, R.W.   460
Gray, Thomas   96
Green Rain   261
Greenlaw, Lavinia   429
Gunn, Thom   298
Haile, Reesom   504
["Happy ye leaves when as those lilly
    hands"] (Sonnet 1)   35
Hardy, Thomas   193
Harlem (2)   241
Harris, Sharon   462
Harwood, Gwen   284
Hawk Roosting   309
Haystack, The   269
Heaney, Seamus   339
Henri, Adrian   324
Heptonstall Old Church   309
Her   427
Herbert, George   54
["here to me from Krete to this holy
    temple"]   468/69

Herrick, Robert 52
High Land 427
Hopkins, Gerard Manley 198
Housman, A.E. 200
["How do I love thee? Let me count the ways"] (Sonnet 43) 137
How this begins 460
Hug, The 300
Hughes, Langston 240
Hughes, Ted 306
[I, being born a woman and distressed] 231
["I celebrate myself, and sing myself"] 166
[I don't want to trip over this in the future from where I'm sitting can you suggest massages] 455
I Hear America Singing 167
["I heard a Fly buzz—when I died"] 172
I Knew a Woman 259
[I'll come when thou art saddest] 165
["I'm Nobody! Who are you?"] 171
Improvement, The 297
In a Station of the Metro 221
In an Artist's Studio 192
[in Just-] 235
In My Country 426
["In my heart she used to stand lovely and live"] 473
In the Park, 284
["In this strange labyrinth how shall I turn?"] (Sonnet 77) 51
In Westminster Abbey 246
It Could Be You 433
Jarrell, Randall 270
Journey of the Magi 229
Kay, Jackie 426
Keats, John 127
Knowledge 505
Kubla Khan 119
[l(a] 239
La Belle Dame sans Merci: A Ballad 128
Lady Lazarus 320
Lady of Shalott, The 142

Lamb, The 105
Lament for the Dorsets 281
Landscape with the Fall of Icarus 219
Larkin, Philip 288
Late Love 428
Latitude, Longitude 257
Leda and the Swan (Bringhurst) 376
Leda and the Swan (Yeats) 207
Lee, Li-Young 417
LePan, Douglas 267
["Let me not to the marriage of true minds"] (Sonnet 116) 43
["Let the world's sharpness like a clasping knife"] (Sonnet 24) 137
Letters & Other Worlds 360
Lines Written a Few Miles above Tintern Abbey 112
Livesay, Dorothy 261
Living in Sin 302
London 110
Look Homeward, Exile 423
Lost Baby Poem, The 327
Lotos-Eaters, The 148
Love Song of J. Alfred Prufrock, The 225
MacEwen, Gwendolyn 348
make it new 356
Marlowe, Christopher 39
Martian Sends a Postcard Home, A 372
Marvell, Andrew 61
McGough, Roger 328
McKay, Don 350
Meditation on a Geode 351
Meditation on Shovels 352
Mid-Term Break 341
Midsummer, from 315
Miki, Roy 353
Millay, Edna St. Vincent 231
Milton, John 57
Minor Miracle 379
Miss Rosie 326
Moore, Marianne 222
Mrs. Albion You've Got a Lovely Daughter 324

Murray, Les   330
Musée des Beaux Arts   249
My Last Duchess   161
["My Life had stood—a Loaded
    Gun"]   173
["My mistress' eyes are nothing like the
    sun"] (Sonnet 130)   43
My Papa's Waltz   258
Negro Speaks of Rivers, The   240
Nelson, Marilyn   379
Nemerov, Howard   285
Neruda, Pablo   483
nervous organism   452
[New performance weightings a bit of a
    moving target the future liability of
    make this sing]   454
Nice   445
Night Feed   367
[No coward soul is mine]   163
Not Just a Platform for My Dance   411
Not Waving but Drowning   242
Nymph's Reply to the Shepherd,
    The   38
Ode on a Grecian Urn   132
Ode to a Nightingale   130
Ode to the West Wind   123
[Often rebuked, yet always back
    returning]   164
Old Fools, The   291
Olds, Sharon   358
On Being Brought from Africa to
    America   104
On Rain   394
On Shakespeare   57
On Sylvia Plath   395
on the sublime   355
On Walking Backwards   395
Ondaatje, Michael   360
One Art   266
["One day I wrote her name upon the
    strand"] (Sonnet 75)   36
One Girl at the Boys Party, The   358
Onions   385
opium   451
Oppen, George   255

Oswald, Alice   440
Owen, Wilfred   233
Ozymandias   122
Page, P.K.   275
Park Drunk, The   414
Passionate Shepherd to His Love,
    The   39
Patten, Brian   381
Persephone, Falling   400
Persimmons   417
Petrarch, Francesco   482
Pigs   330
Pike   307
Pinup   346
Planting a Sequoia   397
Plath, Sylvia   317
Poe, Edgar Allan   138
Poem   431
Poetry   222
Poetry (Revised version)   223
[(ponder,darling,these busted
    statues]   236
Pope, Alexander   68
Porphyria's Lover   159
Portrait of Alice with Christopher
    Robin   457
Portrait of Alice, Annotated   456
Postcard from Kashmir   391
Pound, Ezra   220
Psalm   255
Purdy, Al   279
Raine, Craig   372
Ralegh, Sir Walter   37
Rape of the Lock, The   69
Rapture   409
Rashid, Ian Iqbal   434
Raven, The   138
Red Wheelbarrow, The   217
Rich, Adrienne   301
Rimbaud, Arthur   474
River-Merchant's Wife: A Letter,
    The   220
Road Not Taken, The   210
Robertson, Robin   414
Roethke, Theodore   258

Romance de la luna, luna   480
Root Cellar   259
Rossetti, Christina   175
Ruins of a Great House   313
Sailing to Byzantium   207
Sapphics Against Anger   389
Sappho   467
Scene Set to Music   475
Second Coming, The   206
Self-Portrait in a Series of Professional
    Evaluations   446
September 1, 1939   250
Sex without Love   359
Shakespeare, William   41
["Shall I compare thee to a summer's
    day?"] (Sonnet 18)   41
Shelley, Percy Bysshe   122
Shield-Scales of Heraldry, The   331
Shroud   493
Sick Rose, The   108
Smith, Stevie   242
Solie, Karen   444
Some Functions of a Leaf   350
Somewhere Between Heaven and
    Woolworths, A Song   381
[somewhere i have never travelled,gladly
    beyond]   237
Song for the Song of the Wood
    Thrush   352
Song [Love, a child, is ever crying]   50
Song of Myself, *from*   166
Spenser, Edmund   35
Spring and All   218
["Spring darkness is forgiving. It doesn't
    descend"]   402
Steele, Timothy   389
Stenographers, The   275
Stevens, Wallace   213
Stopping by Woods on a Snowy
    Evening   211
Stories of Snow   277
Sturgeon   444
Subramaniam, Arundhathi   447
Supermarket in California, A   293
Sweep Me through Your Many-

Chambered Heart   383
Talking in Bed   290
Tamer and Hawk   298
["Tell all the Truth but tell it slant"]   174
Tennyson, Alfred Lord   142
Terence, This Is Stupid Stuff   200
Thanks for Remembering Us   396
["That time of year thou mayst in me
    behold"] (Sonnet 73)   42
[The job is to write in 'plain language.'
    No adjectives, adornment or
    surfeit]   454
[The long love that in my thought doth
    harbour]   32
[The moon came to the forge]   481
[The world is too much with us]   116
[There is a garden in her face]   44
There's No Tomorrow   66
[They flee from me that sometime did
    me seek]   33
Thirteen Ways of Looking at a
    Blackbird   213
This Be the Verse   291
This Is Just to Say   218
Thomas, Dylan   271
Thought-Fox, The   306
Three Emilys, The   262
To a Sad Daughter   364
To Autumn   134
To His Coy Mistress   64
To His Cynical Mistress   299
To Rosemounde   29
To the Virgins, to Make Much of
    Time   53
To the Welsh Critic Who Doesn't Find
    Me Identifiably Indian   447
Todesfuge   494
Totenhemd   493
Tourists   502/503
[tous ces mois passés]   500
Treasure   410
Trees at the Arctic Circle   279
Tyger, The   108
Ulysses   154
Un Perro Ha Muerto   488

Unknown Citizen, The   253
Upon Julia's Clothes   53
Vacuum, The   285
Valediction: Forbidding Mourning,
    A   48
Vancouver Lights   243
Variation on the Word *Sleep*   336
Very Simply Topping Up the Brake
    Fluid   432
Vowels   478
Voyelles   478
Walcott, Derek   311
Water Memory   398
Way of Life, A   286
Wayman, Tom   374
We Wear the Mask   209
Wedding   440
[What lips my lips have kissed, and
    where, and why]   232
What the Horses See at Night   415
Wheatley, Phillis   104
When I Come Again to My Father's
    House   387
[When I consider how my light is
    spent]   58
When I Have Fears that I May Cease to
    Be   127
When I Heard the Learn'd
    Astronomer   167

["When in disgrace with fortune and
    men's eyes"] (Sonnet 29)   42
["When our two souls stand up erect
    and strong"] (Sonnet 22)   136
Where Do Poems Come From?   462
White Judges, The   412
Whitman, Walt   166
[Whoso list to hunt, I know where is an
    hind]   34
Why Do Poems Make Me Cry?   463
Wife's Lament, The   26
["Wild Nights—Wild Nights!"]   170
Williams, William Carlos   217
Windhover, The   199
Wolf's Postscript to "Little Red Riding
    Hood", The   392
Wong, Rita   450
Wood   405
Woods etc.   441
Wordsworth, William   111
Wroth, Lady Mary   50
Wyatt, Sir Thomas   32
Yeats, W.B.   203
[you fit into me]   335
Zephaniah, Benjamin   420
Zolf, Rachel   453
Zombies   430

from the publisher

A name never says it all, but the word "broadview" expresses a good deal of the philosophy behind our company. We are open to a broad range of academic approaches and political viewpoints. We pay attention to the broad impact book publishing and book printing has in the wider world; we began using recycled stock more than a decade ago, and for some years now we have used 100% recycled paper for most titles. As a Canadian-based company we naturally publish a number of titles with a Canadian emphasis, but our publishing program overall is internationally oriented and broad-ranging. Our individual titles often appeal to a broad readership too; many are of interest as much to general readers as to academics and students.

Founded in 1985, Broadview remains a fully independent company owned by its shareholders—not an imprint or subsidiary of a larger multinational.

If you would like to find out more about Broadview and about the books we publish, please visit us at **www.broadviewpress.com**. And if you'd like to place an order through the site, we'd like to show our appreciation by extending a special discount to you: by entering the code below you will receive a 20% discount on purchases made through the Broadview website.

Discount code: **broadview20%**

Thank you for choosing Broadview.

Please note: this offer applies only to sales of bound books within the United States or Canada.

LIST
of products used:

4,366 lb(s) of Rolland Opaque50
50% post-consumer

RESULTS
Based on the Cascades products you selected
compared to products in the industry made with
100% virgin fiber, your savings are:

19 trees
1 tennis court

15,140 gal. US of water
164 days of water consumption

3,834 lbs of waste
35 waste containers

11,737 lbs CO2
emissions of 2 cars per year

58 MMBTU
281,492 60W light bulbs for one
hour

35 lbs NOx
**emissions of one truck during 49
days**